A GUIDE TO THE

Battles of the
American Revolution

Books by Theodore P. Savas

The Campaign for Atlanta and Sherman's March to the Sea, 2 vols., editor, with David A. Woodbury (1994)

The Red River Campaign: Union and Confederate Leadership and the War in Louisiana, editor, with David A. Woodbury and Gary D. Joiner (1994)

Silent Hunters: German U-boat Commanders of World War II (editor, 1997)

Nazi Millionaires: The Allied Search for Hidden SS Gold, with Kenneth D. Alford (2004)

Hunt and Kill: U-505 and U-boat War in the Atlantic, editor (2004)

Never for Want of Powder: The Confederate Powder Works in Augusta, Georgia, with C. L. Bragg, Gordon A. Blaker, Charles D. Ross, and Stephanie A. T. Jacobe (2007)

Brady's Civil War Journal: Photographing the War 1861-1865 (2008)

The New American Revolution Handbook:Facts and Artwork for Readers of All Ages, with J. David Dameron (2010)

Books by J. David Dameron

General Henry Lewis Benning: This was a Man (2000)

Kings Mountain: The Defeat of the Loyalists, October 7, 1780 (2003)

Benning's Brigade: A History and Roster of the 2nd, 15th, 17th, and 20th Georgia Regiments, 2 vols. (2003)

Women Air Force Service Pilots of World War II: The WASP (2005)

The New American Revolution Handbook:Facts and Artwork for Readers of All Ages, with Theodore P. Savas (2010)

A GUIDE TO THE

Battles of the
American Revolution

Theodore P. Savas
& J. David Dameron

SB

Savas Beatie

New York and California

Cataloging-in-Publication Data is available from the Library of Congress.

ISBN 978-1-932714-94-4

Second paperback edition, second printing

SB
Published by
Savas Beatie LLC
989 Governor Drive, Suite 102
El Dorado Hills, CA 95762

Phone: 916-941-6896
E-mail: sales@savasbeatie.com

Savas Beatie titles are available at special discounts for bulk purchases in the United States by corporations, institutions, and other organizations. For more details, contact Spccial Sales, P.O. Box 4527, El Dorado Hills, CA 95762, e-mail us your interest at sales@savasbeatie.com, or please visit our website at www.savasbeatie.com.

Printed in the United States of America.

For my beloved and long gone Papou Ted, who arrived at Ellis Island as a penniless young Greek immigrant on the eve of World War I. He came here to be an American, and no one loved this country more than he did. I miss you.

— Theodore P. Savas

For Kevin and Jonathan, in hopes that someday they will love exploring history as much as I do.

— J. David Dameron

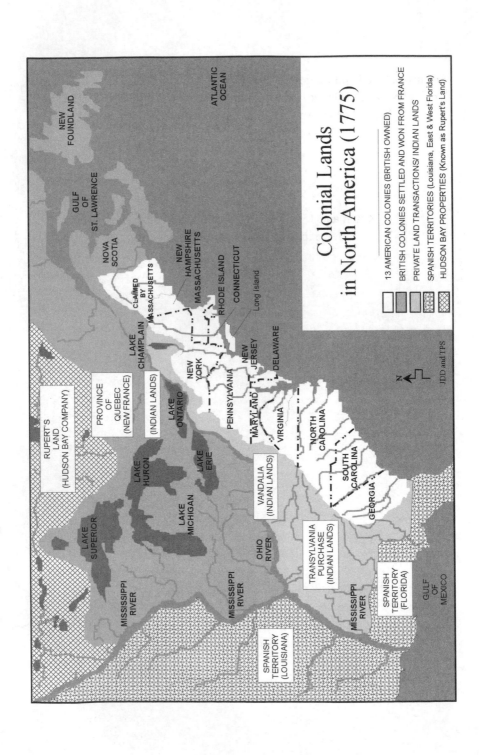

Colonial Lands in North America (1775)

13 AMERICAN COLONIES (BRITISH OWNED)

BRITISH COLONIES SETTLED AND WON FROM FRANCE

PRIVATE LAND TRANSACTIONS/ INDIAN LANDS

SPANISH TERRITORIES (Louisiana, East & West Florida)

HUDSON BAY PROPERTIES (Known as Rupert's Land)

JDD and TPS

NEW FOUNDLAND

ATLANTIC OCEAN

GULF OF ST. LAWRENCE

NOVA SCOTIA

NEW HAMPSHIRE

CLAIMED BY MASSACHUSETTS

MASSACHUSETTS

RHODE ISLAND

CONNECTICUT

Long Island

LAKE CHAMPLAIN

NEW YORK

NEW JERSEY

DELAWARE

PENNSYLVANIA

MARYLAND

VIRGINIA

NORTH CAROLINA

SOUTH CAROLINA

GEORGIA

RUPERT'S LAND (HUDSON BAY COMPANY)

PROVINCE OF QUEBEC (NEW FRANCE) (INDIAN LANDS)

LAKE ONTARIO

LAKE ERIE

LAKE HURON

LAKE MICHIGAN

LAKE SUPERIOR

VANDALIA (INDIAN LANDS)

TRANSYLVANIA PURCHASE (INDIAN LANDS)

OHIO RIVER

MISSISSIPPI RIVER

MISSISSIPPI RIVER

MISSISSIPPI RIVER

SPANISH TERRITORY (LOUISIANA)

SPANISH TERRITORY (FLORIDA)

GULF OF MEXICO

N

CONTENTS

THE BATTLES

CONTENTS (continued)

THE BATTLES (continued)

MAPS AND ILLUSTRATIONS

Original maps have been included with most entries
for the convenience of the reader. A series of regional
maps begins on the following page.

Illustrations begin on page xii.

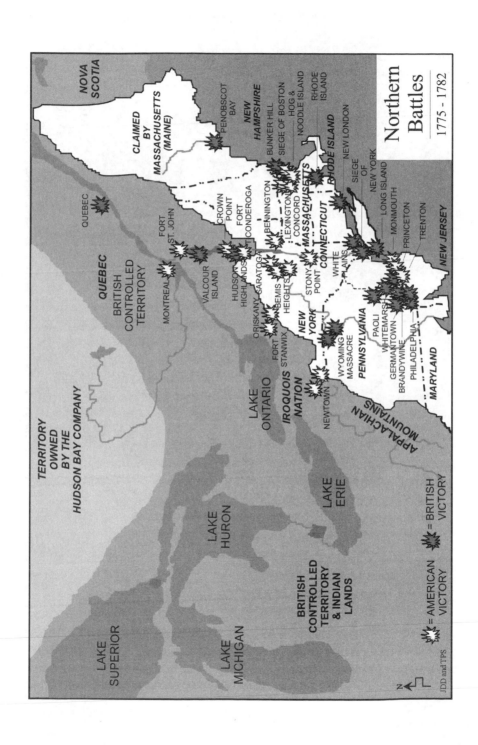

Northern
Battles
1775 - 1782

NOVA SCOTIA

CLAIMED
BY
MASSACHUSETTS
(MAINE)

PENOBSCOT
BAY

NEW
HAMPSHIRE

BUNKER HILL
SIEGE OF BOSTON
HOG &
NOODLE ISLAND
RHODE
ISLAND

QUEBEC

QUEBEC
BRITISH
CONTROLLED
TERRITORY

FORT
ST. JOHN

CROWN
POINT
FORT
TICONDEROGA

BENNINGTON

LEXINGTON
CONCORD

MASSACHUSETTS

RHODE ISLAND

CONNECTICUT

SIEGE
OF
NEW YORK

NEW LONDON

MONTREAL

VALCOUR
ISLAND

HUDSON
HIGHLANDS
SARATOGA

BEMIS
HEIGHTS

STONY
POINT

WHITE
PLAINS

LONG ISLAND

MONMOUTH

PRINCETON

TRENTON

NEW JERSEY

TERRITORY
OWNED
BY THE
HUDSON BAY COMPANY

LAKE
ONTARIO

IROQUOIS
NATION

ORISKANY

FORT
STANWIX

NEW
YORK

PAOLI

WHITEMARSH
GERMANTOWN
BRANDYWINE
PHILADELPHIA

PENNSYLVANIA

MARYLAND

NEWTOWN

WYOMING
MASSACRE

APPALACHIAN
MOUNTAINS

LAKE
ERIE

LAKE
HURON

BRITISH
CONTROLLED
TERRITORY
& INDIAN
LANDS

LAKE
SUPERIOR

LAKE
MICHIGAN

N

= AMERICAN VICTORY   = BRITISH VICTORY

JDD and TPS

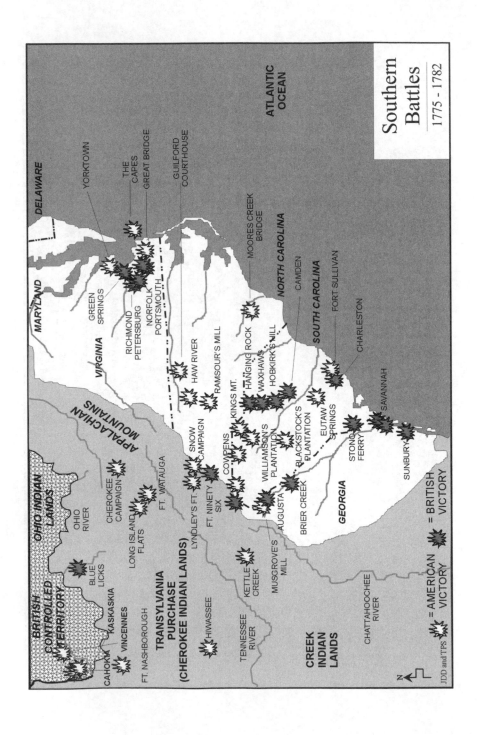

Southern Battles
1775 - 1782

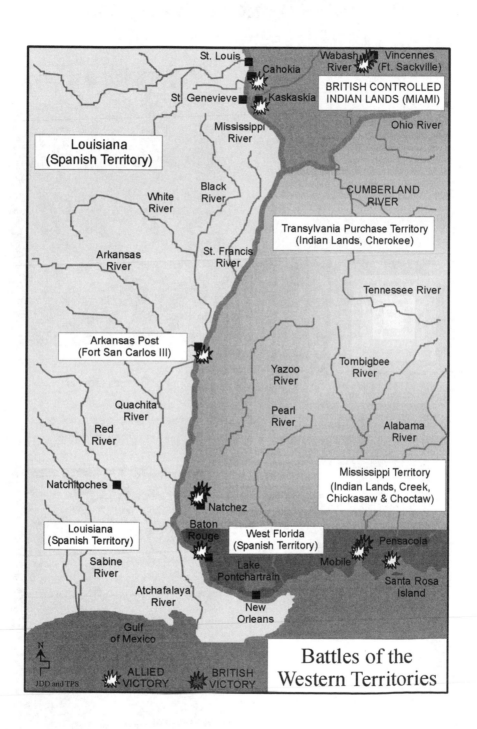

Battles of the
Western Territories

The British & Their Allies

Sir Henry Clinton

*National Park Service, Colonial National
Historical Park, Yorktown Collection*

Admiral Thomas Graves

*National Park Service, Colonial National
Historical Park, Yorktown Collection*

General Sir William Howe

National Archives

General Sir Guy Carleton

Library of Congress

Lieutenant General
Charles Cornwallis

*National Park Service, Colonial National
Historical Park, Yorktown Collection*

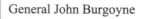

General John Burgoyne

*Independence National Historical
Park Collection*

Major John Pitcairn

Lieutenant Colonel Banastre Tarleton

Chief Joseph Brant

Major General
Baron von Riedesel

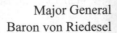

The Americans & Their Allies

General George Washington

Independence National Historical Park Collection

Brigadier General Henry Knox

Independence National Historical Park Collection

Major General Benjamin Lincoln

Independence National Historical Park Collection

Marie Jean Paul Roch Yves Gilbert
Motier, Marquis de Lafayette

*Independence National
Historical Park Collection*

Brigadier General Anthony Wayne

*Independence National Historical
Park Collection*

Colonel "Light Horse Harry" Lee

*Independence National Historical
Park Collection*

General Nathanael Greene

*Independence National Historical
Park Collection*

General Horatio Gates

*Independence National
Historical Park Collection*

General Daniel Morgan

*Independence National Historical
Park Collection*

General Benedict Arnold

*Independence National
Historical Park Collection*

Andrew Pickens

Francois Joseph Paul,
comte de Grasse-Tilly

Thomas Sumter

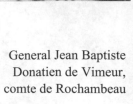

General Jean Baptiste
Donatien de Vimeur,
comte de Rochambeau

Preface

*I*f the number of books being published is any indication, the popularity of the American Revolution is increasing. We think this interest is long overdue. Too many people over too many years rush past the Revolutionary War as if it was a forgone conclusion the Patriots would prevail. Many seem to believe it consisted of little more than a handful of small pitched battles and sporadic guerrilla activity unworthy of study. In fact, the war's killing fields blanketed the North American continent from Canada to the Gulf of Mexico, and from the winding coastal lowlands to the Mississippi River Valley. The naval war stretched from the North Atlantic to the Caribbean, from Lake Champlain in upstate New York all the way to the British Isles—and beyond.

Every young student in America is taught something (though not nearly enough) about the American Revolution. Few come away appreciating the sheer size and scope of the war that gave birth to the United States and spun world history in a different direction. Perhaps this helps explain why this conflict has been elbowed aside in favor of other areas of interest.

The bravery on display at Lexington Green and Concord Bridge is indeed inspiring, and Washington's brilliant victory over Lord Cornwallis at Yorktown more than six years later moved the war from the battlefield to the diplomacy table. Sandwiched between Lexington and Yorktown were the scores of battles, skirmishes, naval engagements, massacres, and expeditions that dictated the course of the war and its eventual outcome. Indeed, fascinating operations associated with the Revolutionary War were conducted *after* the British surrendered at Yorktown. The vast majority of these battles and operations remain obscure to almost everyone.

For example, how many people know the small American navy captured a British fort in the Bahamas, or that a major campaign was undertaken to seize Newport, Rhode Island? John Paul Jones is well known as the captain of *Bonhomme Richard*, but how many remember (or ever learned) his voyage around the British Isles in 1778 included an operation on English soil? Benedict Arnold's name is synonymous with "traitor," but few know that after his defection he returned to lead British troops on American soil and was responsible for burning much of the town of New London, Connecticut. France provided invaluable assistance during the war—but so did Spain and (to a lesser degree) The Netherlands. Because of the assistance rendered by Spanish forces to the American cause of liberty, especially during the 1781 operations in Florida and along the Gulf Coast, descendants of Hispanic troops who served in North America are eligible for membership in the Sons of the American Revolution and the Daughters of the American Revolution.

Outstanding books have been written about many of the major battles of the war. *A Guide to the Battles of the American Revolution* is not intended to supersede a single one of them. Our book is not the last word or definitive treatment of any action, nor did we intend it to be. To our knowledge, no single readily available source has pulled the threads of this vast war together by offering detailed accounts (and in most instances an original map) of nearly every engagement. We believe this method of presentation offers a ready reference guide to the war's conflicts, reinforces the size and global scope of the Revolution, and identifies a wide variety of areas ripe for further study. In order to produce this work, we relied upon quality secondary scholarship, reinforced with light archival and firsthand research and visits to many of the fields.

A Guide to the Battles of the American Revolution presents the war's conflicts in what we believe is a unique way. Each entry offers a wide and rich—but consistent—template of information so readers can find exactly what they are seeking. For example, each entry begins with introductory details including the date of the event(s), the theater and location, campaign with which it is associated, the ranks and commanders, opposing forces, terrain, weather, time of day, and the length of the action.

The body of each entry offers both a Colonial and British perspective of the unfolding military situation, a detailed and unbiased account of the fighting that transpired, a discussion of casualties, an assessment of the consequences of the battle, and what (if anything) remains to be seen where the fighting occurred. Each entry concludes with suggestions for further reading, though we have deliberately limited these suggestions to readily available accounts (as opposed to sending readers to manuscript collections). Nearly every entry is supported with an original map.

Presented in this way, we believe each entry stands entirely on its own and can be read and appreciated accordingly. The Introduction and Authors' Note offer additional information and insights about the respective armies, organizations, and personnel. Familiarity with this material will help readers more fully appreciate the entries that follow.

The methodology we have chosen requires some narrative redundancy, which we have endeavored to minimize as much as possible. We are also aware that many sources conflict—especially regarding numbers engaged and losses suffered. Unlike the Civil War or World War II, records for the American Revolution are scant by comparison. We have tried to follow generally accepted interpretations of events. On occasion we note when and how the sources conflict on important issues.

It is our sincere hope readers find this approach fresh and the entries both informative and entertaining. It is inevitable that mistakes will have slipped through despite our best efforts to spot them, and that some readers will disagree with a particular version of events. We apologize in advance for any errors, factual or otherwise. We have no one to blame but ourselves.

Acknowledgments

As with any book, many people contributed to this one to help make it possible. Unfortunately, it is nearly impossible to remember everyone. If you helped us in some way but don't find your name here, please forgive our oversight and know we cherish your kindness and assistance.

Frank Hanner, Director of the National Infantry Museum, Fort Benning, Georgia and his staff (whose knowledge of 18th century warfare, tactics, and weapons are unexcelled) were especially helpful and filled gaps in our research. The museum's collections are unique, vast, and truly a national treasure. We encourage everyone to visit and explore their holdings.

Chris Revels, Director of the Kings Mountain National Military Park, provided personal assistance in researching archival records of the National Park System (NPS). The rural backwoods of America were fiercely contested during the Revolutionary War, and the NPS files contain unpublished maps, journals, and artifacts that highlight their details.

Dr. Roger Zeimet, whose knowledge of the American Revolution inspired J. David Dameron to explore history, ever deeper, was always available for keen insight and thoughtful discussion.

J. David Dameron's colleagues at Troy University—especially Dr. David White, Dr. Michael Whitlock, and Dr. James Williams—offered assistance and encouragement throughout this project.

We are also indebted to Chief Librarian Ericka Loze and her staff at the Donovan Research Library, U.S. Army Infantry School, Fort Benning, Georgia. Their expertise in locating old military maps and early Army journals proved invaluable to our research. The Donovan Library is filled with rare volumes and is a pleasure to explore.

Sarah Stephan made the manuscript stronger by proofreading our work and offering valuable suggestions, as she always does. She is indispensable. Lee Merideth performed a similar role and prepared the index. He is a good friend, and has been for a long, long time. May it always be so.

We also wish to thank everyone who assisted us while "on the road" locating and exploring the battlefields of our remarkable American Revolution.

Finally, both of us are thankful for our wonderful families and the assistance and patience they demonstrated during the development of this book. They don't come any better.

Authors' Note

Campaigns and Battles of the American Revolution (1775-1783)

The terminology used by those who report and describe military affairs has changed over time. For example, "campaign," "battle," "engagement," "skirmish," or "action" meant different things to different people at different times in our history. Each of these commonly used terms describes a conflict between armed combatants, but their specific usage can sometimes be mis-construed—especially when discussed or presented in narrative form. It is important that readers clearly understand the events set forth in this book, and the framework within which they are presented. To assist in that regard, we utilized the United States Department of Defense (DOD) Dictionary of Military Terms (JCS Pub 1) to define the following:[1]

> *Campaign*: A series of related military operations aimed at accomplishing a strategic or operational objective within a given time and space.

---

1. JP 1-02, DOD *Dictionary of Military and Associated Terms* (Department of Defense (DOD) Dictionary of Military Terms—JCS Pub 1). Washington D. C.: Government Printing Office, April 12, 2001; Alger, John I., *Definitions and Doctrine of the Military Art: Past and Present* (Wayne, NJ: Avery Publishing Group, 1985).

Engagement or *Skirmish*: A tactical conflict or chance meeting, usually between opposing lower echelon maneuver forces.

The following commonly-used related military terms are defined as follows:

Battle: A major confrontation between combatants that usually results in significant casualties.

Action: A small-scale, brief encounter between lower echelon forces that usually results in few casualties and/or little tactical advantage to either side.

The United States military has identified specific battles and campaigns in which its armed forces have engaged in combat against its enemies. During the American Revolution (1775-1783), the first time our nation went to war, the country's national army (known as the Continental Line) and others with an allegiance to separate colonies or states (state militia) fought the British. (Each colony, which became a state by uniting for the purpose of waging war to achieve independence from England, maintained to varying degrees its own militia army and often a small navy.) These Regulars and state militiamen participated together in most of the war's armed engagements. The distinctions about who fought where and when can be, and often are, important. This is because the U.S. Armed Forces traces its roots to specific units and actions through complex lineages and associations. As a result, many smaller but significant armed encounters fought during the Revolutionary War—what we would commonly refer to as battles and campaigns—are not acknowledged in official histories by the modern United States Department of Defense unless Federal (Continental) army and/or navy units participated in the event.

Even this seemingly simple standard, however, can be difficult in its application. For example, the men who fought at Lexington and Concord (April 19, 1775) were New England militia, and not soldiers of the United States Army. However, the U.S. Army traces its inception to these militia units because they went on to form the nucleus of what would become the

2. Wright, Robert K. Jr., *The Continental Army* (Washington D.C.: Government Printing Office, 1983), pp 3-19; Conn, Stetson, ed., *American Military History* (Washington D.C.: Government Printing Office, 1989, p. 44; *U.S. Army Field Manual* (FM 7-21-13) "The Soldiers Guide," Chapter 4, Lineage and Honors (Washington D.C.: Government Printing Office, 2003), 48-56.

Continental Army and conducted the opening events of our first national war.[2]

In contrast, militiamen not connected to specific units of the U.S. Army are looked upon quite differently. For example, one of the most successful offensive operations of the entire war was fought in South Carolina at Kings Mountain on October 7, 1780. There, a combined force of militiamen from several Southern states assembled and conducted a short campaign that culminated in one of the most important battles of the war. They did so without any participation, guidance, or assistance from the Continental authorities. Many campaigns large and small waged in the backwoods and rural villages are not officially acknowledged by US military authorities.

The same is true regarding America's allies. The French (and to a lesser degree, the Spanish) undertook significant campaigns and achieved impressive combat victories that are habitually overlooked even though they played an integral part in winning America's independence. The shots fired on Lexington Green truly were heard around the world because they eventually brought in other countries who shared a common enemy: England. The result was an American Revolution that, for all practical purposes, escalated into a world war. We decided to include Allied armed encounters against the British so readers will better understand the global nature of the Revolutionary War. Students of the period must at least be aware of these Allied-sponsored events to fully appreciate the holistic effect they had upon England's ability to wage war in America. All the combat between the British armed forces and those of the United States and its allies (French, Spanish, and Dutch) from 1775 to 1783 is interconnected to varying degrees, and together contributed to the final field victory at Yorktown, Virginia, in 1781, and the Treaty of Paris in February 1783. The Allied battles and smaller engagements we include in this study were part of the following campaigns: Cherokee, Snow, Spanish, Illinois, and Southern.

Major Land Battles and Campaigns

The American Revolution gave common cause to a group of British colonies rife with substantial differences on nearly every major topic from boundary disputes to tariffs. The coalition that came together to fight to secure its right to exist as a sovereign entity referred to its constituent parts first as colonies, provinces, states, and finally an independent nation. How they referred to themselves mattered not to King George III and Parliament. His Majesty and the Crown's leading politicians looked upon the unrest as ungrateful American colonies in rebellion, and dispatched bits and pieces of the most powerful armed force on the planet to quell it.

After the opening combat in the spring of 1775 in New England between Patriot militiamen and British troops headquartered in Boston, American politicians and other influential voices gathered to formally organize their respective colonial militias into cohesive fighting units. The end result was the creation of a standing national army. Colonial leaders realized very early in the game that the only way they would be able to effectively oppose the professional British army was to combine their resources and fight as one. As Benjamin Franklin cleverly observed when informed of the petty arguments between state and federal leaders, "We must all hang together, or most assuredly we will hang separately." Today's Army was founded by an official act of the Continental Congress on June 14, 1775. This legislation called for the establishment of the "American Continental Army." The next day Congress unanimously appointed Virginian George Washington as its commander in chief. Six days later Washington began his quest to capture or destroy America's armed enemies in what he referred to as the "United Provinces." Authorized by Congress to "take charge of the Army of the United Colonies," he set forth to fuse together a courageous but untrained band of men to fight to secure the independence of the United States of America.[3]

Although others had angled for the job (most notably John Hancock, the flowery signer of the Declaration of Independence), there was little doubt it was Washington's to turn down. Although he had experience in both the British army and Virginia militia, Washington's record was not one that inspired widespread confidence. His rather hasty surrender of Fort Duquesne (Fort Necessity) to the French in 1754 was the opening salvo of the bloody French and Indian War in North America. The next year the 23-year-old Virginian was lucky to survive Braddock's Defeat, one of the worst massacres on American soil. Washington's long and varied experience, however, coupled with his uncommonly keen mind, courage, character, and physical attributes left him unmatched in the selection process.

3. *Journals of the Continental Congress, 1774-1789*. Volume II (May 10-September 20, 1775). Washington DC: Government Printing Office, 1905, pp. 90-95; Fitzpatrick, John Clement. *The Writings of George Washington from the Original Manuscript Sources,* Volume 3, General Orders Head Quarters, Cambridge, July 4, 1775 (Washington: Government Printing Office, 1931-1944).

His task was immense, and one often glossed over. Washington had never led more than small numbers of men, and he knew nothing about leading a large army in the field. But that was only the beginning of his problems. Generally speaking, his overarching task was to gather together untrained men from what were essentially thirteen different "countries" and forge them into an army. It fell to him to convince these farmers, clerks, teachers, lawyers, and laborers to join an ill-supplied and poorly equipped army and risk their lives in a fight against terrible odds. He asked them to fight not for food, wine, gold, or conquest, but for something that could not be eaten, drank, spent, or planted. The ideal of liberty was a new one, and convincing others to fight and die for it was a mighty achievement.

The U.S. Army officially recognizes sixteen campaigns and battles as significant operations conducted during the course of the American Revolution (1775-1783). These operations include:

Lexington (April 19, 1775)
Ticonderoga (May 10, 1775)
Boston (June 17, 1775 - March 17, 1776)
Québec (August 28, 1775 - July 3, 1776)
Charleston (June 28-29, 1776; March 29 - May 12, 1780)
Long Island (August 26-29, 1776)
Trenton (December 26, 1776)
Princeton (January 3, 1777)
Saratoga (July 2 - October 17, 1777)
Brandywine (September 11, 1777)
Germantown (October 4, 1777)
Monmouth (June 28, 1778)
Savannah (December 29, 1778; September 16 - October 10, 1779)
Cowpens (January 17, 1781)
Guilford Court House (March 15, 1781)
Yorktown (September 28 - October 19, 1781)[4]

According to official Army records, between 1775 and 1783 the Continental Army lost 4,044 killed and another 6,004 wounded. It is

---

4. "The Soldiers Guide," pp. 48- 56; U.S. Army Regulation (AR 870-5) "Organizational History," Named Campaigns (Washington DC: Government Printing Office); "Organizational History," U.S. Army Center for Military History (Washington DC: Government Printing Office, 1999); U.S. Army Regulation (AR 600-82), "U.S. Army Regimental System" (Washington DC: Government Printing Office); This information is also found on the U.S. Army website at: http://www.army.mil/cmh-pg/reference/rwcmp.htm.

important to note that state militia—whose battles are not included in Continental Army reports—suffered significant numbers of killed and wounded that are not reflected in these figures.[5] For details regarding the organizations of the Continental Army, please refer to pages xlvii – lxiii.

Major Naval Battles and Campaigns

Like the Army, the Navy and Marine Corps also experienced a difficult genesis. To the seamen of the 18th Century, an American victory at sea seemed even more improbable than success on land. In 1775 England ruled the seas with its vast, efficient, and professional navy. Against these hundreds of warships the newly formed Continental Navy had little to rely upon except courage and persistence.

The U.S. Navy was authorized by an official act of the Continental Congress on October 13, 1775. On November 10 Congress authorized the formation of a Marine Corps composed of two battalions. The construction of the first fleet began December 3, 1775. On March 19, 1776, Congress authorized privateers "to cruise on the enemies of these united colonies."[6]

Against long odds, the small Continental Navy struggled throughout the war to maintain a credible presence on the high seas. Despite crippling losses, the navy vexed British authorities by harassing shipping along the American coast, into the Caribbean, and around the British home islands.

When hostilities erupted in 1775, Boston harbor was a hotbed of waterborne recalcitrance. A wide variety of armed ships was operated there by Patriots anxious to annoy and punish the British. Other colonies organized their own maritime capabilities along inland waterways and in coastal operations. Men, vessels, and equipment were raised to support the nascent Continental Navy. Throughout the colonies privateers also

---

5. *Selected Manpower Statistics and Casualty Reports: Revolutionary War* (Washington: US Department of Defense Directorate for Information, Operations and Reports, DOD M01), Table 2-23; This information is also found on the Department of Defense, Office of the Secretary of Defense website at: http://web1.whs.osd.mil/mmid/m01/SMS223R.htm.

6. Clark, William Bell, ed., *Naval Documents of the American Revolution*, vol. 2, p. 442; *Journal of the Continental Congress, 13 October 1775* (Washington, DC: Government Printing Office, 1966), pp. 965-975; Butterfield, L. H., ed., *Diary and Autobiography of John Adams,* vol. 3 (Cambridge, MA.: Harvard University Press, 1961). This information is also located on the U.S.

conducted support operations by harassing British ships and seizing vessels and supplies critical to the overall war effort.

Numerous small-scale naval expeditions were organized during the war to attack enemy shipping along distant shores. Unfortunately, only one— Valcour Island on Lake Champlain—is routinely mentioned in general histories of the war. Many others were important on several levels, though usually ignored. In 1776, for example, Commodore Esek Hopkins led a small armada to New Providence in the Bahamas, where he launched a successful amphibious assault against British forts and captured invaluable military stores. With French assistance, John Paul Jones boldly led a small armada (including his famous ships *Ranger* and *Bonhomme Richard*) to the British Isles to conduct amphibious operations against enemy coastal strongholds. These were our country's inaugural sea battles, and they deserve to be remembered. The epic War of 1812 battle between USS *Constitution* and HMS *Serapis*, the breathtaking technological innovations witnessed during the Civil War, and the naval engagements in the Pacific Ocean at Midway and elsewhere are built upon a foundation of Massachusetts timber, iron nails, tar, rope, and the blood and sweat of brave men who went to sea in 1775 against the world's most powerful navy.

Because the small navy was not capable of undertaking large-scale pitched naval campaigns against the British navy, its effort was conducted by small fleets of privateers leavened with a sprinkling of Continental ships. However, the Continental Navy did play an important role in several land campaigns, including the fighting around New York in 1776, Philadelphia in 1777, and a variety of operations in Charleston and Savannah. The entrance of France and Spain into the war as American allies forced the Royal Navy to defend more rigorously and thoroughly vast tracks of land and sea and fight large-scale maritime battles against credible deep sea navies as far away as the Indian Ocean and as close as coastal Virginia.

The United States Navy officially recognizes ten campaigns and major battles as significant operations conducted during the course of the American Revolution (1775-1783). These include:

1. New Providence, Bahamas, operation (March 3, 1776)
2. Inland waters and amphibious operations (such as the 1779 Penobscot Bay Expedition)
3. West Indies and European convoy operations
4. Operations in European waters (Jones's Expedition)
5. Commerce raiding operations
6. *Randolph-Yarmouth* (March 7, 1778)
7. *Ranger-Drake* (April 24, 1778)

8. *Bonhomme Richard-Serapis* (September 23, 1779)
9. Other single-ship actions
10. Transport and packet operations[7]

The composition, disposition, and capabilities of the Continental Navy changed during the war, primarily because of the difficulties building, securing, and maintaining ships. The challenges of developing a credible fleet capable of fulfilling its missions was compounded by the domineering presence of the Royal Navy operating in American waters. The result was predictable: most of the American ships were destroyed by the British or scuttled to prevent their capture. According to official naval records, 342 seamen were killed or mortally wounded in action, and another 114 were wounded. The Marines lost 49 killed and 70 wounded. State militia crews suffered additional killed and wounded not reflected in these numbers.[8]

Vessels of the Continental Navy

The following list of sailing ships obtained or built and employed by the Continental Navy during the American Revolution are restricted to those officially listed by the United States Navy as having served in the "Continental" fleet.

Scores of additional vessels served the Patriot cause, some flying state flags and others as privateers. Observant readers will quickly note that famous warships like *Bonhomme Richard* are not included on this list. The reason is simple: John Paul Jones's famous ship was provided to him by the French government; its only direct ties to the Continental Navy were its American captain and crew.

7. Cooney, David M. *A Chronology of the U.S. Navy: 1775-1965* (New York: Franklin Watts, 1965); Neeser, Robert Wilden, *Statistical and Chronological History of the United States Navy, 1775-1907,* 2 vols. (New York: Macmillan, 1909). This information is also located on the U.S. Navy's website at: http://www.history.navy.mil/faqs/stream/faq45-2.htm.

8. U.S. Navy Department, Bureau of Naval Personnel, Casualty Branch. *Navy Casualties Deaths Due to Enemy Action 1776-1937* (Washington, D.C., 1937); Marine Corps Historical Center (US), Reference Section, "Marine Corps Casualties 1775-1995." (Washington, D.C., 1996); Millett, Allan R., *Semper Fidelis: The History of the United States Marine Corps* (New York: Macmillan, 1980); *Selected Manpower Statistics,* Table 2-23. This information is also located on the Department of Defense, Office of the Secretary of Defense website at: http://web1.whs.osd.mil/mmid/m01/SMS223R.htm.

Names	Guns	Type	Placed into Service	Disposition[9]
Alfred	24	Ship	Purchased 1775	Captured March 9, 1778 by HMS *Ariadne* and *Ceres*
Columbus	20	Ship	Purchased 1775	Burned March 27, 1778 after being forced ashore by a British squadron
Andrea Doria	14	Brig	Purchased 1775	Burned to prevent capture, November 21, 1777
Cabot	14	Brig	Purchased 1775	Destroyed 1779
Providence	12	Sloop	Purchased 1775	Destroyed 1777
Hornet	10	Sloop	Purchased 1775	Destroyed 1777
Wasp	8	Schooner	Purchased 1775	Destroyed 1777
Fly	8	Schooner	Purchased 1775	Captured by British cutter Alert 1777

9. Mooney, James L., ed., *Dictionary of American Naval Fighting Ships*, Volume I, A-B, (1959); Volume I, Part A, 1991, GPO Stock No. 008-046-00041-7; Volume II, C-F, 1963, GPO Stock No. 008-046-00007-7; Volume III, G-K, 1968; Volume IV, L-M, 1969, GPO Stock No. 008-046-00009-3, Volume V, N-Q, 1970; Volume VI, R-S, 1976, GPO Stock No. 008-046-00056-5; Volume VII, T-V, 1981, GPO Stock No. 008-046-00100-6; Volume VIII, W-Z, 1981, GPO Stock No. 008-046-00101-4.

Names	Guns	Type	Placed into Service	Disposition
Lexington	16	Brig	Purchased 1776	Captured by British cutter *Alert* 1777
Reprisal	16	Brig	Purchased 1776	Lost at sea 1777
Hampden	14	Brig	Purchased 1776	Sold 1777
Independence	10	Sloop	Purchased 1776	Wrecked 1778
Sachem	10	Sloop	Purchased 1776	Destroyed 1777
Mosquito	4	Sloop	Purchased 1776	Destroyed 1777
Raleigh	32	Frigate	Launched 1776	Captured 1778
Hancock	32	Frigate	Launched 1776	Captured 1777
Warren	32	Frigate	Launched 1776	Destroyed 1779
Washington	32	Frigate	Launched 1776	Destroyed 1777
Randolph	32	Frigate	Launched 1776	Lost in action 1778
Providence	28	Frigate	Launched 1776	Captured 1780
Trumbull	28	Frigate	Launched 1776	Captured 1781
Congress	28	Frigate	Launched 1776	Destroyed 1777

Names	Guns	Type	Placed into Service	Disposition
Virginia	28	Frigate	Launched 1776	Captured 1778
Effingham	28	Frigate	Launched 1776	Destroyed 1777
Boston	24	Frigate	Launched 1776	Captured 1780
Montgomery	24	Frigate	Launched 1776	Destroyed 1777
Delaware	24	Frigate	Launched 1776	Destroyed 1777
Ranger	18	Ship	Launched 1777	Captured 1780
Resistance	10	Brigantine	Launched 1777	Captured 1778
Surprise	?	Sloop	Purchased 1777	Unknown
Racehorse	12	Sloop	Captured 1776	Destroyed
Repulse	8	Xebec (Zebec)	Pennsylvania State Navy gunboat lent to Continental Navy 1777	Destroyed 1777
Champion	8	Xebec	Pennsylvania State Navy gunboat loaned to the Continental Navy 1777	Destroyed 1777

Names	Guns	Type	Placed into Service	Disposition
L'Indien	40	Frigate	Built in Holland 1777	Sold to France; bought by South Carolina Navy as *South Carolina*
Queen of France	28	Frigate	Purchased 1777	Sunk 1780
Dolphin	10	Cutter	Purchased 1777	Unknown
Surprise	10	Lugger	Purchased 1777	Seized by France
Revenge	14	Cutter	Purchased 1777	Sold 1779
Alliance	32	Frigate	Launched 1778	Sold 1785
General Gates	18	Ship	Purchased 1778	Sold 1779
Retaliation	?	Brigantine	Purchased 1778	Unknown
Pigot	8	Schooner	Captured 1778	Unknown
Confederacy	32	Frigate	Launched 1779	Captured 1781

Introduction

British and Allied Soldiers
in the American Revolution

British Soldiers and Organizations
in the American Revolution

During the 18th century, the army of Great Britain served as the "backbone" of the Crown. As the executor of the King's will, these soldiers were both professionally trained and proficient in their duties. The regiments of foot or infantry bore the burden of war and served as the primary military resource on America's battlefields. The infantry was usually supported by light cavalry or dragoons and artillery, but the foot soldier's sole purpose was to close with and destroy his enemy. Marching directly into battle and fighting in tight linear formations required tremendous discipline and confidence in one's officers and comrades. England's army excelled in all these categories and was (and still is) universally recognized as the finest military machine of its age.

When the American Revolution erupted in 1775 there were seventy regiments of foot. During the course of the war that number was expanded to 105 regiments. Each regiment was comprised of eight battalion companies. These companies were supported by one light company and one grenadier company. These were employed on the regiment's flanks or wherever the commander maneuvered them to protect his main force or deploy rapidly for offensive operations. Each regiment was organized with 811 officers and men under the command of a colonel. The commander had 40 officers, 72 non-commissioned officers (NCOs), 24 drummers, two fifers, and 672 privates. Each regiment carried three non-existent men on the rolls to provide adequate pay to maintain uniforms and for whatever else the commander chose to do with the funds to maintain his unit.

The British infantryman carried the .75 caliber flintlock musket known affcctionately as the "Brown Bess." This 15-pound weapon was used with great effect in massed formations and was tipped with a foot-long bayonet, which the soldiers were famous for wielding in battle. The grenadier company was comprised of the largest and strongest men available to the commander. These men typically wore tall bearskin hats and were considered an elite outfit and the most intimidating soldiers on the battlefield. The light infantry was a mobile reserve of maneuverable physically adept men who were normally used as rangers. They were often armed with hatchets and knives and were outstanding in close-quarter fighting.

England was stretched to the breaking point during the American Revolution. In addition to maintaining units at home for defensive purposes, England employed land and naval assets across much of the globe, from the West Indies to the East Indies.

The British regiments that deployed to America and fought there during the war included:

1st Regiment of Foot Guards: Arrived in America in 1776 (New York). Long Island, Fort Washington, Philadelphia Campaign, Brandywine, Monmouth Court House, Charleston, Guilford Court House, Green Spring, and surrendered at Yorktown, Virginia.

3rd Regiment of Foot (*The Buffs*): Arrived in America in 1781 (South Carolina). Charleston, Ninety Six, Eutaw Springs; sent to Jamaica in 1782.

4th (*The King's Own*) *Regiment of Foot*: Arrived in America in 1774 (Boston). Lexington, Concord, Siege of Boston, New York Campaign, Philadelphia Campaign, Charleston, East Florida; sent to Barbados.

5th Regiment of Foot: Arrived in America in 1774 (Boston). Bunker Hill, New York Campaign, Philadelphia Campaign, Brandywine, and Germantown; sent to the West Indies in 1778.

7th Regiment of Foot (*Royal Fusiliers*): Arrived in Québec in 1773. Fort St. John, Chambly, Québec, Forts Clinton and Montgomery, Philadelphia Campaign, Monmouth Court House, Charleston, and Cowpens; split into two sections and assigned to Savannah and New York in 1782.

8th (*The King's*) *Regiment of Foot*: Arrived in Québec in 1768 and assigned to garrison duty in Canada (Niagara, Oswego). Fort Stanwix.

9th (*The East Norfolk*) *Regiment of Foot*: Arrived in Québec in 1776. Lake Champlain, Burgoyne's Campaign (captured at Saratoga).

10th (*The North Lincolnshire*) *Regiment of Foot*: Arrived in America in 1774 (Boston). Lexington, Concord, Bunker Hill, Siege of Boston, New York Campaign, Philadelphia Campaign, and Brandywine. Reorganized into other regiments in 1779.

14th (*Bedfordshire*) *Regiment of Foot*: Arrived in America in 1775 (Virginia). Great Bridge. Reorganized and transferred to Jamaica in 1782.

15th (*The Yorkshire East Riding*) *Regiment of Foot*: Arrived in America in 1776 (North Carolina). Charleston, New York Campaign, Philadelphia Campaign, Brandywine, and Monmouth Court House. Transferred to East Florida in 1778 and St. Kitts in 1779.

16th (*The Buckinghamshire*) *Regiment of Foot*: Arrived in America in 1776 (Georgia). Savannah and Pensacola. Returned to England in 1782.

16th Regiment of (*2nd Queen's*) *Light Dragoons*: Arrived in America in 1776 (New York). Fought in the Philadelphia Campaign, Brandywine, Paoli, and Monmouth Court House. Transferred to Charleston in 1779 and fought at Eutaw Springs. Transferred to the 17th Regiment of Dragoons in 1778.

17th (*The Leicestershire*) *Regiment of Foot*: Arrived in America in 1775 (Boston). Siege of Boston, New York Campaign, Philadelphia Campaign, Brandywine, Germantown, Whitemarsh, Monmouth Court House, Stony Point, and the Siege of Yorktown (captured).

17th Regiment of Light Dragoons: Arrived in America in 1775 (Boston). Fought in the New York Campaign, Long Island, Fort Washington, Princeton, Forts Clinton and Montgomery, Philadelphia Campaign, Whitemarsh, and Monmouth Court House. Elements transferred to Charleston in 1779 as the British Legion (led by Lt. Col. Banastre Tarleton), and fought at Blackstock's Plantation, Cowpens, Guilford Court House, and Yorktown (captured).

18th (*The Royal Irish*) *Regiment of Foot*: Arrived in America in 1774 (Boston). Lexington, Concord, and Bunker Hill. Reorganized in 1776 into other units.

19th (*The 1st Yorkshire North Riding*) *Regiment of Foot*: Arrived in America in 1781 (South Carolina). Charleston, Ninety Six, and Eutaw Springs; sent to St. Lucia in 1782.

20th (*The East Devonshire*) *Regiment of Foot*: Arrived in Québec in 1776. Fought in Burgoyne's Campaign (captured at Saratoga).

21st Regiment of Foot (*Royal North British Fusiliers*): Arrived in Québec in 1776. Lake Champlain and in Burgoyne's Campaign (captured at Saratoga).

22nd (The Cheshire) Regiment of Foot: Arrived in America in 1775 (Boston). Siege of Boston and New York Campaign.

23rd Regiment of Foot (Royal Welch Fusiliers): Arrived in America in 1775 (Boston). Siege of Boston, New York Campaign, Philadelphia Campaign, Brandywine, Germantown, Whitemarsh, Monmouth Court House, Stony Point, Charleston, Camden, Guilford Court House, and the Siege of Yorktown (captured).

24th (2nd Warwickshire) Regiment of Foot: Arrived in Québec in 1776. Lake Champlain, Burgoyne's Campaign (captured at Saratoga).

26th (The Cameronian) Regiment of Foot: Arrived in Québec in 1775. Assigned to garrison duty in Canada (Montreal, Crown Point). Fort St. John, Forts Clinton and Montgomery, Philadelphia Campaign, and Monmouth Court House. Reorganized in 1779.

27th (Enniskillings) Regiment of Foot: Arrived in America in 1775 (Boston). Siege of Boston, New York Campaign, Philadelphia Campaign. Sent to East Florida in 1778 and transferred to St. Kitts in 1779.

28th (North Gloucestershire) Regiment of Foot: Arrived in America in 1776 (North Carolina). Charleston, New York Campaign, Philadelphia Campaign, Brandywine, and Monmouth Court House. Transferred to East Florida in 1778 and St. Kitts in 1779.

29th (Worcestershire) Regiment of Foot: Arrived in America in 1768 (Boston). The Siege of Boston. Transferred to Québec in 1776. Elements participated in Burgoyne's Campaign (captured at Saratoga).

30th (Cambridgeshire) Regiment of Foot: Arrived in America in 1781 (South Carolina). Charleston, Ninety Six, Eutaw Springs; sent to St. Lucia in 1782.

31st (Huntingdonshire) Regiment of Foot: Arrived in Québec in 1776. Lake Champlain and elements participated in Burgoyne's Campaign (captured at Saratoga).

33rd (1st Yorkshire West Riding) Regiment of Foot: Arrived in America in 1776 (North Carolina). Charleston, New York Campaign, Philadelphia Campaign, Brandywine, Germantown, Whitemarsh, and Monmouth Court House. Returned to Charleston in 1779 and Camden, Guilford Court House, Green Spring, and the Siege of Yorktown (captured).

34th (Cumberland) Regiment of Foot: Arrived in Québec in 1776. Lake Champlain, Burgoyne's Campaign (captured at Saratoga).

35th (Dorsetshire) Regiment of Foot: Arrived in America in 1775 (Boston). Siege of Boston, Bunker Hill, New York Campaign; sent to St. Lucia in 1778.

37th (North Hampshire) Regiment of Foot: Arrived in America in 1776 (North Carolina). Charleston. Transferred north and fought in the New York

Campaign, Philadelphia Campaign, Brandywine, and Monmouth Court House. Split into two units and transferred to East Florida and Nova Scotia in 1778.

38th (*1st Staffordshire*) *Regiment of Foot*: Arrived in America in 1774 (Boston). Lexington, Concord, Bunker Hill, Siege of Boston, and New London.

40th (*2nd Somersetshire*) *Regiment of Foot*: Arrived in America in 1775 (Boston). The Siege of Boston, New York Campaign, Philadelphia Campaign, Brandywine, Paoli, and Germantown. Transferred to East Florida in 1778, and Antigua and Barbados in 1779.

42nd Regiment of Foot (*Royal Highland Regiment*): Arrived in America in 1776 (New York). Long Island, Fort Washington, Harlem Heights, Paoli, Whitemarsh, Philadelphia Campaign, Brandywine, and Monmouth Court House. Sent to East Florida in 1778 and fought at Charleston. Sent to fight in India in 1781.

43rd (*Monmouthshire*) *Regiment of Foot*: Arrived in America in 1774 (Boston). Lexington, Concord, Bunker Hill, Siege of Boston, Long Island, Fort Washington, and Green Spring.

44th (*East Essex*) *Regiment of Foot*: Arrived in America in 1775 (Boston). Siege of Boston, New York Campaign, Philadelphia Campaign, and Monmouth Court House. Transferred to Québec in 1779.

45th (*Nottinghamshire*) *Regiment of Foot*: Arrived in America in 1775 (Boston). Siege of Boston and Long Island. Reorganized in 1776.

46th (*Cornwall*) *Regiment of Foot*: Arrived in America in 1776 (North Carolina). Charleston. Transferred north and fought in the New York Campaign, Philadelphia Campaign, Brandywine, and Monmouth Court House. Reorganized and transferred to the West Indies in 1777.

47th (*Lancashire*) *Regiment of Foot*: Arrived in America in 1773 (New Jersey). Lexington, Concord, and the Siege of Boston before being transferred to Québec in 1776. Lake Champlain and Burgoyne's Campaign (captured at Saratoga).

49th (*Hertfordshire*) *Regiment of Foot*: Arrived in America in 1775 (Boston). Siege of Boston, New York Campaign, Philadelphia Campaign, and Monmouth Court House. Transferred to St. Lucia in 1778.

52nd (*Oxfordshire*) *Regiment of Foot* (*Light Infantry*): Arrived in America in 1774 (Boston). Lexington, Concord, Bunker Hill, Siege of Boston, Long Island, and Fort Washington. Reorganized in 1778.

53rd (*Shropshire*) *Regiment of Foot*: Arrived in Québec in 1776. Participated in Burgoyne's Campaign (captured at Saratoga).

54th (*West Norfolk*) *Regiment of Foot*: Arrived in America in 1776 (North Carolina). Charleston, was transferred north, and fought in the New York Campaign and New London. Transferred to Halifax in 1778.

55th (*Westmoreland*) *Regiment of Foot*: Arrived in America in 1775 (Boston). The Siege of Boston, New York Campaign, Philadelphia Campaign, and Monmouth Court House. Transferred to East Florida and St. Kitts in 1779.

57th (*West Middlesex*) *Regiment of Foot*: Arrived in America in 1776 (North Carolina). Charleston, transferred north, and fought in the New York Campaign. Stationed in New York and Halifax until the war's end in 1783.

59th (*2nd Nottinghamshire*) *Regiment of Foot*: Arrived in America in 1774 (Boston). Lexington, Concord, and the Siege of Boston. Reorganized in 1776.

60th (*Royal American*) *Regiment of Foot*: Arrived in America in 1776 (Georgia). Split up during the war, with some companies serving in the West Indies where they fought in Honduras, Nicaragua, and at St. Vincent. Those in America fought at Sunbury, Savannah, Augusta, Briar Creek, Mobile, Baton Rouge, and surrendered during the Siege of Pensacola.

62nd (*Wiltshire*) *Regiment of Foot*: Arrived in Québec in 1776. Participated in Burgoyne's Campaign (captured at Saratoga).

63rd (*West Suffolk*) *Regiment of Foot*: Arrived in America in 1775 (Boston). Siege of Boston, Bunker Hill, New York Campaign, Philadelphia Campaign, Monmouth Court House. Transferred to Charleston in 1779 and fought at Blackstock's Plantation, Hobkirk's Hill, and Eutaw Springs. Transferred to the West Indies in 1782.

64th (*2nd Staffordshire*) *Regiment of Foot*: Arrived in America in 1769 (Boston). Fought in the Siege of Boston, New York Campaign, Philadelphia Campaign, and Monmouth Court House. Transferred to Charleston in 1779 and fought at Eutaw Springs. Transferred to the West Indies in 1782.

65th (*2nd Yorkshire North Riding*) *Regiment of Foot*: Arrived in America in 1769 (Boston). Bunker Hill and the Siege of Boston. Reorganized and transferred to Gibraltar in 1782.

71st Regiment of Foot (*Fraser's Highlanders*): Arrived in America in 1776 (New York). Long Island, Fort Washington, Forts Clinton and Montgomery, Philadelphia Campaign, and Stony Point. Sent to Savannah in 1778 and fought at Briar Creek, Stono Ferry, Augusta, Savannah, Charleston, Camden, Cowpens, Guilford Court House, Green Spring, and Yorktown (captured).

74th Regiment of Foot (*Argyle Highlanders*): Arrived in America in 1779 (New York). Penobscot. Also served in garrison duty at Halifax.

76th Regiment of Foot (*MacDonnell's Highlanders*): Arrived in America in 1779 (New York). Transferred south and fought at Portsmouth, Green Spring, and Yorktown (captured).

79th Regiment of Foot (*Royal Liverpool Volunteers*): Sent to Jamaica in 1779. Served in the West Indies and fought in Honduras and Nicaragua.

80th Regiment of Foot (Royal Edinburgh Volunteers): Arrived in America in 1779 (New York). Transferred south and fought at Portsmouth, Green Spring, and Yorktown (captured).

82nd Regiment of Foot (Lanarkshire): Arrived in America in 1779 (New York). Penobscot. Transferred south and fought at Yorktown (captured).

84th Regiment of Foot (1st Battalion: Royal Highland Emigrants; 2nd Battalion: Young Royal Highlanders): 1775: Organized in North America, comprised of Provincial Loyalists and French and Indian War British veterans who had settled in Canada and New York. Fought in Quebec, the Hudson Valley, and in the Southern Theater at Charleston and Eutaw Springs.

British (Provincial American) Loyalists and Organizations in the American Revolution

During the Revolution, at least 25,000 men sided with England and fought as Tories (Loyalists). Thousands joined the English navy. They fought and died alongside their British counterparts in nearly every battle. Loyalist units with enough men to form companies, battalions, and regiments were organized and equipped just like regular British regiments.

In addition to their services to the Crown, many of these men fought as partisans, especially in the south. Most of the combatants who fought in the backwoods of the Carolinas, Georgia, and Florida were Americans—either Tory or Patriot. For example, Major Patrick Ferguson led the British Provincial Militia (Ferguson's Corps) in South Carolina and served as its brigadier general at Kings Mountain, where every soldier (with the exception of Ferguson) was American. The Loyalists provided invaluable service to the Crown; they knew the terrain better than their English counterparts and their supporting network of informants provided excellent information on enemy activity. Loyalist service divided families and communities. After the war, many Loyalists moved abroad to avoid acts of vengeance and retribution for having supported England.

The list below highlights the larger units raised in America during the war. It offers the year of organization, strength, and a synopsis of service:

American Legion: 1780: 400 men. Raised in New York and fought at Portsmouth and New London.

American Volunteers: 1779: 1,000 men. Raised in New York and South Carolina by Lt. Col. Patrick Ferguson. Savannah and Kings Mountain, where the entire unit was captured or killed.

British Legion: 1778: 775 men. Raised in New York by Lt. Col. Banastre Tarleton. Savannah, Charleston, Cowpens, Guilford Court House, and Yorktown (captured).

Butler's Rangers: 1777: 600 men. Raised in New York and Canada in 1777 by Lt. Col. John Butler. Participated in raids in Pennsylvania and New York.

DeLancey's Brigade: 1776: 1,750 men. Raised in New York by Brig. Gen. Oliver Delancy with three full battalions. The 1st Battalion was commanded by Lt. Col. John Cruger, deployed to Charleston, and defended Fort Ninety Six. The other two battalions fought in New York.

Duke of Cumberland's Regiment: 1781: 600 men. Raised in Charleston from Continentals captured at Camden. Deployed to Jamaica in 1781.

East Florida Rangers (King's Rangers): 1779: 860 men. Raised in Georgia and Florida by Lt. Col. Thomas Brown. Savannah and Augusta. Merged with the Georgia Loyalists in 1782.

Emmerich's Chasseurs: 1776: 250 men. Raised by Lt. Col. Andreas Emmerich in New York. Forts Clinton and Montgomery.

Georgia Loyalists: 1779: 175 men. Raised by Maj. James Wright and was merged with the East Florida Rangers in 1779.

Guides and Pioneers: 1776: 250 men. Raised in New York by Maj. Simon Frazer and attached to the Loyal American regiment in 1777.

Herlyhy's Corps: 1776: 300 men. Raised in Nova Scotia, St. Johns, and Newfoundland. Sent to New York in 1781.

Jamaica Legion & Jamaica Volunteers: 1779: 600 men. Raised in Jamaica by Governor John Dalling. Participated in raids in Nicaragua and Honduras.

Johnson's Royal Greens (King's Royal Regiment of New York or "King's Royal Yorkers"): 1776: 1,290 men. Raised by Col. Sir John Johnson in New York. Fought at Oriskany, Wyoming Massacre, and Fort Stanwix.

King's American Dragoons: 1780: 350 men. Raised by Lt. Col. Benjamin Thompson in New York.

King's American Regiment: 1776: 833 men. Organized by Col. Edmund Fanning in New York and fought at Forts Clinton and Montgomery, Charleston, and Savannah. Elements also served in East Florida, Kings Mountain (captured), and in Georgia.

King's Orange Rangers: 1776: 600 men. Raised in New York and fought at Charleston alongside the "Volunteers of Ireland."

LaMothe's Volunteer Company: 1778: 45 men. Raised in the Northwestern Territory (present-day Indiana) and served at Fort Vincennes.

Loyal American Rangers: 1780: 300 men. Raised in New York from Continental prisoners and deserters. Sent to Jamaica and fought in Honduras.

Loyal American Regiment: 1776: 690 men. Raised in New York by Col. Beverly Robinson. Fought during the Philadelphia Campaign, Forts Clinton and Montgomery, and in the raid on New London.

Loyal Newport Associators: 1777: 180 men. Raised for the defense of Newport, Rhode Island.

North Carolina Loyalists (North Carolina Volunteers, North Carolina Highlanders, Loyal North Carolina Regiment "Highlanders"): 1776: 3,000 men. Organized by exiled Royal Governor Josiah Martin to fight in North and South Carolina. As the units suffered losses, stragglers joined other Tory bands in the Carolinas; some fled to New York and joined other Provincial units.

Maryland Loyalists: 1777: 425 men. Raised by Lt. Colonel James Chalmers in Maryland and Pennsylvania. Served in New York and Halifax until transferred to Pensacola, where they surrendered in 1782.

New Jersey Volunteers (Skinner's Greens): 1776: 2,400 men. Composed of three full battalions raised in New Jersey by Brig. Gen. Cortland Skinner. Fought in New York, East Florida, Savannah, Eutaw Springs, Kings Mountain (one detachment), and Yorktown (captured).

New York Loyalists (Provincial Regiment): 1776: 500 men. Served in battle in New York, East Florida, Forts Clinton and Montgomery, Savannah, Camden, Charleston, and Hobkirk's Hill.

Pennsylvania Loyalists: 1777: 200 men. Organized in Philadelphia and fought alongside the Maryland Loyalists in New York and Halifax until transferred to Pensacola, where it surrendered in 1782.

Philadelphia Light Dragoons: 1777: 120 men. Raised by Captain Richard Hoveden for the British Legion and King's American Dragoons. Savannah, Charleston, Cowpens, Guilford Court House, and Yorktown (captured).

Prince of Wales's American Volunteers: 1776: 600 men from Connecticut and New York. This unit was commanded by Brig. Gen. Monteforte Brown and fought in New York, Charleston, and Hanging Rock, South Carolina.

Queen's Loyal Virginia Regiment: 1775: 600 men. Organized to defend Virginia from Patriot attacks. Great Bridge, Virginia. Transferred to New York and merged with the Queen's Rangers in 1776.

Royal American Reformees: 1777: 120 men. Comprised of Continental deserters and transferred to Canada for the duration of the war.

Royal Ethiopian Regiment: 1775 (Virginia): 300 men. Organized by Virginia's Royal Governor John Murray (Lord Dunmore). This unit was comprised of blacks who were promised freedom in return for their services to the Crown. Norfolk and Great Bridge, Virginia.

Royal Garrison Regiment (Royal Bermudian Regiment): 1778: 800 men. Organized in New York by Maj. William Sutherland. Paulus Hook, New Jersey, and was transferred to garrison duty in Halifax and Bermuda.

South Carolina Dragoons: 1780: 38 men. Organized in Charleston and attached to the South Carolina Royalists.

South Carolina Rangers: 1778: 81 men. Raised in Charleston and assigned to garrison duty at St. Augustine in East Florida, where it served for the duration.

South Carolina Royalists: 1781: 700 men. Raised in East Florida by Maj. Mark Prevost. Savannah, Charleston, Ninety Six, Hobkirk's Hill, and Eutaw Springs. Transferred to New York in 1782.

Volunteers of Ireland: 1777: 871 men. Raised in Pennsylvania and served in the New York Campaign, Charleston, Camden, and Hobkirk's Hill. Assigned to the British Army as the 105th Regiment of Foot in 1782.

West Florida Loyalists: 1779: 75 men. Raised in West Florida and served in the Siege of Pensacola.

West Florida Royal Foresters: 1780: 43 men. Raised in West Florida and served in the Siege of Pensacola.

West Jersey Cavalry: 1778: 160 men. Raised in Philadelphia and served in the New York Campaign. Merged into the King's American Dragoons in 1781.

West Jersey Volunteers: 1778: 200 men. Raised in Philadelphia and served in the New York Campaign. Merged into the New Jersey Volunteers.

Hessian Soldiers and Organizations in the American Revolution

Germany was not yet a nation when the first muskets were discharged on Lexington Green in 1775, but soldiers from independent German states were hired by England to augment its army during the American Revolution. By the time the Treaty of Paris was signed in 1783, nearly 29,000 Germans had served under the Union Jack. These troops hailed from six German states: Hesse-Cassel, Hesse Hanau, Brunswick, Waldeck, Anspach-Beyreuth, and Anhalt Zerbst. The Crown contracted directly with individual German princes for these men, a common protocol during the eighteenth century. The primary core of German (or Hessian) soldiers were provided by Friedrich II, the Landgraf (German noble) of Hesse-Cassel. Friedrich II committed fifteen "Regiments of Foot" (infantry) as well as support troops and resources to assist Great Britain with the rebellion in its American colonies. The professionally trained German soldiers served valiantly and suffered at least 2,300 casualties during the war.

Each Hesse-Cassel regiment was comprised of five companies with a paper total of 650 men. Each of these regiments was reduced by one grenadier company that was used to form four grenadier battalions comprised of 524 men each. An additional Jäger Corps (also known as chasseurs, which translates to "huntsmen") was organized to provide the Hessians with an elite unit of hand-selected warriors. These men were among the tallest and strongest soldiers. The Jägers fielded 600-700 men during the war and achieved notable battlefield success. Three companies of artillery supported the Hesse-Cassel regiments. Thus, the primary Hessian force deployed to fight in America was composed of fifteen infantry regiments, four grenadier battalions, one Jäger Corps, and three artillery companies. The Hesse-Cassel troops were divided into two divisions. Lieutenant General Leopold von Heister commanded the First Division, and Lieutenant General Wilhelm von Knyphausen commanded the Second Division. The Hesse-Cassel units that fought in America arrived in two expeditionary forces at New York in August of 1776.

Troops from the German state of Brunswick formed the second largest Hessian force—five infantry regiments, one grenadier battalion, one regiment of dragoons, a Jäger Corps, and a support artillery unit. The Brunswick troops were initially sent into Québec in June of 1776. These men served the British throughout the war in Canada and participated in Burgoyne's disastrous New York Campaign.

Anspach-Beyreuth provided two infantry regiments, one Jäger Corps, and miscellaneous supporting units. The German states of Hesse Hanau, Waldeck, and Anhalt Zerbst each provided one infantry regiment and their own supporting artillery. All of these units participated in combat with the exception of the Anhalt Zerbst units, which did not arrive in Québec until May of 1778. However, they were stationed in New York from 1781-1783.

Hessian organizations were associated with unique names as opposed to numerical designations. Many units adopted the name of their commander ("Chef"), who was usually a colonel. However, some units were named in honor of fallen commanders or someone else chosen for the honor. The various regiments and the major battles in which they participated are listed below. (1st Div. or 2nd Div. indicates the division to which Hesse–Cassel units were assigned.)

Hesse-Cassel: (12,805 troops)

Field Jäger Corps: This unit or detachments thereof fought in every Hesse-Cassel operation.

Fusilier Regiment von Ditforth: 1st Div., Fort Washington, White Plains, Newport, Charleston.

Fusilier Regiment Erbprinz: 1st Div., Long Island, Fort Washington, Yorktown.

Fusilier Regiment von Knyphausen: 1st Div., Long Island, White Plains, Fort Washington, Trenton (captured; reorganized elements fought at Brandywine).

Fusilier Regiment von Lossburg: 1st Div., Long Island, Fort Washington, White Plains, Fort Washington, Trenton (captured; reorganized elements fought at Brandywine).

Garrison Regiment von Bunau: 2nd Div., Fort Washington, Newport

Garrison Regiment von Huyn: 2nd Div., Fort Washington, Newport, Charleston.

Garrison Regiment von Stein: 2nd Div., Fort Washington, redeployed to garrison at Halifax.

Garrison Regiment von Wissenbach: 2nd Div., Fort Washington, East Florida, Savannah, Stono Ferry.

Grenadier Battalion von Block: 1st Div., Long Island, White Plains, Brandywine, Fort Mercer, Charleston.

Grenadier Battalion von Linsingen: 1st Div., Long, Island, White Plains, Brandywine, Fort Mercer, Charleston.

Grenadier Battalion von Minnigerode: 1st Div., Long Island, White Plains, Brandywine, Fort Mercer, Charleston.

Grenadier Regiment von Rall: 1st Div., Long Island, White Plains, Fort Washington, Trenton, Brandywine, East Florida, Savannah, Charleston.

Grenadier Battalion von Koehler: 1st Div., Fort Washington, Forts Clinton and Montgomery, Charleston.

Grenadier Regiment von Trumbach: 1st Div., Fort Washington, White Plains, Trenton (captured; reorganized elements fought at Guildford Courthouse, Green Spring, and Yorktown.

Lieb Infantry Regiment: 1st Div., White Plains, Brandywine, Germantown, Newport, Springfield.

Musketeer Regiment Prinz Carl: 1st Div., White Plains, Newport, Charleston.

Musketeer Regiment von Donop: 1st Div., Long Island, Fort Washington, Philadelphia Campaign, Brandywine, Germantown.

Musketeer Regiment von Mirbach: 1st Div., Long Island, Fort Washington, Philadelphia Campaign, Brandywine, Fort Mercer.

Regiment (Combined*) von Loos*: Brandywine; composite unit from reorganized troops following debacle at Trenton.

Regiment Landgraf: 2nd Div., Fort Washington, Newport.

Brunswick: (4,300 troops) Arrived at Quebec in June of 1776.

Grenadier Battalion von Breyman: Bennington, Bemis Heights, Saratoga.

Jäger Battalion-Brunswick (aka Light Infantry Battalion von Barner): Bemis Heights, Saratoga.

Musketeer Regiment von Riedesel: Bemis Heights, Saratoga.

Regiment of Dragoons Prinze Ludwig: Bennington, Saratoga.
Regiment Prinz Friedrich: Ticonderoga, Saratoga.
Regiment von Rhetz: Lake Champlain, Bemis Heights, Saratoga.
Regiment von Specht: Saratoga.
Waldeck: (670 troops) Arrived at New York in 1776.
Third Waldeck Regiment: Fort Washington, deployed to West Florida in 1778, Pensacola (captured and imprisoned in Cuba until 1782, redeployed to New York garrison).

Anspach-Beyreuth: (1,285 troops). Arrived at New York in 1777.

1st Regiment Anspach-Bayreuth: Philadelphia, Newport, Yorktown.
2nd Regiment Anspach-Bayreuth: Philadelphia, Newport, and Yorktown.
Hesse Hanau: (2,038 troops). Arrived at Quebec in June of 1776.
Free Corps of Light Infantry: Lake Champlain, Saratoga.
Hesse Hanau Regiment: Lake Champlain, Saratoga.
Hesse Hanau Chasseurs: St. Leger's Expedition to Oriskany and Fort Stanwix.
Anhalt-Zerbst: (600 troops) Arrived at Quebec in May of 1778.
Anhalt-Zerbst Regiment: Garrison duty in Quebec and New York.

American (Continental) Soldiers and Organizations in the American Revolution

Officially formed by an act of Congress on June 14, 1775, the United States Army was formed from volunteer militiamen who initially served their respective colonies/states. Once independence was declared and the nation organized its armed forces, the land component, known as the Continental Line (Army), was reorganized into departments and the individual state regiments were incorporated under the command of Gen. George Washington.

In 1789, Secretary of War Henry Knox reported the following figures as the total number of soldiers who had served in the Continental Line Army (excluding militia):

1775: 27,443
1776: 46,891
1777: 34,820
1778: 32,899

1779: 27,699
1780: 21,015
1781: 13,292
1782: 14,256
1783: 13,476

The congressionally-selected commander in chief, George Washington, followed British doctrine and precedents in the establishment of an army. He organized his 27,000 men into six combat brigades of 2,400 men each, with adequate supporting units to maintain them. Initially the fighting was largely contained in Massachusetts and New York, but the focus shifted south as the war progressed. While the army evolved significantly during the war and its strength declined each year after 1776, General Washington maintained a constant presence in the field. More than any single person, it was his steady hand and clear strategic head that held the army and country together and defeated the largest and most powerful armed force of the 18th century.

American regiments averaged 474 men, though this number generally declined as the war ground on between 1776 and 1783. Although there were also Marines, a small navy, and individual militia units, the bulk of the American armed forces during the Revolution resided in the "American Continental Army."

Most states during the American Revolution organized their military units by regional military districts, which raised individual companies and organized them into regiments. The Continental Congress ordered each state to follow strict guidelines in the way it raised and organized its units. However, differences in population, dialects, communications, war status, and a general reluctance to take commands from a superior federal government (as opposed to a sovereign state) impeded the effort to create a smooth-functioning national army. As a result, Congress allowed the inception of specialty units (such as rangers and partisan militias) in rural areas and generally accepted whatever organizations the states managed to contribute to the war effort.

The bulk of the army was comprised of infantry regiments, dragoons (light cavalry that frequently fought dismounted), and artillery. In an effort to better structure its military, in 1776 Congress reorganized the military areas of the armed forces into four separate territorial departments: Southern, Middle, Northern, and Canadian. In practice, military efforts shifted to meet enemy offensives, so the new departmental structure was largely organized only on paper. The war as experienced by the American army was perhaps best described by Gen. Nathanael Greene when he observed, "We fight, get beat, rise, and fight again." Fighting, losing, and fighting again dampers the morale and bleeds away the strength of any army, and the new American organization was no different. After 1776 the numbers on the muster rolls declined and the Continental regiments underwent many transformations. As the units were reorganized, some regiments disappeared only to reappear with another numerical designation, usually combined from others units in the same situation. Consequently, some men fought in essentially the same regiment, but with a different numerical designation. However, most of these units remained assigned to their original state organizations within the Continental line.

The American regiments listed below by state include their date of organization, the primary battles/sieges/campaigns in which they participated, and how many were present at Yorktown:

Connecticut (twelve companies were present at the Siege of Yorktown)

1st Connecticut Regiment: September of 1776. Fought throughout the New York Campaign, Hudson Highlands, Philadelphia Campaign, Monmouth Court House, and was assigned to duties in New York.

2nd Connecticut Regiment: September of 1776. Fought throughout the New York Campaign, Hudson Highlands, Philadelphia Campaign, Monmouth Court House, and was assigned to duties in New York.

3rd Connecticut Regiment: September of 1776. Fought throughout the New York Campaign, Hudson Highlands, Philadelphia Campaign, Monmouth Court House, and was assigned to duties in New York.

4th Connecticut Regiment: April of 1775. Québec, Fort Ticonderoga, the Philadelphia Campaign, Brandywine, Germantown, Whitemarsh, Monmouth Court House, and the Siege of Yorktown.

5th Connecticut Regiment: September of 1776. Fought throughout the New York Campaign, Philadelphia Campaign, Monmouth Court House, and was assigned to duties in New York, and elements fought at the Siege of Yorktown.

6th Connecticut Regiment: September of 1776. Fought throughout the New York Campaign, Hudson Highlands, Philadelphia Campaign, Monmouth Court House, and was assigned to duties in New York.

8th Connecticut Regiment: September of 1776. Fought throughout the New York Campaign, Hudson Highlands, Philadelphia Campaign, Monmouth Court House, and was reorganized into other regiments.

9th Connecticut Regiment (S. B. Webb's Additional Regiment): January of 1777. The unit defended Connecticut in 1777, then fought at Hudson Highlands, Rhode Island, and was reorganized in 1780 into other units.

10th Connecticut Regiment: April of 1775. The Siege of Boston, throughout the New York Campaign. Unit was reorganized and one company fought in the invasion of Canada.

17th Connecticut Regiment: April of 1775. The Siege of Boston and throughout the New York Campaign. Reorganized, and one company fought in the invasion of Canada.

19th Connecticut Regiment: July of 1775. The Siege of Boston, throughout the New York Campaign, Trenton, and Princeton before being reorganized.

20th Connecticut Regiment: April of 1775. The Siege of Boston, throughout the New York Campaign, Trenton, and Princeton before being reorganized.

22nd Connecticut Regiment: April of 1775. The Siege of Boston, throughout the New York Campaign, Trenton, and Princeton before being reorganized.

Elmore's Regiment: January of 1776. Ft. Stanwix and Oriskany before being disbanded in 1777.

Burrall's Regiment: January of 1776. Ft. Stanwix, Oriskany, and Lake Champlain before being disbanded in 1777.

Ward's Regiment: May of 1776. Fought throughout the New York Campaign, Trenton, and Princeton before being disbanded in 1777.

Westmoreland's (Wyoming) Individual Companies: August of 1776. Fought throughout the New York Campaign, Philadelphia Campaign, and Iroquois Campaign (Sullivan's Expedition). Disbanded in 1781.

Delaware (No units were present at the Siege of Yorktown; assigned to other duties)

The Delaware Regiment: December of 1775. Assigned to the defense of the Chesapeake Bay, fought throughout the New York Campaign, Trenton, Princeton, Monmouth Court House, and Greene's Southern Campaign. Reorganized in 1777, 1778, and 1780.

Georgia (No units were present at the Siege of Yorktown; captured at Charleston in 1780.)

1st Georgia Regiment: November of 1775. East Florida Expeditions, Savannah, and Charleston, where it was captured in 1780.

2nd Georgia Regiment: July of 1776. East Florida Expeditions, Savannah, and Charleston, where it was captured in 1780.

3rd Georgia Regiment: July of 1776. East Florida Expeditions, Savannah, and Charleston, where it was captured in 1780.

4th Georgia Regiment: July of 1776. East Florida Expeditions, Savannah, and Charleston, where it was captured in 1780.

Georgia Continental Artillery Companies: January of 1776. East Florida Expeditions, Savannah, and Sunbury. Disbanded in 1779.

Georgia Regiment of Horse Rangers: January of 1776. East Florida Expeditions, Savannah, and Charleston, where it was captured in 1780.

Georgia Militia: 1775-1783. Several independent units were formed during the war to protect the locals from Indians and British aggression. In northeastern Georgia, Cols. Elijah Clark, John Dooly, Andrew Pickens, and Lt. Col. James McCall raised a 500-man partisan unit that successfully defended their region from both Tory and British forces. The unit launched numerous raids that caused the British a great deal of problems. In the western backwoods, the militia had long been organized to fight Indians and they successfully fought their enemy at Kettle Creek and Augusta. However, they also suffered setbacks in the Siege of Savannah and on expeditions into East Florida. Nonetheless, their service was instrumental in the fight against the Tories and British throughout Georgia and in the neighboring states of North and South Carolina.

Maryland (two regiments were present at the Siege of Yorktown)

1st Maryland Regiment: January of 1776. Assigned to the defense of the Chesapeake Bay, fought throughout the New York Campaign, Trenton, Princeton, Monmouth Court House, and Greene's Southern Campaign.

2nd Maryland Regiment: January of 1776. Assigned to the defense of the Chesapeake Bay, fought throughout the New York Campaign, Trenton, Princeton, Monmouth Court House, and Greene's Southern Campaign.

3rd Maryland Regiment: September of 1776. Assigned to the defense of the Chesapeake Bay, fought throughout the New York Campaign, Trenton, Princeton, Monmouth Court House, Greene's Southern Campaign, and the Siege of Yorktown.

4th Maryland Regiment: September of 1776. Assigned to the defense of the Chesapeake Bay, fought throughout the New York Campaign, Trenton, Princeton, Monmouth Court House, Greene's Southern Campaign, and the Siege of Yorktown.

5th Maryland Regiment: September of 1776. Assigned to the defense of the Chesapeake Bay, fought throughout the New York Campaign, Trenton, Princeton, Monmouth Court House, and Greene's Southern Campaign.

6th Maryland Regiment: September of 1776. Assigned to the defense of the Chesapeake Bay, fought throughout the New York Campaign, Trenton, Princeton, Monmouth Court House, and Greene's Southern Campaign.

7th Maryland Regiment: September of 1776. Assigned to the defense of the Chesapeake Bay, fought throughout the New York Campaign, Trenton, Princeton, Monmouth Court House, and Greene's Southern Campaign.

Maryland State Artillery Companies: September of 1776. Assigned to the defense of the Chesapeake Bay, fought throughout the New York Campaign, Trenton, Princeton, Monmouth Court House, and Greene's Southern Campaign.

Massachusetts (thirteen companies were present at the Siege of Yorktown)

1st Massachusetts Regiment: April of 1775. The Siege of Boston, Canada, Lake Champlain, Trenton, Princeton, Saratoga, Philadelphia Campaign, Monmouth Court House, and Rhode Island.

2nd Massachusetts Regiment: April of 1775. The Siege of Boston, Canada, Lake Champlain, Trenton, Princeton, Saratoga, Philadelphia Campaign, Monmouth Court House, and Rhode Island.

3rd Massachusetts Regiment: April of 1775. The Siege of Boston, Canada, Lake Champlain, Trenton, Princeton, Saratoga, Philadelphia Campaign, Monmouth Court House, and Rhode Island.

4th Massachusetts Regiment: April of 1775. The Siege of Boston, Canada, Lake Champlain, Trenton, Princeton, Saratoga, Philadelphia Campaign, Monmouth Court House, and Rhode Island.

5th Massachusetts Regiment: April of 1775. The Siege of Boston, Canada, Lake Champlain, Trenton, Princeton, and Saratoga.

6th Massachusetts Regiment: April of 1775. Saratoga and in the Iroquois Campaign.

7th Massachusetts Regiment: April of 1775. The Siege of Boston and the New York Campaign. Reorganized into other units.

8th Massachusetts Regiment: April of 1775. The Siege of Boston, Canada, Lake Champlain, Trenton, Princeton, Saratoga, Philadelphia Campaign, Monmouth Court House, and Rhode Island.

9th Massachusetts Regiment: April of 1775. The Siege of Boston, Canada, Lake Champlain, Trenton, Princeton, Saratoga, Philadelphia Campaign, Monmouth Court House, and the Mohawk Valley.

10th Massachusetts Regiment: September of 1776. Saratoga, Philadelphia Campaign, and Monmouth Court House.

11th Massachusetts Regiment: September of 1776. Saratoga, Philadelphia Campaign, and Monmouth Court House.

12th Massachusetts Regiment: April of 1775. The Siege of Boston, Canada, Lake Champlain, Trenton, Princeton, Saratoga, Philadelphia Campaign, and Monmouth Court House.

13th Massachusetts Regiment: April of 1775. The Siege of Boston, Canada, Lake Champlain, Trenton, Princeton, Saratoga, Philadelphia Campaign, Monmouth Court House, and Rhode Island.

14th Massachusetts Regiment: April of 1775. The Siege of Boston, Canada, Lake Champlain, Trenton, Princeton, Saratoga, Philadelphia Campaign, Monmouth Court House, and Rhode Island.

15th Massachusetts Regiment: September of 1776. Saratoga, Philadelphia Campaign, Monmouth Court House, and Rhode Island.

21st Massachusetts Regiment: April of 1775. The Siege of Boston, Canada, Lake Champlain, Trenton, Princeton, Saratoga, Philadelphia Campaign, Monmouth Court House, and Rhode Island.

25th Massachusetts Regiment: April of 1775. The Siege of Boston, Canada, Lake Champlain, Trenton, and Princeton.

Brewer's Regiment: April of 1775. This independently organized unit participated in the Siege of Boston. It was then reorganized and incorporated into the Continental Line in December of 1775.

Bridge's Regiment: April of 1775. This independently organized unit participated in the Siege of Boston. It was then reorganized and incorporated into the Continental Line in December of 1775.

Cotton's Regiment: April of 1775. This independently organized unit participated in the Siege of Boston. It was then reorganized and incorporated into the Continental Line in December of 1775.

Danielson's Regiment: April of 1775. This independently organized unit participated in the Siege of Boston. It was then reorganized and incorporated into the Continental Line in December of 1775.

Doolittle's Regiment: April of 1775. This independently organized unit participated in the Siege of Boston. It was then reorganized and incorporated into the Continental Line in December of 1775.

Fellows's Regiment: April of 1775. This independently organized unit participated in the Siege of Boston. It was then reorganized and incorporated into the Continental Line in December of 1775.

Frye's Regiment: April of 1775. This independently organized unit participated in the Siege of Boston. It was then reorganized and incorporated into the Continental Line in December of 1775.

Henley's Additional Continental Regiment: January of 1777. Saratoga, Philadelphia Campaign, Monmouth Court House, and Rhode Island.

Henry Jackson's Additional Continental Regiment: January of 1777. Saratoga, Philadelphia Campaign, Monmouth Court House, and Rhode Island.

Lee's Additional Continental Regiment: January of 1777. Saratoga, Philadelphia Campaign, Monmouth Court House, and Rhode Island.

Porter's Regiment: April of 1775. This independently organized unit participated in the Siege of Boston. It was then reorganized and incorporated into the Continental Line in December of 1775.

Scammon's Regiment: April of 1775. This independently organized unit participated in the Siege of Boston. It was then reorganized and incorporated into the Continental Line in December of 1775.

Walker's Regiment: April of 1775. This independently organized unit participated in the Siege of Boston. It was then reorganized and incorporated into the Continental Line in December of 1775.

Whitcomb's Regiment: April of 1775. This independently organized unit participated in the Siege of Boston. It was then reorganized and incorporated into the Continental Line in December of 1775.

Woodbridge's Regiment: April of 1775. This independently organized unit participated in the Siege of Boston. It was then reorganized and incorporated into the Continental Line in December of 1775.

New Hampshire (five companies from the regiments below were present at the Siege of Yorktown)

1st New Hampshire Regiment: May of 1775. The Siege of Boston, Lake Champlain, Trenton, Princeton, Philadelphia Campaign, Monmouth Court House, and the Iroquois Campaign (also known as Sullivan's Expedition).

2nd New Hampshire Regiment: May of 1775. The Siege of Boston, Lake Champlain, Trenton, Princeton, Philadelphia Campaign, Monmouth Court House, and the Iroquois Campaign (also known as Sullivan's Expedition).

3rd New Hampshire Regiment: May of 1775. The Siege of Boston, Lake Champlain, Trenton, Princeton, Philadelphia Campaign, Monmouth Court House, and the Iroquois Campaign (also known as Sullivan's Expedition).

Bedel's Regiment: May of 1775. The Canadian Campaign.

Long's Regiment: May of 1775. The Canadian Campaign and Saratoga.

Whitcomb's Rangers: May of 1775. The Canadian Campaign and Fort Ticonderoga.

New Jersey (three regiments were present at the Siege of Yorktown)

1st New Jersey Regiment: October of 1775. Participated in the Canadian Campaign, Lake Champlain, New York Campaign, Philadelphia Campaign, Monmouth Court House, Iroquois Campaign (also known as Sullivan's Expedition), and the Siege of Yorktown.

2nd New Jersey Regiment: October of 1775. Participated in the Canadian Campaign, Lake Champlain, New York Campaign, Philadelphia Campaign, Monmouth Court House, and the Siege of Yorktown.

3rd New Jersey Regiment: January of 1776. Canadian Campaign, Lake Champlain, New York Campaign, Philadelphia Campaign, Monmouth Court House, and the Iroquois Campaign (also known as Sullivan's Expedition).

4th New Jersey Regiment: September of 1776. Philadelphia Campaign and Monmouth Court House. Disbanded in 1779.

New York (thirteen companies from the regiments below were present at the Siege of Yorktown)

1st New York Regiment: October of 1775. Canadian Campaign, Lake Champlain, New York Campaign, Saratoga, Philadelphia Campaign, Monmouth Court House, Iroquois Campaign (also known as Sullivan's Expedition), and the Siege of Yorktown.

2nd New York Regiment: October of 1775. Canadian Campaign, Lake Champlain, New York Campaign, Saratoga, Philadelphia Campaign, Monmouth Court House, Iroquois Campaign (also known as Sullivan's Expedition), and the Siege of Yorktown.

3rd New York Regiment: October of 1775. New York Campaign, Saratoga, Philadelphia Campaign, Monmouth Court House, and the Iroquois Campaign (also known as Sullivan's Expedition).

4th New York Regiment: October of 1775. New York Campaign, Saratoga, Philadelphia Campaign, Monmouth Court House, and the Iroquois Campaign (also known as Sullivan's Expedition).

5th New York Regiment: November of 1776. Hudson Highlands and the Iroquois Campaign (also known as Sullivan's Expedition).

New York Provincial Company of Artillery: October of 1775. Supported the New York regiments on their campaigns.

Nicholson's Regiment: November of 1776. Canadian Campaign.

North Carolina (No units were present at the Siege of Yorktown)

1st North Carolina Regiment: September of 1775. Assigned to the defense of the Chesapeake Bay, fought throughout the Philadelphia Campaign, Monmouth Court House, and Greene's Southern Campaign.

2nd North Carolina Regiment: September of 1775. Assigned to the defense of Charleston, fought in the Florida Expedition, throughout the Philadelphia Campaign, Monmouth Court House, and Charleston, where it was captured.

3rd North Carolina Regiment: January of 1776. Assigned to the defense of the Chesapeake Bay, fought throughout the Philadelphia Campaign, Monmouth Court House, and Charleston, where it was captured.

4th North Carolina Regiment: March of 1776. Assigned to the defense of the Chesapeake Bay, fought throughout the Philadelphia Campaign, Monmouth Court House, Savannah, and Charleston, where it was captured.

5th North Carolina Regiment: April of 1776. Assigned to the defense of the Chesapeake Bay, fought throughout the Philadelphia Campaign, Monmouth Court House, Savannah, and Charleston, where it was captured.

6th North Carolina Regiment: April of 1776. Assigned to the defense of Philadelphia, fought at Monmouth Court House. Disbanded at Valley Forge, Pennsylvania, 1778.

7th North Carolina Regiment: September of 1776. Assigned to the defense of Philadelphia, fought at Monmouth Court House. Disbanded at Valley Forge, Pennsylvania, in 1778.

8th North Carolina Regiment: September of 1776. Assigned to the defense of Philadelphia, fought at Monmouth Court House. Disbanded at Valley Forge, Pennsylvania, in 1778.

9th North Carolina Regiment: September of 1776. Assigned to the defense of Philadelphia, fought at Monmouth Court House. Disbanded at Valley Forge, Pennsylvania, in 1778.

10th North Carolina Regiment: April of 1777. Assigned to the defense of Philadelphia, fought at Monmouth Court House. Disbanded at Valley Forge, Pennsylvania, in 1778.

Corps of North Carolina Light Dragoons: April of 1776. Elements supported the North Carolina regiments during their campaigns.

North Carolina Continental Artillery Company: May of 1776. Supported the North Carolina regiments until it was captured at the Siege of Charleston in 1780.

North Carolina Militia: 1775-1783. Numerous independent units were formed during the war to protect the locals from both Indians and British aggression. In eastern North Carolina, Cols. Alexander Lillington and James Moore raised 1,000 troops that successfully defended their region from both Tory and British aggression at the Battle of Moores Creek. These militiamen later saw service during the Battle of Camden and in Greene's Southern Campaign. In the western backwoods, the militia had long been organized to fight Indians and they successfully fought them during the Cherokee Campaign. As the war encroached into their area in 1780, Cols. Benjamin Cleveland, Joseph Winston, Joseph McDowell, John Sevier, and Isaac Shelby commanded 1,000 men who fought both the Tories and British throughout the Carolina Highlands; they also participated in Greene's Southern Campaign.

Pennsylvania (two battalions were present at the Siege of Yorktown)

1st Pennsylvania Regiment: June of 1775. Siege of Boston, Canadian Campaign, New York Campaign, Trenton, Princeton, and the Philadelphia Campaign. Assigned to the defense of New Jersey and Pennsylvania.

2nd Pennsylvania Regiment: October of 1775. Canadian Campaign, Lake Champlain, New York Campaign, Trenton, Princeton, and the Philadelphia Campaign. Assigned to the defense of New Jersey and Pennsylvania.

3rd Pennsylvania Regiment: December of 1775. Canadian Campaign, Lake Champlain, New York Campaign, Trenton, Princeton, and the Philadelphia Campaign. Assigned to the defense of New Jersey and Pennsylvania.

4th Pennsylvania Regiment: December of 1775. New York Campaign, Trenton, Princeton, Philadelphia Campaign, and the Iroquois Campaign (also known as Sullivan's Expedition). Assigned to the defense of New Jersey and Pennsylvania.

5th Pennsylvania Regiment: December of 1775. Canadian Campaign, Lake Champlain, New York Campaign, Trenton, Princeton, and the Philadelphia Campaign. Assigned to the defense of New Jersey and Pennsylvania.

6th Pennsylvania Regiment: December of 1775. The New York Campaign, Trenton, Princeton, and the Philadelphia Campaign. Assigned to the defense of New Jersey and Pennsylvania.

7th Pennsylvania Regiment: January of 1776. Canadian Campaign, Lake Champlain, New York Campaign, Trenton, Princeton, and the Philadelphia Campaign. Assigned to the defense of New Jersey and Pennsylvania.

8th Pennsylvania Regiment: January of 1776. New York Campaign, Trenton, Princeton, Philadelphia Campaign, and the Iroquois Campaign (also known as Sullivan's Expedition). Assigned to the defense of New Jersey and Pennsylvania.

9th Pennsylvania Regiment: September of 1776. New York Campaign, Trenton, Princeton, and the Philadelphia Campaign. Assigned to the defense of New Jersey and Pennsylvania.

10th Pennsylvania Regiment: January of 1777. New York Campaign, Trenton, Princeton, and the Philadelphia Campaign. Assigned to the defense of New Jersey and Pennsylvania.

11th Pennsylvania Regiment: September of 1776. New York Campaign and the Philadelphia Campaign. Reorganized in 1778.

12th Pennsylvania Regiment: August of 1776. New York Campaign and the Philadelphia Campaign. Reorganized in 1778.

13th Pennsylvania Regiment: September of 1776. New York Campaign, Trenton, Princeton, and the Philadelphia Campaign. Assigned to the defense of New Jersey and Pennsylvania.

Carlisle Independent Companies: October of 1777. Philadelphia Campaign. Disbanded in 1778.

Rhode Island (one regiment was at the Siege of Yorktown)

1st Rhode Island Regiment: April of 1775. The Siege of Boston, New York Campaign, Saratoga, Philadelphia Campaign, Monmouth Court House, Rhode Island, and the Siege of Yorktown.

2nd Rhode Island Regiment: April of 1775. The Siege of Boston, New York Campaign, Saratoga, Philadelphia Campaign, Monmouth Court House, and the siege of Rhode Island.

Rhode Island Train of Artillery: April of 1775. Consolidated into the main Continental Artillery Regiment in October of 1775; its members served throughout the war.

South Carolina (most captured at Charleston in 1780; no units were present at the Siege of Yorktown.)

1st South Carolina Regiment: June of 1775. East Florida Expeditions, Savannah, and Charleston, where it was captured in 1780.

2nd South Carolina Regiment: June of 1775. East Florida Expeditions, Savannah, and Charleston, where it was captured in 1780.

3rd South Carolina Regiment: June of 1775. East Florida Expeditions, Savannah, and Charleston, where it was captured in 1780.

4th South Carolina (Ranger) Regiment: November of 1775. East Florida Expeditions, Savannah, Cherokee Campaign, and Charleston, where it was captured in 1780.

5th South Carolina Regiment (1st South Carolina Rifle Regiment): February of 1776. East Florida Expeditions and Savannah. Reorganized in 1780.

6th South Carolina Regiment (2nd South Carolina Rifle Regiment): February of 1776. East Florida Expeditions, Savannah, and the Cherokee Campaign. Reorganized in 1780.

Beaufort Independent Company of Artillery: February of 1776. Reorganized into the 4th South Carolina Regiment.

Georgetown Independent Company of Artillery: February of 1776. Reorganized into the 4th South Carolina Regiment.

South Carolina Militia: 1775-1783. Numerous independent units were formed during the war to protect the locals from both Indians and British aggression. In eastern South Carolina, Col. Francis Marion (the "Swamp Fox") raised a 300-man partisan unit that successfully defended that region from both Tory and British aggression during numerous raids that harassed and damaged

British interests. In the western backwoods, the militia had long been organized to fight Indians and they successfully fought them during the Cherokee and Snow campaigns. As the war encroached into their area in 1780, Cols. Thomas Sumter, Edward Lacey, and William Hill led 1,000 men against the Tories and British throughout the South Carolina Upcountry at places like Blackstock's Plantation, Ninety Six, and Musgrove's Mill.

Virginia (one militia division, one regiment, and one independent battalion were present at the siege of Yorktown)

1st Virginia Regiment: August 1775. Assigned to the defense of Chesapeake Bay, fought in the New York Campaign, Trenton, Princeton, Monmouth Court House, and at Charleston, where it was captured in 1780.

2nd Virginia Regiment: August1 775. Assigned to the defense of Chesapeake Bay, fought in the New York Campaign, Trenton, Princeton, Monmouth Court House, and at Charleston, where it was captured in 1780.

3rd Virginia Regiment: December 1775. Assigned to the defense of Chesapeake Bay, fought in the New York Campaign, Trenton, Princeton, Monmouth Court House, and at Charleston, where it was captured in 1780.

4th Virginia Regiment: December 1775. Assigned to the defense of Chesapeake Bay, fought in the New York Campaign, Trenton, Princeton, Monmouth Court House, and at Charleston, where it was captured in 1780.

5th Virginia Regiment: December 1775. Assigned to the defense of Chesapeake Bay, fought in the New York Campaign, Trenton, Princeton, Monmouth Court House, and at Charleston.

6th Virginia Regiment: December of 1775. Assigned to the defense of Chesapeake Bay, fought in the New York Campaign, Trenton, Princeton, and Monmouth Court House. Reorganized in 1779.

7th Virginia Regiment: January of 1776. Assigned to the defense of Chesapeake Bay, fought in the New York Campaign, Trenton, Princeton, Monmouth Court House, and at Charleston, where it was captured in 1780.

8th Virginia Regiment: December of 1775. Assigned to the defense of Chesapeake Bay, fought in the New York Campaign, Trenton, Princeton, and Monmouth Court House. Reorganized in 1779.

9th Virginia Regiment: December of 1775. Assigned to the defense of Chesapeake Bay, fought in the New York Campaign, Trenton, Princeton, and Monmouth Court House. Reorganized in 1779.

10th Virginia Regiment: December of 1775. Assigned to the defense of Chesapeake Bay, fought in the New York Campaign, Trenton, Princeton, Monmouth Court House, and at Charleston, where it was captured in 1780.

11th Virginia Regiment: September of 1776. Assigned to the defense of Chesapeake Bay, fought in the New York Campaign, Trenton, Princeton, Monmouth Court House, and at Charleston, where it was captured in 1780.

12th Virginia Regiment: September of 1776. Assigned to the defense of Chesapeake Bay, fought in the New York Campaign, Trenton, Princeton, Monmouth Court House, and at Charleston, where it was captured in 1780.

13th Virginia Regiment: September of 1776. Assigned to the defense of Chesapeake Bay, fought in the New York Campaign, Trenton, Princeton, and Monmouth Court House. Reorganized in 1779.

14th Virginia Regiment: September of 1776. Assigned to the defense of Chesapeake Bay, fought in the New York Campaign, Trenton, Princeton, Monmouth Court House, and at Charleston, where it was captured in 1780.

15th Virginia Regiment: September of 1776. Assigned to the defense of Chesapeake Bay, fought in the New York Campaign, Trenton, Princeton, Monmouth Court House, and at Charleston, where it was captured in 1780.

Virginia Continental Artillery Company: March of 1776. Reorganized along with several state artillery units into the Continental Artillery in November of 1776.

Virginia Independent Companies: January of 1777. Fought in Delaware and were reorganized into other Virginia units.

Virginia Independent Rifle Company: June of 1775. Reorganized into the Virginia line in February of 1777.

Virginia State Artillery Company: January of 1776. Reorganized into the Continental Artillery in November of 1776.

Washington County (Virginia) Militia: Organized in 1776. This 400-man militia unit commanded by Col. William Campbell was the lead element of the "Overmountain Men" that joined with the militia from East Tennessee and Western North Carolina to fight both the British and Indians. These men saw battle in the Cherokee Campaign, Musgrove's Mill, Kings Mountain, and Guilford Court House. Elements also served in the Virginia State Militia in 1780-1781, and were present at the Siege of Yorktown.

Virginia State Militia: Organized in 1780-1781 to defend Virginia against the British invasion led by turncoat Brig. Gen. (British) Benedict Arnold. As Arnold's campaign swept through Virginia, the locals volunteered to defend Virginia and an entire division was formed from volunteers. These units included the 1st Virginia State Regiment (what remained of the Virginia contingent of the Continental Line—most had been captured at Charleston in 1780) commanded by Lt. Col. Charles Dabney (200 men), Brig. Gen. Robert Lawson's Brigade (750 men), Col. William Lewis' Rifle Corps (250 men), Brig. Gen. Edward Stevens's Brigade (750 men), and Brig. Gen. George Weedon's

Brigade (1,500 men). These men fought in the Yorktown Campaign and were one of three allied divisions that helped defeated Lord Cornwallis at Yorktown.

Continental Dragoons

1st Continental Light Dragoon Regiment (Bland's Horse): June of 1776. The Philadelphia Campaign, Charleston, and Greene's Southern Campaign. Reorganized in 1782.

2nd Continental Light Dragoon Regiment (Sheldon's Horse): December of 1776. The New York Campaign, Hudson Highlands, Saratoga, Philadelphia Campaign, and Connecticut.

3rd Continental Light Dragoon Regiment (Baylor's and Lady Washington's Horse): January of 1777. The Philadelphia Campaign, Charleston, and Greene's Southern Campaign.

4th Continental Light Dragoon Regiment (Moylan's Horse): January of 1777. The New York Campaign, Connecticut, Greene's Southern Campaign, and at the Siege of Yorktown.

1st Partisan Corps (Armand's Legion): June of 1778. Commanded by Col. Charles Armand and served in the New York Campaign. Transferred to the Southern Department and joined with Pulaski's Corps in 1780 (five companies). After the Battle of Camden it was reorganized along with Capt. Henry Bedkin's Independent Troop of Light Horse. The units were redesignated the 1st Partisan Corps (three mounted and three infantry troops). This unit also fought at the Siege of Yorktown.

2nd Partisan Corps (Lee's Legion): June of 1776. Fought as three troops of Continental Dragoons during the Philadelphia Campaign, Monmouth Court House, and the New York Campaign. Reorganized in 1779 and was transferred to the Southern Department, where it was redesignated the 2nd Partisan Corps (three mounted and three infantry troops). This unit also fought at the Siege of Yorktown.

Captain Allen McLane's Company: February of 1777. This unit was reorganized in 1778 and 1779 and saw action during the Iroquois Campaign. It was transferred into the 2nd Partisan Corps and served during Greene's Southern Campaign.

Corps of North Carolina Light Dragoons: April of 1776. Philadelphia Campaign. Reorganized in January of 1779.

Ottendorf's Corps: December of 1776. Philadelphia Campaign. Was reorganized in 1777 and again in 1778. Elements of this corps fought at Brandywine, Germantown, Newtown; other elements served as independent troops during the Iroquois Campaign and in the New Jersey Campaign.

Pulaski's Legion: April of 1778. Raised by volunteer troops from Maryland and Pennsylvania, the unit was uniquely comprised of one lancers troop, two dragoon troops, one company of riflemen, and two companies of light infantry. Commanded by professional Polish cavalry officer Count Casimir Pulaski. Fought in the campaigns of New York and New Jersey until it was transferred to the Southern Department in 1779. The legion saw action at Charleston, Savannah (Count Pulaski was killed in action) and at Monck's Corner, where it was nearly decimated in April of 1780. Survivors were absorbed into Armand's Partisan Corps.

Continental Artillery

Continental Artillery Regiment (Gridley's and Knox's Artillery Regiment): May of 1775. The unit was reorganized frequently during the war's early years until it was disbanded in January of 1777. The regiment saw action at the Siege of Boston, New York Campaign, Lake Champlain, Trenton, Princeton, and the Philadelphia Campaign. The bulk of the artillery regiments (1st, 2nd, and 4th) were combined into a Continental Artillery Brigade commanded by Henry Knox, who rose to the rank of brigadier general before war's end. Knox capably commanded Washington's artillery during the Siege of Yorktown.

1st Continental Artillery Regiment (Harrison's Continental Artillery Regiment): November of 1776. The unit was reorganized frequently during the war and saw action during the Chesapeake Campaign (1775-1776), Philadelphia Campaign, and Monmouth Court House. Transferred to the Southern Department, where it served during Greene's Southern Campaign and later played a significant role in achieving victory at Yorktown.

2nd Continental Artillery Regiment (Lamb's Continental Artillery Regiment): January of 1777. Reorganized and transferred frequently during the war, the regiment saw action in the New York and New Jersey campaigns, Hudson Highlands, Philadelphia Campaign, and Iroquois Campaign, and the Siege of Yorktown.

3rd Continental Artillery Regiment (Crane's Continental Artillery Regiment): January of 1777. Reorganized and transferred frequently during the war, the regiment saw action in the New York and New Jersey campaigns, Hudson Highlands, Saratoga, Philadelphia Campaign, Monmouth Court House, and Rhode Island.

4th Continental Artillery Regiment (Proctor's Continental Artillery Regiment): October of 1775. Reorganized and transferred frequently during the war, the regiment saw action in the New Jersey Campaign, Philadelphia Campaign, Iroquois Campaign, Greene's Southern Campaign, and the Siege of Yorktown.

Independent Artillery Units: 1775-1781. The following independent artillery units served with distinction during the war. However, most were incorporated into one of the four main Continental regiments, disbanded, or captured. These units included:

> Captain Sebastian Bauman's Continental Artillery Company
> Captain Issac Coren's Labratory Company
> Captain John Lamb's Company of Artillery
> Captain Benard Roman's Continental Artillery Company
> Georgia Continental Artillery Companies
> Maryland State Artillery Companies
> New York Provincial Company of Artillery
> North Carolina Continental Artillery Company
> Rhode Island Train of Artillery
> Stevens' Provisional Artillery Battalion
> Virginia Continental Artillery Company
> Virginia State Artillery Company

French Soldiers and Organizations in the American Revolution

In June of 1776, France began to secretly provide financial assistance to the rebellious English colonists in America. The French were less concerned with the concept of liberty than causing problems with England, their longtime enemy. When it became apparent the Americans had a chance to actually defeat the British (the victory at Saratoga in late 1777 was the tipping point), France embraced the fledgling democracy with a formal alliance signed in Paris on February 6, 1778. On May 4, 1778, the French government formally recognized American independence. The French saw it as a way to enlarge their empire at England's expense. Thousands of troops and tons of materiel were poured into the colonies and elsewhere to fight England. French officers, most notably Marquis de Marie Jean Paul Joseph Roche Yves Gilbert du Motier Lafayette, volunteered for service in the American army at their own expense. Congress eventually appointed the capable Lafayette to the rank of major general, and he led American troops in the Continental Army.

In the summer of 1778, French Admiral Charles Hector T. d'Estaing sailed his fleet up the northern American coast, confronted a British fleet under Admiral William Howe at Newport, Rhode Island, and engaged in important operations along the coast of New York. The French Navy carried the war to the British across the globe, threatening their far-flung possessions and forcing England to commit precious resources at many other points other than America. In 1779, Admiral d'Estaing assisted the Americans by attacking British land forces at Savannah, Georgia (September 23-October 20). From February through May 1780, the French allies assisted the Americans during their unsuccessful defense of Charleston, South Carolina.

Setbacks during the early joint French-American operations notwithstanding, in July of 1780 Jean Baptiste Donatien de Vimeur, Comte de Rochambeau arrived at Newport, Rhode Island, with an entire corps of troops. A French fleet under Francois Joseph Paul, Comte de Grasse-Tilly inflicted a decisive strategic defeat against Admiral Thomas Graves's British warships at the Battle of the Capes (September 5-8, 1781). The victory isolated Lieutenant General Charles Cornwallis and his army on the Yorktown peninsula in Virginia. Six thousand French soldiers joined with their American allies there in a campaign that led to Cornwallis's surrender on October 5, 1781. Without the assistance of the French during the American Revolution, it is questionable whether the war would have ended in an American victory.

The twenty-three infantry regiments and detachments of engineers, miners, artillerymen, and dragoons committed by France to assist the Americans during the Revolutionary War were arranged in two separate corps. The first French ground campaign deployed to America in September of 1779. These 4,000 soldiers were commanded by Admiral d'Estaing and Count Arthur Dillon. The second major deployment was in July 1780, when Comte de Rochambeau arrived at Newport, Rhode Island, with 6,000 men. Additional French troops were delivered by Admiral de Grasse, who sailed his fleet from the West Indies to participate in the Yorktown Campaign in August 1781. The 3,500 ground troops were led by Major General Marquis Claude Henri de Rouvroy, Comte de Saint-Simon.

The French regiments that served on American soil during the Revolutionary War included:

Agénois Infantry Regiment: (Savannah: d'Estaing, Yorktown: Saint-Simon, Pensacola).
Armagnac Infantry Regiment: (Savannah: d'Estaing).
Auxerrois Infantry Regiment: (Savannah: d'Estaing).
Auxonne Artillery: (Yorktown: Rochambeau).
Bourbonnais Infantry Regiment: (Rhode Island, Yorktown: Rochambeau).

Belzunce Dragoons: (Savannah: d'Estaing).

Cambrésis Infantry Regiment: (Savannah: d'Estaing, Pensacola).

Champagne Infantry Regiment: (Savannah: d'Estaing).

Condé Dragoons: (Savannah: d'Estaing).

Corps Royal du Génie: (Yorktown: Rochambeau).

Dillon Infantry Regiment: (Savannah: d'Estaing, Yorktown: Saint-Simon).

Foix Infantry Regiment: (Savannah: d'Estaing).

Fontanges Infantry Regiment: (Mulattoes & Free Negroes from Saint Domingo) (Savannah: d'Estaing).

Gâtinais Infantry Regiment: (Savannah: d'Estaing, Yorktown: Saint-Simon, Pensacola).

Hainault Infantry Regiment: (Savannah: d'Estaing).

La Guadeloupe Infantry Regiment: (Savannah: d'Estaing).

La Martinique Infantry Regiment: (Savannah: d'Estaing).

La Sarre Infantry Regiment: (Yorktown: Rochambeau).

Le Cap Infantry Regiment: (Savannah: d'Estaing).

Maine Infantry Regiment: (Yorktown: Saint-Simon).

Metz Artillery: (Savannah: d'Estaing, Yorktown: Saint-Simon).

Orléans Infantry Regiment: (Pensacola).

Poitou Infantry Regiment: (Pensacola).

Port au Prince Infantry Regiment: (Savannah: d'Estaing).

Royal Deux Ponts Infantry Regiment: (Yorktown: Rochambeau).

Royal Corps of Engineers: (Yorktown: Rochambeau).

Royal Corps of Miners: (Yorktown: Rochambeau).

Saintonge Infantry Regiment: (Rhode Island).

Soissonnais Infantry Regiment: (Rhode Island, Yorktown: Rochambeau).

Touraine Infantry Regiment: (Yorktown: Saint-Simon) .

1st Legion Marine Volunteers: (Yorktown: Saint-Simon).

2nd Legion of Lauzon Volunteers: (Yorktown: Rochambeau).

Spanish Soldiers and Organizations in the American Revolution

The 16th, 17th, and 18th centuries witnessed the dominant powers in Europe struggling for control of land and resources across much of the Western hemisphere, and especially in North America. Spain had colonies in southern North America and maintained outposts in Florida and Louisiana as well as in the southwestern United States (then wilderness territories) in California, Arizona, New Mexico, and Texas. It also controlled strategic points along the Mississippi River. Spain also had colonies in Cuba, Puerto

Rico, Hispaniola (Dominican Republic and Haiti), and Central America (then called Nueva Espana or New Spain). After the voyages of Cortez and others, Spain conquered and controlled virtually all of South America.

When hostilities erupted in 1775, Spain had already been at war with England for many years. In the Treaty of 1763 (which marked the end of the Seven Years' War) Spain officially ceded Florida to England, even though large numbers of Spanish settlers remained there. Spain managed to wrest "Louisiana" from France, but British opportunists worked against Spanish interests by allying themselves with the Indians who lived throughout that expansive region.

In 1776, the Spanish provided financial and materiel support to the American colonists. Like France, Spain looked for any opening to weaken and harass its enemy. Spanish support became more tangible in 1778 and 1779 when large quantities of gunpowder, arms, and ammunition arrived to directly support Gen. George Rogers Clark in his victories against the British at Kaskaskia, Cahokia, and Vincennes. The Spanish also assisted the Americans in the destruction of British outposts along the Mississippi River. On June 21, 1779, Spain formally declared war against Great Britain and allied itself with America and France. Spain and England engaged in a variety of conflicts across the globe, with King Carlos III encouraging his armed forces to fight the British wherever they could and to exploit opportunities in the wild regions of North America.

During this time the Spaniards continued expanding their influence and settlements in western North America, knowing England had interest in the region as well. When English explorers patrolled the northwest Pacific coast Spain dispatched soldiers to "Alta California" to defend it from enemy incursions. Spanish outposts were constructed at Ventura, Los Angeles, Santa Barbara, San Diego, Monterey, and San Francisco. Settlements were also expanded along the Colorado River, where Yuma Indians fought with the Spanish settlers. British invasions of Nicaragua and Honduras triggered other fighting, as did sea battles in the Caribbean and off Gibraltar.

The Spanish were actively engaged with England around much of the world, but Louisiana and Florida were the battlegrounds they fought over that are closely associated with the Revolution. The war forced England to reinforce Pensacola and East Florida at St. Augustine. Attacks by American expeditionary forces from Georgia against the latter outpost failed to oust the British. In 1779, the Spanish ruler of Louisiana, Governor General Bernardo Gálvez, organized, equipped, and prepared an invasion force to attack the British stationed in West Florida and throughout the Mississippi basin.

The core of Gálvez's command was the "Regimiento Fijo de Infanteria de la Luisiana" (Fixed Infantry Regiment of Louisiana), which he bolstered with militia and regular Spanish troops from the Caribbean. Galvez marched from New Orleans north to Manchac, Louisiana, and attacked the British at Fort Bute and forced their surrender on September 7, 1779. He also captured outposts at Baton Rouge, Louisiana, and Natchez, Mississippi, later that month. Following up on these successes, Gálvez marched into West Florida and laid siege to the British fort at Mobile (now Alabama) from January 28 to March 9, 1780. He was promoted to the rank of Field Marshal and given command of all Spanish forces in America. The king of Spain provided financial support for the American Revolution (several hundred million in today's dollars) and General Gálvez personally collected donations from the citizens of Cuba, which were also handed over to the Americans.

King Carlos III also sent the Spanish fleet to Cuba and appointed Gálvez Spanish Field Marshal for the entire region. Gálvez organized his men and armada for an assault against the main British post in West Florida at Pensacola. With an army of 4,000 men and fifteen ships, he left Havana on October 16, 1780. When a hurricane nearly destroyed the fleet the Spaniards returned to Cuba. Gálvez promptly dispatched two ships and 500 men to bolster his post at Mobile lest the British take advantage of the situation.

On February 28, 1781, Gálvez launched his second expedition to West Florida. From March 9 until May 8, 1781 he laid siege against the British at Pensacola. The 40-ship Spanish armada included four French frigates commanded by Chevalier de Monteil and 725 French soldiers of the Comte de Saint-Simon's command. His army corps also included Indians, Americans, Spaniards, and Germans who had settled in Louisiana; combined, these additional forces (including the French) added nearly 7,000 men to the Spanish expedition. After a long and bitterly contested struggle, the British surrendered nearly 2,000 soldiers (16th and 60th Regiments, Royal Americans, the German Waldeck Regiment, and the Loyalist American Provincial Regiments of Maryland and Pennsylvania).

Once Gálvez's armada secured the Mississippi region and defeated the British in West Florida, the French contingent sailed to the West Indies and rendezvoused with Admiral de Grasse's fleet. Gálvez, meanwhile, obtained funding to pay for French operations in America. While he secured both Spanish and French interests from British attack in West Florida and in the West Indies, the French fleet sailed north for Virginia, where it defeated the British off the Capes, trapped Cornwallis at Yorktown, and assisted in the siege that essentially ended England's commitment to quell the rebellion.

Gálvez's corps and other Spanish units that participated in the American Revolution included:

Battalion of Negroes of Havana (Cuba)
Cavalry Regiment Lusitania
Company of the Morenos Libres (Free Blacks) of Veracruz (Mexico)
Company of the Pardos Riflemen de Yucatan and Campeche (New Spain)
Cuero Dragoons of the Internal Provences
Dragoons of America (Havana)
Fixed Infantry Regiment of Louisiana
Havana Fijo (Fixed) Regiment (Cuba)
Infantry Regiment of Betschart
Infantry Regiment de Hibernia
Infantry Regiment of Guadalajara "El Tigre" (Mexico)
Infantry Regiment of the Line Murtia
Infantry Regiment of Milicias Pardos de Merida y Yucatan (New Spain)
Infantry Regiment of Naples (Spain)
Infantry Regiment of Puerto Rico (de la Raza)
Infantry Regiment of Saboya
Infantry Regiment of Ultonia
Light Dragoons of New Spain
Line Cavalry of the King Foot
Line Cavalry of the Prince
Line Regiment de Burgos
Louisiana Infantry Regiment
Louisiana Dragoon Company
Marine Infantry
Militia of Fusiliers of Tintureros, Arcobuceros, and Bordadores (Mexico)
Militia of the German Coast (Louisiana)
Militia (Mississippi River Volunteers)
Militia of New Orleans (Battalion of Disciplined Militia-Louisiana)
Militia of New Orleans (Distinguished Company of Carabiniers-Louisiana)
Militia of Opelousas (Louisiana)
Militia of Pointe Coupee (Louisiana)
Militia of Urban Mexico (Mexico)
Militia of Veracruz (Mexico)
Mounted Regiment of the Queen
Provincial Dragoons (Mexico)
Regiment of Aragon
Regiment of la Corona

Regiment of Cantabria
Regiment of Dragoons of Villaviciosa
Regiment of Guadalajara (Mexico)
Regiment of Havana (Cuba)
Regiment of Light Cavalry Volunteers of Spain
Regiment of Line Cavalry of the Queen
Regiment of Line Cavalry Bourbon
Regiment of Line Cavalry de Alcaintara
Regiment of Louisiana
Regiment of the Crown
Regiment of the King
Regiment of Mallorca
Regiment of Mercia
Regiment of Montesa
Regiment of Navarra
Regiment of the Prince
Regiment of the Royal Walloon Guards
Regiment of Sagunto
Regiment of Soria
Regiment of Spain
Regiment of Zamora
Royal Corps of Artillery
Royal Artillery of Louisiana
Spanish Frontier Dragoons

THE BATTLES

Lexington and Concord, Battles of (Boston Campaign)

Date: April 19, 1775.

Region: Northern Colonies, Massachusetts.

Commanders: British: Lieutenant Colonel Frances Smith, Major John Pitcairn, Major (Lord) Hugh Percy; American: Captain John Parker (Lexington), Colonel James Barrett (Concord and along British retreat to Charlestown-Boston).

Time of Day / Length of Action: Early morning (Lexington and Concord), morning and afternoon (retreat to Boston)

Weather Conditions: Unremarkable, clear and pleasant.

Opposing Forces: British: 700-man force of infantry, grenadiers, Royal marines with cavalry escort (reinforced with 1,000 soldiers and two cannons during retreat phase); American: 70 at Lexington; 200 at Concord, with more along British retreat to Charlestown (loosely organized local militia units).

British Perspective: By the spring of 1775, the American colonies were on the verge of revolt. Nowhere was this radical energy more fervent than in Boston and the surrounding countryside, where British troops eyed the locals with justifiable suspicion. In the port of Boston, British authorities focused closely on the export businesses as local merchants sought ways around the numerous tariffs imposed by the Crown. Smuggling was rampant. New Englanders avoided high taxes by trading illegally with the Dutch and French. Violent protests in the streets of Boston reached a new phase on March 5, 1770, when British troops fired into a mob killing five protestors. Anti-British sentiment escalated over the next few years.

In May of 1774, Lt. Gen. Thomas Gage, the commander-in- chief of the British Army in America, returned to the colonies after a leave in England and assumed command as the military Royal Governor of Massachusetts. Rebellion loomed as the Crown implemented additional retaliatory measures for what it deemed rebellious acts against the King's authority.

The colonials established a Massachusetts Provincial Congress in May 1774, which met illegally in Concord. Its leadership included John Hancock and Samuel Adams. In February of 1775, Parliament declared the colony of Massachusetts to be in open rebellion and authorized British troops to kill violent rebels. General Gage was ordered to quell the rebellious behavior.

He was instructed to arrest the membership of the Massachusetts Provincial Congress, but decided instead to seize arms and munitions stored at Concord. During the early hours of April 19, he dispatched troops under Lt. Colonel Frances Smith and Maj. James Pitcairn to seize these munitions.

American Perspective: Burdensome taxes imposed by the Crown were enacted to recoup expenditures of the French and Indian War, but the American colonists despised the British authorities for their heavy-handed tactics. Between 1763 and 1765, the Americans were hit with the Sugar Act, Currency Act, and Quartering Acts. In 1767, the Massachusetts House of Representatives officially denounced a new tax known as the Townshend Act. Hailing these acts passed in England as "taxation without representation," disgruntled colonials subject to the Crown expressed their displeasure loudly and frequently. Royal Governor Sir Francis Bernard sought assistance from British authorities and on October 1, 1768, Boston was occupied by British soldiers. Parliament eventually repealed the Townshend Act, but its tax remained on imported tea. In 1773, the East India Trading Company enjoyed British favor as the primary importer of colonial tea, and an official decree known as the Tea Act was established to enforce it as policy. The colonists consumed tea with a passion, and the increased prices served only to further anger them.

On December 16, 1773, colonists covertly boarded an East Indian merchant ship laden with tea and poured it into the harbor. The consequence of what came to be known as "The Boston Tea Party" was the passage of a new imposition known as the Intolerable Acts, which included the closure of the port of Boston until restitution for the lost tea was made to the Crown. Previously elected officials were replaced with appointed British authorities, and private homes were seized to quarter British troops.

The establishment of the Massachusetts Provincial Congress in May 1774, coupled with the increased rhetoric against the Crown's authority, left the region a dry tinderbox awaiting a spark that arrived in the form of British troops marching from Boston to Concord.

Despite British efforts to march in secret to Concord, a network of local spies sounded the alarm. Two Bostonians, Paul Revere and William Dawes, avoided capture and slipped out of the city into the countryside. Before his departure Revere placed lanterns in the Old North Church to signal movement details of his enemy (which resulted in the well-known mantra "One if by land or two if by sea"). Dawes and Revere traversed different routes to warn colonials in Lexington that the British were on the march toward Concord. In Lexington, which lay on the road to Concord, another colonist named Samuel Prescott joined the "midnight riders" in order to

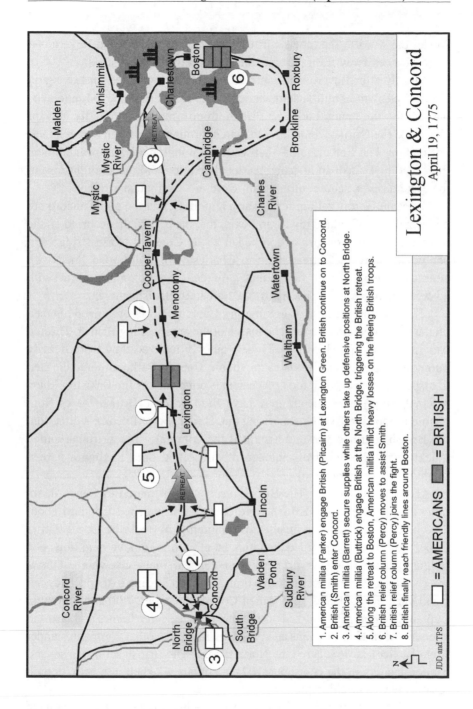

Lexington & Concord
April 19, 1775

1. American militia (Parker) engage British (Pitcairn) at Lexington Green. British continue on to Concord.
2. British (Smith) enter Concord.
3. American militia (Barrett) secure supplies while others take up defensive positions at North Bridge.
4. American militia (Buttrick) engage British at the North Bridge, triggering the British retreat.
5. Along the retreat to Boston, American militia inflict heavy losses on the fleeing British troops.
6. British relief column (Percy) moves to assist Smith.
7. British relief column (Percy) joins the fight.
8. British finally reach friendly lines around Boston.

☐ = AMERICANS   ▩ = BRITISH

JDD and TPS

spread the word to the rebels. British cavalry patrols captured Revere and forced Dawes away from the area, but Prescott reached Concord.

Shortly after Revere was captured the rebels assembled on Lexington Green. Led by their militia commander Capt. John Parker, the "Minutemen" waited for the main body of British troops marching rapidly toward Concord. The British would have to march through Lexington to reach their destination. The first clash of what would be a long hard war awaited them there. As the British approached the rebel position and the sunlight rose in the eastern sky, a scout returned with word the enemy had arrived.

Terrain: Gently rolling fertile farm region. Lexington and Concord are both small New England towns. In Lexington, the brief fight occurred on the town green. The Concord action began at the Concord North Bridge and continued along the retreat route to Charlestown, a dirt road lined with alternating forests and fields that provided the colonial militia with advantageous areas for picking off the retreating British soldiers.

The Fighting: (Battle of Lexington): Captain Parker organized his men on the town green to interrupt the march of the approaching British. The sun was just rising. The handful of rebels quickly realized they were heavily outnumbered and that defeat was inevitable. Captain Parker ordered his men to disperse. Exactly what took place next is not clear. As the British soldiers reached the green, someone may have fired into the British forces from behind a stone wall. Other shots rang out. Under Major Pitcairn's direction, the British returned fire and assaulted the colonials. The skirmish ended quickly with the blood of eighteen rebels spilled onto Lexington Green (eight killed, ten wounded).

(Battle of Concord): The British resumed their march to Concord, six miles distant. News the British were coming had reached Concord about 2:00 a.m., and several companies of minutemen turned out. Local militia leader Col. James Barrett led a contingent of men to remove munitions and military stores from his property and conceal them elsewhere. Others watched for the enemy from a ridge lining the road leading to town. They fell back when the Redcoats approached Concord between 7:00 and 8:00 a.m. Captain Lawrence Parsons led three companies to search homes and farms to uncover the hidden weapons and powder while three other companies under Capt. Walter Laurie secured the North Bridge. The British set fire to several cannon mounts in the courthouse. The colonials watched in horror, certain the enemy was torching the town.

By this time (perhaps 9:30 a.m.), 300 to 400 militia had gathered on the high ground above the North Bridge. With fife and drum Maj. John Buttrick led his motley group of farmers and merchants toward Laurie's companies defending the span. Laurie ordered his men to fall back to the opposite side of the bridge, where they deployed in a tight in-depth defensive formation that allowed only one of the three companies to fire on the approaching rebels, who continued advancing unaware of the brief fight at Lexington. When the British opened fire the rebels confidently returned it. The exchange lasted for several minutes and eventually drove the Crown's professional soldiers back in some disorder into Concord. They left three killed and eight wounded on the field. The Americans, who suffered two killed and three wounded, made no real attempt to pursue Laurie or cut off the column of British out searching Barrett's farm. A chagrined Lieutenant Colonel Smith led his men out of Concord about noon, cognizant that the force of Massachusetts militiamen was growing.

(Retreat to Charlestown): The British passed through a hail of enemy lead as they withdrew from Concord to Lexington. Just outside Lexington, Captain Parker, who had earlier led the militia on Lexington Green, organized an ambush known today as "Parker's Revenge." Parker's surprise attack inflicted many casualties and wounded key British leaders, including Lt. Col. Francis Smith. A British relief force led by Maj. (Lord) Percy joined Smith's column at Lexington. Without Percy's men, artillery, and leadership, the colonials may have overwhelmed and destroyed Smith's expeditionary force. Using his cannon to disperse the advancing rebels, Percy regained some control of a difficult withdrawal. Although Percy managed to lead the British column back to the safety of Charlestown, the rebels fired on it from the woods throughout much of the march, inflicting several hundred casualties. By the time the march ended, some 6,000 colonial militiamen had assembled on the outskirts of Boston.

Casualties: British: 73 killed, 174 wounded, and 26 missing; American: 49 killed, 41 wounded, and five missing (most losses on both sides incurred during the running battle to Charlestown).

Outcome / Impact: The battles of Lexington and Concord ("The Shot Heard Round The World") initiated armed hostilities between the British and American forces. The bloodshed was exactly what many in the colonies were hoping for to raise popular support for an armed revolution. The colonial fighting style was unconventional and disorganized, but the asymmetric form of warfare had a tremendous impact upon the morale of the British soldiers, who suffered nearly 20 percent casualties. The seemingly invincible British army suddenly found itself in a war fighting an enemy who used tactics as foreign to them as the soil upon which they were fighting. Colonial Gen. William Heath organized the thousands of militiamen milling about outside Boston and established a quasi "siege" around Gage's shocked British command. The war was now on in earnest.

Today: The Minute Man National Historical Park in Concord interprets and preserves these opening battles of the war through exhibits and living history programs.

Further Reading: Tourtellot, Arthur Bernon, *Lexington and Concord: The Beginning of the War of the American Revolution* (Norton, 2000); Forthingham, Richard, *History of the Siege of Boston and the Battles of Lexington, Concord, and Bunker Hill; Also, An Account of the Bunker Hill Monument with Illustrative Documents* (Scholars, 2005); Hibbert, Christopher, *Redcoats and Rebels: The American Revolution Through British Eyes* (Norton, 2000).

Boston, Siege of (Boston Campaign)

Date: April 19, 1775 – March 17, 1776.
Region: Northern Colonies, Boston, Massachusetts.
Commanders: British: General Thomas Gage; American: General Artemas Ward.
Time of Day / Length of Action: Eleven months.
Weather Conditions: Unremarkable.
Opposing Forces: British: 4,000 in April to 9,500 in March of 1776; American: 7,000 in April to 24,000 in March of 1776.

British Perspective: By the time night fell on the evening of April 19, 1775, England was at war with the American colonists. After barely escaping from Concord the British suffered heavy casualties at the hands of untrained colonial militia during the retreat to the outskirts of Boston. The sudden turn of events restricted the British garrison of about 4,000 men to the city, though its powerful navy controlled Boston harbor. While rations and information about the rebels were in short supply, the British retained a strong and virtually unassailable position in the port city. General Thomas Gage was in overall charge of British forces in the American colonies with his headquarters in Boston.

Events in the American colonies were of great concern to King George III (it was said he had Boston "on the brain"). On May 25, 4,500 British reinforcements arrived there to help Gage put down the rebellion. With them were Generals William Howe, Henry Clinton, and John Burgoyne. Plans to break through the siege and crush the rebellion were quickly drafted. The plan was carried out on June 17 with a victorious (but very costly) assault on the colonists across the Charles River at the Battle of Bunker (Breed's) Hill.

American Perspective: After driving the British back to Boston and pinning them against the sea, the thousands of colonists who joined forces around the city were placed under the command of American General Artemas Ward, a prominent leader of the Massachusetts militia. Ward established his headquarters at Cambridge (west of Boston) and the surrounding area swelled quickly with troop concentrations at Charlestown, Roxbury, and Dorchester Heights. Within a short time the colonial army had 7,000 soldiers to confront the military professionals marking time in Boston.

On June 14, 1775 the Continental Congress officially created a Continental Army and the following day selected George Washington to serve as its commander in chief. General Ward, meanwhile, strengthened his lines, drilled his fresh troops, and maintained his loosely organized Patriots in a quasi-siege of Boston. Ward's plans to strengthen the colonial works near Charlestown led to the June 17 Battle of Bunker Hill. Although the British won a costly victory in that engagement, the area around Charlestown was retaken without opposition when General Washington arrived on July 3. The Continental Army continued to grow in strength and its lines around Boston were tightened. The arrival of heavy siege artillery finally forced the British to evacuate the city. The King's army sailed for Halifax, Nova Scotia, ending the "siege" of Boston on March 17, 1776. The next month Washington shifted the bulk of the Continental Army to fortify New York City.

Terrain: Boston and its environs was a well developed and populated colonial city surrounded by several small towns at Charlestown, Roxbury, Cambridge, and Dorchester Heights. As a flourishing port city, the harbor was filled with sailing vessels of many types, including merchant ships and fishing fleets.

The Fighting and *Casualties*: Not applicable (see separate entry for Bunker Hill).

Outcome / Impact: The siege of Boston was the first large scale operational phase of the American Revolution. Events in and around the city during this siege were critical in shaping the character of the emerging nation and forced Great Britain to deal with threats to its authority in the colonies. The siege and fighting set the stage for what followed. The firm display by the militia at the Bunker Hill fight, demonstrated that local militias, properly handled, could be used to advantage against the greatest military machine of its day. The Patriot stand confounded the British and went against the

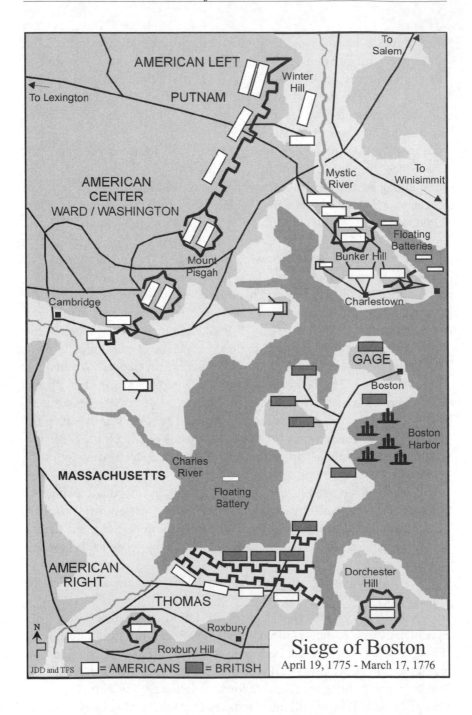

AMERICAN LEFT

PUTNAM

Winter Hill

To Salem

To Lexington

AMERICAN CENTER
WARD / WASHINGTON

Mystic River

To Winisimmit

Mount Pisgah

Bunker Hill

Floating Batteries

Cambridge

Charlestown

GAGE

Boston

Boston Harbor

MASSACHUSETTS

Charles River

Floating Battery

AMERICAN RIGHT

THOMAS

Dorchester Hill

N

Roxbury

Roxbury Hill

JDD and TPS   ☐ = AMERICANS   ■ = BRITISH

Siege of Boston
April 19, 1775 - March 17, 1776

military doctrine of the day. Most of the British had initially perceived the Patriots as little more than rustic rebels with no real military ability; the early battles and the siege forced the King's troops to at least privately acknowledge their bravery.

The fighting during the war's early weeks bought additional time for politicians and civilians alike to debate crucial questions associated with independence, sovereignty, and ideals that forged the foundations of the United States of America.

Today: The Boston National Historical Park in Boston interprets and preserves the colonial history of the city.

Further Reading: Hibbert, Christopher, *Redcoats and Rebels: The American Revolution Through British Eyes* (Norton, 2000); Haskell, Caleb. *Caleb Haskell's Diary, May 5-May 30, 1776: A Revolutionary Soldier's Record before Boston and With Arnold's Quebec Expedition*. Edited by Lothrop Withington. Newburyport, Mass.: W. H. House & Co., 1881.

Fort Ticonderoga, Battle of (Canadian Campaign)

Date: May 10, 1775.
Region: Northern Colonies, New York.
Commanders: British: Captain De La Place; American: Colonel Ethan Allen and Captain Benedict Arnold.
Time of Day / Length of Action: Dawn.
Weather Conditions: Unremarkable, spring morning.
Opposing Forces: British: 85; American: 100 Vermont militiamen.

British Perspective: Hostilities in Massachusetts were far removed from the stone ramparts of Fort Ticonderoga. Although the revolution had been underway for several weeks, most of the British outposts and garrisons in North America, including Ticonderoga, remained undermanned and isolated. As with any frontier outpost, the drudgery of daily routine and isolation dulled the senses and lulled inhabitants into a false sense of security. Fort Ticonderoga was built by the French in 1755. By 1775 the post was armed with 79 pieces of heavy artillery but had a garrison of only 85 soldiers. British authorities, however, believed it was adequately defended. There was no indication local citizens were preparing for an assault on the fort or that any hostile force was approaching.

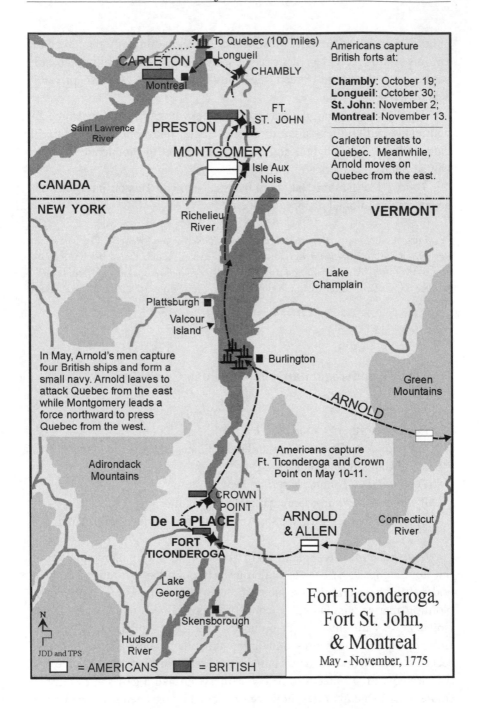

To Quebec (100 miles)

CARLETON

Longueil

CHAMBLY

Montreal

FT. ST. JOHN

Saint Lawrence River

PRESTON

MONTGOMERY

Isle Aux Nois

CANADA

NEW YORK

Richelieu River

VERMONT

Americans capture British forts at:

Chambly: October 19;
Longueil: October 30;
St. John: November 2;
Montreal: November 13.

Carleton retreats to Quebec. Meanwhile, Arnold moves on Quebec from the east.

Lake Champlain

Plattsburgh

Valcour Island

Burlington

In May, Arnold's men capture four British ships and form a small navy. Arnold leaves to attack Quebec from the east while Montgomery leads a force northward to press Quebec from the west.

Green Mountains

ARNOLD

Adirondack Mountains

Americans capture Ft. Ticonderoga and Crown Point on May 10-11.

CROWN POINT

De La PLACE

FORT TICONDEROGA

ARNOLD & ALLEN

Connecticut River

Lake George

Skensborough

N

JDD and TPS

Hudson River

☐ = AMERICANS   ■ = BRITISH

Fort Ticonderoga, Fort St. John, & Montreal

May - November, 1775

American Perspective: Following the battles of Lexington and Concord, the Second Continental Congress called up a national standing army, naming George Washington as its commander. Washington opened a quasi-siege against the British in Boston, Massachusetts. He and his officers realized from the outset they were short on nearly everything an army required, especially artillery and ammunition. The British outpost at Fort Ticonderoga 200 miles to the north had both guns and powder in substantial quantities. If the fort could be taken, its resources and strategic location would meet other needs as well. Colonel Ethan Allen organized a 100-man force of Vermont militiamen (known as the Green Mountain Boys) to conduct the difficult mission. Joined by Connecticut militia leader Captain Benedict Arnold, the Patriot force launched its effort to capture the British fort.

Terrain: Located in Essex County, New York, 95 miles north of Albany, Ticonderoga derived its name from the Indian word *Cheonderoga*, or "Place between two waters." Fort Ticonderoga was strategically located on dominating high ground surrounding the area between Lake Champlain and Lake George in the Hudson River Valley.

The Fighting: Before dawn on May 10, the Green Mountain Boys stealthily crossed Lake Champlain from Vermont into New York. The Vermonters crept undetected up to the fort's stone walls. To their surprise, the raiders discovered an unmanned and unlocked entrance, through which they quietly entered the bastion. As they hoped, except for a single guard the garrison was sound asleep. A brief fight broke out during which the lone British guard and a Vermonter were wounded. The Americans moved quickly to the commander's quarters, where Captain De La Place awoke slowly to the realization that his fortress had been captured by the enemy. When Colonel Allen demanded his surrender, the sleepy De La Place, who was still in his bedclothes, asked, "To whom and why?" Colonel Allen recalled in his memoirs that he replied in a firm, loud voice, "In the name of the Great Jehovah and the Continental Congress!" The startled British commander ordered his men to stand down and surrendered the fort.

Casualties: British: one wounded; American: one wounded.

Outcome / Impact: In addition to the vast supply of munitions and 79 artillery pieces that went with the capture of Fort Ticonderoga, the fledgling Patriot army achieved a magnificent public relations victory. The artillery that could be moved was hauled overland to Boston and emplaced in the siege works. Fort Ticonderoga became an important base for the Americans. Had it remained in British hands, it would have posed a dangerous threat to operations in the Hudson River Valley. On May 11 (the day after Ticonderoga fell), the Vermont raiders also captured the British fort at

Crown Point several miles north of Ticonderoga. The embarrassment of these twin military failures humiliated the British while offering an invaluable morale boost for the nascent Continental army and the Patriot movement throughout the colonies.

Today: Fort Ticonderoga National Historic Landmark hosts nearly 100,000 visitors each year and includes a wide variety of living history programs and interpretive events. Fort Crown Point in New York preserves and interprets American, British, and French history.

Further Reading: Hamilton, Edward Pierce. *Fort Ticonderoga: Key to a Continent* (Ft. Ticonderoga, 1995); Pell, Stephan H. P. *Fort Ticonderoga: A Short History Compiled from Contemporary Sources* (n.p., 1957).

Hog and Noodle Islands, Battles of (Boston Campaign)

Date: May 27-28, 1775.

Region: Northern Colonies, Massachusetts.

Commanders: British: General Thomas Gage (actual ground commander unknown); American: Colonel Israel Putnam.

Time of Day / Length of Action: Late afternoon until midnight (sporadic fighting for seven hours).

Weather Conditions: Unremarkable, spring weather.

Opposing Forces: British: 100 marines escorted by one schooner, one sloop, and eight barges (all armed with cannon); American: 300.

British Perspective: By the time the siege of Boston was in its fifth week the embattled 4,000 British soldiers were facing severe shortages of meat and other food supplies. The British navy moved freely in and out of port, but the onset and early course of the war had taken the British by surprise. Rebels frequented the small islands within the harbor. British spies watched their movements carefully. The islands were used by local Bostonians to graze livestock. The British raided these islands to meet their heavy subsistence needs. Two successful raids that April against Governor's and Thompson's islands brought in significant food supplies, but the British requirements quickly outstripped these small additions to the Crown's commissary. Several large herds were known to be grazing on Hog and Noodle islands, and the British decided to try and capture them. At least eight barges were prepared for both the movement of British troops and the retrieval of the livestock. An armed naval escort included a schooner and a sloop with a combined strength of six guns. On the afternoon of May 27, a 100-man detachment of British marines and their armed naval escort left for what they believed would be a routine mission.

American Perspective: After driving the British into a restrictive enclave around Boston, the largely green 7,000-man colonial army pressed their enemy into a quasi-siege. Although five weeks had elapsed since the rebel army began arriving outside Boston, there were no indications that General Washington's besiegers would be able to sustain and complete their mammoth effort. Without a real navy, the rebels could not prevent supplies and reinforcements from reaching the enemy. Washington faced serious logistical quandaries of his own, and depended upon local farmers for much of his subsistence. These logistical arrangements included much of the livestock grazing freely on the islands dotting Boston harbor.

Stunned by the British raids against Governor's and Thompson's islands, the Patriots promptly arranged for the defense of their remaining animals. When local citizen-spies provided information of an impending British attack against Hog and Noodle islands, Gen. Artemus Ward dispatched 300 men under Col. Israel Putnam to defend the livestock.

Terrain: In 1775, Hog Island and Noodle Island were located adjacent to one another in Boston harbor, two miles northeast of Boston and two miles east of Charlestown. Both islands extended into the harbor from northeast to southwest. Noodle Island measured three miles wide and six miles long. Hog Island measured three miles wide and three miles long, and was located between Noodle Island and the mainland. The islands featured gently elevated knolls in the northeast, while the southwest regions sloped gently toward the shore and docking areas. In the 18th century, Hog and Noodle islands were used as livestock pens and fields where sheep and cattle roamed freely. The islands were connected to the mainland on their north sides via a short ferry crossing near the village of Winnesimit. The two islands were also separated by less than one mile, and the crossing between them was easily accomplished with small boats.

The Fighting: When the British landed on Noodle Island, a detachment of 30 Patriots was there to meet them. The Americans had taken up positions on the heights and opened a sharp musket fire against the surprised British as they disembarked from their barges. The British landed in force and brushed aside and chased the Patriots back toward Hog Island. The running stopped when the British came up against Colonel Putnam's main command. Putnam had deployed his men in a large ditch, from which they poured an effective small arms fire into the advancing enemy. The Americans also opened fire

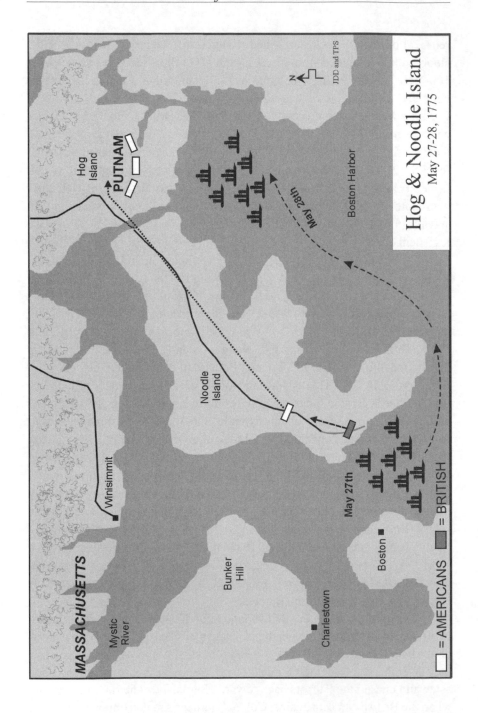

Hog & Noodle Island
May 27-28, 1775

with two small 3-pounder field pieces, which lobbed rounds into both the troops and the ships waiting below them. The artillery destroyed one of the British barges. The British warships responded with an ineffective supporting fire. The Americans were well protected. Because the naval guns did not have the right angle of fire, they contributed nothing to the combat.

The odd little battle sputtered fitfully for nearly seven hours. The rebels were too strong to attack directly, and could not be successfully flanked. It was late in the evening before the British finally gave up the effort and returned to their barges. At dawn on May 28, the British attempted another attack from the sea off the coast of Hog Island near the Winnesimit Ferry crossing. Once again the Americans were waiting for their enemy and enjoyed the advantage of good terrain. When Patriot artillery destroyed another British barge, the battle quickly came to an end. The British retreated back to Boston and the Americans retained possession of the islands and their livestock.

Casualties: British: 20 killed and 50 wounded; *American*: one killed and three wounded.

Outcome / Impact: The Americans retained possession of at least 400 sheep, 30 cows, and several horses. By keeping the livestock away from the British, the Americans eliminated a large source of food the British desperately needed. Many soldiers and civilians around Boston witnessed the battle, and the Patriots were the obvious victors.

Within several weeks of these small actions, Gen. George Washington was appointed by the Continental Congress to command the American army. Colonel Putnam, the Patriot commander who had led the troops so well at Bunker Hill and on Hog Island and Noodle Island, was promoted to major general. In this manner Putnam and his peers, Gens. Artemus Ward, Charles Lee, and Philip John Schuyler became General Washington's primary early-war battlefield commanders.

Today: The islands on which the battle occurred have been connected with landfill and reshaped by urban growth. The area is known today as East Boston and Logan International Airport.

Further Reading: Allen, Gardner. *A Naval History of the American Revolution* (Corner House Publishing, 1970); Frothingham, Richard. *History of the Siege of Boston* (Scholar's Bookshelf, 2005); Moore, Frank. *Diary of the American Revolution*, volume I (Washington Square Press, 1968).

Bunker Hill, Battle of (Boston Campaign)

Date: June 17, 1775.

Region: Northern Colonies, Charlestown (Boston), Massachusetts.

Commanders: British: Lieutenant General Thomas Gage, Major Generals William Howe, Henry Clinton, John Burgoyne; American: Colonel William Prescott, Generals Israel Putnam, Artemas Ward.

Time of Day / Length of Action: All-day artillery fire, afternoon infantry fighting.

Weather Conditions: Clear, hot, and oppressive.

Opposing Forces: British: 2,500; American: 3,000 on the peninsula; 1,400 engaged. In and around Boston: 10,000 Americans and 6,500 British.

British Perspective: After the battles of Lexington and Concord on April 19, 1775, the colonial militiamen laid siege to British-occupied Boston. While restricted to Boston and the heights along Copp's Hill, the British still retained access to the sea and within a few months attained improved strength, additional leadership, and naval warships. General Gage met with Generals Howe, Clinton, and Burgoyne and his war council to decide how best to control the harbor and retain access to the sea. They decided control of the key terrain on Dorchester Heights and Charlestown on the northern side of Boston was critical to their success.

Plans were developed to occupy the high ground on the Charlestown peninsula, including the strategic high points of Bunker Hill and Breed's Hill. The British were astounded when the sun rose on June 17 to reveal the colonists had not only taken the heights, but managed to construct a rather elaborate redoubt worthy of an organized army.

American Perspective: After surrounding Boston the Americans learned on June 13 of the British plan to take the heights on Charlestown. On June 16 Colonel Prescott led some 1,200 men to fortify this strategic locale before the British could move on the high ground. Other commands joined him. The plan was to seize Bunker Hill, construct fortifications during the night, and prepare to meet an anticipated British assault.

When they arrived on the scene a long discussion ensued before it was decided to establish the redoubt on Breed's Hill, the mound southeast of Bunker Hill. (Bunker Hill could have been made nearly impregnable while Breed's Hill, closer to the harbor, was essentially untenable and offered nothing of strategic value not found in former.) Fortifications were also dug on Bunker Hill. Exactly who was in command of the American troops is unclear; Putnam was likely in nominal command, but Prescott seems to have exercised tactical control. Ward remained in Cambridge.

Terrain: The Charlestown peninsula is across the Charles River from Boston and measures one mile long (northeast to southwest) and just more than one-half mile wide. Three pieces of high ground dominate the peninsula. At the northern end is Bunker Hill (110 feet), followed by Breed's Hill near the middle (75 feet) and Moulton's Hill (35 feet) in the southeastern corner. A narrow point in the northeastern corner (the "Neck") connects Charlestown peninsula with the mainland. Charlestown was located in the northwest section, but the bulk of the land consisted of open ground.

The Fighting: On the morning of June 17, 1775, General Gage ordered General Howe to attack the colonists and remove them from Charlestown peninsula. While the troops prepared for action the British navy and artillery continued its largely ineffective bombardment that had lasted for much of the day. British troops landed unopposed at Moulton's Point on the southeastern end of the peninsula about 1:00 p.m. The plan was to push around the open American left flank along the Mystic River beach and envelop the redoubt while a holding attack pinned the enemy in the fort. Prescott reinforced his exposed left by dispatching men to take position behind a stone and rail fence. A breastwork of stone extended the line from where the fence ended down to the river bluff and beach area.

In columns of fours the fully equipped British infantry marched against the beach breastwork and John Stark's New Hampshire men. Ordered to fire low and pick off British officers, the defenders held their fire until the heavy scarlet British formations stepped within 50 yards. Organized in three ranks, one of which was always firing, the colonists opened deadly volleys against the British ranks. The stalled primary attack angered Howe, who personally moved forward to lead the assault against the American center at the rail fence. The heavy and accurate fire stunned the Regulars, who stopped to wage an uphill battle against a well-defended position. Unable to advance and taking fearful casualties, Howe withdrew but reorganized for a second attack. The holding attack against the main redoubt did not fare any better.

The defenders withstood a second British assault fifteen minutes later aimed primarily against the redoubt. It was repulsed in much the same manner. The frustrated fully equipped professional soldiers organized yet again and, with reinforcements, launched a third push against the redoubt—this time without heavy knapsacks and personal baggage. The Americans were running low on ammunition when the third attack was launched. At some point Putnam famously ordered his men to not "fire until you see the white of their eyes." With close artillery cover the British made it

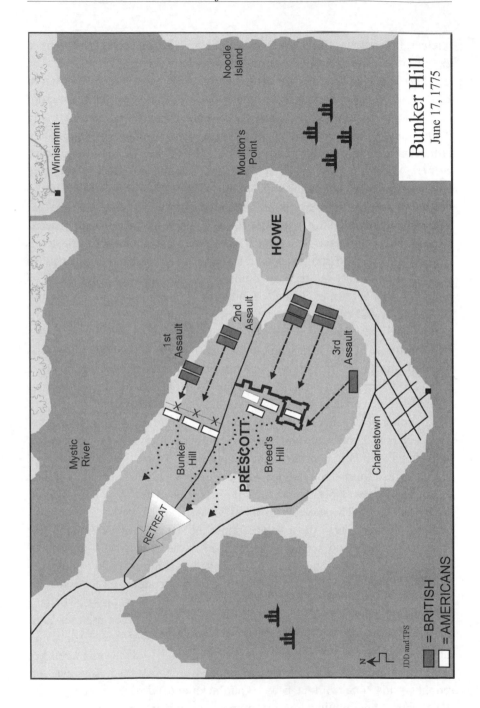

Bunker Hill
June 17, 1775

up to the fort and spilled into the redoubt. Desperate hand-to-hand bayonet and clubbed musket fighting ensued. Prescott barely escaped with his life. The colonists waged a fighting retreat to Bunker Hill and then, utterly exhausted, across the "Neck" to the mainland.

Casualties: British: This early battle was one of the bloodiest fights of the entire war. Though General Howe emerged tactically victorious, he lost 1,154 killed and wounded of the 2,500 men fed into the fight—or about 46%. This broke down to a reported 226 killed and 828 wounded (38th Foot losses were not reported; estimated at 125). Casualties among officers were extraordinarily heavy. According to one credible source, 1/8 of those killed and 1/6 of those wounded during the *entire* war were lost at Bunker Hill. American: The Putnam-Prescott defenders numbered about 1,400 effectives and suffered 140 killed and 301 wounded (30 of the latter were captured). Most of these losses were suffered during the retreat from the redoubt.

Outcome / Impact: American willpower and morale soared as the hope for reconciliation and an early end to the fighting ebbed. Undeterred by the ominous strength of the British military machine, the colonists demonstrated their ability to stand in the face of Europe's finest soldiers, albeit behind breastworks. As other historians have noted, the key to the defensive action was the effective veteran leadership of Prescott, Putnam, and others. In turn, the British realized the war would be long and bloody and for the better part of a year did not launch another offensive action.

Today: The Boston National Historical Park and Charlestown Navy Yard Visitor Center interpret and preserve the Bunker Hill fighting.

Further Reading: Green, Samuel Abbott. "Colonel William Prescott; and Groton Soldiers at the Battle of Bunker Hill." Proceedings of the Massachusetts Historical Society, 43 (November 1909), pp. 92-96; Hibbert, Christopher, *Redcoats and Rebels: The American Revolution Through British* Eyes (Norton, 2000); Ketchum, Richard M., *Decisive Day: The Battle for Bunker Hill* (Owl Books, 1999).

Fort St. John, Siege of (Canada Campaign)

Date: September 4 – November 2, 1775.

Region: St. John, Québec Province, Canada (Canadian Campaign- American expedition beyond the Northern Colonies).

Commanders: British: General Sir Guy Carleton and Major Charles Preston; American: General Richard Montgomery.

Time of Day / Length of Action: Eight weeks.
Weather Conditions: Cold and wet.
Opposing Forces: British: 800; American: 2,000.

British Perspective: In the summer of 1775, the British governor of Canada and commander of all British forces there, Gen. Sir Guy Carleton, made preparations to counter any invasion by American forces. The loss of British outposts south at Fort Ticonderoga and Crown Point provided the Americans with an excellent base of operations from which to threaten other British possessions. Rebel raiders also attacked and seized British ships on Lake Champlain. By June of 1775, the Americans controlled the entire lake. The naval losses provided the Americans with ships to threaten British outposts along the northern corridor into Canada. The British realized Fort St. John, a stronghold on the Richelieu River, was the next likely target if the Americans continued advancing.

General Carleton began a methodical preparation to counter the potential threat against Fort St. John, but his resources were limited to a few thousand soldiers and a handful of ships. At St. John, Carleton posted as many as 800 men under the command of Maj. Charles Preston. This force included several hundred Indian and Canadian volunteers. Carleton bolstered the fort's defense by posting a 16-gun warship in the river below the fort. By the 1st of September Carleton knew the Americans were establishing a base below St. John at Isle aux Noix, and that a siege would be underway soon.

American Perspective: Encouraged by the capture of British outposts at Fort Ticonderoga and Crown Point, Col. Benedict Arnold continued his brazen attacks against British possessions. After seizing a schooner at Skenesborough (Whitehall) on Lake Champlain, Arnold launched a series of naval raids in mid-May that resulted in the capture of four ships (including a 70-ton sloop) and the destruction of five others. This Patriot victory secured complete control of Lake Champlain, prompting the Continental Congress to encourage a push northward into Canada. Part of the reason for doing so was a hope that Canadians would join the Americans as a fourteenth colony in a revolt against the Crown. Additionally, the control of Canadian outposts minimized a British threat from that direction.

An expedition to invade Canada was launched in late August and early September under the command of Gens. Philip Schuyler and Richard Montgomery. This Northern army consisted of 3,100 men divided into a two-prong invasion force intended to converge at Québec. General Montgomery was tasked with leading 2,000 men along the main lake and river connections northward through St. John, Montreal, to threaten Québec from the southwest. Colonel Benedict Arnold, meanwhile, would lead the second wing of 1,100 men on a circuitous route across the wilds of Maine and approach Québec from that direction.

In early September Schuyler left because of ill health and Montgomery assumed command of the campaign. Montgomery's troops built entrenchments at Isle aux Noix and placed a barrier across the Richelieu River to keep British ships from moving south into Lake Champlain and Lake George. This obstacle was important because the British had two vessels posted below their fort at St. John. Meanwhile, the Patriots made plans to defeat their enemy and continue their mission to Canada.

Terrain: (Please refer to the Northern Battles map following the Table of Contents). Fort St. John dominated the fertile valley carved by the Richelieu River, which empties Lake Champlain (U.S. border) into the St. Lawrence River. This strategic 80-mile waterway has served as a major commerce route for centuries and has been the subject of many American and Canadian disputes. The stone forts at St. John and Chambly were erected on the shore of the Richelieu River to provide their defenders with strategic outposts capable of controlling shipping on the waterway. They were originally built by the French, who lost them to the British in 1763 in the Treaty of Paris, which ended the French and Indian War.

The Fighting: On September 6, 1775, the Americans conducted their first offensive operation of the Canadian Campaign by attacking the British defenses and fort located at St. John, Québec. Heavy British gunfire prevented the Americans from getting close to seriously threatening the stronghold, and they retreated to their base at Isle aux Noix. However, the thrust did seize some supplies at Chambly, where the British had an outpost and supply facility. Undeterred, Montgomery launched another effort against Major Preston's defenders on the evening of September 10. This one involved fourteen boats and 1,100 men intent on investing the fort from the north. It, too, ended in failure after the main ground assault force became confused in the darkness and marshy terrain below the fort and British cannon fire killed and wounded several men. The leader of the foray, Lieutenant Colonel Rudolphus Ritzema, ordered a retreat. A follow-up assault scheduled the next day was canceled.

By this time the Americans were becoming demoralized and many were ill. Luckily for Montgomery, 300 reinforcements arrived to bolster the army's flagging spirits. On September 17 the Americans launched another combined strike against the British fort that was also repelled, though not before the capture of valuable supplies. The Americans suffered another setback on September 24-25 when Col. Ethan Allen launched a premature assault without adequate support designed to capture Montreal. This flawed escapade resulted in Allen's capture and the loss of his small army (see Battle of Montreal). The rest of September passed with the Americans digging traditional siege lines to constrict and crush the defenders. Although they could fire into the British lines, they could not capture the stronghold without a proper ground attack. Without sufficient supplies, discipline, and equipment, the task began to look impossible.

The tide turned in October when small successes and the opening of an artillery battery forced Preston to scuttle his main warship *Royal Savage*. On the 18th, 90 soldiers defending the British fort at Chambly capitulated. The victory provided the Americans with more artillery, small arms, gunpowder, and other badly needed supplies—everything they needed to finish the job against St. John. In an effort to rescue St. John's beleaguered defenders, General Carleton tried to punch through the American siege lines at Longueil, but Col. Seth Warner and the Green Mountain Boys repelled the effort. Warner's force numbered only 350 men and Carleton's 1,100, but American artillery in commanding positions, bolstered by entrenchments, convinced the British commander he could not successfully cross the St. Lawrence River. Carleton retreated to Montreal.

After conferring with American authorities about the hopelessness of the British position at Fort St. John, Preston surrendered his garrison to Montgomery on November 2, ending the long siege.

Casualties: British: 43 killed and wounded, several hundred captured; American: 11 killed and wounded (scores more died or suffered from disease).

Outcome / Impact: This first Patriot victory of the Canadian Campaign was a tremendous success and requisite first step to wresting Canada from the British. If Montgomery's forces had failed at Fort St. John, continued movement northward would have been impossible. Victory at Fort St. John provided the catalyst for General Carleton to evacuate Montreal and isolate his forces at Québec City. This, in turn, made it possible for Montgomery to capture Montreal without a fight and focus his efforts on Québec City, where he intended to link up point with Benedict Arnold's command. However, Preston's gallant defense of the St. John's bastion delayed Montgomery's expedition by two months, forcing Montgomery and Arnold to fight a major winter campaign, for which they were ill equipped.

Further Reading: Shelton, Hal T. *General Richard Montgomery and the American Revolution*. New York: New York Press, 1996.

Montreal, Battle of (Canada Campaign)

Date: September 24-25, 1775.

Region: Montreal, Québec Province, Canada (Canadian Campaign-American expedition beyond the Northern Colonies).

Commanders: British: Major General Sir Guy Carleton; American: Colonel Ethan Allen.

Time of Day / Length of Action: Late night into pre-dawn, several hours

Weather Conditions: Unremarkable, cool.

Opposing Forces: British: Composite force of 235 British, Canadian, and Indian; American:110 American and Canadian volunteers.

British Perspective: With the siege of Fort St. John having been underway since September 4, General Carleton knew that Montreal would soon be threatened. He initiated plans to relieve his forces there and protect his interests in the region. Spies informed Carleton that Americans had been recruiting Canadians outside of Montreal with the intent of capturing the city on the evening of September 24. Carleton formed an ad-hoc command of 235 men to close with his enemy and remove the threat before it could fully mature. When he learned Col. Ethan Allen had fashioned a small army of Canadian sympathizers and it was isolated near Montreal, Carleton moved quickly to trap Allen on the outskirts of the city.

American Perspective: From the siege works surrounding Fort St. John, Gen. Richard Montgomery dispatched Colonel Allen and Maj. John Brown to gather Canadians to fight against the British. While both parties recruited small elements of Canadian sympathizers, they did not achieve the numbers they had hoped to enlist. Nonetheless, Allen decided to try and invest Montreal, an overly ambitious plan that quickly fell apart. Allen and Brown joined forces on the way back to St. John and decided an effort to capture Montreal should be undertaken. Their composite strength was only 300 men. The bold plan called for Allen to lead his 110 men across the St. Lawrence River below the city while Brown did likewise above it. Allen successfully crossed the river under the cover of darkness on September 24. When he realized Brown would not meet his deadline, Allen took up a defensive position a few miles from the outskirts of Montreal because he could not cross back to safety before daylight.

Terrain: (Please refer to the Northern Battles map following the Table of Contents).The city of Montreal is situated on a large island 40 miles long by

20 miles wide. The Prairies River in the west; the St. Lawrence River wraps around the city in the south, east, and north.

The Fighting: Carleton moved out against Allen's trapped force with about 35 Regulars and another 200 volunteer militiamen and Indians. As Carleton pressed forward, firing into Allen's Canadian recruits, they fled the field in a panic. Allen attempted to organize a fighting withdrawal, but unsure of his whereabouts and how best to escape, he could not affect it and was forced to surrender.

Casualties: British: none reported; American: undetermined killed and wounded, 40 captured.

Outcome / Impact: On November 13, 1775, Montgomery captured Montreal without firing a shot. Ethan Allen's ill-planned September raid against the city damaged the American cause in Canada by making it appear as though the Americans could never win the war. Many Canadians either sat on their hands or decided to fight with the British rather than rally to a losing cause. Indian tribes also evaluated the small affair with a similar eye toward allying with the winning side. When the British learned Colonel Allen had led the capture of Fort Ticonderoga that May, they sailed him to England and threw him into prison. Calls to hang him were not acted upon in fear that the Americans would do likewise to British prisoners, and Allen was shipped back to Canada and paroled in New York City in October 1776. He was eventually exchanged for British officer Archibald Campbell in 1778, mounted a horse, and sought out General Washington at Valley Forge.

Today: A wide variety of sites incorporate to varying degrees Montreal's Revolutionary War history, including Montreal's tourist center and Fort Ticonderoga National Historic Landmark.

Further Reading: Jellison, Charles Albert, *Ethan Allen: Frontier Rebel* (Syracuse University Press, 1983); Shelton, Hal T. *General Richard Montgomery and the American Revolution: From Redcoat to Rebel* (New York University Press, 1996).

Snow Campaign, Battles of the (Ninety-Six and Great Cane Brake)

Date: October through December 1775.
Region: Southern Colonies, South Carolina.
Commanders: British (Tory militia): Colonel Thomas Fletchall and Patrick Cunningham; American (North and South Carolina militia): Colonel

Richard Richardson, Colonel William "Danger" Thomson, and Major Andrew Williamson.

Time of Day / Length of Action: Ongoing, three months.

Weather Conditions: Cold and wintry mix in October and November followed by heavy snow in December.

Opposing Forces: British (Tory militia): 600 to 2,000; American (North and South Carolina militia): 562 to 4,000. Both militia forces increased in strength as the campaign progressed.

British Perspective: The battles conducted during the 1775 Snow Campaign were all waged by American colonists living in a wild region of northwestern South Carolina known as the Upcountry. Within these forested foothills the colonists had pushed the Indians westward and established settlements. The beginning of the American Revolution divided these people into Loyalists (Tories) who supported the Crown and English rule and Rebels or Patriots, who desired independence. The Loyalist movement within this backwoods region was led by Col. Thomas Fletchall, who organized a loose military organization to counter pro-Patriot militia operating in the area. Another fervent Loyalist leader was Maj. Patrick Cunningham. While these Upcountry Loyalists received little support from the British, they maintained a dogged presence and engaged in brutal fighting against Patriot militia throughout the American Revolution.

In October of 1775, in District Ninety-Six, Loyalist leader Patrick Cunningham and 60 of his men seized a South Carolina colonial militia wagon train laden with 2,000 pounds of lead and 1,000 pounds of gunpowder. Intended as a peace gesture, the supplies were being delivered to the Cherokee Indians from Charleston, South Carolina. The Loyalists not only gained a fat prize but threatened to upset the delicate balance of peace the local settlers needed to maintain with their Indian neighbors. Throughout the war British Indian agents also maintained a delicate relationship with the Cherokees, and Cunningham worked diligently to keep the Indians aligned with the British and Tories and opposed to the Patriots. The seizure of the wagons prompted the South Carolina militia to organize; the Loyalists decided to attack and destroy them.

American Perspective: Prior to 1755, Indians occupied the Upcountry region of South Carolina and the land northwest of it. However, as pioneers moved into the area in the mid-1750s, the settlers made close friends with the friendly Siouan Catawbas and established a peace treaty with the more aggressive Cherokees. The result was a steady influx of white settlers and the establishment of outposts throughout the area during the next twenty years. Occasional war parties attacked white settlers when the latter encroached into favorite Indian hunting grounds. The ever-westward push of the pioneers created friction between the Indians and the settlers.

When the American Revolution began, the Upcountry region was still remote and dangerous. In order to provide protection for the settlers, a string of forts were constructed by the colonial government throughout District Ninety-Six. These forts included Fort George, Fort Prince, Earle's Fort, Poole's Fort, Anderson's Block House, Nichols' Fort, and Thickety Fort. After the war began, the Patriot inhabitants found themselves fighting Indians, British Regulars, and the local Tory militia. An especially contested region was a large district known as Ninety-Six, where Tory raiders in October of 1775 seized colonial militia supply wagons. This action prompted Maj. Andrew Williamson to call out the local Patriot militia, which mustered a respectable 562 men. Major Williamson and his men established a hastily constructed fort near the settlement of Ninety-Six (in District Ninety-Six).

Terrain: (For a general map of this region, see page 52.) The northwestern corner of South Carolina steadily rises in elevation from southeast to northwest as the terrain transitions from foothills to mountains. Rivers drain the area from northwest to southeast. Lower areas along the waterways are filled with thick undergrowth. The region has hot humid summers and chilly and wet winters. Settlers carved out farms in the valley regions, where they grew and cultivated flax, grains, and tobacco. The battlefields during the Snow Campaign were in District Ninety-Six, which includes the present-day counties of Edgefield, Abbeville, Greenville, Newberry, Spartanburg, Pickens, Union, and Laurens.

The Fighting: On November 19, 1775, the Loyalists attacked the Patriot fort at Ninety-Six. For the next two days the Patriots defended an 85' x 150' log palisade, reinforced with earthen berms on the north and northwestern walls. The two-day siege ended with just one man killed and four men wounded. The battle, however, marked the beginning of a lengthy and bloody struggle.

Neither side was prepared for war in the Upcountry, especially a long one. A temporary truce gave each time to better organize. During the next few weeks, volunteers joined either Tory or Patriot militias and prepared for battle. Colonel Richard Richardson and Col. William "Danger" Thomson rushed to the assistance of Major Williamson at Fort Ninety-Six. Their combined force numbered about 4,000 men. After adequately manning and improving their defensive posts, they planned to assault Tory militia.

Meanwhile, Maj. Patrick Cunningham and Col. Thomas Fletcher combined their own militia and the Tory force in District Ninety-Six also swelled to several thousand. Knowing they were not as strong as their Patriot opponents, however, the Tories or "King's Men" did not aggressively seek to fight as an army.

Despite the cold winter weather, in December of 1775 the Patriot army attempted to surprise the enemy by attacking Tory camps. The Loyalists avoided battle by moving deeper into the forests. Patriot scouts were dispatched to find them, and a large Tory encampment was discovered on Great Cane Brake, a tributary of the Reedy River. This area was located in Cherokee Territory. On December 22 Colonel Thomson led his 3rd Ranger Regiment on a surprise assault of the Tory encampment. Despite heavy rain, sleet, and frigid temperatures, the Rangers moved stealthily through the dark hours of the early morning and crept toward their enemy. By dawn they had surrounded the Tories, but alert sentinels in the Tory camp detected the approaching Patriots. A brisk battle erupted. The Tories had at least one eye focused on escape, and after a short running fight the combat ended with the Patriots in possession of the field.

Casualties: British (Tory): Seven killed, 12 wounded, 130 prisoners; American: three wounded.

Outcome / Impact: As the Patriot militia withdrew eastward to the safety of their forts and settlements, a winter storm blanketed the area with two feet of snow, providing the campaign with its name. Throughout the American Revolution, Tories in the Southern Theater fought primarily as partisan warriors. With the exception of several battles in which they joined their British allies during the latter years of the war, the primary tactics used by Tories were hit and run raids. Captain Thomas "Gamecock" Sumter and Col. Francis "Swamp Fox" Marion also participated in the Snow Campaign. While it achieved little in strategic terms, the effort forged the beginning of a long proud Patriot militia in the Carolinas. Throughout the revolution, a fratricidal civil war raged in the western wilderness regions of Virginia, both Carolinas, and northeast Georgia. The Snow Campaign was just the beginning of this bitter protracted struggle in what was then a wild and often lawless region.

Further Reading: Lumpkin, Henry. *From Savannah to Yorktown: The American Revolution in the South* (Paragon House, 1981).

Great Bridge, Battle of (1st British Southern Expedition)

Date: December 9, 1775.

Region: Southern Colonies, Chesapeake, Virginia (10 miles south of Norfolk).

Commanders: British: John Murray (Earl of Dunmore), and Captain Samuel Leslie; American: Colonel William Woodford, Lieutenant Colonel Edward Stevens (Virginia militia), Colonel Robert Howe (North Carolina militia).

Time of Day / Length of Action: Early morning, 30 minutes.

Weather Conditions: Cold and rainy.

Opposing Forces: British: 672; American: 1,275.

British Perspective: As the rebellion gathered strength throughout the colonies, Virginia's Royal Governor John Murray (Lord Dunmore) fled from the capital at Williamsburg seeking the safety of the British navy at Norfolk. An unpopular ruler, Dunmore had two British grenadier companies to provide him protection in Norfolk. He raised an additional two regiments of Loyalists, including the "Royal Ethiopians," an outfit composed of runaway slaves who served the Crown in return for their freedom.

The early war in the Northern colonies was not going well for the British, and it was Dunmore's hope to crush the rebellion in Virginia and win favor with King George III. Dunmore imposed martial law, erected entrenchments around Norfolk, and constructed Fort Murray, a small log palisade at Great Bridge to control the causeway connecting Norfolk with the Virginia mainland. This strategic thoroughfare and trade route linked eastern Virginia with North Carolina. His position could not be flanked because of swampy terrain. Only a headlong attack could dislodge him. In late November a small force of Patriots arrived to defeat him.

American Perspective: While Lord Dunmore was driven into isolation at Norfolk, his control of the port city and its entrance at Great Bridge depended upon the fort he had constructed there, which posed a threat to the Virginians. While many of the local citizens of Norfolk were sympathetic to the Crown, many more Virginians supported the campaign for independence. Two Virginia regiments of militia infantry under Col. William Woodford prepared to engage Lord Dunmore and drive him and his soldiers away. Colonel Robert Howe and 150 men from North Carolina joined their neighbors in the quest to defeat Dunmore. Comprised of some 700 militiamen, this composite Patriot force included a young John

Marshall, the future Chief Justice of the US Supreme Court, as well as Marshall's father.

In late November, Colonel Woodford ordered entrenchments built south of the British fort to block the other end of the causeway and isolate and threaten Dunmore's army. The Virginians expertly threw up parapets within musket range of the fort. Ninety marksmen were left to hold the end of the narrow causeway while the rest camped several hundred yards in the rear. Shots were exchanged over the next few weeks and a handful of minor skirmishes occurred. Several homes between the combatant forces were destroyed.

Terrain: This area of Tidewater Virginia is swampy coastal plain with narrow sandy passages through which flows the southern branch of the Elizabeth River. Great Bridge lies between the Chesapeake to the south and Norfolk, Virginia, to the north.

The Fighting: Dunmore's outnumbered command was armed with several field pieces and protected by a palisade. The Virginia and North Carolina militiamen had nothing more than small arms and determination. The Virginians had nothing but contempt for Dunmore's "Fort Murray," which they referred to as the "Hog Pen." The fort had been hastily constructed with planks from local houses, logs, and mud, and was not a bastion of great strength. Additionally, the weather was rainy and cold and the British suffered accordingly in their damp "fortress." The Americans suffered as well, exposed to the wintry weather that made the standoff a frigid nightmare for everyone involved. Concerned that time favored the Americans (some credit a deserter who lied about Patriot strength), Lord Dunmore decided to attack and drive away the militia. An assault was planned for the morning of December 9. Captain Fordyce was ordered to lead a mixed force of 60 grenadiers and another 140 regular infantry while Captain Samuel Leslie supported the attack with his 230 Royal Ethiopians.

Fordyce's British grenadiers led the attack before dawn, but it was quickly thrown back in some confusion. The British field pieces were now in position and opened fire on the militia, who were by this time all at their posts. Some of the remaining houses between the lines caught fire and smoke rolled across the American position. Aligned in rows six men wide, the British infantry stepped off a second time to the beat of their drums, crossed the causeway, and approached the reinforced rebel position with parade-like precision. The bulk of the British slated for the attack, however, waited in reserve near the fort while the grenadiers and light infantry marched on. There is some evidence that Fordyce believed the light field works had been abandoned because no fire was coming from them. In reality, the Patriot

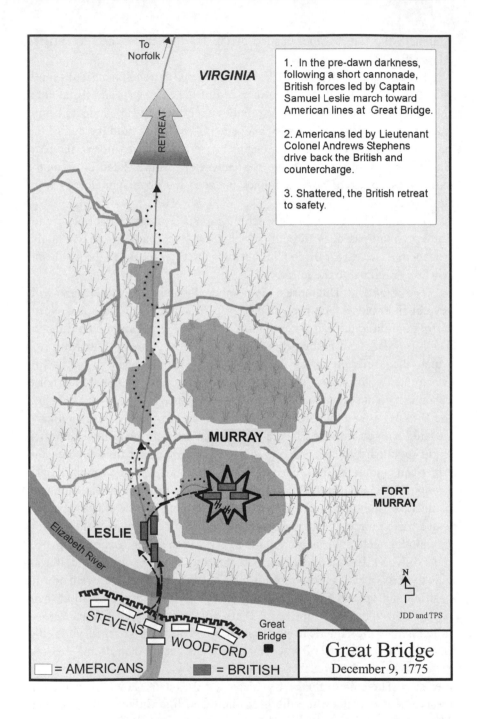

To Norfolk

VIRGINIA

RETREAT

1. In the pre-dawn darkness, following a short cannonade, British forces led by Captain Samuel Leslie march toward American lines at Great Bridge.

2. Americans led by Lieutenant Colonel Andrews Stephens drive back the British and countercharge.

3. Shattered, the British retreat to safety.

MURRAY

FORT MURRAY

LESLIE

Elizabeth River

N

JDD and TPS

STEVENS

WOODFORD

Great Bridge

= AMERICANS   = BRITISH

Great Bridge
December 9, 1775

militia had orders to hold their fire until the enemy tramped within point blank range. Fordyce is said to have yelled, "The day is our own!" as he neared the entrenchments. When the order to fire was given, the colonial militia unleashed several disciplined volleys into the grenadiers. The British attack faltered as shattered bodies collapsed upon one another. Fordyce fell riddled with musket balls a few yards from the enemy lines. The survivors stumbled back across the causeway in shock.

When the British artillery ceased firing, the American militia counterattacked. Led by Lt. Col. Edward Stevens, the 100 men of the "Culpeper Minutemen" forced the British between the causeway and the fort to fall back into a shrinking enclave, capturing the cannons in the process. The Virginians fought their enemy "Indian style," firing individually as they maneuvered closer to the grenadiers. The unconventional tactics worked well against the British, who were unaccustomed and ill-prepared for such unorthodox warfare. The carnage was later accurately described as a slaughter, with the Virginians picking off their trapped and hapless enemy.

Well aware of the disparity of forces available for action, the Virginians retreated to their own defensive works instead of continuing their assault into the strongly held fort. Lord Dunmore sent out a flag of truce to recover the wounded. The day ended as it began, with both sides holding the same positions. That evening Lord Dunmore ordered his troops to abandon Fort Murray and retreat into Norfolk.

Casualties: British: 12 dead, 90 wounded; American: one wounded

Outcome / Impact: The small and largely forgotten battle was disastrous for the British. Lord Dunmore's slim popularity waned after his embarrassing defeat at Great Bridge, and the local populace, bolstered by his humiliation, began shooting at his men during and after the retreat. Within a few weeks Dunmore was forced to seek refuge offshore on British ships. In retaliation for the American victory, British ships shelled Norfolk on January 1, 1776. Their bombardment burned about two-thirds of the town and destroyed nearly 800 structures. The British retreated from Virginia and Lord Dunmore escaped to England.

Great Bridge was the first battle fought in the South. It was a tremendous morale-boosting victory for the nascent revolution and the ideals of liberty. Following Dunmore's retreat from Virginia, colonial authorities extended emancipation and full pardons to Dunmore's former "Royal Ethiopians." The colonials forged stronger bonds, and in many cases race and ethnic differences were cast aside in their common quest for independence. Significantly, the North Carolinians and Virginians had defeated some of the finest soldiers in what was recognized as the greatest army in the world. The combat has been referred to as the "Bunker Hill of the South."

Today: The Great Bridge Waterway Foundation is working to create a Battlefield Waterway Visitor Center to interpret the 1775 battle and the historical Albermarle & Chesapeake and Dismal Swamp canals. In 2003, a $24,000 cash grant was awarded by the American Battlefield Protection Program to provide for historic research and to study surviving battlefield features.

Further Reading: Eckenrode, H. J., *The Revolution in Virginia* (Archon Books, 1964).

Québec, Battle of (Canada Campaign)

Date: December 31, 1775.

Region: Québec City, Québec Province, Canada (Canadian Campaign-American expedition beyond the Northern Colonies).

Commanders: British: Major General Sir Guy Carleton; American: General Richard Montgomery and Colonel Benedict Arnold.

Time of Day / Length of Action: Initial pre-dawn assault followed by intermittent combat actions throughout the day.

Weather Conditions: Bitter cold and strong snowstorm.

Opposing Forces: British: 1,800; American: 950.

British Perspective: Only after losing valuable outposts in the Hudson River Valley in May of 1775 did British commanders fully realize how vulnerable these positions were to surprise attacks. After the capitulation of Fort St. John and Montreal, Gen. Sir Guy Carleton prepared his forces stationed in Canada for whatever the rebels might undertake next to threaten British interests there. Quebec City was a likely target. Carleton's proactive and prudent thinking proved invaluable as the Americans were preparing to do just as he suspected.

American Perspective: After capturing Fort Ticonderoga (May 10, 1775) and Crown Point two days later, the Continental Congress decided rather optimistically to launch an expedition aimed against British strongholds in Canada. The hope was that continued victories large or small would not only reduce the British threat from the north but rally Canadian support for the American Revolution. On September 5, Brig. Gen. Richard

Montgomery established a forward operating base with 1,000 men at Ile Aux Noix, Québec. After winning his lengthy siege of Fort St. John (November 2, 1775) and taking Montreal, Montgomery was eager to strike at Québec City. Thus far his Canadian Campaign had achieved more success than many thought possible. Before more could be achieved, he would have to consolidate his command with Col. Benedict Arnold's force.

Colonel Arnold had begun his own expedition into Canada on September 13 with about 1,000 men. While Montgomery moved north, Arnold traversed a difficult route across Maine. Harsh winter weather, sickness, desertions, and the necessity of hauling heavy equipment conspired to make the journey difficult, dangerous, and frustratingly slow. On November 8, Arnold arrived opposite Québec City at Point Levis on the St. Lawrence River. Montgomery left 650 of his men at Montreal and moved his remaining 300 men to Point-Aux-Trembles on December 3.

With the combined American forces poised to threaten Québec City, Montgomery spent the next few weeks in a quasi-siege of the place. On the evening of December 30, he made up his mind to attack. Many of the enlistments of his men were about to expire, and his army would never be as strong as it was then. The high thick walls of the upper town opposite the Plains of Abraham were too strong to assail, but he believed the lower city vulnerable. He decided to use a snowstorm as cover and launch a surprise attack early the next morning. He needed the snow and the darkness to get close enough to the walls to have a chance of winning. Arnold would strike the lower city at the same time from the opposite direction—one of the most difficult maneuvers to pull off. Time, though, was running out for on January 1, 1776, the Continentals in his army would be free to return home. Montgomery would have only one opportunity to capture the important city.

Terrain: Québec City is in the province of Québec on the northern shore of the St. Lawrence River. It occupied strategic terrain that dominated the area. Much of the fighting would be done on city streets with a gently sloping incline to the main target (upper Québec City).

The Fighting: On December 31, at 2:00 a.m., Montgomery mustered his troops for his daring surprise assault. Montgomery (300) and Arnold (600) maneuvered their men through a blinding snowstorm toward the lower city from opposite directions. The plan was to combine and force Prescott Gate, carry the lower city and, in a single formation deep in the business district near the outskirts of town, move en masse to attack the British positions in the Upper Town district. Unbeknownst to the Patriots, however, a deserter warned Sir Guy Carleton of their impending attack.

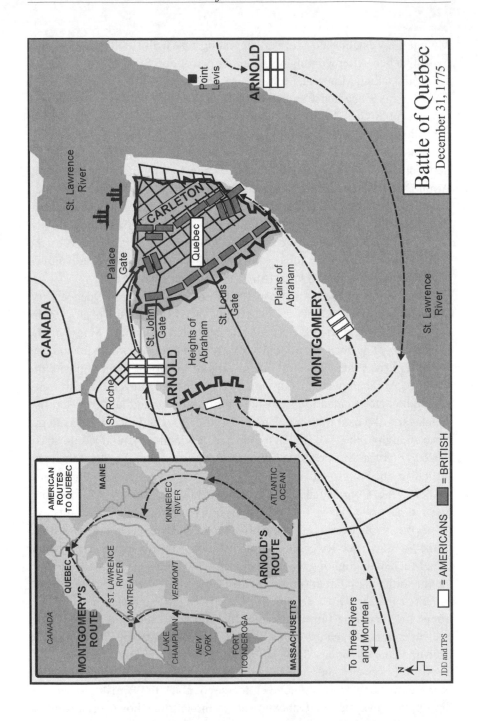

Battle of Quebec
December 31, 1775

Montgomery moved his column south from the Plains of Abraham about one mile to Wolfe's Cove, and then along the icy edge of the St. Lawrence River. Before he reached his objective Montgomery ran into a fortified position. It was nearly dawn. In an effort to surprise the defenders, the brave officer led 17 men in a mad dash to storm the barricade. The position was in reality an ambush, and artillery and musket fire cut them down at point blank range, killing the general and several men instantly. Aaron Burr, future vice president of the United States, participated but escaped unscathed. (There are several slightly different versions of how Montgomery met his death, and some have him firing signal rockets to notify Arnold.) Lieutenant Colonel Donald Campbell assumed command and ordered a retreat. Montgomery's column would not be available to assist Arnold.

On the other side of lower Québec City, meanwhile, Arnold was moving with his men (New Englanders, Virginians, Pennsylvanians, and a handful of Indians and Canadians) forward along the walls through St. Roque. After slipping past an advance artillery outpost and beyond one of the city's gates on the northwest corner of the urban center, his advance was fired upon from riflemen posted atop the walls. Arnold was wounded early with a shot to the leg and Capt. Daniel Morgan assumed command. The wet snow rendered most of the muskets unusable, but the Americans relied upon musket butts and bayonets to overrun the enemy. Morgan led the Patriots through the barricade, capturing dozens of enemy soldiers in the process.

Morgan's advance drove into the Sault au Matelot a few hundred yards to the next major barricade. It was lightly defended, but he had no way of knowing this. Arnold was down, his men were strung out and confused, and he was burdened with many prisoners. To his everlasting disgust, he listened to pessimistic subordinates and decided to wait before attacking the 12-foot walls to move deeper into the city. Perhaps an hour passed as he consolidated his position. Morgan did not know anything of Montgomery's fate and the sun was now up. He finally decided to renew the attack.

By this time Carleton had repositioned his men at strategic positions on the walls and in buildings above the Patriots. After several failed breakthrough attempts Morgan ordered a retreat, only to discover the British were moving against his rear. Morgan's men were trapped within a maze of sharpshooter-filled streets waiting in vain for Montgomery to put in an appearance. Amidst the confusion Morgan lost control of his command. His men escaped in small groups, were taken prisoner, or shot down in the streets of Québec City. Morgan was finally persuaded to surrender, but he refused to do so directly with the British. Instead, he turned over his sword to a French priest to end the slaughter of his troops. It was about 9:00 a.m.

Casualties: British: five killed, 13 wounded; American: 60 killed and wounded, 426 captured.

Outcome / Impact: While Morgan led the Americans and bore the brunt of battle, the wounded Colonel Arnold escaped and reached Montgomery's shaken command just beyond Québec City. The Americans dug hasty entrenchments along the outskirts of town and waited for a British counterattack that never came. Carleton's victorious British retained control of Québec City while the Americans occupied their trenches in brutal winter weather. Despite the disaster, Arnold was promoted to brigadier general on January 10, 1776. Even if the attack had been successful the Americans could not have held the city without a larger army and control of the river. The battle serves as a reminder that concentrating separated columns for a combined attack offers little hope of success. In May 1776 the American army began retreating from Canada when British Gen. John Burgoyne arrived there with 4,000 reinforcements. Arnold was the last American soldier to leave Canada on June 18. Once the withdrawal was complete, American military operations in Canada ended for the duration of the war.

Today: Québec City offers plaques, monuments, tours, living history programs, and other outstanding opportunities to step back into time.

Further Reading: Roberts, Kenneth, *March to Québec: Journals of the Members of Arnold's Expedition* (Doubleday, 1945); Shelton, Hal, *General Richard Montgomery and the American Revolution (New York University Press, 1996).*

Moores (Moore's) Creek Bridge, Battle of (1st British Southern Expedition)

Date: February 27, 1776.

Region: Southern Colonies, Moores Creek Bridge, North Carolina (20 miles northwest of Wilmington).

Commanders: British (Tory): Brigadier General Donald MacDonald, Lieutenant Colonel Donald McLeod; American: Colonels Richard Caswell and Alexander Lillington.

Time of Day / Length of Action: Dawn, one-quarter hour.

Weather Conditions: Cold and damp.

Opposing Forces: British (Tory militia): 1,600; American: 1,000.

British Perspective: Early Patriot successes in the North (Lexington, Concord, and Bunker Hill) triggered an outbreak of sympathy in the Old

North State that had led to the ouster of Josiah Martin, the Royal Governor of North Carolina. Martin initially sought refuge at Fort Johnston near Cape Fear. The rebels were determined to remove him from the colony and so threatened, Martin fled for safety offshore on the British warship *Cruizer*.

Martin and other refugee office holders saw a major British expedition as a means of returning to office and securing the rebellious Southern colonies for the Crown. They convinced British authorities that such a move would be greeted by a massive uprising of Loyalist sympathizers. The result was a campaign led by Gen. Sir Henry Clinton, who was tasked with opening the Southern front of the war by sailing a 2,500-man expeditionary force on a campaign to take Charleston, South Carolina. Clinton was to secure the colonies, turn over control to the Loyalists, and sail north to join General Howe. When the British expedition reached Cape Fear, North Carolina, Clinton would join forces with Gen. Charles Cornwallis and seven British regiments recently arrived from Europe, and then proceed with his mission.

Before the conjoining of Clinton and Cornwallis occurred, events in North Carolina ruined the Crown's plans. By February 18, more than 1,000 Scottish Highlander Loyalists mustered into service and were soon joined by another 500. Together they marched from Cross Creek (modern-day Fayetteville) to rally with their British allies at Cape Fear off Wilmington. They were weeks ahead of schedule and the fleet well behind its timetable. As the Tories moved toward the coast, scouts informed Tory leader Gen. Donald MacDonald that a sizable rebel force intended to fight them before they could join forces with Clinton. MacDonald recommended avoiding a battle, but his zealous younger subordinate commanders argued otherwise.

American Perspective: In the Southern colonies, news of the battles in Massachusetts created a firestorm of activities that firmly divided the colonists into two camps: Tories (British Loyalists) and Patriots (pro-American colonists). Pressure from rebels forced Royal Governor Josiah Martin to flee from the capital. Martin made plans to return to power by combining with British seaborne forces led by Cornwallis and Clinton and reorganizing his fellow Tories into a credible ground force. With the ex-governor no longer in the colony, the Patriots established their own government and raised two regiments and several battalions of militiamen.

In Wilmington, Patriots organized a defense complete with redoubts to face any approaching enemy. A large Loyalist column made up primarily of Scottish Highlanders was moving in their direction. The North Carolinians organized under the Continental Line at New Bern. Led by Cols. James Moore, Richard Caswell, and Alexander Lillington, they decided to move into a blocking position to delay, isolate, and perhaps destroy the

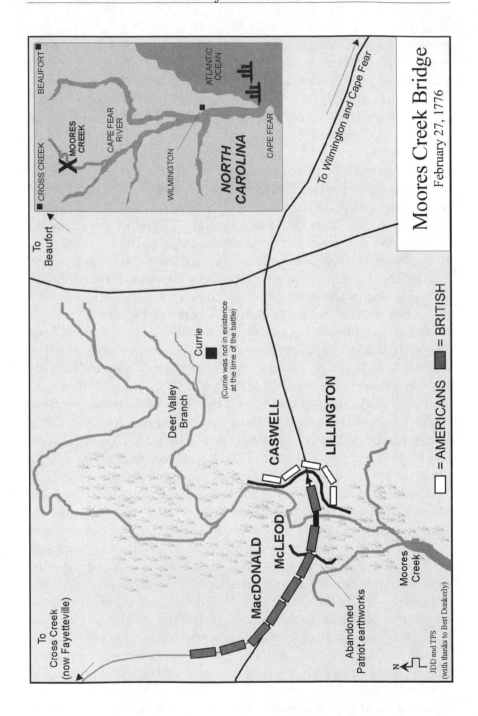

Moores Creek Bridge
February 27, 1776

approaching enemy. They decided to meet them at a bridge spanning the narrow but deep and swift Moores Creek twenty miles outside Wilmington. (Moore, in overall command, would not arrive until the fighting was over.)

Terrain: Generally flat coastal savannah with pine trees, brushy marshes, and brackish waters. The creek is 35-feet wide at the bridge, which was bordered by swampy terrain that funneled traffic across the span.

The Fighting: The Loyalist leader decided to assault the Patriots moving to block his journey to Wilmington, even though neither side seems to have fully appreciated the strength of the other. Loyalist leaders held a council of war the night before the assault. Desertions had whittled their column down to only 800-850 men, but they decided to attack early the next morning. When the old and feeble leader of the small Tory army, General MacDonald, fell ill during the night, command passed to Lt. Col. Donald McLeod.

The Tories broke camp at 1:00 a.m. on February 27 and marched for Moores Creek. Captain John Campbell and 80 men held the advance. The Loyalists, divided into two wings, reach the abandoned Patriot entrenchments and campsite on the near side of the stream. Orders were given to pull back and bring up the wagons and remaining soldiers. The right wing pulled back, but the left wing under Capt. Alexander McClean, continued moving ahead and reached the bridge. As one participant later wrote, "the left wing did not know that the right wing had marched back."

At the bridge, McLean and his Loyalists encountered American pickets on the opposite shore, but the darkness prevented him from discovering their true identity. He called to them, but no response was forthcoming. Had the rebels withdrawn? The planks had been pulled up from the bridge, indicating that they had. It was at this point that the rebels on the far side of the creek opened fire on the Loyalists, who promptly returned it. The entire Loyalist force surged forward, thinking that attack orders had been given.

Campbell's 80 handpicked men, each wielding a Scottish Claymore broadsword, dashed across to secure the bridge. Campbell and McLeod each led a column across the two main bridge stringers. According to some sources, the bridge stringers had been smeared with grease, though the Loyalists would not know this until it was too late.

With Scottish pipes screeching and drums beating, the Loyalists stormed across what was left of the bridge yelling "King George and broadswords!" They were unaware that as many as 1,000 rebels were waiting for them behind recently dug entrenchments. At a range of only thirty yards the rebels opened fire with light artillery and muskets. Protected by mounds of earth the Patriot fire devastated the small attacking force. The survivors of the initial volley milled about in confusion as they tried to come to grips with the defenders. McLeod, Campbell, and 28 others were mowed down, many killed outright. The remainder fell in the few minutes of combat that followed. Some were trampled in the melee; others were shot off or slipped from the greasy stringers and tumbled into the creek, where they drowned or were taken captive.

A brisk rebel counterattack surged over the bridge and pursued the fleeing Loyalists while a rebel flanking move across a nearby ford helped block part of the retreat. A previous order to other North Carolina units to seize Cross Creek (Fayetteville) led to the capture of hundreds of soldiers. The fight ended decisively. General MacDonald was among the captured.

Casualties: British (Tory): 30 dead, 40 wounded, and 850 prisoners; American: one mortally wounded and one wounded.

Outcome / Impact: Moores Creek was the first of several battles to pit Loyalists against rebel militia. The immediate impact was the end of organized Loyalist activity in North Carolina for nearly two years. Sir Henry Clinton was dismayed by the inept tactics that had led to the annihilation of his Tory supports at the hands of a hastily prepared Patriot force. Afterward, he declared the colony of North Carolina to be in rebellion. Within a few months North Carolina would become the first colony to become an independent state. The defeat hurt Clinton's effort to open a Southern front for England, and effectively kept the boots of both armies out of the state for five years. The battle was a small affair with significant consequences.

Today: Moores Creek National Battlefield features a small visitor center, interpretive trails, and living history programs.

Further Reading: Rankin, Hugh, *The Moores Creek Bridge Campaign* (Ft Washington, 2004); Wilson, David K., *The Southern Strategy* (Columbia, 2005);

Nassau, Battle of (Naval Campaign, Caribbean)

Date: March 3, 1776 (Campaign: February 18 – April 8, 1776).
Region: Atlantic Ocean (Bahamas and offshore Northern Colonies).
Commanders: British: Royal Governor Montfort Browne; (HMS *Glasgow*) Captain Tyringham Howe; American: Commodore Esek Hopkins and Captain Samuel Nicholas.
Time of Day / Length of Action: (Nassau): Morning, 30 minutes; (Battle with *Glasgow*): 2:00 a.m. to 5:00 a.m..
Weather Conditions: Warm in the Caribbean, cold in New England.
Opposing Forces: British: 42; American: 284 marines.

British Perspective: For Governor Montfort Browne and his small Loyalist militia, the arrival of American ships in the Bahamas was something of a shock. The British had constructed two forts on New Providence Island in the 1740s to guard the harbor entrance. When the enemy vessels arrived on March 2, 1776, the forts engaged them with solid shot. Governor Browne's problem, however, was how to properly man the 104 guns at his disposal, for he only had one British officer, 40 militiamen, and a few British sloops offshore to defend New Providence. The light artillery barrage convinced the enemy squadron to move out of range, leaving the governor with his dilemma. If the Americans pressed for a decisive battle, the Loyalists could not hope to hold out for long. To keep valuable gunpowder out of enemy hands, Browne sent the bulk of his supply to St. Augustine, Florida, aboard one of his sloops.

When the sun rose the next morning, the small American fleet was spotted anchored well offshore beyond the range of Browne's guns. To the horror of the island defenders, an amphibious assault by American marines was underway.

American Perspective: The Continental Navy was officially formed on October 13, 1775. By December its small fleet was comprised of five ships: *Alfred*, *Columbus*, *Cabot*, *Providence*, and *Andrea Doria*, all under the command of Commodore Esck Hopkins. The tars spent November and December rigging the small ships with cannon while recruiting seamen to man the vessels. On November 10, Congress authorized the formation of two battalions of marines (which inaugurated the US Marine Corps) to defend the ships and provide the navy with both offensive and defensive infantry capability. The first marine commanders were Capt. Samuel Nicholas, (aboard *Alfred*) and Lt. Isaac Craig (aboard *Andrea Doria*).

On December 22, Commander Hopkins and his neophyte navy were officially tasked to defend American commerce on the open seas. However, the Delaware River was frozen solid and the fleet remained inactive for the next few months. Three other ships, *Fly*, *Hornet*, and *Wasp* joined the fleet and Captain Nicholas recruited and organized five companies of marines to sail with them.

On February 18, 1776, Hopkins maneuvered his ships into the Atlantic Ocean for the navy's first open water cruise. The American fleet was comprised of the following eight vessels: *Alfred* with 30 guns; *Columbus* with 28 guns; *Andrea Doria* with 14 guns, *Cabot* with 14 guns, *Providence* with 12 guns, *Hornet* with 10 guns, *Wasp* with eight guns, and the *Fly* with six guns. Considering that most ships of the line in that era were armed with at least 74 guns, the American fleet was sallying forth with little more than raw courage. With orders that provided him with freedom to maneuver as he saw fit, the commodore wisely decided against seeking out British warships and instead sailed for the West Indies. His specific target was the British port at Nassau, on New Providence Island in the Bahamas. His objective was to obtain badly needed gunpowder being stored there.

After conducting a rendezvous on March 1 at Great Abaco Island, north of New Providence Island, the American ships sailed to an area known as "Hole-In-The-Wall," where they seized two small Loyalist ships. The captured sailors were forced to guide the Americans through the local waters. The next day the fleet sailed into Nassau Harbor.

Terrain: New Providence Island is part of the chain of islands known as the Bahamas, and Nassau is its capital. Located in the Atlantic Ocean, the islands are just 50 miles southeast of Florida. Fort Montagu (named for the Duke of Montagu) was the larger of the two forts, constructed of stone and shaped in a sturdy square. The fort had been erected just above the shoreline and was easily accessible, which prompted later forts to be constructed elsewhere. Fort Nassau was also constructed of stone and shaped like a 4-pointed star; two of its high-walled points jutted northward into the harbor. Fort Montagu (which is still standing) guarded the eastern end of the harbor, and Fort Nassau (no longer standing) the opposite end. The bastions were about four miles apart, which provided for interlocking fields of fire within the harbor.

The Fighting: As the Americans sailed within view of Nassau, British artillery from the two forts opened fire, but the shots fell short. Maintaining his fleet beyond the range of the British guns, Commodore Hopkins surveyed the situation and decided to attack the forts by land instead of engaging in a risky naval bombardment. The next morning, March 3, with the American ships anchored in Hanover Sound about nine miles east of Nassau, 284 marines and sailors led by Captain Samuel Nicholas disembarked for an amphibious assault of the island. Governor Browne, a British lieutenant, and 40 Loyalist militiamen went out to oppose the landing but upon reconsideration returned to the fort. Browne decided instead to concentrate his limited resources and defend the opposite end of the harbor at Fort Nassau. He ordered his men to spike the artillery at Fort Montagu. When the Americans drew near the fort, however, several Loyalists deserted—a rather inauspicious sign for the already outnumbered defenders. After a quick debate with his remaining men, Governor Browne decided to surrender his command. Without firing a single shot the Americans captured both forts and their small garrison.

Unbeknownst to the Americans, 160 barrels of gunpowder had been hauled aboard a sloop the night before and sailed off to Florida. Still, the

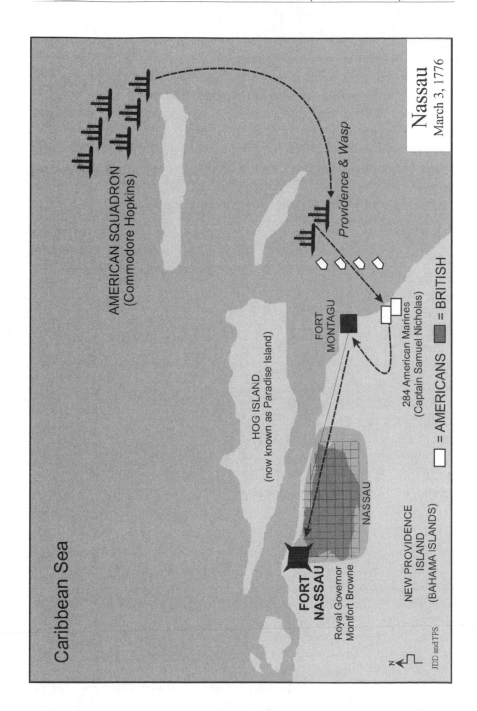

Nassau
March 3, 1776

AMERICAN SQUADRON
(Commodore Hopkins)

Providence & Wasp

Caribbean Sea

HOG ISLAND
(now known as Paradise Island)

FORT
MONTAGU

284 American Marines
(Captain Samuel Nicholas)

□ = AMERICANS   ■ = BRITISH

FORT
NASSAU

Royal Governor
Montfort Browne

NASSAU

NEW PROVIDENCE
ISLAND
(BAHAMA ISLANDS)

N

JDD and TPS

Americans managed to seize two forts, 88 cannon, 15 mortars, and valuable supplies that were badly needed for the war effort.

Governor Browne, the British lieutenant, and a Loyalist official from South Carolina were taken prisoner and the fleet sailed for America on March 17. During the return journey two British merchant vessels were captured and incorporated into the fleet as prizes.

On April 4, the Americans met and engaged the small British warships *Hawk* and *Bolton*; both capitulated to Commodore Hopkins's larger and stronger fleet. From their new prisoners Hopkins learned a strong British fleet was nearby at Newport, Rhode Island. The commodore turned his own ships toward New London, Connecticut.

In the pre-dawn darkness of April 6, the American fleet came across the British warship *Glasgow*. The 20-gun vessel was commanded by Capt. Tyringham Howe and had a crew of 150 men. She was sailing to Charleston with dispatches. Howe carefully approached the American vessels to confirm their nationality. When the mystery ships answered his curiosity with gunfire, Howe replied in kind. Unlike the captains of *Hawk* or *Bolton*, he was not about to raise the white flag just because he was outgunned. For the next three hours a running fitful combat ensued. Although raked with iron that damaged her rigging and weakened her masts, *Glasgow* was well handled and outmaneuvered her slower American opponents. Howe returned fire as well as he could and did not break off contact until he had inflicted more damage than he had received.

Unable to prevent *Glasgow's* escape, Commodore Hopkins continued his homeward journey. On April 8 the American fleet arrived safely in port, ending the first American naval campaign.

Casualties: British: (Nassau): no casualties, three prisoners (including the governor); (Battle with *Glasgow*): one killed and three wounded; American: (Nassau): none; (Battle with *Glasgow*): 10 killed and seven wounded. (*Cabot's* Capt. John B. Hopkins, the son of Commodore Esek Hopkins, was among the dead).

Outcome / Impact: The Continental Navy achieved perhaps more success than it had a right to expect in its first venture out to sea. The small victories bolstered morale and served as grist for the American propaganda mill. For young naval officers like Lt. John Paul Jones, his service aboard *Alfred* prepared him for bold future maritime combat. Commodore Hopkins, however, was popular neither with his men nor with Congress, and his command was terminated in January of 1777.

Although generally overlooked, the first American naval campaign did have a minor strategic impact on the course of the war. The raid forced the

Crown to reevaluate how and where it distributed resources in the West Indies and elsewhere. After France allied itself with America, the West Indies became a magnet for warships. Both British and French fleets focused their endeavors in that region.

Today: Although overshadowed by modern construction, Fort Montagu, Nassau, Bahamas, is open to tourists. It is still a magnificent structure in a stunning setting.

Further Reading: Dupuy, Trevor Nevitt. *The Military History of Revolutionary War Naval Battles* (Franklin Watts, Inc., 1970); Allen, Gardner. *A Naval History of the American Revolution* (Houghton, 1913).

Fort Sullivan, Battle of (also known as the First Battle of Charleston and Battle of Sullivan's Island) (1st British Southern Expedition)

Date: June 28, 1776.

Region: Southern Colonies, Charleston, South Carolina.

Commanders: British: Major General Sir Henry Clinton and Commodore Peter Parker; American: Colonel William Moultrie, Major General Charles Lee (Francis Marion and Thomas Sumter were junior leaders).

Time of Day / Length of Action: 11:30 a.m. to 9:30 p.m. (a 10-hour running battle).

Weather Conditions: Beautiful summer day with a seaward breeze.

Opposing Forces: British: 2,900 men (20 ships, 262 guns); American: 425 men (Fort Sullivan: 26 guns, south end of island), 750 men (north end of island).

British Perspective: Disappointing setbacks in North Carolina, including the Tory defeat at Moores (Moore's) Creek Bridge and the loss of the Royal governorship, prompted the British to move their operations to South Carolina, from which colony they launched their Southern Campaign. The British plan was to seize the ports of Savannah, Georgia, and Charleston, South Carolina. After securing the ports and enlisting Tory support, they intended to move aggressively inland and pacify the colonies of South Carolina and Georgia. Once that was complete, Clinton would march north into North Carolina and Virginia and do the same thing.

The initial assault against a southern colonial port focused on Fort Sullivan, an unfinished fortification on Sullivan's Island at the entrance to Charleston Harbor (north shore). The British arrived off the Charleston bar on June 4, where they remained out of range of American guns as they carefully maneuvered their warships into position. From June 7-15, the British landed infantry on Long Island (now known as Isle of Palms), a narrow piece of land north of Sullivan's Island. American troops prevented the British from transferring the infantry via small boats to Sullivan's Island. British ships, meanwhile, were now in position at Five Fathom Hole, a channel entrance through which the vessels could readily move into the harbor and engage the Patriot land defenses.

American Perspective: Fort Sullivan was the primary Patriot defensive work established to protect the entrance to Charleston harbor. Commanding on Sullivan's Island was Col. William Moultrie, whose subordinates included future prominent leaders Francis Marion and Thomas Sumter. The commander of the Continental Southern Department, Maj. Gen. Charles Lee, arrived at Fort Sullivan on June 2, 1776. In anticipation of the British naval assault Lee ordered additional fortifications constructed around the city, but there was little else he could do.

Terrain: The port city of Charleston sits on a peninsula at the confluence of the Cooper, Wando, and Ashley rivers, all of which empty together into the Atlantic Ocean. The conjunction of these waterways forms a natural harbor surrounded by marshy lowlands and shifting sand bars. The harbor entrance is narrow and shallow and protected by a large sandbar that in the 18th century was impassable during low tide. At high tide there were only five channels through which ships could pass into the harbor. The British had charts of the harbor and knew of these navigational difficulties. Maneuvering under fire, however, would be difficult because Fort Sullivan dominated the harbor entrance channels.

The Fighting: With a favorable wind Commodore Parker ordered his armada into action about 10:30 a.m. on June 28. The long range artillery ship *Thunder* (bomb ketch with mortar) opened the battle by commencing fire with her 10-inch mortars against Fort Sullivan. The ship was too far away to inflict much damage, and many of the shells buried themselves in the sand or swampy morass inside the fort and exploded with little or no impact. The *Thunder* was eventually disabled and withdrawn from the action. British warships *Bristol, Experiment, Active, Solebay, Acteon, Syren, Sphynx, Friendship, Ranger,* and *St. Lawrence* also went into action, anchoring at various distances and showering the forts with cannon fire. The *Acteon, Sphynx,* and *Syren* set sail in an attempt to gain entrance to the harbor along

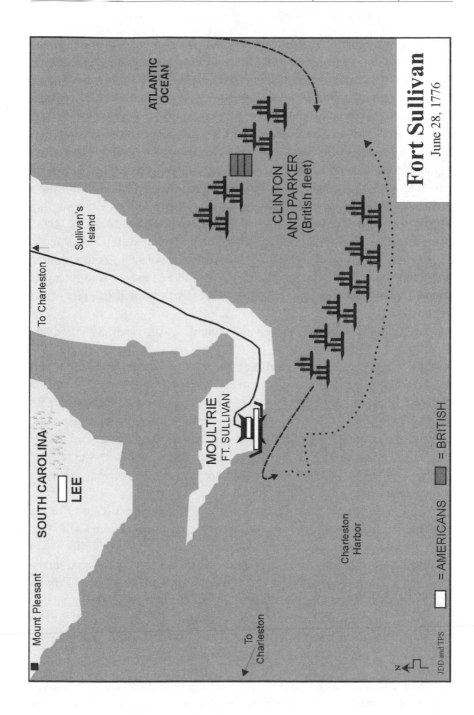

Fort Sullivan
June 28, 1776

the opposite shore of Fort Sullivan to enfilade the bastion, but luckily for the defenders all three ran aground on Middle Ground shoal (where Fort Sumter would later be constructed). *Syren* and *Sphynx* eventually managed to dislodge themselves and withdraw for repairs. *Acteon*, however, was caught fast and unable to slip off the bar.

The British poured a relentless fire with more than 100 pieces into Fort Sullivan. However, the stronghold was constructed of sand and spongy palmetto logs, which absorbed the pounding without great difficulty or much damage. Although hampered by a lack of gunpowder, Colonel Moultrie's artillerists returned fire with deadly accuracy. Commodore Parker's flagship *Bristol* was struck 70 times and had to be withdrawn from the fight. Moultrie's fire killed 64 and wounded another 170 on that ship alone. When the sun began setting the battle fell into a fitful exchange before ending altogether about 9:30 p.m. A stunned Parker ordered his ships to retreat to Five Fathom Hole. The next morning *Acteon* was burned to prevent her capture.

Casualties: British: 195 killed and wounded; American: 37 killed and wounded.

Outcome / Impact: The repulse of the world's most powerful navy was the first major American victory of the war and spun the conflict in a different direction. Sir Henry Clinton, who had spent the battle ashore on Long Island, was dumbfounded by the pounding his ships had taken and ordered a withdrawal from Charleston. His ground forces remained ashore until the third week of July, when they embarked on ships for the ten day voyage to New York. Charleston would not face another serious threat for several years.

General Charles Lee returned north also to assist Gen. George Washington in his defense of the Northern Department. Colonel Moultrie, the victorious Patriot commander, was honored when Fort Sullivan was renamed in his honor to Fort Moultrie. The victory convinced many Americans (including Moultrie defenders Francis Marion and Thomas Sumter) that the British military machine could indeed be beaten.

Today: Fort Moultrie National Monument (a unit of the Fort Sumter National Monument) is open for tours. The current fortifications were erected in 1809 (the third fort constructed on that general site).

Further Reading: Allen, Gardner. *A Naval History of the American Revolution*. Boston: Houghton, 1913; Christopher Ward, *The War of the Revolution*, 2 vols. (MacMillan, 1952).

Cherokee Campaign, Battles of the
(also known as the Second Cherokee War)

Date: July 1, 1776 through December 1782.

Region: Southern Colonies: Virginia, Georgia, North and South Carolina.

Commanders: British: (Indian Agents) Alexander Cameron, Henry Stuart, and John McDonald. (Cherokee Chiefs) Attakullakulla, Dragging Canoe, Old Tassel, and Okonostota; American (militia commanders): Brigadier General Griffith Rutherford, Colonels Arthur Campbell, Isaac Shelby, John Sevier, Elijah Clarke, James Williams, Andrew Williamson, and Andrew Pickens.

Time of Day / Length of Action: Fitful action over a period of six years.

Weather Conditions: Various, unremarkable seasons.

Opposing Forces: British (Indians): 4,000; American: (Militia) 4,000.

British Perspective: One of the results of the French and Indian War was the ceding of land west of the Appalachian Mountains to the Indians. Colonial settlers were supposed to remain east of the Proclamation Line of 1763. However, the western expansion of white settlements and Indian raids and fighting for frontier lands in the Southern colonies continued unabated. On March 17, 1775, the largest private real estate transaction in American history was consummated when the Cherokee agreed to the "Henderson Purchase." Through this exchange, the Cherokee gave the Transylvania Land Company the bulk of what are today Kentucky and Tennessee (20,000,000 acres) in exchange for 2,000 pounds sterling and 8,000 pounds of gunpowder, lead, clothing, and various trinkets. The deal also provided the settlers and Indians with the Treaty of Sycamore Shoals, which guaranteed peace (on paper, at least) between the parties. The elder chiefs of the Treaty Council, Old Tassel, Oconostota, Savanooka, and Attakullakulla agreed with the deal and the contract with the white men was confirmed. Chief Dragging Canoe, the son of Attakullakulla, vehemently opposed the transaction, pledging that the deal would provide the whites with a "dark and bloody ground."

Once the American Revolution began, many northern Indian tribes, including the Mohawk, Shawnee, and Ottawa, made pacts with the British who, in turn, encouraged the southern tribes to also ally with them. Some Cherokee tribal factions did work with and ally themselves with these Indians along the Ohio River, but most of the southern Cherokee remained neutral. However, British Indian agents Alexander Cameron, Henry Stuart, and John McDonald supported the Chickamauga Cherokee and Chief Dragging Canoe. Many of the Tory sympathizers in and around the frontier settlements provided the Indians with intelligence concerning Patriot settlements and outposts. On several occasions Tories dressed as Indians and joined them on their raids. Despite various peace treaties, throughout the war Indian war parties and punitive expeditions conducted by the whites made the frontier in the Southern colonies a brutally contested campaign. Chief Dragging Canoe and several thousand Cherokee warriors made a pact with the Shawnee and waged war against the settlers throughout the remainder of the war (and for many years thereafter).

American Perspective: Until the British opened an offensive in the Southern colonies in 1779, colonial settlers in that region faced few threats from a British invasion. Though many of the men in the frontier settlements joined the cause of liberty and served in both the Continental Line and local militia units, the battles in the Northern colonies were far removed from their daily lives and thus not as important to them as the constant threat of Indian attacks on their homes.

Just as the war with England got underway in 1775, the pioneers in the southern reaches of the colonies achieved a peace treaty with the Cherokee. The Henderson Purchase opened former Indian lands to white settlements and new opportunities. Richard Henderson, the man who brokered the deal, was nothing more than a land speculator, and legal issues concerning the transaction's validity festered. Legal or not, men like Daniel Boone (who worked for Henderson) led settlers into the fertile lands of Kentucky and Tennessee to establish homesteads. As promised by Chief Dragging Canoe, the settlements became targets for the Indians, which in turn prompted settlers to conduct retaliatory raids. The result was a vicious though low-profile backwoods fight waged simultaneously with the larger and more visible campaigns of the American Revolution.

The settlements of western Virginia and what is today Kentucky and Tennessee were especially contested as the Indians fought fervently to drive the settlers from their lands. The Watauga and Nolichucky settlements (present-day East Tennessee) and the Clinch River and Holston River settlements of southwest Virginia were particularly isolated and frequently attacked. The militia leaders in these areas were Cols. Arthur and William Campbell (cousins), Isaac Shelby, and John Sevier. The raids they conducted destroyed at least 36 Indian villages and killed scores of Cherokee. In western North and South Carolina and northern Georgia, punitive militia raids were led by Brig. Gen. Griffith Rutherford and Cols.

James Williams, Elijah Clarke, Joseph Winston, Andrew Williamson, and Andrew Pickens. Many of these expeditions focused on Indians who had committed themselves to neutrality. Once the whites pillaged and destroyed their villages, however, neutrality was abandoned in favor of war.

During the American Revolution there were approximately 25,000 Cherokee living on the frontier divided into three primary geographic divisions: Lower, Middle, and Over-the-Hill. Within these divisions, the Cherokee were organized into at least 170 villages, where they planted crops and raised their families. These Indians were no longer nomadic and loved the land they had settled. From their perspective, factional tribes and leaders such as Dragging Canoe caused problems, but the white settlers and their aggressive nature made a harmonious existence impossible.

Terrain: The region under discussion was primarily west of the Appalachian Mountains and comprised of the fertile agriculturally rich breadbasket of southwestern Virginia, eastern Tennessee, eastern Kentucky, northern Georgia, western North Carolina, and northwestern South Carolina. The bulk of the land consisted of river valleys on both sides of the Appalachian range. During the late 18th Century, the forests and valleys in this region were filled with wild game including buffalo, bear, elk, and deer. The area could only be traversed by a combination of canoe or flat boat on the rivers and along foot trails through the forest.

The Fighting: Numerous battles were waged during this campaign and precise information about them is vague at best; many important details were never recorded. Most of the confrontations involved one side or the other conducting surprise raids against an enemy camp or settlement. Throughout the summer of 1776, the Indians conducted an offensive campaign with approximately 4,000 warriors. While the Indians had the element of surprise, the settlers were prepared because frontier scouts detected the large scale movements days before they descended upon the white settlements. Most of the attacks were launched piecemeal by disjointed bands against settlers protected within log palisades. July and August of 1776, however, witnessed the western edge of the frontier (from present-day Sullivan County, Tennessee in the north as far south as Abbeville County, South Carolina), erupt in bloody violence.

British Agent Alexander Cameron accompanied a 2,000-man Indian war party into South Carolina, where it joined with several hundred Tories dressed as Indians. They attacked Lyndley's Fort (Abbeville County, South Carolina) on July 15, but the 600 defenders were able to hold the stronghold and beat back the assault. During the next few weeks Indians terrorized much of the Upcountry. Although they killed many people, their objective of

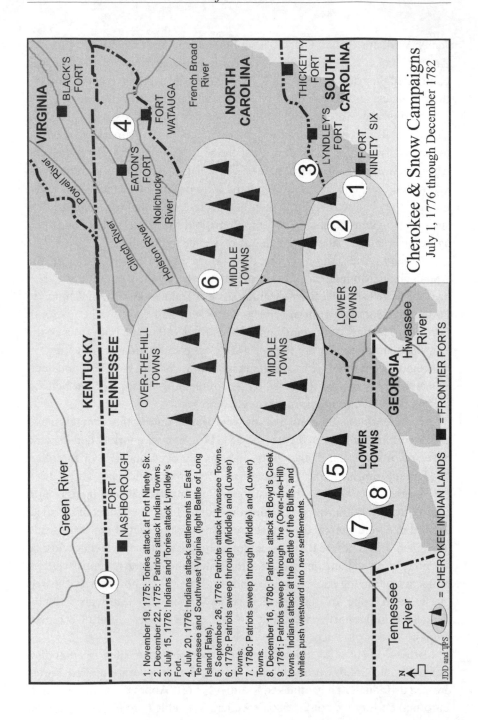

Cherokee & Snow Campaigns
July 1, 1776 through December 1782

1. November 19, 1775: Tories attack at Fort Ninety Six.
2. December 22, 1775: Patriots attack Indian Towns.
3. July 15, 1776: Indians and Tories attack Lyndley's Fort.
4. July 20, 1776: Indians attack settlements in East Tennessee and Southwest Virginia (fight Battle of Long Island Flats).
5. September 26, 1776: Patriots attack Hiwassee Towns.
6. 1779: Patriots sweep through (Middle) and (Lower) Towns.
7. 1780: Patriots sweep through (Middle) and (Lower) Towns.
8. December 16, 1780: Patriots attack at Boyd's Creek.
9. 1781: Patriots sweep through the (Over-the-Hill) towns. Indians attack at the Battle of the Bluffs, and whites push westward into new settlements.

■ = FRONTIER FORTS

= CHEROKEE INDIAN LANDS

▲ = CHEROKEE INDIAN TOWNS

JDD and TPS

driving out the white settlers failed miserably because the Indian summer 1776 offensive lacked a coherent plan and utilized disjointed methods.

Farther north, meanwhile, Dragging Canoe led his main war party against the settlements at Fort Watauga and Eaton's Fort in modern-day East Tennessee. The pioneer militiamen were ready and Fort Watauga survived a three-week siege by the Indians before the effort was abandoned. Farther north at Long Island Flats on the Holston River, the militiamen were positioned west of Eaton's Station. On July 20, the militia attacked the enemy as the Indians moved toward the fort in a fight known today as the Battle of Long Island Flats. Many of the Indians were killed, Dragging Canoe was wounded, and the result was a resounding victory for the white settlers. During the next few weeks the Indians attempted similar operations against forts and outposts in southwestern Virginia, with the same disappointing results.

After the Indian offensive of 1776, the militias of all the associated Southern colonies initiated punitive expeditions against the Cherokee villages. Marching and riding into Cherokee lands from their respective colonies, the Americans combined forces deep in Indian Territory at Hiwassee, Tennessee, on September 26. The united force of 4,000 men pillaged and burned Indian villages throughout the area to eliminate the Cherokee threat. An unknown number of Indians (including women and children) were slaughtered. Conservative estimates suggest the American militia suffered 300 casualties, but the Cherokee lost several thousand.

The bloody expedition convinced the Cherokee to sign a peace treaty. Dragging Canoe and the Chickamauga branch of the Cherokee refused to discuss peace or surrender. Colonel George Rogers Clark, meanwhile, conducted his expedition against the Indians in the north along the Ohio River, an effort designed to keep most of the northern and southern tribes separated and thus weak. For the next few years, harassing raids by the Chickamauga (who ultimately banded with the Shawnee and white Tories) continued terrorizing Patriot settlements.

In 1779 and 1780, Col. Isaac Shelby and Col. John Sevier launched raids deep into Chickamauga territory, burning villages and destroying vast amounts of property. Female hostages were taken and male warriors were killed. Dragging Canoe and his followers, however, continued their own operations against white settlements. During the summer of 1779, Colonel Shelby traveled as far south as Lookout Mountain, Tennessee, and attacked Chickamauga villages throughout the area, destroying crops, killing braves, and taking hostages. Dragging Canoe and his band escaped by dissolving into the forest, only to emerge again after Shelby's offensive ended. On

December 16, 1780, Colonel Sevier and a large contingent of militiamen attacked a large camp of Indian warriors at Boyd's Creek (Sevierville, Tennessee). The victory was decisive and came just two months after the stunning militia victory at Kings Mountain against Loyalist troops.

On April 2, 1781, Dragging Canoe led an assault against the settlers at Fort Nashborough (present-day Nashville, Tennessee), which nearly ended in a disaster for the white frontiersmen, who beat back the assault at a very high cost. While these battles constituted significant military victories for the white settlers, they were difficult to follow up because the Indians simply vanished by moving deeper into the forest, only to reappear later to launch counterstrikes.

Casualties: Compiling accurate estimates of casualties for the long Cherokee Campaign is impossible because records do not exist. The best estimate is that the Patriot militia suffered at least 500 killed and wounded during these war years, and the Indians many thousands (including women and children).

Outcome / Impact: The battles fought between the Indians and white settlers in the Southern Theater had little or no direct strategic impact on the war with England. However, the constant threat of Indian attacks and the need to deal with them forced the colonial militia to commit resources that could otherwise have been used to fight the British elsewhere. This impact was especially burdensome in 1776 when the Cherokee went on the offensive. The ongoing fight with the Indians became more onerous in 1779 when the British invaded South Carolina. With the Indians threatening their homes from the west, and the British marching inland from the east, the American pioneers faced tremendous challenges that for some time seemed unsolvable. These threats forced the settlers to contribute their frontier militias (usually referred to as the "Overmountain Men") to the American army. These men were experienced Indian fighters, and their well-honed skills and courageous fighting abilities proved invaluable in dealing with the Indian threat during the long war.

Further Reading: Hatley, Tom, *Dividing Paths: Cherokees and South Carolinians Through the End of the Revolution* (Oxford University Press, 1995); Lumpkin, Henry, *From Savannah to Yorktown: The American Revolution in the South* (Paragon House, 1981).

Long Island, Battle of (New York Campaign)

Date: August 27-29, 1776.

Region: Northern Colonies, New York.

Commanders: British: General Lord William Howe, Lieutenant Generals Henry Clinton, Charles Cornwallis, and Lieutenant General Leopold Philip von Heister; American: General George Washington, Major General Israel Putnam, Brigadier Generals John Sullivan and William (Lord Stirling) Alexander.

Time of Day / Length of Action: 3:00 a.m to 2:00 p.m.

Weather Conditions: Unseasonably cool summer weather with heavy rain and fog.

Opposing Forces: British Army: 24,600 plus 5,000 Hessians; British Navy: 10,000; American Army: 19,000.

British Perspective: After evacuating Boston, the British reorganized and focused their efforts on New York. On June 25, 1776, Gen. William Howe, who replaced Thomas Gage as the Crown's commander-in-chief in the colonies, led an armada to Sandy Hook, New Jersey, which guarded the southern entrance to New York harbor. From that station the Royal Navy could guard the harbor entrance while the army disembarked to prepare for land operations. On July 12, Admiral Richard Howe joined his brother William and delivered to him additional troops and 150 more ships. Augmenting these forces was Maj. Gen. Sir Henry Clinton and his armada, fresh from the ill-fated attempt to take Charleston (Fort Sullivan, June 28, 1776). With a combined arms task force of nearly 40,000 men and several hundred warships, the Crown was finally well prepared to stamp out the war wrought by her rebellious colonies.

From local Loyalists British intelligence learned the rebels were deployed in defensive positions along Brooklyn (Guian) Heights, where they had prepared a series of forts and interconnecting trenches to protect New York City from invasion. Spies also provided the British with information about weaknesses in the lines that offered tempting targets. Howe promptly made plans to exploit them. Mindful of the stiff resolve the Americans had demonstrated in Massachusetts, Howe planned his offensive operations in New York with more deliberation and care.

Early on the morning of August 22, Howe led the first batch of 20,000 men in an amphibious assault against Long Island. The initial part of Howe's force (about 4,000 men) launched from Staten Island and landed on the southwest side of Long Island near New Utrecht. The rest of the army followed while powerful naval warships provided cover. None was needed. By noon, more than 15,000 men and dozens of artillery pieces had been put ashore. A march four miles inland to Flatbush resulted in a sharp skirmish on August 23 with advance elements of the Patriot command on Long Island. On August 25, more British landed southeast of Denyse's Point, augmenting Howe's effective force to more than 20,000 men. He split his army into two roughly 10,000-man wings. By the morning of August 27 he was in position to begin his offensive.

American Perspective: Having successfully defended Massachusetts, General Washington anticipated the British would move to New York. He established a defensive network around that city's harbor, a vast undertaking for a fledgling army supported by only a tiny and untried navy. Still, recruits flooded to the cause and by August of 1776 the nascent colonial army filled fortifications and defensive positions around the city with 19,000 troops.

The terrain on Long Island was similar to that of Boston and its harbor, though much larger in area. For Washington and the Patriots, the devil was in the vexing details: how to defend a vast area against overwhelming land and naval forces. Washington's men were predominantly inexperienced and inadequately trained and equipped for the task Washington set for them, which was to hold both New York City and Brooklyn (on Long Island), or at least extract precious blood and treasure from the Crown before giving them up. The architect of Long Island's defense was Nathanael Greene, a capable field commander who had a decent grasp of the terrain and the men assigned to defend it.

Greene concentrated his resources in a line anchored by three small forts named Putnam, Greene, and Box along Guian Heights (also called Brooklyn Heights). The line was reinforced by felled trees and good fields of fire. It offered a three-mile barrier along a natural neck of strategic terrain that would have to be taken if New York was to be threatened by a ground assault. Other forts positioned along the harbor shore defended against any maritime assault directed at New York. As the Americans were about to learn, however, things could go very wrong in a hurry.

Two days before the British began landing operations against the southwest coast of Long Island Greene fell sick with a fever and was replaced by John Sullivan. The change erased Greene's extensive knowledge of the terrain and disposition of the defenders from the battle about to unfold. Four days later Sullivan was superseded by Maj. Gen. Israel Putnam. Putnam was a hard fighter, a trait amply demonstrated at Boston, but most observers agree he was not capable of managing the large scale field action presented by the Long Island campaign; he knew even less about Long Island's terrain than Sullivan.

Howe began landing troops on August 22. Washington was in New York City. Though he shuttled over reinforcements, he was unsure whether Howe's Long Island effort was his primary attack or merely a large diversion. Within less than one week (August 20-26), however, Howe had landed a mammoth army and marched several miles inland, seriously threatening the Guian ridge. By the time sunset arrived on August 26, Washington knew the hammer was about to fall on Long Island.

Israel Putnam, who had no idea where the British would attack his front, was tasked with overseeing essentially two defensive lines perpendicular to one another. Exactly how many Americans were deployed on Long Island is open to some speculation. The main line held approximately 6,500 men deployed around Brooklyn and faced generally southeast. This line ran north for one and one-half miles from the mill dam–Gowanus Creek area that emptied into Gowanus Bay to Wallabout Bay. The remaining 3,000 soldiers were deployed to guard four strategic natural passes cut by major roads leading to the top and beyond the heights. About 550 men were on the far left guarding Gowanus Road overlooking the bay of the same name. About one and one-half miles east were 1,100 men guarding Flatbush Pass. One mile farther east, 800 soldiers blocked Bedford Pass. Still farther east on the far left flank of Putnam's attenuated line were another 500 riflemen. They were tasked with picketing a thin line stretching toward Howard's Tavern at Jamaica Pass—Putnam's extreme (and very vulnerable) left flank.

Terrain: New York City occupied the land on Manhattan Island, where the Hudson, Harlem, and East rivers converge to empty into New York harbor. Long Island (now part of New York City) measures 118 miles long (roughly north to south) and 20 miles at its widest point (roughly east to west). There was only one connector to the mainland of New York, which was on the north side of Manhattan at Kingsbridge on the Harlem River. In 1776, Long Island was a mixture of heavily forested hills and pastoral rolling farmland that included several small towns such as Flatbush, Bedford, and Brooklyn.

The battle took place in the northwestern section of the island on Guian (or more popularly Brooklyn) Heights. This high ground ran generally west to east. It was anchored on the west above Gowanus Bay and ran east by northeast several miles into Long Island. The heights were more abrupt on their southern (British) side, towering at some points 80 feet above the lower approaching elevations. The result was an imposing natural barricade to

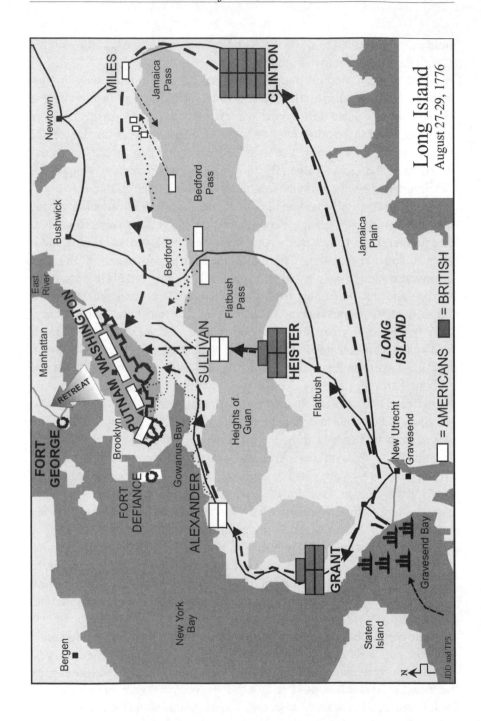

Long Island
August 27-29, 1776

General Howe's advance. The high ridge was cut by four major roads, which dictated to a large degree where the Patriot defenders deployed.

The Fighting: General Howe's plan was simple. A strong 5,000-man column under Gen. James Grant would move against Putnam's far right flank above Gowanus Bay to divert Patriot attention to the western end of the line. In conjunction with Grant, a Hessian column of similar strength under von Heister would move against and hold in place the enemy center around Flatbush. While the enemy focused attention on their center-right, Howe (with Generals Cornwallis and Clinton) would march east and then north with 10,000 men beyond and behind Putnam's left flank, rolling up and crushing the Patriot army strung out along the high ridge.

The battle opened just after midnight on the morning of August 27, when General Grant moved his 5,000 British soldiers north along the Gowanus Road and began skirmishing with rebel defenders. Putnam was advised about 3:00 a.m. of the enemy move and ordered Gen. William (Lord Stirling) Alexander to advance to the far right with reinforcements. He did so and deployed about 1,600 men to confront his much stronger opponent. Grant stopped his column in front of the rebel line and shelled the Patriots, threatening them with an infantry attack. General Sullivan, meanwhile, had reached the center of the line near Flatbush Pass, where he discovered von Heister's Hessians menacing his front with artillery—but nothing more. Playing into Howe's hands, Sullivan dispatched troops west to reinforce Alexander. By 8:00 a.m. Washington arrived on Long Island.

When the firing began early on the Patriot right and center, Col. Samuel Miles moved his Pennsylvania riflemen west toward the combat, leaving Jamaica Pass (Putnam's extreme left flank) unguarded. Ordered to return to the pass, Miles arrived just in time to spot the tail end of Howe's column (his baggage train) rolling through the defile. Miles realized the peril of the unfolding situation and sent about half his men toward the main line to warn their comrades and escape the closing trap. With his remaining men (about 250) he attacked the baggage train. It was a forlorn hope, though a brave effort. In addition to killed and wounded, 160 of the riflemen were captured, including Miles. Howe's plan was working perfectly.

The large British turning column marched completely behind Putnam's line and reached Bedford about 8:30 a.m. Thirty minutes later (after Miles's attack) Howe fired a pair of signal guns to alert Grant and von Heister to attack the front of the heights while Howe advanced against the rear. However, only the Germans attacked. Von Heister's advance north up the main road in the center of the battlefield struck General Sullivan's defenders, who faced pressure from both front and rear. Within minutes the Patriot line unraveled east to west (left to right) as men dashed along the wooded heights in an effort to reach the safety of the main Brooklyn line. Sullivan and many of his men were captured near Baker's Tavern, where a stout but short defense was attempted. Pressed by the Hessians in front and Howe's column behind them, the defenders had nowhere to run and surrendered or were shot down.

By 11:30 a.m., Alexander's infantry holding Putnam's far right flank above Gowanus Bay were overwhelmed by Grant's numerically superior command, which finally moved forward in a decisive attack that broke apart the Patriot line. Most of the fleeting Americans headed for Gowanus Creek in an effort to escape the closing enemy jaws. When Cornwallis and the 71st Regiment of Highlanders were discovered blocking their route of retreat, Alexander launched a series of daring counterattacks with about 250 Maryland riflemen led by Maj. Mordecai Gist. The bold tactical effort allowed some of his men to escape across Mill Dam Road, but Alexander was unable to clear a path of retreat for the bulk of his command. Most of the attackers, including Alexander, were captured.

After soundly sweeping Putnam's defenders off the Guian high ground, Howe interrupted his own brilliantly conceived and executed battle plan. Hours of daylight were still left to him, but instead of regrouping and attacking the last line of Patriot defense, he halted his army, reorganized his command, and ordered entrenchments dug facing the Patriot defensive works. With control of the East River, Howe apparently believed Washington was trapped and at his mercy. The two armies remained in place as rain curtailed aggression throughout the next day. Luckily for the Patriots, heavy winds prevented Howe's warships from moving behind Washington's trapped army. On the evening of August 29, Washington ordered boats to be gathered to withdraw his troops from Brooklyn Heights. A heavy fog, rain, and wind helped mask his narrow escape. By the next morning the Americans were safely across the river. That same day, Howe's warships moved up the river, a few hours too late to effectively end the American Revolution in 1776.

Casualties: British: 63 killed, 314 wounded; American: Estimates vary widely, from 800 (Washington) to 6,000 (Clinton). A reasonable tabulation is 300 killed, 650 wounded, and 1,100 captured (2,050 all causes).

Outcome / Impact: The fight on Long Island was a terrible defeat for the colonial army. The loss of Greene to fever and the consequent elevation of Putnam to command weakened what was otherwise a reasonably sound defensive deployment. The failure to properly guard the far left allowed a 10,000-man column to slip around unnoticed, ensuring defeat. The failure to effectively use cavalry to watch the flank was inexcusable. The resounding military defeat sent morale plummeting and caused many to question Washington's fitness for high command. The British war machine—large, well supplied, and supported by the world's most powerful navy—seemed unstoppable. Howe's star was ascendant (though his hesitation after his initial victory let Washington slip from his grasp). Only weeks earlier, the colonists had declared to the world their intent to break away by signing the Declaration of Independence. After Long Island, the freedom-seeking Americans were not as confident of final victory.

Further Reading: Bliven, Bruce, Jr. *Under the Guns: New York: 1775-1776* (Harper & Row, 1972); Gallagher, John J. *The Battle of Brooklyn, 1776* (Da Capo, 2001).

New York (Kip's Bay, Harlem Heights, Ft. Washington) (New York Campaign)

Date: September - November, 1776.

Region: Northern Colonies, New York (New York Campaign).

Commanders: British: General Lord William Howe, Lieutenant Generals Henry Clinton, Charles Cornwallis, and Lieutenant General Leopold Philip de Heister; American: General George Washington.

Time of Day / Length of Action: three months, see various actions

Weather Conditions: Unremarkable rainy fall weather.

Opposing Forces: British: Army: 24,300 + 5,000 Hessians (German mercenaries); British Navy: 10,000; American: 18,000.

British Perspective: After thoroughly defeating the American army on Long Island (August 27, 1776), General Howe moved deliberately to strengthen his grip on New York City. Through the use of spies and reconnaissance, he gathered intelligence in preparation for a pending assault against the enemy stationed in New York City across the East River on Manhattan Island. The cautious commander expended two weeks maneuvering his army and navy into positions that would offer him greater flexibility and striking power in the days ahead. Because of the size and quality of the British navy, he was able to move his transports, supply vessels, and warships virtually unopposed throughout the harbor and along the strategic maritime route to Lake Champlain via the Hudson River. Control of the Hudson River Valley was especially important for the British because they planned to use it to dominate and isolate New England from the rest of the rebellious colonies.

Confident the defeat on Long Island would bring the Americans to their senses, Howe delayed offensive action to arrange a peace negotiation with the rebel authorities. He released American Gen. John Sullivan from captivity and urged him to persuade the Continental Congress to discuss peace terms. John Adams, Benjamin Franklin, and Edmund Rutledge met with Howe at his Staten Island headquarters on September 11, 1776. This meeting, known as the Staten Island Peace Conference, had no chance of success because the British demanded a retraction of the American Declaration of Independence, something the American delegates refused to seriously entertain. Thereafter Howe focused on seizing control of the rest of New York City and crushing the enemy army.

His plan was to land a strong force north of the city at Kip's Bay to effectively cut Manhattan Island in two and thus divide Washington's army, capture the southern portion, and/or force a general engagement. Kip's Bay was a thinly protected area on the island's eastern shore. Preliminary moves included pushing warships and transports up the East River. On the 13th of September, several warships sailed north up the Hudson past American shore batteries, threatening to land forces above Washington's command and severing waterborne communications with the mainland.

American Perspective: By all rights the American Revolution should have ended after the August 27 battle on Long Island, where the bulk of George Washington's nascent army was outflanked, routed, and cut off against the East River. Howe, however, had underestimated his opponent's resolve. His hesitation in finishing the job allowed Washington to slip across the river to fight another day. Still, the August battle exposed several serious problems for Washington. In addition to losing valuable commanders, the loss sapped his army's morale. Desertions skyrocketed and thousands of militia simply went home. The defeat also caused many inside and outside the army to question his leadership abilities. Washington's problems were compounded by the fact that many of the inhabitants on Manhattan Island were Loyalists, which made life much more difficult for his occupation force.

Washington had little recourse but to defend New York City as well as possible while he searched for opportunities to improve his situation. Although his army was not completely surrounded, his ability to freely maneuver was limited and decreasing by the day. General Howe not only had a strong professional army but a powerful navy that provided the British with agility and mobility. Washington's command was again isolated on an island, much as it had been on Long Island.

The strength of the army approached 20,000 men, but at least one-quarter of his soldiers were ill. The new Patriot army needed a thorough reorganization, better muskets and more artillery, equipment of all kinds, and a better strategic operational area than Manhattan Island. Most of what was required was simply not readily available to Washington in 1776, though he could reorganize his command, work on increasing morale, and strengthen his position. The army was reorganized into three wings or "grand divisions" led by Gens. Israel Putnam, Nathanael Greene, and William Heath. When it was determined the city would be defended, Washington deployed his new organizations for defensive operations. Putnam's 5,000-man wing was in the city itself; Greene's command was assigned to defend eastern Manhattan Island, which included Turtle and Kip's bays (about mid-island, east side); Heath's wing, about 9,000 men, was ordered to defend the western side of the island and secure the high ground in the north known as Harlem Heights. On the western shore, Fort Washington, an old citadel guarding the Hudson River, was strengthened to prevent enemy ships from moving upriver and cutting off the American defenders.

As inexperienced field commanders are often wont to do, Washington overextended his army. There was too much terrain that needed defending and not enough troops, artillery, and naval resources available for the task. The British could land at will almost anywhere. A meeting of army officers on September 12 concluded the entire island below Fort Washington should be evacuated and the equipment and supplies hauled to safety. Unfortunately for the Americans, this could not be accomplished before British offensive operations began.

Terrain: Manhattan Island, the heart of modern New York City, is 12.5 miles long (north to south) and 2.5 miles wide (east to west). In 1776, New York City occupied the island's southern tip. The rest of the island was still rural and sparsely populated. The terrain on the island gently rises from south to north. Harlem Heights, which does not exceed 250 feet in elevation, dominated the narrow northern end of the island. Along the western shore was the strategic Hudson River, an important trade route between Canada and New York Harbor that spilled into the Atlantic Ocean. Along Manhattan's eastern shore ran the Harlem River, and along its southern fringe the East River separated New York City from Long Island. In 1776, only one bridge, on the extreme northeast corner of Manhattan Island at Kings Bridge on the Harlem River, connected the island to the mainland.

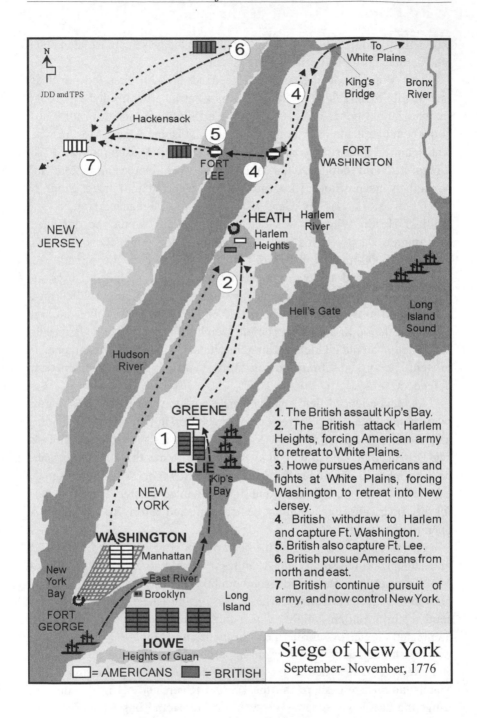

N

JDD and TPS

To White Plains

King's Bridge   Bronx River

Hackensack

FORT WASHINGTON

Hackensack

FORT LEE

NEW JERSEY

HEATH   Harlem River

Harlem Heights

Hell's Gate

Long Island Sound

Hudson River

GREENE

NEW YORK

LESLIE   Kip's Bay

WASHINGTON

Manhattan

New York Bay

East River

Brooklyn   Long Island

FORT GEORGE

HOWE
Heights of Guan

☐ = AMERICANS   ■ = BRITISH

1. The British assault Kip's Bay.
2. The British attack Harlem Heights, forcing American army to retreat to White Plains.
3. Howe pursues Americans and fights at White Plains, forcing Washington to retreat into New Jersey.
4. British withdraw to Harlem and capture Ft. Washington.
5. British also capture Ft. Lee.
6. British pursue Americans from north and east.
7. British continue pursuit of army, and now control New York.

Siege of New York
September- November, 1776

The Fighting: One of the opening moves in the New York campaign was also one of the most bizarre: a submarine attack. On the night of September 6, 1776, Sgt. Ezra Lee stealthily maneuvered a small one-man American submarine affectionately named "The American Turtle" beneath HMS *Eagle*. His intent was to drill a hole in the British hull, insert an explosive charge, and slip away before it detonated. Unable to accomplish his mission, the frustrated young officer withdrew but was spotted by British seamen who opened fire on the strange vessel. Sergeant Lee released his bomb and escaped. Unfortunately, the sub was hidden aboard a colonial warship that was sunk trying to run the British blockade. It took to the bottom the first submarine used in a combat operation.

During the early morning hours of September 15, British warships moved into Kip's Bay with a flotilla of transports filled with 4,000 soldiers. The warships pummeled Patriot positions with a heavy cannonade for about one hour, after which the British debarked and assaulted the beach about 1:00 p.m. The defenders in this sector were commanded by Col. William Douglas, whose troops consisted largely of raw Connecticut militia hunkered down in an ill-placed shallow trench. Douglas attempted to mount a credible defense, but his undisciplined soldiers, together with others defending nearby, panicked in the face of the stunning display of firepower and fled for the rear after barely firing a shot.

A dumbfounded Washington arrived on scene with several other generals and tried to rally the fleeing troops. According to some accounts, he struck several fugitives with the flat side of his sword, spoke mockingly of their fighting abilities, and finally spurred his horse in an effort to charge the British line, a foolhardy bit of bravado that ended when his aides grabbed the reins and persuaded him that retreat was a better option. (Though described in flowery terms in several sources, these actions cannot be verified.) Fortunately for the Patriots, the troops deployed in the city below Kip's Bay were notified of the mid-island disaster soon enough to march north quickly before Howe expanded his beachhead and cut off their line of retreat. Easily driven from the eastern and lower portions of the island, the Patriot army retreated northward along the western shore to fortified positions on Harlem Heights. The British mirrored the withdrawal, marching north up the eastern shoreline in one of the oddest foot races of the war.

The next day, advance elements of both armies clashed on the plain southeast of Harlem Heights. Brigadier General Leslie's command approached the new Patriot position. Washington dispatched Lt. Col. Thomas Knowlton's Connecticut Rangers (Congress's Own), about 150 men, to develop the advance. After easy victories at Long Island and Kip's

Bay, Howe's men had little regard for colonial fighting abilities. When the Rangers ran into light infantry a small fight developed. Knowlton's men comprised a specially formed unit that answered directly to General Washington. Unlike the militia defenders at Kip's Bay, these men fought with great zeal and steadfastness until reinforcements from the 42nd Regiment of Foot arrived, prompting Knowlton to withdraw.

After his men had twice failed to stand and deliver a credible fight, Washington was more than a little anxious about engaging in a pitched action. However, when word reached him that Knowlton's Rangers were fighting well and the British were mocking the Americans with fox hunting calls, Washington decided to set a trap. He ordered 150 men under Lt. Col. Archibald Crary (John Nixon's Brigade) to initiate a limited counterattack while Knowlton and his rangers, together with three companies from the 3rd Virginia under Maj. Andrew Leitch (230 men) executed a flanking movement around the advancing British right to cut them off. Washington's front line was kept too far distant to be effective on purpose to lure the British closer. Washington fed the balance of Nixon's men, about 800 Pennsylvania infantry, into the line. General Leslie took the bait and advanced, triggering an energetic musketry action.

Leslie realized something was amiss when premature firing on his right flank alerted him to the danger of envelopment. The British fell back a couple hundred yards behind a fence line followed closely by the Americans. The fighting raged at close range while Washington fed in troops from Maryland and New England, including Douglas's Connecticut militia who had failed so miserably at Kip's Bay. Two guns were also brought forward. Both Knowlton and Leitch were mortally injured early in the fighting while urging their men to stand tall against the world's finest infantry. Leslie reinforced his light infantry and Scottish Highlanders (42nd Regiment) with Jägers and field artillery. The fighting was more than Leslie had bargained for, and he fell back from Harlem Plains, stopping after a short distance to fight a rearguard action. By this time reinforcements from several miles away had arrived, swelling Leslie's command to more than 5,000 men. Unlike so many battles, darkness did not end the fighting, which stopped by 2:30 p.m. Worried Howe was planning a larger assault, perhaps with naval support, Washington ordered his troops to withdraw to the relative safety of Harlem Heights. The Americans also still held Fort Washington, but Howe had secured New York City with relative ease.

Harlem Heights was a small but morale-boosting victory—exactly what the American army needed. It was also the last combat action of consequence for the next four weeks. Washington used the gift of time to refit his men and weigh a significant strategic issue: should he abandon Fort Washington? As long as the Americans held Harlem Heights the fort (located on the northwest side of Manhattan Island) was secure. Howe would almost certainly try to turn Washington's army out of its position, and when he did the American army would have to move to the mainland, exposing Fort Washington (and a stronghold built across the river in New Jersey called Fort Lee) to capture. Washington wanted the large garrison and invaluable artillery and tons of supplies withdrawn, but his subordinate officers convinced him the fort could withstand assault. General Greene urged it be held, claiming the garrison could be evacuated in time if necessary. Events would prove the advice unsound.

The move Washington feared began on October 12, when Howe launched an envelopment of the Harlem Height's position. Washington had no choice but to order a tactical withdrawal from the heavily wooded northern end of Manhattan Island. Organized into four divisions led by Gens. Charles Lee, William Heath, John Sullivan, and Benjamin Lincoln, Washington maneuvered his army through the west end of the Bronx northward into mainland New York. Stretching his army along a 13-mile route from Fordham to White Plains, Washington moved his headquarters from Manhattan to the vicinity of White Plains on October 21.

After the White Plains operation (October 28, 1776) failed to live up to Howe's expectation, he turned back to deal with Fort Washington. On November 13-14 the British launched a combined operation with nearly 8,000 men to capture the stronghold. The British attacked from several directions, with several thousand German troops comprising the primary attacking column. Washington crossed over the river from Fort Lee during the fighting and quickly determined that saving the fort and Col. Robert Magaw's 2,800-man garrison and precious artillery was no longer possible. He returned to New Jersey and by 3:00 p.m. the fort was under the control of the British. The fall of Fort Washington (Fort Lee fell four days later, though the garrison had already fled) brought the New York Campaign to a close.

Casualties: Kip's Bay: British: 12 killed and wounded; American: 60 killed and wounded, 300 captured; Harlem Heights: British: 14 killed and 154 wounded (including Hessians); American: 30 killed, 100 wounded and/or missing; Fort Washington: British: 130 British and 320 Hessians killed and wounded; American: 53 killed, 250 wounded, and 2,818 captured.

Outcome / Impact: The British "siege" of New York was a disaster of significant magnitude for the American army. Though the string of defeats provided the Crown with several opportunities to quell the rebellion outright or at least fatally wound it, they did neither. The opposing commanders demonstrated significant strengths and weaknesses. General Howe's ability to craft elegant victories was marred by his inability to win decisively. Unlike Howe, Washington and his leading generals demonstrated again they had much to learn about commanding large bodies of troops. Washington had twice barely avoided complete annihilation (Long Island, Manhattan). Greene, who would survive the war with a sterling reputation, was responsible for convincing Washington that the garrison in Fort Washington was safe.

The complex campaign was important for several reasons. It secured New York City for the Crown for the balance of the war. It also stripped valuable men (thousands in prisoners alone), tons of critical supplies, and 146 artillery pieces from Washington's army, sapping Patriot resolve in the process. In the eyes of the world, the American rebellion appeared on its last legs. Fresh troops from England, including additional Hessian mercenaries, were already riding the Atlantic on their way to the conquered port of New York City.

Several noteworthy events occurred during the British siege of New York. During the evening of September 20, a great fire swept through the city destroying a large number of buildings. On the 21st, Patriot Capt. Nathan Hale, a member of Knowlton's Connecticut Rangers, was captured and hanged as a spy the next day by British authorities. On the gallows Hale proclaimed the famous line, "I only regret that I have but one life to lose for my country."

Today: Much of the fighting during this siege took place in what is today Manhattan. Little evidence of the fighting remains. The Morris-Jumel Mansion (West 160 Street at Edgecombe Ave., Manhattan) was the house occupied by General Washington during the Harlem Heights battle. Fort Lee State Historic Site is a 33-acre park with a visitor center and living history programs.

Further Reading: Bliven, Bruce, Jr., *Under the Guns. New York: 1775-1776* (Harper & Row, 1972); Golway, Terry, *Washington's General: Nathanael Greene and the Triumph of the American Revolution* (Henry Holt, 2005); Johnston, Henry P., *Campaign of Seventeen Seventy Six and Around New York and Brooklyn* (Da Capo, 1971).

Lake Champlain (Valcour Island), Battle of (Canadian Campaign)

Date: October 11-13, 1776.
Region: Northern Colonies, Lake Champlain, New York.
Commanders: British: Governor-General Sir Guy Carleton and Captain Thomas Pringle; American: Brigadier General Benedict Arnold and General David Waterbury.
Time of Day / Length of Action: 48-hour running naval battle.
Weather Conditions: Cold and overcast, frigid winds from the north.
Opposing Forces: British: 697; American: 873.

British Perspective: In 1775, the British lost control of their outposts along the Hudson River Valley at Fort Ticonderoga, Crown Point, and Fort St. John. Rebel raiders also seized or destroyed British ships operating on Lake Champlain, which considerably weakened the Crown's control of the region. After successfully thwarting the American Canadian offensive the British followed their defeated foe south into the American colonies. Control of Lake Champlain was essential to both sides, and in order to threaten the Americans from the north the British knew they had to control that important waterway.

Because the long and narrow lake was closed to deep water traffic on both ends, Gen. Sir Guy Carleton was forced to organize a large flotilla of ships to be hauled in for duty on the inland lake. Most of the ships were small vessels with rows and sails, and thus unsuited for moving against the wind. The ships were dismantled at Chambly and transported overland across the river narrows to St. John, where they were reassembled—a tremendous feat accomplished in a mere 28 days. In the wake of the larger ships were 400 smaller vessels loaded with 7,000 British soldiers and Indians preparing for an invasion of New York.

General Carleton's naval commander, Capt. Thomas Pringle, finally set off from St. John on the 4th of October, moving slowly south down Richelieu River in search of the Patriot ships they knew had been operating on the lake. One week later the British fleet sailed past Cumberland Head and below Valcour Island before realizing the American flotilla was arrayed between the island and the lake's western shore. Once Captain Pringle maneuvered his fleet to block southern access to Arnold, the battle for Lake Champlain was underway.

The British fleet was comprised of the following ships:

Vessel	Crew	Armaments	Commander
Inflexible, 3-masted flagship	120	Eighteen12-pounders	Captain Thomas Pringle
Maria, schooner	120	Fourteen 6-pounders	Unk.
Carleton, schooner	Unk.	Twelve 6-pounders	Unk.
Thunderer, redeau	Unk.	Six 24-pounders, six 12-pounders, and two howitzers	Unk.
Loyal Convert, gondola	Unk.	Seven 9-pounders	Unk.
20 Gunboats	Unk.	1 cannon each (various sizes)	Unk.
28 Longboats	Unk.	None	Unk.

American Perspective: On May 14, 1775 at Skenesboro (now Whitehall), New York, 50 Patriots led by Col. Benedict Arnold captured a British schooner. Arnold sailed the vessel to St. John on the Richelieu River, where on the 18th of May he discovered 10 more British ships of varying size. His men destroyed five and captured the remaining five, among them a 70-ton sloop. Arnold's amazing feat wiped out the Crown's maritime supremacy on Lake Champlain while simultaneously establishing an American ad-hock naval presence on the key lake. Although luck played a part in his success, Arnold was an experienced sea captain before war and was skilled on the water.

During the summer and fall of 1775, the Americans conducted an unsuccessful campaign to wrest Canada from British occupation. Rebuffed, the Patriots retreated in the spring of 1776, with the tiny American fleet following as it sailed south down Lake Champlain toward New York. In an effort to hold the lake and delay the British, Arnold set about building a larger fleet nearly from scratch. Although the odds were long, he pulled the tools and craftsman together and used available timber to construct his small ships in the southern reaches of the waterway at Crown Point and Skenesboro.

The backbone of his "fleet" comprised four stout flat-bottomed galleys, each crewed by 80 men. These galleys were about 70 feet long and 20 feet across, with a short mast and lanteen sail. Their armament is open to some dispute, but it is likely each possessed one or more of the following: 18-pounders, 12-pounders, 9-pounders, and 4-pounders, together with swivel guns on the quarterdeck. Eight smaller "gondolas" were also cobbled together. These flat-bottomed vessels were 53 feet long with a beam of 15.5 feet and a draft of four feet. Each had a small single mast with two small sails and a crew of 45 working three guns: a 12-pounder in the bow and two 9-pounders amidships. Like the larger galleys, the gondolas were also equipped with oars.

With his fleet finished and the British approaching, Arnold cleverly moved his motley flotilla into the narrow strait between southwest portion of Valcour Island and the New York shore. He knew his fleet was not evenly matched with that of the enemy, and decided instead to rely on stealth and unexpected tactics to make up for his lack of artillery and numbers. With a scout ship he watched the main channel and waited for the more powerful British fleet to appear. Arnold took the galley *Congress* as his flagship, while his second in command, Gen. David Waterbury, took station on the galley *Washington*.

Although there is some dispute as to the number of vessels Arnold had with him, his flotilla likely consisted of the following 15 ships:

Vessel	*Crew*	*Armaments*	*Commander*
Enterprise, sloop	50	Twelve 4-pounders and 10 swivel guns	Captain Dickenson
Royal Savage, schooner	50	Four 6-pounders and eight 4-pounders, and 10 swivel guns	Captain Hawley
Revenge, schooner	35	Four 4-pounders, four 2-pounders, and 10 swivel guns	Captain Seaman

Vessel	Crew	Armaments	Commander
Four galleys: *Lee, Congress, Washington,* and *Trumbull*	376 men	30 cannons, incl. several 18-pounders, and 58 swivel guns	Unk.
Eight gondolas: *New Haven, Providence, Boston, Spitfire, Philadelphia, Connecticut, Jersey,* and *New York*	360 men	24 cannons and 8 swivel guns	Unk.

Terrain: Lake Champlain is the sixth largest fresh water lake in the United States and the country's largest mountain lake. Located between Vermont (Green Mountains), upper New York State (Adirondack Mountains), and the Province of Québec, Canada, Lake Champlain is 120 miles long from north to south and 12 miles wide east to west at its widest point, with a basin measuring 8,200 square miles. The lake's depth averages 64 feet, and winds blow predominantly from the north.

The Fighting: Inexplicably, Captain Pringle and General Carleton failed to conduct a proper reconnaissance and on the morning of October 11 overshot their enemy. The result was that the American fleet was not spotted until the British ships had sailed past the southern tip of Valcour Island. This mistake gave Arnold's small fleet the wind and at least some advantage he otherwise would not have enjoyed. Fearing Carleton would move north and use the wind to come around Valcour Island and down the passage behind him, Arnold ordered several ships to sally out and engage the British, hoping to lure them into the southern channel off the island's southwest tip. When he saw how large the enemy flotilla was, however, Arnold pulled back and prepared to fight with his ships arrayed in a line across the narrow channel.

About 11:00 a.m. the British pressed the attack. The American schooner *Royal Savage* was the engagement's first casualty. Enemy fire damaged the ship early when it ripped away the schooner's rigging and shattered a mast. During the attempt to escape, *Royal Savage* ran aground off the southwestern corner of the island. (Captain Hawley may have deliberately pushed his crippled ship aground to save the lives of his men, who stood to their guns until they were eventually driven away.) Losing the schooner, especially so early in the fight, was a blow the Americans could ill afford.

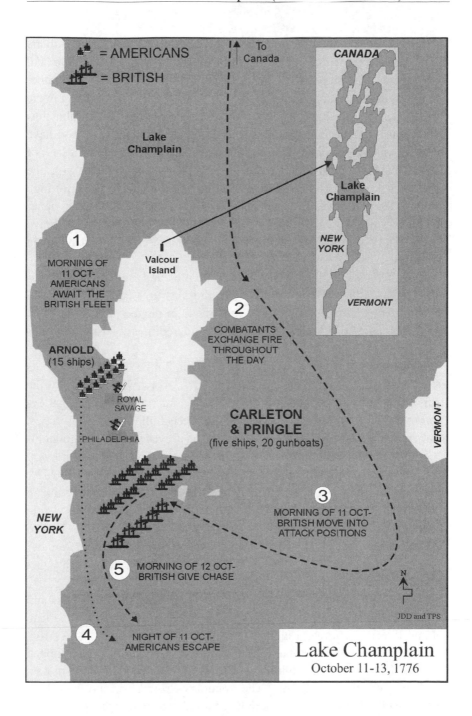

= AMERICANS
= BRITISH

To Canada

Lake Champlain

CANADA

Lake Champlain

NEW YORK

VERMONT

1 MORNING OF 11 OCT-AMERICANS AWAIT THE BRITISH FLEET

Valcour Island

2 COMBATANTS EXCHANGE FIRE THROUGHOUT THE DAY

ARNOLD (15 ships)

ROYAL SAVAGE

PHILADELPHIA

CARLETON & PRINGLE (five ships, 20 gunboats)

3 MORNING OF 11 OCT-BRITISH MOVE INTO ATTACK POSITIONS

NEW YORK

VERMONT

5 MORNING OF 12 OCT-BRITISH GIVE CHASE

N

JDD and TPS

4 NIGHT OF 11 OCT-AMERICANS ESCAPE

Lake Champlain
October 11-13, 1776

Arnold's navy stood fast and exchanged artillery fire for hours with the larger enemy fleet, with much of the action unfolding at a range of about 350 to 400 yards. The ships were small, difficult to handle under the weather conditions of the day, and battle smoke obscured much of the fighting in the narrow channel. These factors contributed to poor shooting, the combat thus lasting much longer than it otherwise would have. Arnold is said to have personally aimed many of the guns aboard *Congress* because of a lack of trained gunners. Both sides suffered direct hits and losses, with the Americans taking the lion's share of the iron. One of the key Patriot high points of the battle was the damage inflicted against the British schooner *Carleton*, which killed and wounded many of her crew. Only the brave actions of a 19-year-old midshipman who found himself in command saved the vessel.

Dusk fell on Lake Champlain about 5:00 p.m. and the British warships pulled back another 300 or 400 yards. During this time Pringle's powerful flagship *Inflexible* let loose with five medium-ranged broadsides that crippled many of the American ships and rendered most of Arnold's guns unserviceable. Darkness ended the action.

Arnold was justifiably proud of the fight his flotilla had waged, but his losses were significant. The grounded *Royal Savage* was burned by the British. Enemy gunfire had torn apart masts and rigging on the galleys *Congress* and *Washington*. Each had also been hulled numerous times. Neither would be fit for action anytime soon, if ever again. The gondolas *New York* and *Philadelphia* had also fared poorly. The former lost every officer except her captain, while the crew of the latter had been decimated by flying iron balls and wooden splinters, the ship itself crippled; she sank an hour after the artillery fell silent. The darkness had also masked a less visible American weakness. The fighting had not only cut many Patriot ships to pieces, but had nearly exhausted Arnold's supply of ammunition. Another round of fighting could only end in defeat for the Americans, a reality that prompted Arnold to prepare an escape.

Beneath an overcast night sky the Americans muffled their oars and lined their ships into single file. At 7:00 p.m. the *Trumbull* led the American column directly southward along the western shore through a heavy fog. When the sun rose on October 12 the battered American fleet had slipped away safely, but was only eight miles distant from Valcour Island. Arnold's problems were only beginning. The gondolas *Providence* and *New York* were so badly damaged they had to be scuttled. The *Jersey* hit a rock and, coupled with previous battle damage, had to be abandoned.

The daring escape angered the British commanders, who had gone to sleep that night believing Arnold was trapped and ripe for destruction. An immediate pursuit was launched. All that day the British rowed after Arnold, both sides fighting the wind now blowing up from the south. Early on the morning of October 13 the wind changed back to the north and Pringle's warships overtook the crippled American fleet near Split Rock Point. The fighting began anew with a focused attack by *Inflexible* and *Maria* against Arnold's larger ships. General Waterbury's *Washington* and more than 100 men surrendered when the pair of British ships bracketed the crippled galley. The galley *Lee* ran up against rocks near shore and was left to her fate. *Inflexible*, *Maria*, and the badly damaged but still dangerous *Carleton* moved alongside Arnold's flagship *Congress*, spraying her decks with grapeshot that ripped apart rigging and bodies while cannon balls smashed their way through the flagship's already porous hull. Woefully outgunned, Arnold knew if he did not get away his entire fleet and every crewman would be killed or captured.

In a stunning display of seamanship and leadership, Arnold ordered his remaining ships to turn into the wind and make a run past the British for Buttonmould Bay on the Vermont shore. His enemy could not sail into the wind, and some reports claim the bay was too shallow for the larger British vessels to safely enter. Once inside this sanctuary, the Americans stripped the ships of everything of value and scuttled them. Their mission at an end, Arnold and his men marched overland to Crown Point. He could not hold that position and so continued his journey to Fort Ticonderoga, which he and his 200 survivors reached at 4:00 a.m. on the morning of October 14.

Casualties: British: 50 killed, wounded, and missing; American: 673 casualties (estimate); only 200 survived the escape to Fort Ticonderoga.

Outcome / Impact: Except for *Enterprise* and a handful of battered gondolas, the American naval fleet was destroyed or captured, leaving the British once again in control on Lake Champlain. However, the fact that Arnold was able to build a credible flotilla and stall the British offensive for so long turned the tactical defeat that was America's first major naval battle into a major colonial strategic victory. The Americans still held Fort Ticonderoga and heavy winter snow and cold weather in the Hudson River Valley prevented the British from mounting their long planned invasion of New York. Carleton and his British expeditionary ground force withdrew to winter in Canada. Arnold's brilliant endeavor also bought time for the Americans to better organize their army and navy and prepare for the British New York spring offensive they knew would be coming in 1777.

Today: Some of the sunken boats on Lake Champlain have been studied, cannons have been raised, and *Philadelphia* has been located, preserved, and can be seen in the Smithsonian Institute. For more information regarding these fascinating and worthwhile efforts, see the Valcour Bay Research Project online.

Further Reading: Allen, Gardner. *A Naval History of the American Revolution* (Houghton, 1913); Fowler, William M., Jr., *Rebels Under Sail: The American Navy during the Revolution* (Scribners, 1976); Hill, Ralph Nading, *Lake Champlain: Key to Liberty* (Countryman Press, 1995); Nelson, Paul David, "Guy Carleton versus Benedict Arnold: The Campaign of 1776 in Canada and on Lake Champlain," in *New York History* (July 1976, LVII), No. 3.

White Plains, Battle of (New York Campaign)

Date: October 28, 1776.
Region: Northern Colonies, New York (New York Campaign).
Commanders: British: General Lord William Howe, Lieutenant General Sir Henry Clinton, Brigadier General Alexander Leslie, Brigadier General Wilhelm von Knyhausen, and Lieutenant General Leopold Philip von Heister; American: General George Washington, Major General Joseph Spencer, Major General Alexander McDougall, and Major General Israel Putnam.
Time of Day / Length of Action: 10:00 a.m. to 12:00 p.m.
Weather Conditions: Clear and comfortable autumn day.
Opposing Forces: British (including Hessians): 13,000 of a total 30,000-man force; American: 5,000 of a 14,000-man force.

British Perspective: After forcing the Patriot army off Manhattan Island (October 12, 1776), General Howe pursued his enemy slowly out of New York City into the countryside north toward Scarsdale. An opportunity to strike a strung-out enemy column quickly and hard was not undertaken. In order to parallel the movement of Washington's army, Howe extended his own command in a line running from New Rochelle in the south through Eastchester and on toward Scarsdale in the north. Howe found Washington's army deployed west of his own men in a thinly manned 13-mile defensive line stretching from Fordham Heights in the south to White Plains in the north. In an attempt to get behind Washington's lines, Howe launched a surprise amphibious assault with 4,000 men at Pell's Point (Pelham) on October 18. The enemy guarding the strategic landing point in Pelham Bay, however, discovered the move, fought tenaciously, and repelled the effort.

Howe continued marching northward. Occasional skirmishing erupted , (the most notable on October 22 at Mamaroneck) and dozens of casualties were incurred on both sides. On the morning of the 28th, Howe entered the village of Scarsdale and advanced toward White Plains. Reconnaissance revealed that Washington had concentrated his army and deployed it in a large shallow crescent below the village, the narrow swollen Bronx River protecting his right flank. Howe decided to engage his enemy.

American Perspective: After retreating from Manhattan Island, General Washington's army deployed in a lengthy defensive line in Westchester County on the mainland of New York. Washington's objective was to escape the encircling grasp of his adversary, whose superior forces dominated the region, while evacuating tons of local supplies before they could be captured by the British. Washington left about 1,500 men behind at Fort Washington and another 3,500 under Gen. Nathanael Greene to defend the opposite shore of the Hudson River at Fort Lee, New Jersey. With cannons in the forts above and obstacles placed in the river below, Washington hoped to prevent enemy warships from moving upriver above the forts and into the Hudson River Valley. This left Washington and his recently reorganized army with about 14,500 men to confront Howe. His plan was risky, however, because it split his army and overextended his lines, leaving his various commands vulnerable to defeat in detail if Howe moved quickly. In addition, many of Washington's men were demoralized, ill-equipped, and improperly trained. Desertions steadily eroded the combat strength of his army.

On October 18 the British attempted to get behind Washington's lines with a surprise amphibious assault at Pell's Point in Pelham Bay. A stalwart brigade led by Col. John Glover successfully blocked 4,000 British and Hessian soldiers in a crucial day-long defense of their assigned sector. Although the Patriot victory maintained the integrity of Washington's extended defensive front, Howe simply moved his army northward to exploit the overstretched American position.

Probing British advances over the next week triggered skirmishes as the two armies maneuvered toward Scarsdale and a potentially major battle. On October 27 Washington's concave double-line front covered the town of White Plains. Facing generally south, it was anchored on the right flank (west) on Purdy Hill along the Bronx River and on the left beyond the town on Hatfield Hill near a large pond. The center was directly in front of the village. One-half mile beyond Washington's right on the far side of the Bronx River was Chatterton's Hill, which the American commander did not initially perceive as important enough to occupy.

Terrain: The White Plains battlefield is located 20 miles northeast of New York City in Westchester County. In 1776 the area was a rural and sparsely populated farming community. The White Plains refers to the fertile plateau east of the Bronx River, which flows southward toward New York City. The average elevation in the area is 150 feet, and the terrain consists of gently rolling hills through which runs the Bronx River Valley. The battleground consisted of Chatterton's Hill (primary Patriot position), and its wooded ridgeline nearly three-quarters of a mile in length with an elevation of 180 feet. This high ground commanded the approaching plain below (British position), which separated the villages of Scarsdale to the south and White Plains to the north. The terrain slopes downward from Scarsdale to the Bronx River before rising steadily to the crest of Chatterton's Hill one mile north of Scarsdale.

The Fighting: At 10:00 a.m. on October 28, General Howe ordered his army to advance in two columns (one British and the other Hessian) into the village of Scarsdale. General Henry Clinton commanded the British; the Hessians were led by General von Heister. Washington advanced Gen. Joseph Spencer and about 1,500 men (some sources say as few as 500) to block the advancing British in the plains (known locally as Greenacres) between Chatterton's Hill and Scarsdale. Spencer's men fought bravely, delivering a steady musket fire as they fell back from one low stone wall to another. When the Hessians under Col. Johann Gottlieb Rahl (or Rall) advanced and threatened Spencer's left flank, however, the advanced American infantry could not hold their position and were driven back across the river onto Chatterton's Hill.

With Howe's army now in close proximity, Washington suddenly realized the critical nature of the high ground beyond his right and decided to strengthen it. He dispatched about 1,600 Delaware troops and Maryland militiamen, which brought the total defensive force there to about 2,500 (sources disagree, allowing as few as 1,600 to as many as 2,500). Major General Alexander McDougall assumed command of the high ground.

After Spencer's delaying force was knocked rearward, Howe moved his 13,000 men into the flat land below the high ground and in front of White Plains village in clear view of the Americans. It was a stunning display of the Crown's powerful military machine. None of the Americans who witnessed the spectacle ever forgot it, and many wrote about how the sun glimmered on the newly-polished enemy equipment and bayonets. Howe broke apart his

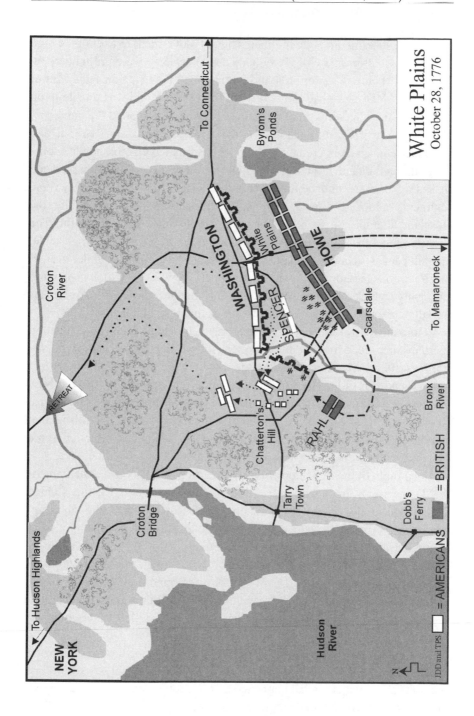

White Plains
October 28, 1776

command, shaking out eight regiments (about 4,000 men) to assault the high ground of Chatterton's Hill. Twenty pieces of artillery were unlimbered on Fisher Hill below Chatterton's and commenced firing against the Patriot positions. McDougall had but two small field pieces, and was unable to do more than fire a handful of shots before his crews abandoned the guns.

As the artillery fire smothered the American position, British and Hessian troops maneuvered under fire to the Bronx River, crossed with some difficulty in the face of musket fire (some by a downriver ford; others over a makeshift bridge), and deployed to attack Chatterton's Hill. The British regiments attacked directly against the American positions while the Hessians attempted a flanking maneuver against the American right. The British regiments found scaling the heights under the terrific fire impossible, and fell back with heavy casualties. The Hessians also suffered under the hail of fire from Captain Alexander's American New York Colony Artillery Company, which had reinforced the ridge that morning. The Americans initially appeared to be getting the better of the defensive battle.

Colonel Rahl and his Hessian regiment, however, took up a position (perhaps unnoticed) beyond the American left. Using that tactical advantage Rahl assaulted McDougall's exposed flank, which was held by largely inexperienced militia. The fight lasted only a few minutes before the New Yorkers and Massachusetts men broke and fled; the appearance of a British cavalry unit charging down on them helped convince the militia that standing in the face of the enemy was a death sentence. Although some escaped, many were killed, wounded, and captured.

The flight of the right elements on Chatterton's Hill exposed the flank of the Delaware troops, who were thrown into confusion by the sudden appearance of the enemy from an unexpected direction. Although many companies formed and repulsed several attacks, pressure against their front continued and supporting troops were breaking for the rear. Unable to sustain a credible defense, the remnants of the Delaware regiment withdrew from the field in good order. Howe's troops stopped on Chatterton's Hill, ending the battle about 5:00 p.m., with darkness falling a short time later.

Casualties: British (including Hessians): 313 killed and wounded; American: 150-500 killed, wounded, and captured.

Outcome / Impact: Given the size and proximity of the two opposing armies, the fighting at White Plains ended up being a smallish affair. The accounts about exactly what happened and when it occurred often disagree. Many cannot be reconciled at all.

The fight was a clear British victory, but Howe was once again unable to capitalize on his success. He remained in possession of the high ground on

October 28, but heavy rains and winds hampered further aggressive maneuvers by either army. On the 31st Howe planned to attack Washington, but the rain prevented the offensive. By November 1 Washington was gone. The American army retreated into the hills north of White Plains. Instead of following his enemy and forcing a decisive battle, the cautious Howe allowed Washington to safely retreat westward into New Jersey.

On November 4, Howe withdrew from White Plains and returned to New York City. Twelve days later his forces soundly defeated the American defenders holding Fort Washington. Although New York would remain in British control throughout the remainder of the war, its occupation could not alone win the lengthening and expensive war for the Crown. Washington would use the grace period Howe extended to resurrect the waning cause of independence with twin victories at Trenton and Princeton that December and January.

Today: A monument with an artillery piece marks the spot where the British forded the Bronx River. Unfortunately, there is little else in the way of interpretation on the site of this interesting engagement.

Further Reading: McCullough, David, *1776* (Simon & Schuster, 2005); Coffin, Charles, *The Boys of '76: A History of the Battles of the Revolution* (Harper & Brothers Publishers, 1924); Ward, Christopher, *The War of the Revolution*, 2 vols. (MacMillan, 1952).

Trenton, Battle of (New Jersey Campaign)

Date: December 26, 1776.

Region: Northern Colonies, New Jersey.

Commanders: British: Colonel Johann Rahl (Rall); American: General George Washington, Major General Nathanael Greene, Major General Hugh Mercer, and Major General John Sullivan.

Time of Day / Length of Action: Morning: 8:00 a.m. to 9:30 a.m.

Weather Conditions: Snowstorm, cold, windy.

Opposing Forces: British (Hessians): 1,500 with six cannon; American: 2,400 with two cannon.

British Perspective: After the Battle of White Plains (October 28, 1776), General Howe returned to Manhattan Island but dispatched General Cornwallis with 8,000 British and Hessian troops to take Fort Washington on the Hudson River. On November 16, Fort Washington fell in what was to date the most overwhelming victory of the war. The Patriot citadel touted as impregnable surrendered 2,800 defenders, tons of supplies, and nearly 150 pieces of artillery. With commendable swiftness, Cornwallis made a daring night crossing of the Hudson to engage Fort Lee on the New Jersey side of the river. The Americans withdrew from Fort Lee and joined Washington's retreating army moving southward toward Trenton. Cornwallis set forth in pursuit. British control and navigation of the Hudson River was now unimpeded.

Howe moved the bulk of his army into winter quarters, but ordered Cornwallis to continue pursuing the American army across New Jersey. Cornwallis moved his command swiftly, but the Americans did what they could to obstruct and harass his march with delaying attacks across the southern end of New Jersey from Fort Lee to Trenton. By the time Cornwallis caught up with Washington's rag-tag army on December 8, the Americans were safely across the Delaware River in Pennsylvania.

Cornwallis spent days searching for boats to cross, but the Patriots had destroyed nearly everything that floated for miles up and down the river. With cold weather setting in across the middle colonies Cornwallis ordered his men into winter quarters. He decided to station his troops across New Jersey in several strategic locations. Colonel Johann Rahl's Hessians occupied Burlington and Trenton. Other British troops were garrisoned at Princeton, Perth Amboy, Bordentown, and Pennington. Cornwallis established his headquarters at Brunswick and ordered his commanders to keep a vigilant guard and establish good defensive positions.

Colonel Rahl failed to adhere to his commander's orders. He and his men settled in at Trenton for the winter with little obvious regard for security issues. The Hessian garrison consisted of three 400-man regiments: von Rahl (grenadiers), von Knyphausen, and von Lossberg. Rahl was an experienced soldier with a reputation for hard fighting (his service at Fort Washington earned him the honor of holding Trenton), but he was also known for his fondness of drink and celebration. The Hessians embraced the Christmas holiday as an excellent opportunity to imbibe beer and hard liquor, and the night was spent in boisterous revelry. Rahl and his men were completely oblivious to Patriot movements around Trenton, even though deserters had informed him of the exact date and time the attack would come. The German either did not believe his source or thought the effort would be nothing more than a small raid.

American Perspective: Following the standoff at White Plains, New York, General Washington decided to move west into New Jersey for the winter. General Charles Lee remained at White Plains with the bulk of the Patriot army while Washington withdrew 4,400. His column crossed the Hudson River and marched southward to Hackensack, New Jersey. In this position he could await the arrival of Lee with the bulk of the Patriot army (about 12,000 men) and remain abreast of events transpiring well to the east at Forts Washington and Lee.

Fort Washington was stormed and captured by the British on November 16 . Fort Lee fell four days later, but not before Washington ordered Gen. Nathanael Greene to evacuate the bastion. The combined forces moved through Newark and to Brunswick, New Jersey. The results of steady defeat and retreat manifested themselves while in Brunswick, where Washington not only had trouble enlisting New Jersey men to fight as militia, but 2,000 of his own men refused to reenlist; hundreds of others deserted. The onset of cold weather and severe shortages of food and equipment only complicated the plight of the Patriot army. Washington was also well aware that Cornwallis was pursuing him across the state. By the time General Lee finally moved into New Jersey with the main Patriot army he was too far north to help Washington.

On December 2 Washington left General Greene with a small force in Princeton to destroy bridges, delay Cornwallis's advance, and act as a rear guard while Washington moved to Trenton. The next day at Trenton Washington was joined by 2,000 Pennsylvania volunteers. Moving swiftly, he ferried his contingent across the Delaware River into Pennsylvania while simultaneously destroying every other boat his men could find within miles of Trenton. After Greene arrived from Princeton the last of Washington's force crossed safely into Pennsylvania and went into camp. The head of the British column reached Trenton on December 8. From the far shore of the Delaware River the Patriots greeted their arrival with cannon fire. With no boats to cross the river, the frustrated and naturally aggressive Cornwallis established defensive camps for the winter across New Jersey, including a Hessian outpost at Trenton.

Meanwhile, Charles Lee and the main Patriot army were moving across New Jersey in an effort to link up with Washington. The army bled deserters and ill soldiers with every step. On December 13, General Lee was captured by a British patrol and was replaced by Maj. Gen. John Sullivan. What was left of the main army (about 2,000 men) reached Washington's encampment on December 20. Major General Horatio Gates arrived that same day with another 800 men from Fort Ticonderoga. To Washington's satisfaction, Pennsylvania militiamen continued arriving and soon the strength of the army climbed to a respectable 6,000 capable soldiers.

Knowing he had to seize the initiative, fight on his own terms, and keep his men occupied, Washington decided to go over to the offensive. When intelligence reported the situation around the isolated post at Trenton, he organized a surprise attack against Rahl's unsuspecting Hessians. Believing the Germans would be vulnerable the day after Christmas, he made plans for a daring night crossing of the Delaware River and an early morning assault.

Beginning at 2:00 p.m. on December 25, 2,400 Patriots and 18 field pieces led by General Washington moved to positions nine miles northwest of Trenton at McConkey's Ferry on the Delaware River. After dark they began crossing the river into New Jersey. As a diversion and to prevent the reinforcement of Trenton, Washington dispatched Col. John Cadwalader with 2,000 militiamen to attack Gen. Carl von Donop's British garrison at Bordentown. However, a violent snowstorm that began around 11:00 p.m. prevented Cadwalader from getting his artillery across the river. He did not get into position in time to affect the battle about to unfold. Another 1,000 men led by Brig. Gen. James Ewing tried to cross the Delaware and establish a blocking force south of Trenton at the Assunpink Creek bridge just below the town. However, General Ewing's men were also unable to cross the Delaware River due to the harsh wintry weather.

Washington's troops crossed the Delaware at McConkey's Ford but the blinding snow and powerful winds delayed the move by several hours. Washington had planned to have his troops across the river by midnight, but they did not get fully across until 3:00 a.m., and they were not ready to begin marching toward Trenton until 4:00 a.m. At the tiny hamlet of Birmingham (also known as Bear's Tavern) four miles northeast of the crossing point, the Patriot force split into two columns, which then moved toward their assigned assault positions.

Major General John Sullivan led one wing to the west end of Trenton along River Road to attack the Hessians from that direction. Moving along a more northerly but parallel route toward Trenton was Maj. Gen. Nathanael Greene's column along the Pennington Road. This wing, which Washington accompanied, would attack Trenton from the north. For the next two hours the Patriots battled the cold and snow as they trudged toward Trenton. Although the icy winds and blinding snow made the march difficult, the weather concealed the move and all but guaranteed that pickets would be sheltered indoors and no one would be picketing any of the approaches.

Terrain: The battlefield is located in the city of Trenton, New Jersey, on the northern bank of the Delaware River twelve miles south of Princeton. In 1776, Trenton was a small village with just a few hundred inhabitants.

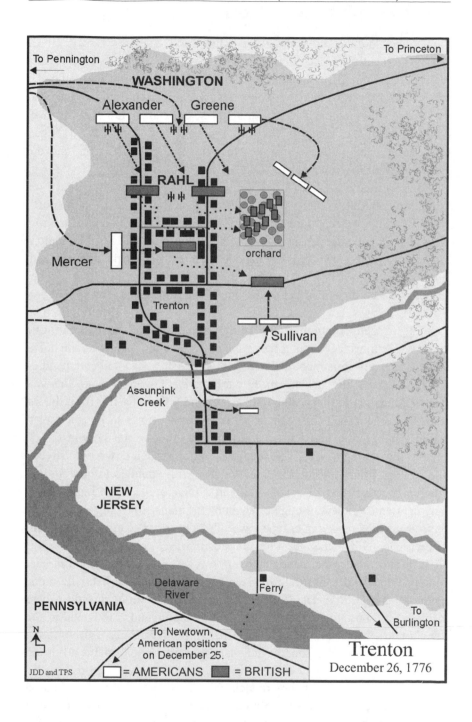

To Pennington

To Princeton

WASHINGTON

Alexander   Greene

RAHL

orchard

Mercer

Trenton

Sullivan

Assunpink
Creek

NEW
JERSEY

Delaware
River

Ferry

PENNSYLVANIA

To
Burlington

N

To Newtown,
American positions
on December 25.

JDD and TPS

☐ = AMERICANS ◼ = BRITISH

Trenton
December 26, 1776

Constructed at the conflux of the Assunpink and Delaware rivers, the town was methodically arranged with several north-south and east-west roads.

The Fighting: The sun was well above the horizon on December 26 when Hessians posted in a house on the outskirts of town fired into the head of Greene's Pennington Road column about one-half mile north of town. Minutes later the head of Sullivan's column on River Road began exchanging shots with Hessian sentries. It was about 8:00 a.m., and the Battle of Trenton was underway.

The Patriots moved quickly into their assault positions and aligned for battle, unlimbering artillery to sweep the long straight streets. On the north side of Trenton, General Greene skillfully deployed four regiments to cover King and Queen streets, the main routes leading into and out of Trenton. General Sullivan's men blocked the southern end of Queen Street near its intersection with First Street and the bridge over the Assunpink, while other troops in his command stretched the line of battle southeast toward Second Street.

The sudden eruption of fire roused the Hessians from their foggy slumber. Within a few minutes they were organized into regiments and out in the streets ready for action. Colonel Rahl sluggishly assumed command of the situation and the men advanced north against Greene's men. The well placed American artillery, small arms fire, and a flanking fire from the far left of Greene's men threw them back. German efforts to get their own artillery into action failed when Patriot guns drove away the gun crews. Infantry belonging to Capt. Alexander Hamilton rushed down both streets, and Lt. (and future president) James Monroe was wounded in the fighting. On the southern end of town, Sullivan's men drove back most of the Knyphausen Regiment, though a few hundred managed to slip away, cross the Assunpink Creek, and escape toward Bordertown because of the failure of Ewing to get his blocking force into position.

The snow and wind made firing muskets difficult, and the fighting that followed, much of it house to house, depended upon bare fist, rifle butts, bayonets, and swords. The Germans retreated east to an open field, where Rahl did his best to reorganize his stunned command. From within the town's houses and buildings Patriot riflemen poured a hail of fire into the exposed ranks of the Hessian formations. Other fire came from the north and west.

When efforts at a counterattack failed, and with the Knyphausen Regiment essentially out of the picture, Rahl ordered his two remaining regiments (Rahl and Lossberg) to fall back southeast into an orchard. An effort to counterattack was broken up by artillery and small arms fire. When

Colonel Rahl fell mortally wounded, the nearly surrounded Hessians began surrendering. By 9:30 a.m. the fighting was over (some sources claim the fighting lasted little more than 40 minutes). Washington gave serious thought to following up his victory with an immediate march against Princeton, but the freezing weather, hundreds of prisoners, and lack of supply convinced him to recross the Delaware into Pennsylvania.

Casualties: British: 40 killed, 66 wounded, and 918 captured; American: eight wounded and four killed.

Outcome / Impact: The lopsided Trenton fight was the first meaningful American victory of the war. With the American army approaching collapse after the debacle in New York City, its impact on morale and enlistments is difficult to overstate. Many historians consider the tremendous improvement in morale that swept through the colonies after Trenton to be the turning point of the war. In addition to heavy losses in manpower, Rahl's Hessians forfeited 40 horses, six field pieces, and 1,000 muskets and ammunition, all of which were put to good use by the Patriots. The professional Hessian soldiers, who had held the American soldiers in contempt, looked upon the colonial fighters with a new level of respect. Many in the British ranks also took note of the bold nature of the well-planned American assault. Cornwallis, perplexed and a bit embarrassed by the humiliating nature of the defeat, ordered his remaining outposts on high alert.

Today: Washington Crossing State Park in Titusville, New Jersey, offers an outstanding visitor center, museum, and a host of related events (including living history programs) that interpret this and related battles. Old Barracks Museum in Trenton once housed Hessian soldiers and is open to the public.

Further Reading: Dwyer, William. *The Day is Ours! November 1776-January 1777: An Inside View of the Battles of Trenton and Princeton* (Rutgers University Press, 1998); Stryker, William, *Battles of Trenton and Princeton* (Houghton Mifflin, 1898); Weintraub, Stanley, *Iron Tears: America's Battle for Freedom, Britain's Quagmire: 1775-1783* (Free Press, 2005).

Princeton, Battle of (New Jersey Campaign)

Date: January 3, 1777.
Region: Northern Colonies, New Jersey.

Commanders: British: Lieutenant General Charles Cornwallis, Brigadier General Alexander Leslie, and Colonel Charles Mawhood; American: General George Washington, Major General Hugh Mercer, Major General Nathanael Greene, Major General John Sullivan, Colonel John Cadwalader, and Colonel David Hitchcock.

Time of Day / Length of Action: 8:00 a.m. to 10:00 a.m.

Weather Conditions: Clear and cold.

Opposing Forces: British: 1,200; American: 4,600 men and artillery.

British Perspective: On the cold evening of January 2, 1777, General Cornwallis and a 5,500-man force reached Trenton, New Jersey. His arrival at the distant outpost in the dead of winter was triggered by General Washington's surprise attack against the isolated town just one week earlier on December 26, 1776. The strike decimated Col. Johann Rahl's Hessians, the highly touted heroes of the Battle of White Plains (October 28, 1776), and killed Rahl. The positioning and defense of the string of New Jersey posts were Cornwallis's responsibility. Like most other observers, after the debacle of the New York campaign the general believed the American army was on its last legs. Angry that the first decisive Patriot victory of the war had come against part of his own command, Cornwallis set out to catch and destroy Washington. His disposition was not helped by the cancellation of his scheduled leave to visit England, brought about by the Hessian humiliation.

Cornwallis left Princeton for Trenton on the morning of January 2 with about 6,700 men. In Princeton he left 1,200 men, three regiments, and a small contingent of light dragoons under Col. Charles Mawhood. General Leslie and a force of similar strength were dropped off at Maidenead (now Lawrenceville), midway between Princeton and Trenton. Both men had orders to join Cornwallis on January 3. More than 5,000 additional troops were posted across New Jersey at other outposts. However, Cornwallis felt confident his strength and arrangements were sufficient for the immediate task at hand.

When an enemy line of battle was spotted a few miles above Trenton, Cornwallis spent precious hours deploying and skirmishing with it as the Patriots fell back in good order. The enemy was delaying his march, and doing a fine job of it. By the time he reached Trenton it was nearly dark. Washington's army had taken up a position southeast of the town below the Assunpink River. A light feint to test the resolve of those guarding the bridge demonstrated the Americans intended to obstruct the crossing. Cornwallis established a defensive line from Trenton stretching east along the northern bank of the river facing the Americans on the opposite shore. The Patriot army was aligned in defensive positions along a ridge overlooking the small river and the town of Trenton beyond. Local intelligence convinced Cornwallis if he pressed ahead with a superior force, Washington would be trapped between the Assunpink and Delaware.

With his enemy in a box of their own choosing, hemmed in by rivers, freezing weather, and difficult terrain, a pleased Cornwallis bedded down for the night in preparation for a battle of elimination the following day.

American Perspective: The sudden and heavy blow delivered against the British outpost at Trenton the day after Christmas 1776 had, as General Washington suspected it would, serious repercussions. He knew Cornwallis was not about to sit on his hands until spring before moving swiftly to punish the Patriot army, and the Crown could not risk another similar defeat or the boost it would provide to the cause of independence.

After the battle at Trenton Washington crossed back to the west bank of the Delaware River to rest and re-supply his men. Opportunities against Cornwallis's scattered New Jersey outposts beckoned the aggressive Virginia commander. General Cadwalader's 1,200 men had reached the eastern shore on December 27 and were still there below Trenton. Cadwalader urged Washington to return and take the offensive. With many enlistments set to expire at midnight on December 31 (the America army at the beginning of 1777 numbered just 1,600 Continentals), Washington authorized an illegal $10.00 bounty to keep hundreds of men in the ranks for another six weeks. Reinforcements from Philadelphia (about 500 newly raised militia under Brig. Gen. Thomas Mifflin) were also marching his way. On December 30 Washington crossed back to the east side of the river and marched his tired men to Trenton, where he ordered Cadwalader and Mifflin to join him.

When word arrived that Cornwallis was at Princeton with a large army intent on finding and crushing him, Washington dispatched a sizeable force to block the road from Princeton (about twelve miles northeast of Trenton) in order to effect his concentration below the Assunpink River. This command consisted of Gen. Matthias Fermoy's brigade, Colonel Hand's Pennsylvanians, Colonel Haussegger's German battalion, Colonel Scott's Virginians, and a pair of light field guns.

Cornwallis's approach on the road to Trenton sent General Fermoy riding for the rear, but Colonel Hand stood tall and demonstrated his tactical ability. He forced the British to deploy into battle formation, slowing down their advance to a crawl and burning away several hours. The German allies fled quickly and Haussegger was captured (and spent the balance of his captivity urging cooperation with the British). Hand nimbly withdrew after some light skirmishing and fell slowly back toward Trenton. Washington, meanwhile, had established his army's primary position south of the Assunpink, where Hand joined him later that afternoon near dusk. Cornwallis's halfhearted thrust at the bridge leading over the waterway was thrown back easily as the sun set on January 2.

Both armies were now facing one another across the Assunpink in what could be roughly described as conventional battle lines. An engagement similar to those waged during the recent New York campaign seemed in the offing. Although he had narrowly avoided what would have been a disastrous attack during daylight, Washington knew he was in a terrible strategic situation. His army of mostly green militia could not withstand a direct attack, his right flank was vulnerable, and the Delaware River on his left might as well have been the ocean, for he did not have enough boats to affect a speedy escape. Retreat south along the river would buy him hours, or perhaps a day or two of relief before Cornwallis caught him. A fight seemed inevitable, but Washington had no intention of fighting Cornwallis on his terms. The early war battles had convinced the American general his army was not yet ready to stand in a pitched battle against the Crown's finest. However, he had found a recipe for success in his unconventional strike against Trenton. Washington decided to stir the same pot again. Sources disagree as to who came up with the plan, but it was Washington who had to find the courage to execute it.

Under the cover of darkness on January 2-3 he prepared his army for a strategic envelopment of Cornwallis's weak left flank. In order to guarantee secrecy, only Washington and his senior commanders knew the details of the march and its objectives. The soldiers simply did as they were ordered. Wagon wheels were wrapped with rags and 400 men remained behind to keep fires burning to deceive the enemy. About 1:00 a.m. on the 3rd of January, 4,600 men began marching east along Sandtown Road in a broad arc across Miry Run and then northeast on the Quaker Road toward Princeton. Washington ordered Gen. Hugh Mercer and 350 infantry to act as a blocking force two miles southwest of Princeton on the Post Road at Stony Creek Bridge. Mercer's objective was to prevent Cornwallis or Leslie from reinforcing Mawhood and to prevent an escape from Princeton toward Trenton. With Mercer in place, Washington intended to move the balance of his army north and east along the Back Road and close rapidly with the unsuspecting 1,200-man garrison.

Terrain: The battlefield is located in and around Princeton, New Jersey. In 1777, Princeton was a sleepy village a dozen miles north of Trenton. The surrounding rural countryside consisted of open gently rolling fields with intermittent farmsteads and forested areas. Fighting also occurred at Stony Creek, two miles southwest of Princeton.

The Fighting: Cornwallis awoke on January 3 to two unpleasant facts: his opponent had slipped away during the night, and artillery and small arms fire could clear be heard in the direction of Princeton. Messengers soon arrived with word that Washington was assaulting Mawhood. Exactly what went through Cornwallis's mind when he realized he had been utterly outgeneraled will never be known, but the realization could not have pleased him. With the commendable speed that was always his trademark, Cornwallis drove his army rapidly northeast to catch the Patriots between his own and Mawhood's men.

The fighting he heard was the heavy rattle of musketry and artillery fire of Mawhood's infantry and a Patriot militia force sprinkled with Continentals in and around an orchard south of the Post Road one and one-half miles west of Princeton. Unbeknownst to Washington, Cornwallis had ordered Colonel Mawhood to send 800 of his men to Trenton that morning. Had Washington been thirty minutes later he would have missed his objective entirely. As he drew near Stony Creek, Mawhood spotted General Mercer's column to the south marching northeast toward the bridge to take up his blocking position. For reasons still unclear, both commands changed the direction of their march, Mawhood's to the southeast and Mercer's to the northeast. The opponents made a dash for a large orchard, which Mercer's men reached first, leaving the British to form in an open field on slightly lower ground between the Post and Back roads. Much of the 55th Regiment of Foot ended up on a patch of high ground farther to the east and did not play a significant role in the fighting. The frost-laden fields made it easy to spot the bright scarlet uniforms worn by Mawhood's 17th and 55th infantry regiments. (The 40th had been left behind to guard Princeton.)

Both sides deployed quickly into line and began killing one another at a range of only 50 yards while unlimbering a pair of field pieces each. The British were fresh and alert, while the Patriots had marched all night in freezing temperatures. After one volley Mawhood ordered a bayonet charge. Mercer was fighting on foot after his horse was injured and was mortally wounded in a melee that left him with at least seven stab wounds. Unable to withstand British steel, the militia retreated south toward the Back Road. When Mawhood spotted the head of another Patriot column arriving on the field behind Mercer's men, he fell back and took up a defensive position. The men Mawhood spotted belonged to Cadwalader, who tried to engage the

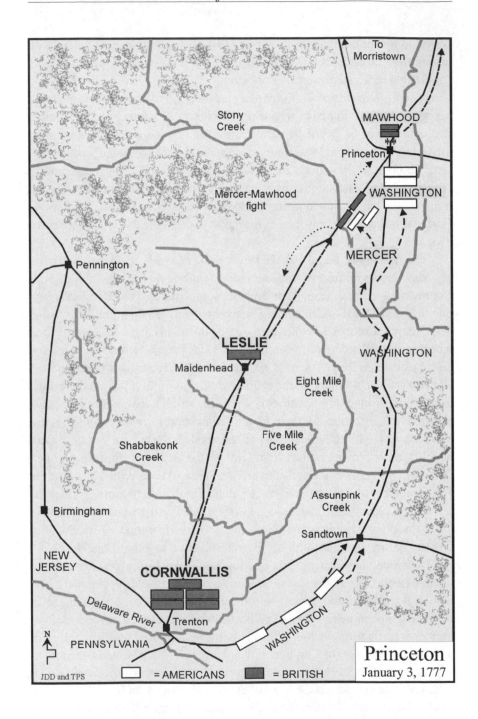

To Morristown

Stony Creek

MAWHOOD

Princeton

Mercer-Mawhood fight

WASHINGTON

MERCER

Pennington

WASHINGTON

LESLIE

Maidenhead

Eight Mile Creek

Five Mile Creek

Shabbakonk Creek

Birmingham

Assunpink Creek

Sandtown

NEW JERSEY

CORNWALLIS

Delaware River

Trenton

WASHINGTON

N

PENNSYLVANIA

JDD and TPS

□ = AMERICANS   ■ = BRITISH

Princeton
January 3, 1777

British infantry with militia in the open, failed, and began falling back in disorder. Thus far the Princeton fight was not going well for the Patriots.

As if by script, Washington arrived on the scene. The general had been riding toward Princeton with Sullivan's division on Back Road when he heard the heavy firing. He and a few aides rode cross-country to evaluate its significance. Washington rode in the midst of the disorganized militia, encouraging them to stand firm, align themselves, and fight the enemy. He did so with only 30 yards separating himself and the British front rank. Luckily for Washington, additional reinforcements from Sullivan's command in the form of Rhode Island Continentals from Col. David Hitchcock's brigade, Hand's experienced Pennsylvanians, and Virginians under Scott, had trotted across the same fields to throw back Mawhood's advance. The presence of these veterans helped the militia remain in line, as did a pair of Patriot artillery pieces that had been firing since nearly the beginning of the action.

The combined Patriot attack triggered an intense firefight at close range that nearly enveloped Mawhood's infantry (the 17th and part of the 55th) before breaking apart its cohesion; some scattered in the direction of New Brunswick, while others, Mawhood with them, broke through the lines and headed for the bridge and Trenton. The Americans gave chase and secured 50 prisoners before Washington recalled his men and continued advancing toward Princeton. The British 17th Regiment had performed the bulk of the fighting and suffered the vast majority of the casualties. The entire action consumed less than one hour.

The "battle" that followed was anti-climactic. The main Patriot army flooded into the area to find about 200 enemy soldiers, most from the 40th Regiment and a few from the 55th, barricaded inside Nassau Hall, a thickly walled building that served as the College of New Jersey (now Princeton University). A single round from one of Capt. Alexander Hamilton's field pieces brought about their surrender. Princeton belonged to the Patriots.

Washington had no desire to hold the town, and indeed his army was too weak and too exhausted to do so. His goal had been to launch another surprise attack against a New Jersey outpost. The rout of Mawhood and capture of Princeton accomplished his goal. His additional dream of marching eighteen miles northeast to capture the enemy supply depot at New Brunswick was beyond his reach. The Patriot infantry were freezing, exhausted after forty hours of marching and fighting on slim rations. Many were already dropping to the ground to sleep. Knowing Cornwallis would even now be marching quickly in his direction, Washington ordered his men to secure food, supplies, and equipment, round up their prisoners, and move with as much haste as possible to the American base in the wooded hills at Morristown, New Jersey.

Washington left a detachment of soldiers to destroy Stony Creek Bridge to delay the British army, but Cornwallis simply fed his men across the icy stream and pressed ahead. Although Cornwallis had marched with speed, and his vanguard spotted the tail of Washington's army evacuating Princeton, he could not catch the victorious Patriots.

Casualties: British: 28 killed, 58 wounded, 187 missing/captured; American: 23 killed and 20 wounded.

Outcome / Impact: With Washington on the move Cornwallis had little time to absorb the shocking defeat at Princeton. Worried the American army was marching for New Brunswick (which housed the British treasury and supply depot), Cornwallis drove his army another eighteen miles to secure the post. Washington had instead marched west of New Brunswick and reached Morristown on January 6, where he established a winter encampment in a secure and pro-Patriot stronghold.

Washington's bold New Jersey Campaign (called by one historian "The Nine Days' Wonder") changed the face of the American Revolution. He had driven the British out of most of New Jersey in the dead of winter with an ill-fed and woefully outnumbered army composed largely of inexperienced militia. Except for Amboy and New Brunswick, the entire state had been wiped clean of the Crown's troops. The man who had been laughed at as a bumbling fool was now looked upon by both his opponents and European onlookers as a general of some brilliance. Princeton sent a second shock wave of pride rippling through the colonies. In France, talk of supporting the American rebellion took on a more serious tone.

The loss of General Mercer was a blow to Washington's army. After suffering his terrible wounds, Mercer was removed to the nearby Thomas Clarke house, where he lingered in agony until January 11 before expiring. Many contemporaries and postwar historians believe Mercer was one of the Patriot army's legitimate rising stars, and his loss was keenly felt.

Today: The battle is commemorated and interpreted by the 85-acre Princeton Battlefield State Park, which includes the Thomas Clarke house.

Further Reading: Dwyer, William, *The Day is Ours! November 1776-January 1777: An Inside View of the Battles of Trenton and Princeton* (Rutgers University Press, 1998); Stryker, William, *Battles of Trenton and Princeton* (Houghton Mifflin, 1898); Weintraub, Stanley, *Iron Tears: America's Battle for Freedom, Britain's Quagmire: 1775-1783* (Free Press, 2005).

Fort Ticonderoga, Battle of (Saratoga Campaign)

Date: June 30 – July 7, 1777.
Region: Northern Colonies, New York and Vermont.
Commanders: British: Major General John Burgoyne, Major General Friedrich von Riedesel, and Brigadier General Simon Fraser; American: Major General Philip Schuyler, Major General Arthur St. Clair.
Time of Day / Length of Action: Fort Ticonderoga: June 30 – July 5.
Weather Conditions: Clear and warm.
Opposing Forces: British: 9,100; American: 4,000.

British Perspective: In the spring of 1777, Maj. Gen. John Burgoyne was dispatched to Québec, Canada, to take charge of British forces in that country and lead an offensive south into western New York. His mission was to crush Patriot forces in that region. After destroying rebel resistance in western New York, Burgoyne intended to march south to Albany, where he would join with Gen. William Howe's army for additional offensive operations. Burgoyne himself designed this ambitious scheme, which was fully supported by his superiors.

Burgoyne assigned 3,700 troops to remain with Gen. Sir Guy Carleton in Québec while he led a 9,100-man expeditionary force southward along Lake Champlain to eliminate the Patriots defending Fort Ticonderoga. This success would clear the rebels from Canada all the way to the Hudson River Valley. Simultaneously, another British force, about 2,000 men commanded by Lt. Col. Barry St. Leger, would march around to the west and attack Patriots operating in the Mohawk Valley before moving to Albany. Howe, meanwhile, would lead the main British army northward up the Hudson River from New York City to join with St. Leger and Burgoyne at Albany. If successful, the three-pronged British offensive would crush the rebellion in New York and separate the New England colonies from the middle and lower colonies. It was an ambitious plan, and offered perhaps the best way to cripple the rebellion and turn the tide of the war decisively in the Crown's favor.

Burgoyne's expeditionary force departed St. Johns, Canada, on June 20, 1777. His troops consisted of 5,500 British soldiers, 3,000 Hessians commanded by Maj. Gen. Friedrich von Riedesel, 400 Indians, 150 Canadians, and 100 Tory sympathizers. Burgoyne also had 37 naval ships of various size, 138 artillery pieces, and 250 British artillerymen.

American Perspective: When he learned of the arrival of General Burgoyne and his army in Canada, Maj. Gen. John Thomas, the commander of American forces stationed on the outskirts of Québec, retreated southward into western New York. An outbreak of smallpox decimated American ranks during the retreat and Thomas was one of those who died from the disease. Brigadier General John Sullivan replaced Thomas, and the army marched southward to Fort Ticonderoga to join there with the forces led by Maj. Gen. Philip Schuyler, who commanded all the Patriot troops in western New York (Northern Department of the Continental Army). One of Schuyler's subordinates, Gen. Arthur St. Clair, was assigned to defend the key terrain overlooking Lake Champlain at Fort Ticonderoga and Mount Independence.

Fort Ticonderoga had been in Patriot hands since its capture by Benedict Arnold and Ethan Allen on May 10, 1775. The fort dominated the terrain on the western shore of Lake Champlain, where it intersected with the narrow waterway linking it to Lake George. This area was a mainstay in the Patriot defensive northern network, and 2,500 troops led by Maj. Gen. Arthur St. Clair were busy there preparing for the arrival of the British. Artillery and supplemental positions were also prepared on Mount Independence, which overlooked the lake from the southeast. High ground west at Mt. Hope, southwest of Mt. Defiance, the lake itself, and wide northern and northwestern approaches, meant that without a large force Ticonderoga was indefensible. Its importance in the minds of Americans, however, made its defense professionally and politically necessary.

On June 20, Schuyler and his generals decided to hold the fort as long as possible before falling back southeast across a quarter-mile span of boats to Mt. Independence, where a line of retreat led south near the lakeshore to Skenesboro. The line of British operations was unknown, and the American plan was at best uninspired.

Terrain: Fort Ticonderoga was a large stone fort studded with artillery strategically located on dominating high ground on the western side of Lake Champlain on a point of land between that body of water and the narrow waterway leading to Lake George in the Hudson River Valley. Fort Ticonderoga was in Essex County, New York, 95 miles north of Albany. Ticonderoga derived its name from the Indian word *Cheonderoga*, or "Place between two waters."

The Fighting: General Burgoyne arrived outside the walls of Fort Ticonderoga on June 30. His British had marched or landed on the western shore of the lake, while von Riedesel's Hessians landed and marched down the eastern side toward Mt. Independence. The Hessians faced a difficult mission as East Creek and its surrounding marshes dominated the terrain in

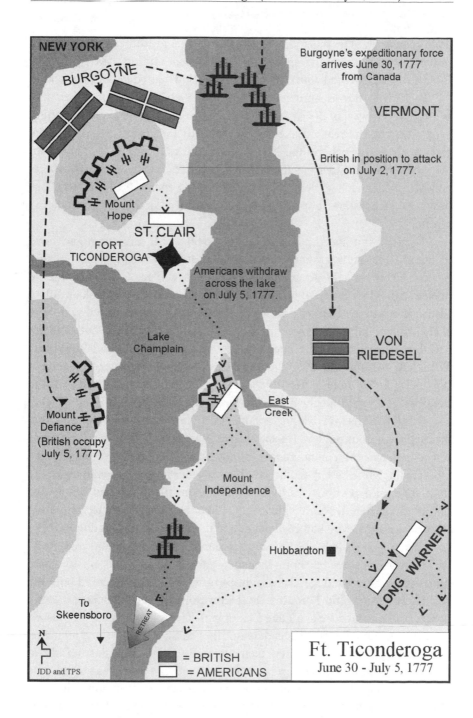

NEW YORK

BURGOYNE

Burgoyne's expeditionary force
arrives June 30, 1777
from Canada

VERMONT

British in position to attack
on July 2, 1777.

Mount
Hope

ST. CLAIR

FORT
TICONDEROGA

Americans withdraw
across the lake
on July 5, 1777.

Lake
Champlain

VON
RIEDESEL

East
Creek

Mount
Defiance
(British occupy
July 5, 1777)

Mount
Independence

Hubbardton

LONG   WARNER

To
Skeensboro

N

RETREAT

JDD and TPS

= BRITISH
= AMERICANS

Ft. Ticonderoga
June 30 - July 5, 1777

their sector. The Hessians planned to sweep around to the south and then move up into the high ground, but American artillery fire from Mt. Independence, coupled with swampy East Creek thwarted their movements.

By July 2 troops commanded by Brig. Gen. Simon Fraser secured positions northwest of the American fort on Mount Hope, effectively cutting off an American retreat to Lake George. St. Clair and his officers knew if the British moved to occupy the high ground one mile farther south on Mt. Defiance, Fort Ticonderoga, the bridge of boats leading to the eastern shore, and Mt. Independence would be within range of enemy artillery. St. Clair, however, lacked the troop strength to adequately defend the surrounding terrain.

The British initiated plans on July 4 to occupy Mt. Defiance. The move to mount the high ground and unlimber artillery there was foolishly performed in front of American eyes, which gave St. Clair the time he needed to hold a council of war and decide his next move. At dusk on July 5 St. Clair began evacuating Fort Ticonderoga, the move masked by a large scale artillery barrage. As long as the Hessians did not move south and cut off the route below Mt. Independence, the route to Skenesboro (now Whitehall) remained open. Critical supplies and artillery pieces were moved downriver; two hours later the balance of the garrison crossed the boat-bridge to Mt. Independence and marched south.

Burgoyne discovered his opponent's escape the next morning and ordered a vigorous pursuit. He split his army into three parts. One wing was left to occupy Fort Ticonderoga and other strategic locations around Lake Champlain, while he led another section by water in pursuit south down the lake. The third portion was placed under General Fraser and ordered to march down the western side of the lake in pursuit of the retreating Americans. Burgoyne had easily captured the important stronghold.

Casualties: British: one killed, one wounded; American: none reported.

Outcome / Impact: Fort Ticonderoga was the initial phase (with hindsight) of the Saratoga Campaign. Burgoyne's victory secured both the fort and Crown Point, Fort Ann, Fort Edward, Mt. Independence, and the control of Lake George and Lake Champlain. Ticonderoga's loss depressed the Patriots, but inept British leadership allowed St. Clair's command to slip away, though several hundred men were lost in the rearguard fight at Hubbardton on July 7. Today it is clear von Riedesel's Hessians should have been reinforced to cut off the only viable route of evacuation. Instead, Burgoyne had drawn men away from von Riedesel. If St. Clair's retreat is viewed as a tactical withdrawal, it can be argued the Patriot position was improved by the loss of Fort Ticonderoga because its disjointed outposts were consolidated into a larger, more lethal army that would play a significant role in defeating Burgoyne's New York offensive.

During this same period (June 26), a pre-dawn skirmish broke out at Metuchen Meeting House (Short Hills) between Lord Cornwallis's 5,000 men marching from Amboy, New Jersey, and 1,400 soldiers under Brig. Gen. William (Lord Stirling) Alexander. General Alexander broke off the fight, but not before losing three field pieces, 100 killed and wounded, and 70 prisoners.

Today: Fort Ticonderoga National Historic Landmark hosts nearly 100,000 visitors each year, with a wide variety of living history and interpretive programs.

Further Reading: Cook, Fred J., *Dawn Over Saratoga: The Turning Point of the Revolutionary War* (Doubleday, 1973); Ellis, Davis M., *The Saratoga Campaign* (McGraw, 1969); Luzader, John: *Saratoga: A Military History of the Decisive Campaign of the American Revolution* (Savas Beatie, 2007).

Hubbardton, Battle of (Saratoga Campaign)

Date: July 7, 1777.

Region: Northern Colonies (New York and Vermont).

Commanders: British: Major General John Burgoyne, Major General Friedrich von Riedesel, and Brigadier General Simon Fraser; American: Lieutenant Colonel Seth Warner.

Time of Day / Length of Action: Early morning, three hours.

Weather Conditions: Clear and warm.

Opposing Forces: Total: British: 1,030 (advance guard); American: 1,100 (rear guard).

British Perspective: In the spring of 1777, Maj. Gen. John Burgoyne was dispatched to Québec to take charge of British forces in Canada and lead an offensive into western New York, where he was to crush Patriot forces in that region. He would then march south to Albany and join forces with Gen. William Howe's army for additional offensive operations. Burgoyne left 3,700 troops in Canada with Gen. Sir Guy Carleton while he led a 9,100-man expeditionary force south along Lake Champlain to capture Fort Ticonderoga. At the same time, another British force, about 2,000 men led by Lt. Col. Barry St. Leger, would march around to the west and attack

Patriots operating in the Mohawk Valley before moving to Albany. Howe, meanwhile, would lead the main British army north up the Hudson River from New York City to join St. Leger and Burgoyne at Albany. If successful, the three-pronged offensive would crush the rebellion in New York and separate New England from the rest of the colonies. It was an ambitious plan, but if successful offered perhaps the best way to cripple the rebellion and turn the tide of the war decisively in the Crown's favor.

Burgoyne reached Fort Ticonderoga in late June, and after initial captured critical high ground that made the occupation of the fort untenable. General Arthur St. Clair evacuated Fort Ticonderoga on the night of July 5. When Burgoyne discovered the withdrawal the next morning, he ordered a vigorous pursuit to catch and destroy the Patriot army. Brigadier General Simon Fraser's British and Maj. Gen. Friedrich von Riedesel's Hessians joined forces on the afternoon of July 6 and camped later that day just three miles from the American rear guard. When the enemy was discovered so close, Fraser determined to attack them in the morning.

American Perspective: General Burgoyne's invasion from Canada forced the scattered Patriots to funnel south to Fort Ticonderoga, where they joined with men led by Maj. Gen. Philip Schuyler, the commander of American troops in western New York (Northern Department of the Continental Army). One of his subordinates, Gen. Arthur St. Clair, was assigned to defend Fort Ticonderoga and the surrounding region. When Burgoyne arrived and secured high ground southwest of the fort on Mt. Defiance, St. Clair ordered his men to evacuate (some by water, others by land) after dark on July 5. Colonel Pierce Long, tasked with covering the main withdrawal route of American forces, was nearly trapped in Skenesboro on the afternoon of July 6, but he set fire to the town and slipped off in the confusion toward Hubbardton (now East Hubbardton), Vermont.

St. Clair, meanwhile, led the largest contingent of his army, about 2,500 men, overland south through Castleton with the intention of joining up with Colonel Long and much of the army's artillery train at Skenesboro. On the way they passed through the tiny village of Hubbardton. Militia officer Seth Warner was left behind on a piece of high ground to guide trailing regiments on to Castleton. Instead of the 150 men St. Clair intended, Warner ended up with about 1,000 soldiers in a camp around which he failed to post pickets.

Terrain: Warner's troops occupied a 1,000-foot elevation east of what is today known as East Hubbardton. This hill is the dominant terrain feature in an area known for its thickly wooded hills.

The Fighting: Warner's men held an advantageous position (known today as Monument Hill), but without a proper advance guard the position was nearly worthless against a determined and veteran enemy. Fraser attacked with 750 men from the west at 4:40 a.m. The initial wave struck a regiment of New Hampshire troops commanded by Col. Nathan Hale (not the better-known Hale) while they were cooking breakfast along a small stream. The assault routed the New England infantry. Warner and another regimental commander, Col. Turbott Francis, hastily formed their regiments and unleashed a volley into the front line of attackers, killing and wounding two dozen including some high ranking field officers. The fighting front stabilized into a 900-yard line stretching from 1,200-foot rocky and wooded Zion Hill on the American left into the woods on the far right. Forced to advance under fire uphill, the redcoats had a harder time of it.

A good tactician, Fraser quickly realized the hill was the key terrain on the field and stripped his own left flank to increase the punch on his right. Either forced back or by design, the American left flank on the hill slowly bent backward, which made it harder for the British to find the flank and turn and collapse it. Colonel Francis commanded on the American right and gained ground there with his Massachusetts infantry against the weakened British left flank. All along the line the Patriot infantry enjoyed the advantage of fighting Indian-style from behind trees and rocks—tactics the British did not fully understand or train for. The fighting was at close quarters and the result was mounting British losses.

Fortunately for Fraser, von Riedesel arrived with his grenadiers and jägers. He, too, was a capable officer and quickly realized the difficulties they were facing that morning. Without wasting time, the German general pitched in his troops as quickly as they arrived, some directly forward and others around to find and roll up the American flank. Von Riedesel ordered his band to play and his men to sing, which had a tendency to unnerve enemy troops and convince them they were facing overwhelming numbers. Within a few minutes Colonel Francis was shot dead (after the battle von Riedesel saw to it he received a Christian burial), the grenadiers had found Francis's flank, and the Massachusetts regiment was falling back. When Fraser's men finally launched a bayonet attack against the Vermont troops on the high ground, Warner knew he had pushed his luck as far as possible. Instead of ordering a traditional withdrawal, he spread the word to "scatter and meet me back at Manchester." Most of Warner's men managed to reassemble and continue evading the enemy southward to Bennington, Vermont.

The heavy battle had seesawed back and forth in the Vermont thickets for more than two hours. One of the war's leading historians claims the forgotten battle of Hubbardton was "as bloody as Waterloo" when one

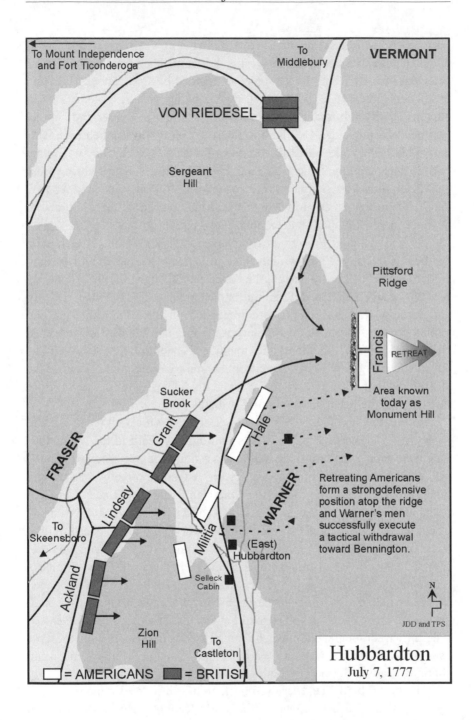

To Mount Independence
and Fort Ticonderoga

To
Middlebury

VERMONT

VON RIEDESEL

Sergeant
Hill

Pittsford
Ridge

Francis

RETREAT

Area known
today as
Monument Hill

Sucker
Brook

Grant

Hale

FRASER

WARNER

Retreating Americans
form a strongdefensive
position atop the ridge
and Warner's men
successfully execute
a tactical withdrawal
toward Bennington.

Lindsay

To
Skeensboro

Militia

(East)
Hubbardton

Selleck
Cabin

Ackland

N

JDD and TPS

Zion
Hill

To
Castleton

☐ = AMERICANS ▨ = BRITISH

Hubbardton

July 7, 1777

considers the proportion of casualties to the numbers involved (roughly one in four of those involved in the fighting was either killed, wounded, or captured). However, estimates of the losses on both sides vary considerably.

Casualties: British: 35 killed and 150 wounded; American: 40 killed, 40 wounded, and 234 captured (estimates), and 12 artillery pieces lost.

Outcome / Impact: The delaying action combat at Hubbardton was a British tactical success but an American strategic victory. Warner's initially inept stand succeeded in delaying Burgoyne's advance long enough to put a more comfortable distance between the British army and St. Clair's main American column. St. Clair marched southward in Vermont to Fort Ann and farther south to Fort Edward on the Hudson River. His route to the frontier outposts along the Hudson River wound through a thickly forested region, throughout which the Patriots felled trees from Skenesboro to Fort Edward. They also dug ditches and emplaced obstacles at strategic locations along the route, all of which slowed pursuit. The British eventually covered the 20 miles, but it took them three weeks to perform the arduous task. On July 29 Burgoyne and his army reached the outskirts of Fort Edward, but the Americans were by this time in the vicinity of Sarotoga. In hindsight, we know today that the evacuation of the American garrison from Fort Ticonderoga, coupled with the delaying action at Hubbardton, signaled the beginning of the end of Burgoyne's campaign. He would surrender his entire army to Horatio Gates just three months later at Saratoga.

Today: The Hubbardton battlefield is a Vermont State Historic Site that hosts an annual reenactment of the battle. The visitor center offers period artifacts, a fiber-optic map of the engagement, and other interpretive information.

Further Reading: Cook, Fred J. *Dawn Over Saratoga: The Turning Point of the Revolutionary War.* Garden City, NY: Doubleday, 1973; Ellis, Davis M. *The Saratoga Campaign.* New York: McGraw, 1969; Luzader, John: *Saratoga: A Military History of the Decisive Campaign of the American Revolution* (Savas Beatie, 2007); Williams, John, *The Battle of Hubbardton: The Americans Stem the Tide.* Vermont Division of Historic Preservation, 1988.

Fort Stanwix and Oriskany, Battle of (Saratoga Campaign)

Date: August 6, 1777.
Region: Northern Colonies, New York.

Commanders: British: Lieutenant Colonel Barry St. Leger; Indians: Joseph Brant; Tories: Sir John Johnson and Colonel John Butler; American: Colonel Peter Gansevoort, General Nicholas Herkimer, Brigadier General Benedict Arnold.

Time of Day / Length of Action: 10:00 - 11:00 a.m., and 2:00 - 3:00 p.m. (two hours of intermittent fighting between rain storms).

Weather Conditions: Warm, overcast with intermittent hard rain.

Opposing Forces: British: 2,000; American: 1,550.

British Perspective: On June 23, 1777, Lt. Col. Barry St. Leger departed Canada with a 2,000-man British force. His command was an integral part of Gen. John Burgoyne's grand three-pronged campaign to crush the rebellion in western New York. St. Leger's force was comprised of 340 British soldiers, 650 Canadians and Tories, and 1,000 Indians. His men hauled with them four small cannons and four mortars. St. Leger's column began moving by boat southwest from Montreal into Lake Ontario, landed at Fort Oswego, and began a 75-mile trek east toward the Patriot outpost at Fort Stanwix. For the next week his troops traveled an average of ten miles per day and arrived outside the walls of Stanwix on August 4.

American Perspective: Fort Stanwix was a strong frontier guard post designed to slow down or stop the British from entering western New York through the Mohawk River Valley. Originally built by the British in 1758, the bastion was allowed to deteriorate after 1763 until Continental troops rebuilt it thirteen years later (initially naming it Fort Schuyler). By April 1777 it was defended by 600 New York Continental soldiers under Col. Peter Gansevoort. The fort had undergone substantial improvements just that spring and was well prepared for defensive warfare. Friendly Indians in the region informed New York militia Gen. Nicholas Herkimer that the British had invaded the Mohawk Valley and were marching east. To meet this threat, the New York militia rallied an additional 800 men and 60 Oneida Indians and marched to aid their comrades at Fort Stanwix. By August 5, the relief column was in camp ten miles from the fort. A messenger was sent to let Gansevoort know of their pending arrival.

Terrain: The thickly forested and lightly populated Mohawk River Valley made Fort Stanwix (present-day Rome, New York) an isolated outpost. Located along a strategic route through Iroquois country in western New York, the fort served as the regional hub of travel between Canada's huge lakes and waterways to the west, and the main route into the American colonies in the east. The fort was surrounded by the Mohawk River in the north and west, Wood Creek and Lake Oneida to the east, and marshy lowlands to the south, all of which were surrounded by hills. The strategic fort commanded a natural canoe portage trail that connected Wood Creek and Lake Oneida to the west with the Mohawk River to the east. Although isolated, the strategic location of the outpost cannot be overstated because it was impossible to travel west to east through the Mohawk River Valley without moving past the fort.

The terrain at the ambush site near the Oneida Indian village of Oriskany included a channeled trail through a deep 200-yard wide ravine surrounded by high ground and woods on all sides.

The Fighting: The British did not expect Fort Stanwix to be more than a small outpost, and so were surprised to find a stronghold in good condition and well manned. St. Leger failed when he attempted to intimidate the defenders by parading his troops before the American fort. Realizing his command was too small for a direct assault, he undertook siege operations by surrounding the fort in a rough triangular formation. The British regulars took up a position about one-quarter of a mile northeast of the fort on commanding ground. A large contingent of Indians and Tories were about double that distance from the fort, southwest of it near the west bank of the Mohawk River. Other outfits of Tories and Indians cordoned off the balance of the siege line. Because St. Leger did not have enough men to tightly seal every avenue of escape and still detach enough men to cut a 16-mile supply track, his siege line was not tightly drawn. Sharpshooters picked off curious defenders while St. Leger's remaining troops manned the lines and cut his supply trail. On August 5 St. Leger learned that rebel reinforcements were were just 10 miles to the east. He dispatched Joseph Brant and 400 Indians (and a few white troops) to attack the marching Americans. It was a major gamble because the besiegers were already thinly deployed.

When dawn rose on August 6, General Herkimer was looking for a Patriot detachment from Fort Stanwix to act as a guide for his American relief column. He was not aware that sympathetic informers had already warned the British of his approach. Six miles from the fort at Oriskany, St. Leger's men arranged an ambush with the British and Tories aligned to strike the front of Herkimer's command and the Indians arrayed to attack its flanks and rear. Herkimer's men were stretched out in a column about one mile long and did not detect the ambush in time to avoid it or take proper defensive action.

Exactly how the battle unfolded and how long it lasted will never be known. After the initial surprise attack (about 10:00 a.m.) the Americans probably formed a defensive perimeter and fought off attacks for the first hour of the action. Herkimer was badly wounded in the leg early in the fight,

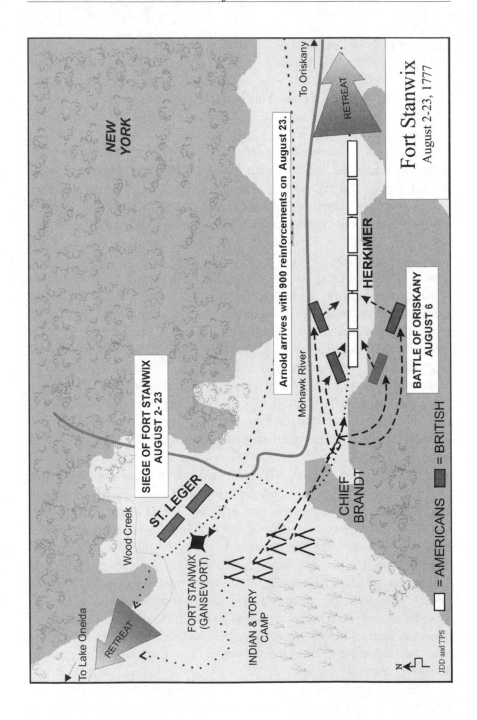

NEW YORK

Arnold arrives with 900 reinforcements on August 23.

To Oriskany

RETREAT

Fort Stanwix
August 2-23, 1777

HERKIMER

Mohawk River

BATTLE OF ORISKANY
AUGUST 6

SIEGE OF FORT STANWIX
AUGUST 2- 23

CHIEF
BRANDT

ST. LEGER

Wood Creek

FORT STANWIX
(GANSEVORT)

INDIAN & TORY
CAMP

To Lake Oneida

RETREAT

= AMERICANS   = BRITISH

N

JDD and TPS

but is said to have sat on the saddle removed from his dead horse, smoking his pipe and directing his men to fight on. The combat was a gruesome, often hand-to-hand brawl with clubbed muskets, tomahawks, knives, and bare hands. It dribbled to a close under a torrent of blinding rain that may have saved Herkimer's command from annihilation.

The Indians withdrew into the forest to regroup, leaving the German-American commander to pull back his men. After rearranging the militia the fighting began anew once the rain stopped. At one point the Tories turned their coats inside out in an effort to deceive Herkimer's militia into thinking they were a relief force from the fort, but someone recognized his Tory neighbor and more bloody hand-to-hand fighting broke out. Indians were not trained or accustomed to fighting sustained engagements, and by the middle of the afternoon were more than willing to break off the fighting. Unable to eliminate Herkimer's command, the Indians and Tories withdrew and made their way back to British lines. Herkimer and his few remaining soldiers withdrew to Fort Dayton, 23 miles to the southeast. After suffering for ten days, the general's infected leg was amputated by a French surgeon. He did not survive the surgery.

While the Oriskany battle raged the Americans at Fort Stanwix sortied beyond the walls and destroyed the Indian and Tory encampments south of the fort. The offensive strike demoralized many of enemy when they returned from the Oriskany combat. They had been sent by the British commander, had suffered the bulk of the casualties, and their camps had been sacked during their absence.

For the next two weeks a standoff ensued before the walls of Fort Stanwix, during which Colonel Gansevoort sent off messengers to the east requesting assistance. On August 10, Maj. Gen. Philip Schuyler, stationed at Stillwater, New York, dispatched Brig. Gen. Benedict Arnold with 800 men to assist Gansevoort's beleaguered defenders. Arnold's approaching reinforcements prompted St. Leger's Indians to desert (they were so frustrated they killed a few British soldiers before departing). Arnold arrived at Fort Stanwix on August 23 without incident in the wake of St. Leger's withdrawal. After a brief pursuit he left about 700 men to man the fort and marched east with 1,200 to join Horatio Gates's army as it prepared to battle Burgoyne at Saratoga. St. Leger's expedition, part of Burgoyne's New York campaign, ended with a retreat back to Canada.

Casualties: Losses for this fighting are particularly difficult to calculate. Reasonable estimates are as follows: British: (Indians: up to 100 killed; Tories: 50 killed and wounded); American: up to 150 killed, 50 wounded, and as many as 200 captured.

Outcome / Impact: The Oriskany battle was, according to one historian, the bloodiest encounter in proportion to the numbers engaged during the entire war. The fight was a tremendous strategic victory for St. Leger, who succeeded in turning back the American reinforcement column from Fort Stanwix. However, it was also obvious the British could not clear rebels from the Mohawk Valley without more fighting than they had planned for. St. Leger's defeat before Fort Stanwix kept him out of western New York and off Burgoyne's order of battle at Saratoga. His hasty retreat as Arnold approached also allowed that general to return to successfully battle the British invasion.

Today: Both battles have outstanding historic interpretive sites: Fort Stanwix National Monument, in Rome, New York, and the Oriskany Battlefield State Historic Site in Oriskany, New York. The former is part of the National Park Service system and includes a working replica of the fort and historic interpretation that brings the 18th century to life. Visitors can also explore the past at the Marinus Willett Collections Management and Education Center with exhibits that reflect the story of Fort Stanwix and the Mohawk Valley through the eyes of the people who lived in New York during the American Revolutionary War.

Further Reading: Ellis, Davis M. *The Saratoga Campaign* (McGraw, 1969); Herkimer, Gil. *Roads to Oriskany* (Alfa Publications, 1996); Luzader, John. *The Construction and Military History of Fort Stanwix* (Washington, D.C.: GPO, 1969).

Bennington, Battle of (Saratoga Campaign)

Date: August 6-16, 1777.

Region: Northern Colonies (Vermont/New York border). The battlefield is located in Walloomsac, New York, but is traditionally listed as the Battle of Bennington because of its proximity to the larger town of the same name. (In 1777, the border in this area was disputed by New York and New Hampshire).

Commanders: British: Major General John Baum and Lieutenant Colonel Heinrich Breymann; American: Brigadier General John Stark, Major General Benjamin Lincoln, and Colonel Seth Warner.

Time of Day / Length of Action: 3:00 p.m. to 7:00 p.m.

Weather Conditions: Hot and humid, overcast with intermittent rain.

Opposing Forces: British: 1,450; American: 1,100.

British Perspective: After securing the key facilities and terrain surrounding Lake Champlain and the outposts of the northern Hudson River Valley, Maj. Gen. John Burgoyne and his army faced myriad problems of logistics and communications. They were unable to procure adequate resources in the sparsely inhabited forest, and so suffered serious shortages of food and supplies. Moreover, the American forces were retreating southward from Lake Champlain and procuring most of the resources they needed along the way. On June 20, Burgoyne issued a desperate proclamation to the few locals in the region that if they did not assist his army he would authorize his Indian allies to wreak havoc throughout the valley. British raiding parties, meanwhile, were organized to sweep through the surrounding countryside in pursuit of subsistence. Burgoyne's logistical crisis threatened to turn his campaign into an epic failure.

To meet British needs, a large raiding party was organized by Maj. Gen. Friedrich von Riedesel. The German officer dispatched Col. Friedrich Baum of the Brunswick dragoons with 800 men (375 Hessian dragoons, 50 British infantry, and a mixed force of 375 Indians, Tories, and Canadians). As more than one observer has commented, appointing an officer who could not speak a word of English to rally support in an English-speaking region was shortsighted at best.

Baum launched his mission on August 9, moving east through the fertile farming communities of Fort Miller, Batten Kill, and into Cambridge four days later. He intended to link up with Burgoyne farther south near Albany. During these raids the Indians with Baum's column freely took civilian life and destroyed and confiscated the property of the region's inhabitants. While he was in Cambridge, Baum learned a band of 400 rebel militiamen was camped in the village of Bennington. He decided to move against them the next day.

About 9:00 a.m. on the morning of August 14, a brief skirmish broke out between Baum's advance and the men of Col. John Stark's colonial militia at Sancoick Mill (also San, Saint, and Van Schaick's Mill) about eight miles west of Bennington. The rebels retreated east across the Walloomscoick River and on to Bennington, where they made camp for the evening. The initial fighting convinced Baum the rebel force was larger than he originally believed. He sent a messenger back to Burgoyne requesting reinforcements. Baum, meanwhile, moved to secure a fording site on the Walloomscoick River, where he established hasty fortifications on either side of the waterway and retired for the evening. That night Burgoyne learned of Baum's request for reinforcements and the next morning dispatched Lt. Col. Heinrich Breymann with 650 men. A heavy summer rain delayed a second confrontation with the rebels on August 15, though it also delayed the arrival of Breymann's reinforcements.

American Perspective: As planned, by July 30, 1777, Brig. Gen. John Stark and his men regrouped in Manchester, Vermont, following the July 7 combat at Hubbardton. Colonel Seth Warner's Green Mountain Boys also reorganized there, allowing the militia to coalesce into a viable fighting force. Northern Department commander Maj. Gen. Philip Schuyler dispatched Maj. Gen. Benjamin Lincoln to join with Stark's men and lead them from Manchester back to the main army at Stillwater, New York. The Patriot leaders at Manchester sent a 400-man unit to Bennington to keep an eye on hostile Indians reportedly operating in the area. However, when the men learned that Baum's raiding party was threatening the region, they moved to the vicinity of Bennington. Heavy rain delayed the arrival of the Americans until August 16, by which date they faced the British and their hastily prepared defensive positions along the banks of the Walloomscoick River. Stark's position was about one and one-half miles east of Baum's, with a loop of the river dividing the opponents.

General Stark divided his column into three units for a difficult double envelopment. The first column under Col. Moses Nichols with about 250 men was tasked with moving around the British left into Baum's rear against what would be called the "Dragoon Redoubt." The second arm of the pincer numbered about 300 men under Col. Samuel Herrick. This column would have to cross the river twice to get into position behind or west of the British defensive works. The third unit of about 300 men was ordered to launch a more straightforward assault against the "Tory Redoubt." This column divided into two arms, one under Col. David Hobart and the other under Col. Thomas Stickney. Their movement was designed as a smaller version of the larger plan. Once the men were in position, Stark planned to bolster the movement around the right with another 200 men. He put his plan into action early that afternoon.

Terrain: The area where the fighting occurred was ten miles southwest of Bennington, Vermont (now Walloomsac, New York). The British fortifications were erected atop the dominant high ground just east of the village of Walloomsac. Another smaller British earthwork was established at the road entrance of the village where it crosses the river. As the Americans encircled the defending British soldiers, the river restricted Baum's safe movement and trapped his men within their positions.

The Fighting: Somehow, Stark's nearly impossible plan was executed flawlessly, assisted along the way by Baum's incompetence. Although he had seen men leave the American camp, Baum thought they were retreating.

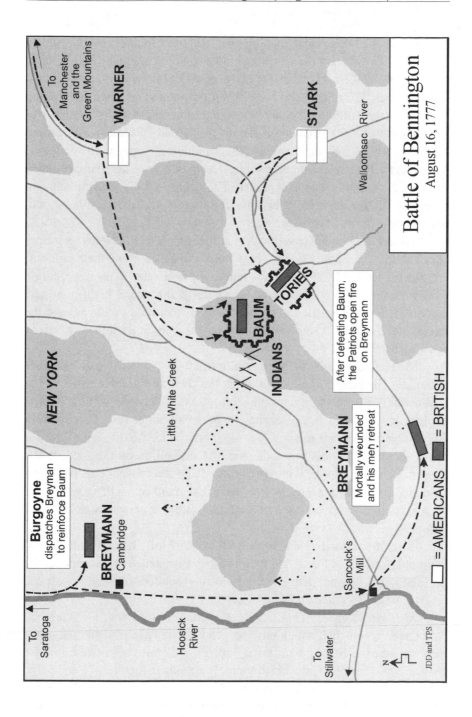

Battle of Bennington
August 16, 1777

When he spotted them again moving toward his rear he mistakenly believed they were Tory allies. When the attack opened about 3:00 p.m., the Hessian dragoons stood their ground and many were killed and wounded while most of the Tories, Canadians, and Indians put up but a short resistance before fleeing. As the battle raged, Stark moved out of his camp with the balance of his men (about 1,200) down the Bennington Road. Within two hours the Hessians within the fortifications (their numbers augmented by fleeing allies) had exhausted their ammunition. The only chance at re-supply ended when an ammunition wagon exploded. The Brunswick Germans tried to cut their way out, but when Colonel Baum fell mortally wounded with a shot to the stomach, the survivors surrendered.

Colonel Breymann arrived with reinforcements from Burgoyne's army shortly after the battle ended. They were exhausted from their arduous, lengthy (and painfully slow) march, much of it conducted in the rain. Stark's men were also tired and scattered. Stark decided to stand his ground and fight. At one point he tried to use captured British field pieces against the enemy but found to his dismay that he was the only one who knew how to operate them.

The second part of the fighting was much more confused than the earlier action. At one point it looked as though the German reinforcements would swamp the American right flank and defeat Stark. For a long while the battle settled down into a heavy exchange of small arms fire, but by dusk Breymann's men were running low on ammunition. An attempt to ask for terms for surrender was not understood by the militia on the field. When Breymann ordered a retreat the battle turned into a confused rout. The badly wounded British commander bravely led a rear guard action that saved much of his column from capture. Like Baum, Breymann was also mortally wounded.

Casualties: British (Hessian and Allies): 207 killed and wounded; 700 captured; American: These figures are widely disputed. Some sources claim 30 killed and 40 wounded, but the ratio of wounded-to-killed is suspect. Stark reported 14 killed and 42 wounded.

Outcome / Impact: This largely forgotten victory was a resounding American success that, with hindsight, echoes today as the beginning of the turning of the war in America's favor. Indians and Tories began deserting the British ranks, making General Burgoyne's already difficult 1777 campaign even more problematic. The loss was a humiliating and costly setback, and Burgoyne's logistical situation only continued to deteriorate. The spoils included hundreds of muskets and four small brass cannon. The waves of American pride that resulted rolled all the way across the Atlantic Ocean and spilled against European shores. Many in England were dismayed by the defeat, while officials in France acknowledged that the American rebellion (especially after the winter victories at Trenton and Princeton), was beginning to look more bankable. Coming as it did on the heels of Fort Stanwix, Bennington sent British hopes for a successful campaign that year spiraling out of control.

Today: Visitors can tour the scene of this fighting at the scenic Bennington Battlefield State Historic Site. This lovely 276-acre park includes a visitor center, historic interpretive markers and extensive walking trails.

Further Reading: Cook, Fred J., *Dawn Over Saratoga: The Turning Point of the Revolutionary War* (Doubleday, 1973); Ellis, Davis M., *The Saratoga Campaign* (McGraw, 1969); Lord, Philip, Jr., *War over Wallomscoic,* New York State Bulletin, No. 473, (Albany, New York, 1989); Luzader, John: *Saratoga: A Military History of the Decisive Campaign of the American Revolution* (Savas Beatie, 2007).

Brandywine, Battle of (Philadelphia Campaign)

Date: September 11, 1777.

Region: Northern Colonies, Pennsylvania.

Commanders: British: Lieutenant General Sir William Howe, Major General Earl Charles Cornwallis, and Lieutenant General Baron Wilhelm von Knyphausen; American: General George Washington, Major General Nathanael Greene, Major General Adam Stephens, Major General William (Lord Stirling) Alexander, Major General John Sullivan, Brigadier General William Maxwell, and Brigadier General Anthony Wayne.

Time of Day / Length of Action: From sunrise to sunset (three main actions occurring at 9:30 a.m., 4:00 p.m., and 6:00 p.m.).

Weather Conditions: Foggy morning, hot and humid all day.

Opposing Forces: British: 16,500 (including 5,000 Hessians); American: 11,000.

British Perspective: Lieutenant General William Howe had not fought General George Washington since the August 1776 Battle of Long Island. That action and the later combats at Kips's Bay, Harlem Heights, and Fort Washington had secured New York City for the Crown. Portions of Howe's army had clashed with Washington's forces at White Plains, New York, and again at Trenton and Princeton, New Jersey. However, decisive victory over the Rebels had thus far eluded Howe, who longed for the opportunity to destroy his enemy in a pitched battle. He was as well aware as anyone that he had let Washington off the hook at least twice.

During the spring of 1777, minor skirmishes erupted in New Jersey as both sides maneuvered for advantage. On March 8, Brig. Gen. William Maxwell's American troops faced off against the British at Amboy, and on April 13 Maj. Gen. Earl Charles Cornwallis conducted a surprise assault against American troops led by Brig. Gen. Benjamin Lincoln at Bound Brook. Neither action was decisive, though the British were able to strip valuable resources from the rebels (in the latter engagement, for example, the Americans lost an entire artillery unit).

Howe knew that General Washington had used the first half of 1777 to rebuild, train, and reinvigorate his army while defending the de facto American capital at Philadelphia, Pennsylvania. The American general was happy with the status quo, and so wise not to move hastily back into New Jersey or New York to seek a decisive battle, though Howe wished he would do so. Now a campaign against Washington and the rebel capital became inevitable.

Farther north, Gen. John Burgoyne's British army was moving into western New York on an offensive designed to split apart the northern colonies. Howe had promised his superiors in London that he would assist Burgoyne, but the general's pledge became impossible once he gained approval to launch his own campaign against Washington. On May 1 at Crooked Billet, Pennsylvania, 700 British soldiers tried to surround the isolated outpost of Brig. Gen. John Lacey and force a battle, but Lacey skillfully led his troops out of the trap at a cost of 36 lives and his supply trains. On May 20 at Barren Hill, Pennsylvania, another isolated rebel unit under Lafayette maneuvered out of harm's way, again without having to engage in a major fight.

General Howe launched his campaign against Washington at Philadelphia on July 8, 1777, when he loaded 16,500 soldiers aboard a 265-ship armada commanded by his brother, Admiral Richard Howe. The armada sailed for Delaware Bay. When General Howe learned the Delaware River was filled with obstacles he decided to instead make for Chesapeake Bay. The journey was longer than originally planned, but Howe wanted to move his army by water as far north as possible before marching overland to Philadelphia. After six difficult weeks at sea Howe's expedition landed unopposed near Elkton, Maryland. The journey debilitated soldiers and animals alike.

Howe's army moved north in two divisions commanded by Cornwallis and Hessian Lt. Gen. Baron Wilhelm Knyphausen. The expedition marched into enemy territory without too much difficulty, moving through northern Maryland, across the northern tip of Delaware, and into Pennsylvania. Washington's rebels harassed the invaders at several key locations and offered a sharp skirmish in Delaware at Cooch's Bridge on September 3. After another week of harassing fire and marching the British reached Kennett Square, Pennsylvania, three miles west of Chadd's Ford on Brandywine Creek. Washington was discovered on the far bank, his army posted in strategic blocking positions opposite the waterway's many fords. Philadelphia was just twenty-five miles distant. Howe was about to get his battle with Washington.

The plan Howe devised for his 12,500 men was a good one. General Knyphausen would lead a "grand division" of about 5,000 men in a diversionary attack against Chadd's Ford while Howe and Cornwallis led the remainder of the army northward along the Great Valley Road in a 17-mile button hook turning movement aimed at crossing the creek at Jeffries' Ford and flanking the American position. If Howe could convince Washington his main effort was at Chadd's Ford, he could slip the bulk of his army behind the rebels and deliver his *coup de main*. The flanking column got underway at 5:00 a.m. on September 11. A heavy morning fog combined with the darkness to make visibility all but impossible. One hour later Knyphausen's men commenced marching east along Nottingham Road to locate and press the Americans at Chadd's Ford.

American Perspective: The summer of 1777 was a critical time for Washington and the Continental Army. After doggedly defending New York City in 1776 when the Continental Congress was located there, he withdrew his army with some skill into New Jersey. Washington watched for opportunities to strike back and did so quickly and hard later that year. The battles at Trenton (December 26, 1776) and Princeton (January 3, 1777) surprised his enemy, demonstrated the fighting abilities of his own soldiers, and helped bolster flagging American morale. Though emboldened, Washington was also wise enough to know he could not commit to a true offensive strategy until his army was stronger and more experienced. Determined to avoid a large battle if at all possible, he spent his time drilling and organizing his army while protecting the young nation's capital at Philadelphia. His Northern Department, meanwhile, was gathering men and resources to fight against British Gen. John Burgoyne's New York offensive. When news reached Philadelphia that Howe's army had landed in

Maryland, Washington had little choice but to move his army into the field to meet it. American morale was high and his soldiers were eager to fight.

Brigadier General William Maxwell was assigned to lead the Patriot advance guard. His light infantry forces observed and harassed the British as they moved northward. The series of running skirmishes culminated in a well-planned ambush by Maxwell's 700 men at Cooch's Bridge on September 3. Using hit-and-run tactics, the Americans fought well until forced back. When it became obvious the British were pressing toward Philadelphia, Washington recalled Maxwell.

Washington decided to deploy his army along the fords of meandering Brandywine Creek three miles west of Kennett Square. The long defensive front would eventually stretch six miles along the eastern shore, with large concentrations of men behind most of the possible crossing points. Three primary routes (and several secondary roads) led east into Philadelphia, but it was Washington's hope to force a fight at Chadd's Ford, the southernmost crossing point along the main route on Nottingham Road.

Behind Chadd's Ford Washington posted two divisions, one on either side of the road. One was commanded by Maj. Gen. Nathanael Greene (1st and 2nd Virginia Brigades) and the other by Brig. Gen. "Mad" Anthony Wayne (1st and 2nd Pennsylvania brigades). Maxwell's light infantry was ordered to move west of the creek (on the British side), where it deployed on the high ground between the ford and Kennett Square. These divisions were supported by Col. Thomas Procter's Continental Artillery Regiment, which had unlimbered on a piece of commanding terrain northeast of Chadd's Ford where Washington also established his headquarters. A pair of brigades led by Brig. Gen. John Armstrong were posted one-half mile south of Chadd's Ford. Armstrong's men held the army's far left.

North of Chadd's Ford Washington's line of battle angled northwest following Brandywine Creek in an attempt to cover its various crossing points. Immediately above Chadd's, Maj. Gen. John Sullivan's Division (1st and 2nd Maryland brigades) covered Brinton's Ford, while Maj. Gen. Adam Stephens' Division (3rd and 4th Virginia brigades) and Brig. Gen. Francis Nash's North Carolina brigade (collocated with Stephen's Division) extended the line northward. Major General William ("Lord Stirling") Alexander's Division, comprised of one New Jersey brigade, one Pennsylvania brigade, and a company of Delaware troops, was posted bchind Painter's (Jones's) Ford. The northernmost positions at Wistar's and Buffington's fords were each guarded with a single battalion (about 200 men each), both of which were under the command of Col. Moses Hazen. Colonel Theodorick Bland's light Virginia cavalry unit patrolled the northern reaches of the creek to warn of any turning movement from that direction. Once these dispositions were complete, Washington and his men waited for the enemy to arrive.

Terrain: In 1777 the battlefield was twenty-five miles southwest of colonial Philadelphia. The gently rolling terrain—renowned for its beautiful meadows and orchards—was dotted with rural villages and farms carved from thickly vegetated forests. Many of the region's inhabitants were Quakers. The swiftly flowing Brandywine Creek was from three to five feet deep. With a few major exceptions its bows and bends run generally north to south, cutting their way through the countryside before emptying into the Delaware River several miles below Chadd's Ford. The width of the creek varied from as little as thirty feet at the northern fords to as much as 150 feet at Chadd's Ford in the south. Three main roads running east to west cut the battlefield, though Washington had to defend as many as eight different crossing points. The eastern shore was higher than the western side, which provided the Americans with excellent positions for artillery.

The Fighting: Once the sun broke over the horizon and the fog lifted, it was apparent to Washington that the British were approaching Chadd's Ford in force. Knyphausen's column was led by a crack force of riflemen armed with unique breech-loading rifles designed by their commander, Maj. Patrick Ferguson. Accompanying them was a unit of Tories known as the Queen's Rangers, who skirmished with Maxwell's infantry posted along the road and heights west of the ford. As the British vanguard approached Chadd's, a deadly hail of small arms fire raked the Tory line. Captain Andrew Porter's company of Col. Thomas Proctor's Continental Artillery (4th Battalion) opened fire east of the creek, but the artillery was poorly sighted and the fire generally ineffective. Several units from Greene's division crossed to the west side of Brandywine Creek and escalated the fighting at close quarters. Knyphausen's Tories, Hessians, and Ferguson's riflemen, however, gradually overwhelmed the rebels. By 10:30 a.m. the Americans were falling back across Brandywine Creek, leaving Knyphausen in command of the west side. The fighting settled down to long range musket fire and a fitful artillery duel.

Knyphausen's diversion effectively locked Washington's attention to the left side of his line while Howe's turning column marched north and then east. Howe crossed Jeffries' Ford about 2:30 p.m. Once across, Howe marched his men to Osborne's Hill, where they stopped to prepare for a thrust southward into and behind Washington's right flank. The move was not a complete surprise to Washington. Once Knyphausen's aggressive thrust opposite Chadd's Ford petered out at mid-morning, the American

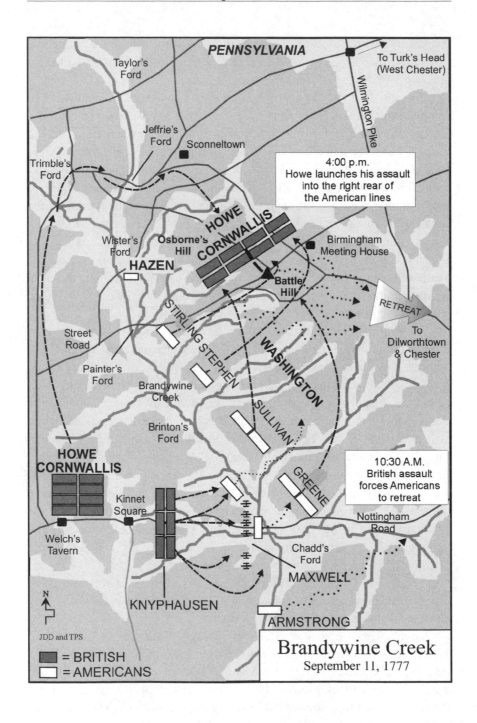

PENNSYLVANIA

Taylor's Ford

To Turk's Head (West Chester)

Wilmington Pike

Jeffrie's Ford

Sconneltown

Trimble's Ford

4:00 p.m.
Howe launches his assault into the right rear of the American lines

HOWE

CORNWALLIS

Wister's Ford

Osborne's Hill

Birmingham Meeting House

HAZEN

Battle Hill

STIRLING STEPHEN

RETREAT

Street Road

To Dilworthtown & Chester

Painter's Ford

WASHINGTON

Brandywine Creek

SULLIVAN

Brinton's Ford

HOWE
CORNWALLIS

GREENE

10:30 A.M.
British assault forces Americans to retreat

Kinnet Square

Nottingham Road

Welch's Tavern

Chadd's Ford

MAXWELL

KNYPHAUSEN

N

ARMSTRONG

JDD and TPS

■ = BRITISH
□ = AMERICANS

Brandywine Creek
September 11, 1777

general began to suspect Howe was moving to cross at another point. As early as 11:00 a.m. reports of a British column marching north reached Washington. Once these reports were confirmed, he ordered Alexander and Stephens to move with their divisions to Birmingham Hill, about three and one-half miles north and east of Chadd's Ford. This would bolster his right flank and rear.

Washington's aggressive nature revealed itself when he decided to cross the creek and destroy the enemy force opposite Chadd's Ford. If Howe had divided his army, then the smallest portion was alone and ripe for destruction. Before Washington could do so, however, a fresh report from Sullivan denied the existence of a British turning movement. The news placed Washington squarely on the horns of a strategic dilemma. He decided to cancel the attack order and stop Alexander and Stephens until the situation could be clarified. Maxwell's probes west of the creek did not glean enough intelligence to shed light on the confusing situation.

About 2:00 p.m. the confirmation Washington needed arrived in the form of a local farmer and a report from Colonel Bland's scouts. The former warned Washington the British were about to fall upon his rear, while the latter reported Howe's column forming on Osborne Hill well north of Sullivan's right flank. Washington ordered Sullivan north to meet the threat while Alexander and Stephens swung their divisions northeast in an effort to form on the right of Sullivan's line atop several small knolls known as Birmingham Hill and Battle Hill. Still uneasy about the unfolding situation Washington, together with Greene's division and two brigades, remained near Chadd's Ford.

To his dismay, Sullivan—who was temporarily in charge of all three divisions on that part of the field—realized his men were out of position; the two divisions meant to reinforce his line were well to his right and rear. Before he could reform properly, however, Howe attacked him about 4:00 p.m. The effort to cobble together a strong line on unfamiliar terrain threw the inexperienced Americans into confusion, though they put up a credible defense that impressed enemy observers. American artillery was particularly effective. For the next hour and forty minutes Howe and Cornwallis pressed the rebel lines. The heavy noise of battle in his right rear convinced Washington that the real battle was raging far from Chadd's Ford, and he made fast for Birmingham Hill with Greene's Division. Washington reached the scene of the fighting about 5:00 p.m., just as Sullivan's front was beginning to collapse.

Greene demonstrated his tactical abilities when he threw his men into line and allowed Sullivan's exhausted and now ineffective remnants to withdraw without the ensuing chaos one would expect from such a maneuver. Before darkness fell the Americans, after waging a magnificent fighting withdrawal, were in full retreat on the road to Chester. Knyphausen, meanwhile, had attacked across Chadd's Ford while Howe was assaulting Sullivan. Knyphausen overwhelmed the defenders at the ford. Both wings of the British army followed the retreating Americans as best as possible to Dilworthtown, when darkness put an end to the pursuit.

Casualties: British: 89 killed, 488 wounded, six missing; American: 200 killed, 500 wounded, and 400 captured.

Outcome / Impact: Brandywine Creek was a disaster for the American army. The losses were enormous (1,100 men and 11 cannons) and the capital at Philadelphia was now in danger of falling into enemy hands. Washington's intelligence service was abysmal, and he failed utterly to use his interior lines to defeat two widely separated enemy wings. However, just as at Long Island and again after the fighting around New York, Washington managed to escape with his army. Although badly beaten, for the time being he would remain in the field between the British army and Philadelphia. Knyphausen failed to keep up sufficient pressure against Chadd's Ford, allowing Washington to nearly stop Howe's flanking movement.

Today: In 1961, the Department of the Interior set aside a 10-square mile area that became the Brandywine Battlefield National Historic Landmark (most under private ownership). Within this area is the 50-acre Brandywine Battlefield Park (www.brandywinebattlefield.org), established in 1949 and administered by the Pennsylvania Historical and Museum Commission in partnership with the Friends of Brandywine Battlefield. The Chadd's Ford Historical Society also offers information about this and other area battles.

Further Reading: Freeman, Thomas J. McGuire, *Brandywine Battlefield Park* (Stackpole, 2011); and *The Philadelphia Campaign, Vol 1: Brandywine and the Fall of Philadelphia* (Stackpole, 2006); David R. Palmer, *George Washington's Military Genius* (Regnery, 2012).

"The Clouds," Battle of (Warren or White Horse Tavern), Philadelphia Campaign

Date: September 16, 1777.
Region: Northern Colonies, Pennsylvania.
Commanders: British: Lieutenant General Sir William Howe, Major General Earl Charles Cornwallis, Brigadier General William Maxwell, and

Lieutenant General Baron Wilhelm von Knyphausen; American: General George Washington and Brigadier General Anthony Wayne.

Time of Day / Length of Action: 1:00 p.m. to 2:00 p.m.

Weather Conditions: Cold wind and heavy rain.

Opposing Forces: British: 18,000 (including 5,000 Hessians); American: 10,000.

British Perspective: After defeating Gen. George Washington's army at the Battle of Brandywine (September 11, 1777), General Howe's British army spent the next several days treating the wounded and burying the dead. Although the rebels had initially retreated toward Chester, once out of immediate danger Washington had circled around in a great arc and was again maneuvering his army into position between the British lines and Philadelphia. Howe, meanwhile, focused his immediate concerns on securing a safe port at Wilmington on the Delaware River. By the 14th of September the British Navy was unloading supplies and taking on wounded British soldiers for evacuation.

On the 15th, Howe resumed his march toward Philadelphia. To his surprise, intelligence gleaned from scouts and local spies indicated the rebel army was holding positions along the upper fords of the Schuylkill River just ten miles to the north. Generals Howe, Cornwallis, and Knyphausen made plans to attack Washington. The British army crept forward in two separate columns in the pre-dawn darkness of September 16. Cornwallis led one wing with 13,000 men toward enemy deployed around White Horse Tavern; Knyphausen led the second smaller wing of about 5,000 men in two sections, one along the Wilmington Pike toward Boot Tavern and the other along the Pottstown Pike to Indian King Tavern.

American Perspective: After his humiliating defeat along the Brandywine, George Washington withdrew his exhausted army toward Chester, Pennsylvania. Early the next morning he ordered his soldiers to fall out at 4:00 a.m. The grueling march that followed consumed 17 hours in an effort to place the army in a blocking position between the British army at Brandywine Creek and the colonial capital in Philadelphia. The Continental force reached the falls of the Schuylkill River without incident and was once more in position to defend Philadelphia against Howe's British. Washington allowed his men to spend September 13 recuperating and preparing for battle.

On September 14, Washington marched his army another 14 miles west and took up several key locations along likely enemy approach routes. The leading element of his army deployed at White Horse Tavern, with the rest of the army taking up positions along a three-mile stretch of ground running east and terminating at Warren Tavern. Washington established his headquarters near the center of the line at Malin Hall. From this position the Americans could defend the important supply centers at Reading, Valley Forge, Warwick, and Coventry, and still cover Philadelphia. As far as Washington could discern, Howe's army was still camped around Chadd's Ford 10 miles to the south. Washington's brilliant and aggressive maneuver had effectively nullified the British victory at Brandywine. His Continentals were once again arrayed in a viable defensive line with their foe in front and the capital in their rear.

On the morning of September 16, Washington received intelligence that the British were advancing. In an effort to better meet his enemy, Washington altered his alignment by extending his three-mile long line southward a short distance. This allowed him to occupy key terrain along the crest of the South Valley Hills parallel with the Indian King Road from Three Tuns Tavern in the east to Boot Tavern in the west.

Terrain: The battlefield of September 16 is 20 miles west of Philadelphia in the town of Planebrook and a few miles east at modern-day Malvern. In 1777, the gently rolling terrain was dotted with rural villages and farms carved from thickly vegetated forests. The Schuylkill River provided a natural barrier between the combatants similar to their previous positions at Brandywine Creek. The river runs from Reading, Pennsylvania, in the west to Philadelphia in the east, where it empties into the Delaware River. Three main roads on the battlefield led eastward toward Philadelphia and several strategic fords, which the Continental forces manned.

The Fighting: About 1:00 p.m. Washington ordered cavalry led by Count Casimir Pulaski, supported by 300 light infantry, to move forward, find the advancing enemy, and delay the advance. Cornwallis countered this move by dispatching his own light infantry ahead of his column. The American infantry refused to stand and skirmish and was easily brushed aside. More American infantry led by Brig. Gens. "Mad" Anthony Wayne and William Maxwell clashed with General Knyphausen's advancing Hessian Jägers near Boot Tavern. The American line of battle ran through cornfields along the high ground overlooking the road below, and from this point they poured a heavy fire into a large advance party of infantry under Count von Donop's command. When Hessian grenadiers reinforced the Jägers the Americans withdrew rather precipitately into the forest. The brief fight against Knyphausen's troops had held the Americans in position while a British column under General Edward Matthew to the west moved

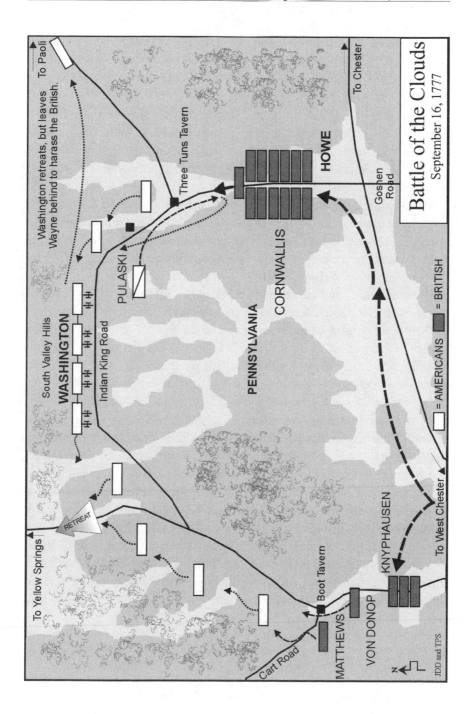

Battle of the Clouds
September 16, 1777

unopposed and swung into position on the American right flank. The British columns advanced in a brilliant triple pincer maneuver that rapidly carried them onto the high ground west of White Horse Tavern. Washington's extended lines were no longer tenable.

Just when it looked as if another major disaster similar to the fight at Brandywine Creek was about to erupt, a heavy rainfall cut the day's events short. Many participants left vivid descriptions of the torrent of rain that fell so fast and furious that, within minutes, the already saturated terrain was a lake of mud so thick it rendered movement nearly impossible. The rain and high winds ruined gunpowder and paper cartridges. Although the British contemplated making a bayonet assault, the sticky ground quickly made the option impossible. Washington wisely took the opportunity to evacuate the field in a strategic retrograde to the northwest while maintaining a defense of the fords across the Schuylkill River.

The rain and wind gave the surreal scene its nickname: "The Battle of the Clouds." Washington reformed his army along the high ground near Yellow Springs (now Chester Springs), and the day's fight ended as it had begun: in a standoff.

Casualties: British: two killed and five wounded; American: 18 killed and 13 wounded.

Outcome / Impact: The outcome of the battle was of little consequence. The Americans remained within striking distance of Howe's army. The torrential rain temporarily flooded the Schuylkill River, which prevented the British from crossing and marching on to Philadelphia. Meanwhile, Washington hurriedly moved his supplies to safety at Reading and replenished his army with ammunition. Both Washington and Howe dispatched scouts and spies to determine where and when their next clash would most likely occur.

Today: Little remains where the almost-major battle took place. Independence Visitor Center in Philadelphia, includes artifacts and other information about this action, as well as the other battles small and large fought during the Philadelphia Campaign.

Further Reading: Buchanan, John, *The Road to Valley Forge: How Washington Built the Army that Won the Revolution* (Wiley, 2004); Reed, John F., *Campaign to Valley Forge: July 1, 1777 – December 19, 1777* (Pioneer Press, 1980); Taaffee, Stephen R., *The Philadelphia Campaign, 1777-1778* (University of Kansas, 2003).

Freeman's Farm, Battle of (Saratoga Campaign)

Date: September 19, 1777.

Region: Northern Colonies, New York.

Commanders: British: Major General John Burgoyne, Major General Friedrich von Riedesel, Brigadier General Simon Fraser; American: Major General Horatio Gates, Brigadier General Benedict Arnold, and Colonel Daniel Morgan.

Time of Day / Length of Action: 12:45 p.m. to nightfall.

Weather Conditions: Cold and foggy in the morning; clear and warm by midday.

Opposing Forces: British: 6,000; American: 7,000.

British Perspective: By September of 1777, Maj. Gen. John Burgoyne's offensive, known today as the Saratoga Campaign, was not going well. His expedition had lost valuable material resources and more than 1,000 casualties. Although he had regained Fort Ticonderoga and Crown Point, and had secured the terrain surrounding Lake Champlain and the outposts of the northern Hudson River Valley, the British were too thinly stretched to be effective while the strength of their opponents was growing in terms of war materiel, unit strength, and morale. Moreover, Burgoyne's subordinates had suffered a humiliating defeat at the Battle of Bennington (August 16, 1777) and forces led by Col. Barry St. Leger in the Mohawk River Valley had returned to Canada. To make matters worse, Burgoyne's problems with logistics and communications worsened with each passing day.

Burgoyne, however, decided to press his operations southward toward Albany, New York, where he hoped to link up with Maj. Gen. William Howe's main British army, which Burgoyne believed was moving northward up the Hudson River from New York City to meet him. Burgoyne's army was moving toward Albany when he received word that General Howe had decided not to move there as planned, but instead had deployed his army to attack Washington and capture Philadelphia. Howe's decision bewildered the rather inflexible Burgoyne, who decided to continue moving south in New York.

On September 13 Burgoyne and 6,000 British troops crossed the Hudson River and halted at Saratoga, New York. By this time most of Burgoyne's Indian scouts had deserted him and British intelligence concerning the location and intentions of enemy forces was woefully inadequate. His supply line, too, was long and inadequate. Burgoyne continued moving southward and from September 16-18, his forces moved within a short distance of the Americans, who had occupied fortifications on Bemis Heights overlooking the Hudson River. Poor communications and inadequate intelligence continued to hamper the British. Burgoyne had no idea he was outnumbered and did not fully understand how the rebels were deployed.

The aggressive-minded Burgoyne decided to move forward from Sword's Farm, four miles north of Bemis Heights, and attack the enemy. He began his advance at 10:00 a.m. on September 19, a three-pronged movement south by southwest. On the right (west) was Brig. Gen. Simon Fraser and 2,000 men. Fraser's orders were to sweep in an arc and clear the fields and byways of Freeman's farm. On the left (east) were Maj. Gens. Friedrich von Riedesel and William Philips with 1,100 men. Their orders were to approach the Americans by marching south along the main road to Bemis Heights, which ran parallel to the Hudson River. Burgoyne rode with the center column, about 1,100 men under Brig. Gen. James Hamilton. The center column moved generally in the same direction as Fraser's wing; Hamilton's movements would be governed by the reactions of the Americans. Although Burgoyne's movement offered tactical flexibility, the massive reconnaissance-in-force would necessarily stumble blindly through the forest in search of the American lines. By about 12:30 Burgoyne's center column had reached the Freeman cabin, where a halt was called to await word from the remaining columns.

American Perspective: In the summer of 1777, with General Burgoyne cutting a swath southward through western New York, George Washington dispatched key leaders to help Maj. Gen. Philip Schuyler's Northern Department. Forces commanded by Maj. Gen. Benjamin Lincoln and Col. Daniel Morgan joined with Schuyler at Stillwater. In mid-August, within days of the Patriot victories at Bennington and Fort Stanwix, Maj. Gen. Horatio Gates assumed command of the entire Northern Department. The Continental Congress dispatched Gates to replace Schuyler because of political infighting and friction. Gates wisely moved his army to occupy strategic positions on Bemis Heights, adjacent to Hudson River.

Gates deployed his men within entrenchments along the high ground just west of the Hudson at Bemis Heights, about one mile south of Freeman's Farm. Some 3,000 troops and the majority of his artillery, which overlooked the river, occupied the positions on the east. General Ebenezer Learned and his 2,000 men defended the center of the American positions farther to the northwest at Nielson's Farm. General Benedict Arnold and Col. Daniel Morgan commanded another 2,000 men west and south of Learned. This latter sector was especially vital to the integrity of the American position because the terrain there was higher; if the British captured heights on the western flank, their artillery would be able to force the Americans to flee, just as they had at Fort Ticonderoga.

As Burgoyne's army felt its way toward Freeman's farm and the western approaches to Bemis Heights, Arnold finally convinced Gates to move out and meet him. Morgan's riflemen and Dearing's light infantry, with Arnold in support, advanced and deployed in the forest surrounding the Freeman fields to await the arrival of their foe.

Terrain: Freeman's farm consisted of gently rolling open fields surrounded by forests. Bemis Heights one mile to the south is a natural plateau east of the Hudson River and south of Mill Creek. Militarily this was key terrain that served as a gateway south to Albany, New York. The dense forest surrounding Bemis Heights provided the combatants with stealthy maneuver room as well as cover and concealment. At Bemis Heights, high ground extended north, west, and east, while the south remained flat and open. In the northwestern corner of Bemis Heights was Nielson's farm, a piece of land owned by a Patriot supporter. The fields of fire inherent in the open farmlands were excellent for both small arms and artillery.

The Fighting: At 12:45 p.m., the Americans opened fire from the trees on Burgoyne's advance guard. Morgan's men were expert marksmen. They trained their muskets on the British officers and knocked many out of the fighting early, demoralizing the foot soldiers. Caught in the open, the British were unable to effectively fight back and broke for the rear. Morgan's men gave chase but stopped when they met Hamilton's main force, fell apart, and then regrouped. By 1:00 p.m. Burgoyne had moved his command into the Freeman clearing with the 20th, 62nd, and 21st regiments in line from left to right, and the 9th Regiment behind in reserve.

The battle opened anew with a thunderous exchange that lasted for several hours, with neither side able to gain a decided advantage. More American regiments gave the rebels a decided numerical advantage and forced the British to spread their line thin to avoid being outflanked. Repeated British bayonet charges were thrown back with heavy loss; the 62nd Regiment was especially exposed and suffered terribly. Riedesel, who was leading Burgoyne's left wing near the Hudson River, heard the fighting and learned of the circumstances from a courier. Burgoyne ordered the German to leave men to hold the road and move west to strike the Americans in the flank. Riedesel moved out, reconnoitered the enemy position, and attacked with two companies. Burgoyne renewed his attack as Riedesel

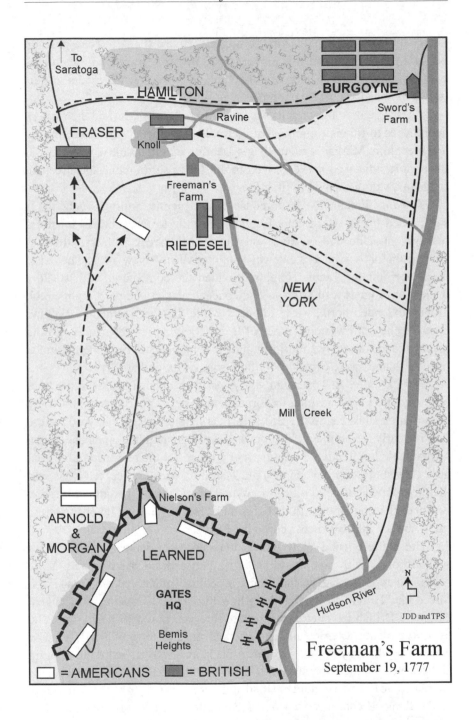

To Saratoga

HAMILTON

BURGOYNE

Sword's Farm

FRASER

Ravine

Knoll

Freeman's Farm

RIEDESEL

NEW YORK

Mill Creek

Nielson's Farm

ARNOLD & MORGAN

LEARNED

GATES HQ

Bemis Heights

Hudson River

JDD and TPS

☐ = AMERICANS   ◼ = BRITISH

Freeman's Farm
September 19, 1777

struck. Darkness was falling and by this time Arnold was with Gates in the rear. The Americans held for a time before withdrawing to Bemis Heights.

There are differing accounts of Arnold's role in the fighting. Almost certainly he was present and directing the tactical issues for much of the early action. According to some, he sent a messenger back to Gates requesting reinforcements, but Gates refused and insisted Arnold and Morgan return their men to their assigned defensive positions. Gates's role during the entire affair was defensive-minded. A strong attack from the defenders on the heights in the rear might have caught and easily overwhelmed Burgoyne's dispersed columns. General Learned's brigade had moved out to support the Americans late in the action, but drifted northwest into Fraser's wing, where a brief skirmish erupted that did not contribute to the main combat on the Freeman Farm.

Casualties: British: 600 killed, wounded, and captured; American: 65 killed, 218 wounded, and 36 missing.

Outcome / Impact: Burgoyne occupied the battlefield and could claim a tactical victory. However, the fight eroded British morale and chipped away at his dwindling resources. Because of the wooded terrain and his woeful lack of intelligence, Burgoyne did not yet realize that Gates outnumbered him, and his tactical "victory" that afternoon convinced him to continue moving against his enemy. On the other side of the line, the sharp punch the Americans delivered against Burgoyne's advancing column further emboldened the warrior spirit in the defenders of Bemis Heights. From within their strong positions the rebels awaited the next move of their foe.

Today: Saratoga National Historical Park on the upper Hudson river offers an outstanding visitor center, living history programs, and other cultural and historical activities.

Further Reading: Cook, Fred J., *Dawn Over Saratoga: The Turning Point of the Revolutionary War* (Doubleday, 1973); Ellis, Davis M., *The Saratoga Campaign* (McGraw, 1969); Luzader, John: *Saratoga: A Military History of the Decisive Campaign of the American Revolution* (Savas Beatie, 2007).

Paoli, Battle of (also known as the Massacre of Paoli), Philadelphia Campaign

Date: September 21, 1777.
Region: Northern Colonies, Pennsylvania.

Commanders: British: Major General Charles Grey; American: Brigadier General Anthony Wayne.
   Time of Day / Length of Action: 1:00 to 2:00 a.m.
   Weather Conditions: Cool, damp night.
   Opposing Forces: British: 5,000; American: 1,500.

British Perspective: After the "Battle of the Clouds" (September 16, 1777) ended prematurely due to heavy rain, the British went into camp at Tredyfferin. From this position, General Howe could move his army across the Schuykill River and attack Philadelphia to the east or the Patriot supply depot at Reading to the west. While in camp, local Tory spies reported that although the main army under General Washington had crossed over the Schuykill, a strong force of Americans had remained behind near Paoli Tavern to assault the flank of any British pursuit. In addition, the Americans left valuable supplies at Valley Forge. Howe, who rarely acted quickly, moved with commendable celerity by dispatching a veteran force under a capable leader to destroy the detached Patriots and retrieve the supplies.

   The officer in charge of the operation was Maj. Gen. Charles Grey, a distinguished officer with a string of accomplishments to his credit. Grey sifted through the intelligence and settled upon a stealth march within striking range of the Americans, followed by a daring night attack with only bayonets, musket butts, and swords. In order to achieve maximum stealth, Grey ordered his men to remove their flints lest an accidental rifle shot warn the enemy of their approach (hence his nickname "No Flint"). He moved out on September 20 about 10:00 p.m. with the 2nd Light Infantry Battalion and the 42nd and 44th Regiments of Foot. Although another pair of regiments followed a few hours later, but neither played a role in the fighting.

   American Perspective: After losing at Brandywine (September 11, 1777) and escaping a potential disaster at the aptly named "Battle of the Clouds" five days later, General Washington withdrew his army west across the Schuykill River toward Reading to refit and re-supply his men. In his wake was Brig. Gen. "Mad" Anthony Wayne's division of about 1,500 men and four pieces of light field artillery. Wayne acted as a quasi-rearguard to harass and delay any British attempt at pursuit. He took up a position two miles southwest of Paoli Tavern. Because he grew up in the area, he knew its roads and fields well. Despite the advantage afforded by operating in familiar terrain in an area filled with kith and kin, Tories also lived there. Anxious to see their rebellious neighbors quelled by their British allies, the Loyalists had no qualms about sharing intelligence on Wayne's dispositions.

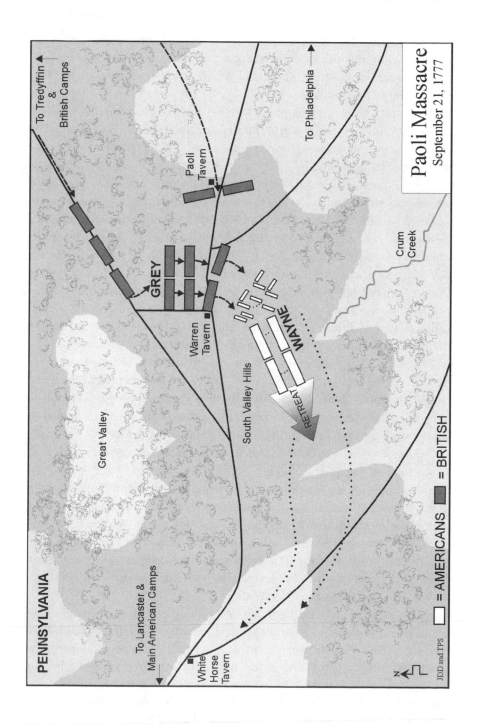

PENNSYLVANIA

Great Valley

To Lancaster &
Main American Camps

White
Horse
Tavern

South Valley Hills

Warren
Tavern

GREY

Paoli
Tavern

To Tredyffrin
&
British Camps

To Philadelphia

Crum
Creek

WAYNE

RETREAT

N

Paoli Massacre
September 21, 1777

JDD and TPS

□ = AMERICANS   ■ = BRITISH

By the time the sun set on September 20, Wayne and his men were settled comfortably in their tents. A light cool rain fell in the fields outside. Guards were posted in the camp and on the roads leading to it. Nothing seemed out of the ordinary.

Terrain: The battle took place 18 miles west of Philadelphia. In 1777, the gently rolling terrain was dotted with rural villages and farms. The American encampment was located in the South Valley Hills in a large field surrounded by thick woods.

The Fighting: General Grey marched his men quickly and was in position to strike about 1:00 a.m. He arranged his men accordingly and advanced east toward the sleeping bivouac, knowing a night attack was difficult to execute and even more difficult to control. A few American sentries posted on the outskirts of the rebel camp opened fire on the advancing British before turning to flee and raise the alarm. A surprised Wayne ordered his men into battle formation, but he could not get his soldiers into fighting form before the enemy was upon him. The British had followed Grey's directive to the letter, and the only British weapons used in the first few minutes of the fight were the bayonet and the sword.

Illuminated by their campfires, the Americans were shot down quickly by an unseen enemy who relied on cold steel to rouse men from tents and finish the bloody work. Unable to rally their men into proper formations, Wayne and his officers saw to it the four artillery pieces were hauled to safety while the bulk of the army fled west in search of safety.

Casualties: British: four killed, seven wounded; American: 53 killed, 100 wounded, and 71 captured.

Outcome / Impact: Luckily for Wayne and the American cause, the bulk of his surprised division escaped to safety and rallied at the various taverns and houses west of the battlefield. A few days later Wayne's division rejoined Washington's army. A court of inquiry completely cleared Wayne of any negligence or blame for the embarrassing debacle. After acquitting himself well, General Grey led his men back to rejoin the main British Army on its campaign to capture Philadelphia.

Although the surprise night assault quickly ended any possibility of harassing Howe's army, the attack had repercussions few would have predicted. The Patriots viewed an attack against a sleeping enemy as cowardly, which in turn *increased* American morale. Outrage followed when word spread that the dead had been "mangled" before being buried in a mass grave. Rumors circulated that Grey's men had not offered quarter to those attempting to surrender. The name "Paoli Massacre" was used to describe the fighting. In reality, there was no massacre. Attacking at night with bayonets and swords could only result in hacked up and "mangled" dead and mortally wounded men, and the fact that Grey left the most seriously injured in houses for better care (and ended the action with 71 prisoners), belies the report that no quarter was given. However, the dead were now martyrs and the British were concerned that Wayne's hearty infantrymen would attempt to get even whenever the opportunity arose.

Today: The battle took place on ground that is now part of an expensive Philadelphia suburb. The Paoli Massacre Preservation Fund is trying to purchase the land for 2.5 million dollars. A monument was erected on the field forty years after the battle.

Further Reading: Lossing, Benson J., *Pictorial Field Book of the Revolution* (New York, 1850); Reed, John F., *Campaign to Valley Forge: July 1, 1777 – December 19, 1777* (Pioneer Press, 1980).

Germantown, Battle of (Philadelphia Campaign)

Date: October 4, 1777.

Region: Northern Colonies, Pennsylvania.

Commanders: British: Lieutenant General Sir William Howe and Lieutenant General Baron Wilhelm von Knyphausen; American: General George Washington, Major General Nathaniel Greene, Major General John Armstrong, Major General William Alexander, Major General John Sullivan, Major General Adam Stephen, Major General William Smallwood, Brigadier General Thomas Conway, Brigadier General William Maxwell, Brigadier General Francis Nash, and Brigadier General Anthony Wayne.

Time of Day / Length of Action: Attack: (6:00 a.m. to 9:00 a.m.); withdrawal (11:00 a.m. to 9:00 p.m.).

Weather Conditions: Thick fog and cool.

Opposing Forces: British: 10,000 (including 3,000 Hessians); American: 11,000.

British Perspective: For the British, the Battle of Paoli (September 21, 1777) eliminated the Patriot threat that had been plaguing their rear. General Howe was now free to focus his attention west against General Washington's main army at Reading or east against Philadelphia. Howe decided to establish his army along the southern banks of the Schuylkill

River from Gordon's Ford (now Phoenixville) in the west to Fatlands Ford and Valley Forge in the east. The construction of a bridge across the river at Gordon's Ford was undertaken, which enticed Washington to focus his attention on Reading instead of Philadelphia. The British ruse worked well, and on the 22nd of September Howe ordered his army to cross the fords at both ends of the river and move toward the colonial capital. Marching unopposed in two columns along the Ridge Road and Germantown Pike, Howe's British occupied Germantown on September 25. This move placed his army between Washington's command and Philadelphia. The British were now within five miles of the city. Howe dispatched scouts to reconnoiter routes leading southward into the colonial capital.

On September 26, while Howe remained in Germantown five miles north of the city with 9,500 men, Lord Cornwallis and 3,000 troops moved south and occupied Philadelphia without resistance about 10:00 a.m. Local Tories were all that remained in the capital, the rebels and their Congress having evacuated the city. It had taken Howe 80 days and a great expenditure of lives and treasure to capture the Patriot capital. Unlike in Europe, however, there was no request for surrender terms and no discussion of ending the war. As they had in the past when the British captured New York and Boston, the Americans simply moved their capital elsewhere, this time to York, Pennsylvania.

Howe's success offered a new problem for his command: supply. While he focused efforts to eliminate bands of rebels operating in the area, he also had to feed his army. The enemy maintained a small naval fleet and two forts south of Philadelphia that prevented the British from moving supply ships up the Delaware River. Supplies had to be hauled from Head of Elk. On October 3, Howe learned Washington's army was advancing toward Germantown. The British general did not believe his enemy capable of striking a serious blow so soon after several defeats. His response was to order his outposts advanced with a warning to be observant.

American Perspective: September 1777 had been a month of setbacks and defeats for the Patriot cause. The fight at Brandywine on September 11 had thrown aside General Washington's army and exposed Philadelphia to capture. The inconsequential fiasco known as the battle of the Clouds five days later was followed by a more substantial disaster at Paoli on the 21st.

General Washington reorganized his forces at his main supply depot at Reading. Scouts were posted along the northern bank of the Schuylkill River to watch the enemy and guard the fords while Washington contemplated his next move. He could defend Reading or Philadelphia, but not both. It was a difficult decision because he had no idea what Howe would do next, and to a large degree his own actions had to be dictated by Howe's unfolding strategy. Washington's scouts reported information that led him to believe Howe would attack his army at Reading, but by September 23 it was obvious the British were marching toward Philadelphia. Riders were dispatched to warn the citizens there, and Col. Alexander Hamilton led a small force into the city to retrieve valuable supplies, such as blankets, horses, shoes, and food. Cornwallis paraded his command into the city on September 26.

Although embarrassed about the loss of Philadelphia, Washington formulated a plan to turn the tables on Howe. Washington ordered the commander of the Pennsylvania navy, Commodore John Hazelwood, to vigorously defend the approaches to Philadelphia on the Delaware River at Forts Mifflin and Mercer. With the British supply fleet denied access to Philadelphia from the south, Howe was forced to disperse foraging teams into the countryside to feed his army in the city and to escort vulnerable supply trains from Head of Elk. Washington planned to choke off land routes to the north and west, locking the British into an ever-tightening enclave. He also decided Howe's position at Germantown was vulnerable to a surprise attack. Washington's own army had been reinforced and now consisted of 8,000 Continentals and another 3,100 militia.

Washington moved his army to Pennypacker's Mill. On the 29th he marched five miles east to the village of Skippack, where he remained until October 2, when he moved his army a few more miles to Centre Point. The Patriot army was now just 15 miles north of Germantown. American naval losses in the Delaware River, meanwhile, including the capture of the 32-gun American frigate *Delaware*, gave the British maritime capabilities above and below Forts Mercer and Mifflin.

With his army ready to attack Germantown, Washington moved out at dusk on October 3 to get into position for the assault. The operation was bold, but too complex for an amateur army to carry out. The plan called for a confusing night march executed in several columns over difficult terrain. General Greene's wing comprised about two-thirds of the army's strength. It was ordered on a wide envelopment toward Lucken's Mill against the British right flank. General Sullivan would advance from the north along Shippack Road to attack the British center. General William (Lord Stirling) Alexander moved behind Sullivan as a central reserve. Militia was stationed on either side of the army. General William Smallwood's Maryland and New Jersey infantry was ordered to march beyond Greene's left and get behind the British flank. On the other side of the army was General Armstrong's Pennsylvania militia, which would move along Ridge Pike along the Schuylkill River toward the British left. Every unit was to be in position to attack by 2:00 a.m., with preparations for the attack completed by 4:00 a.m. The attack itself would commence at dawn. The men of the Continental Army carried only their arms, ammunition, and pioneer tools. Each was directed to pin a piece of white paper on his hat for recognition purposes.

Although the Patriot army moved out about 7:00 p.m., the march was slowed by bad roads and other difficulties. Chestnut Hill, two miles north of Germantown, was not reached until dawn. The army was hours behind schedule and no one was in position as planned. Just as the sun was rising Patriot light cavalry ran into a British outpost at Mt. Airy on the Shippack Road, triggering the first shots of the battle of Germantown.

Terrain: The battlefield was five miles north of colonial Philadelphia, Pennsylvania. In 1777, Germantown was a small village where the main roads converged before leading into Philadelphia. The gently rolling terrain was dotted with rural villages and farms carved from thick forests. The Schuylkill River provided a natural barrier southwest of Germantown. It flows from west to southeast and empties into the Delaware River at Philadelphia. Three main roads passed through Germantown from the north and west to the city of Philadelphia in the south. The main British lines were established along these routes; Howe's headquarters was established at the southeast corner of the town behind the main lines.

The Fighting: Washington was traveling with the American center column when the fighting began. He ordered General Sullivan's center wing to lead the attack even though he was unsure whether General Greene was in position on the American left (he was not). Sullivan extended Anthony Wayne's division on the east or left flank, Thomas Conway's in the middle, and his own on the right (west). With a strong line of battle Sullivan advanced south against Lt. Col. Thomas Musgrave's British 40th Regiment of Foot, which had arrived to bolster the light infantry pickets. It was about this time that a dense fog descended and smothered Germantown. The fog and thick powder smoke reduced visibility to a handful of yards and slowed Sullivan's advance to a crawl.

Although the fog made it difficult for Sullivan to control his line of battle, it also hid his men from British musket balls. Musgrave's infantry veterans, outnumbered and outflanked on both sides, counterattacked briefly before falling slowly back as they delayed Sullivan's advance, using each fence line and obstacle to advantage. Believing themselves cut off, Musgrave and 120 of his men took up a position in a stone mansion that belonged to former provincial Chief Justice Benjamin Chew. Sullivan's infantry washed around the position and continued moving slowly south. On Washington's right flank, meanwhile, General Armstrong's militia located

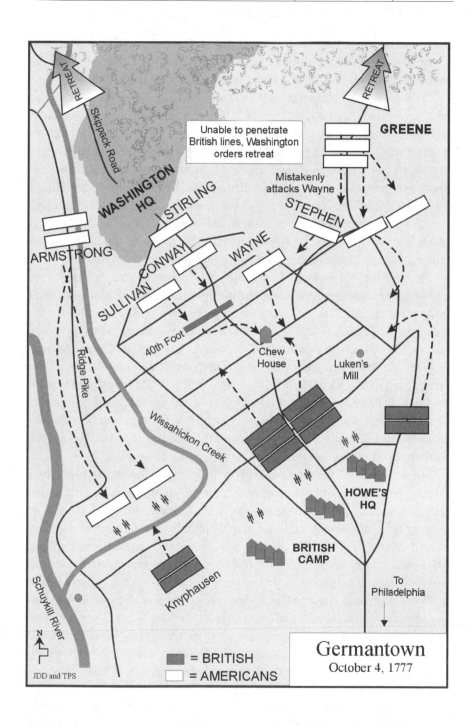

RETREAT

RETREAT

Skippack Road

Unable to penetrate
British lines, Washington
orders retreat

GREENE

Mistakenly
attacks Wayne

WASHINGTON
HQ

STIRLING

STEPHEN

ARMSTRONG

CONWAY

WAYNE

SULLIVAN

40th Foot

Chew
House

Luken's
Mill

Ridge Pike

Wissahickon Creek

HOWE'S
HQ

Knyphausen

BRITISH
CAMP

Schuykill River

To
Philadelphia

N

JDD and TPS

■ = BRITISH
☐ = AMERICANS

Germantown
October 4, 1777

the left of Howe's line, which was held by Hessians under Wilhelm von Knyphausen. Armstrong unlimbered a few light artillery pieces to hold the enemy's attention, but little else was achieved on that flank.

Matters on the American left were not going well. Both Greene and Smallwood had taken the wrong road and for a time were lost. Eventually Greene reached his assigned position north of Lucken's Mill about 45 minutes after the fighting began. He deployed Stephen's division on his right (west), his own in the center, and Alexander McDougall's brigade on the left (east) and advanced. However, the British line had been extended farther east than Greene expected. As his men bore down southwest toward Meeting House with the intent of converging with Sullivan at Market Square, General Stephen's men veered sharply west toward the sound of the Chew house fighting—directly toward Sullivan's (Wayne's) exposed left flank.

While Armstrong was lobbing shells and Greene was struggling to hold his battle line together and turn the British right flank, the fighting continued in the center where British infantry was using the houses and fences to form a defensive line. Artillerist Henry Knox convinced Washington that the Chew bastion needed to be isolated and captured, not bypassed and ignored. William Maxwell's brigade was bought up for that purpose. When a man carrying a flag of truce was shot down, light artillery was brought up to shell the Chew house. Unable to inflict sufficient damage, an infantry charge was launched. That, too, failed. Howe, meanwhile, was preparing to order the evacuation of not only Germantown but Philadelphia under belief that the wide American front threatened to overwhelm his command.

General Wayne, meanwhile, holding Sullivan's left flank, was thrusting forward beyond the Chew house, cutting deeply into the British defensive line. The climax of the battle was at hand. Without warning a body of infantry fired into Wayne's left and rear. Stephen's men (Greene's wing) had arrived, mistaken Wayne's men for the enemy, and engaged them. Fighting was now taking place behind both of Wayne's flanks. Tired, running low on ammunition, and believing they were being cut off, Wayne's infantry began to retreat. As they streamed rearward out of the fog they announced to anyone who would listen that the enemy was flanking them. The promising attack through the British center was over. Wayne's retreat exposed Conway's left and his troops also fell back; Sullivan's men followed shortly thereafter, leaving behind a mortally wounded Gen. Francis Nash, who fell leading his North Carolina brigade near the Chew residence.

Within this confusion Greene continued pushing his men southwest into Germantown until his left flank was attacked by British reinforcements. A large portion of the 9th Virginia Regiment was trapped and cut off in front of the main advance. The fighting signaled a large-scale British counterattack, and Cornwallis arrived about this time from Philadelphia with additional reinforcements. When Greene realized he was fighting the battle alone he ordered a withdrawal, which was skillfully executed. The British followed the diverging American columns for about ten miles before stout rear guard actions and bad roads ended the pursuit.

Casualties: British: 71 killed, 450 wounded, and 14 captured; American: 152 killed, 521 wounded, and 400 captured.

Outcome / Impact: The sharp American tactical defeat at Germantown had consequences far beyond the battlefield. The immediate result was that the British maintained their grip on Philadelphia. Except for the American holdouts led by Commodore Hazelwood on the Delaware River, Howe remained master of the region as winter approached. Once the British fleet established control of the Delaware River, the strategic situation in the Northern colonies threatened to change dramatically.

Washington's complex battle plan with amateur soldiers was unwieldy and almost doomed to failure. However, his army retreated intact and the men sensed they had nearly won a decisive battle under difficult conditions. Though outgeneraled at Brandywine, they had also fought well on that field. They were well on the way to becoming hardened veterans. Two weeks later, British Gen. Johnny Burgoyne surrendered his entire army to Horatio Gates at Saratoga in upstate New York. All of these facts were not lost on foreign observers. The French relied upon the enhanced American fighting capabilities, together with the important victory at Saratoga, to enter the war against England in 1778.

One other smaller consequence of the battle was the courts-martial of General Stephen, who was found to have been drunk during the battle and dismissed from the service. He was replaced with Frenchman Marquis de Lafayette.

Today: The battle is interpreted by the Germantown Historical Society and visitor center, located in Market Square in downtown Germantown. The two-story Chew house, which is in private hands, still stands.

Further Reading: Golway, Terry, *Washington's General: Nathanael Greene and the Triumph of the American Revolution* (Henry Holt, 2005); MaGuire, Thomas J., *The Surprise of Germantown: Or, the Battle of Cliveden, October 4th, 1777* (Thomas Publications, 1996).

The Hudson Highlands, Battle of (also known as the Battle of Fort Montgomery and Fort Clinton) (Saratoga Campaign)

Date: October 6, 1777.

Region: Northern Colonies, New York.

Commanders: British: Major General Sir Henry Clinton, Sir James Wallace (naval commander), Major General John Vaughan, and Lieutenant Colonel Archibald Campbell; American: Brigadier General George Clinton and Brigadier General James Clinton.

Time of Day / Length of Action: 5:00 p.m. to 8:00 p.m.

Weather Conditions: Cold and rainy.

Opposing Forces: British: 3,100 (composite British, Hessian, and Loyalists Provincials); American: 600 (composite Continental Line and local militia).

British Perspective: After fighting a costly tactical victory at Freeman's Farm on September 19, 1777, General Burgoyne was for pressing southward toward Bemis Heights to engage Horatio Gates's Patriot army. General Simon Fraser, however, urged caution. The soldiers were tired and apprehensive after the sharp and narrowly won affair. Burgoyne's army had dwindled to just 5,000 men, supplies were dangerously low, and replenishment of food, ammunition, and manpower were not close at hand. Fraser's counsel was prudent and warranted—and especially understandable since Fraser's column had been designated to lead the offensive the next day against American defensive positions on Bemis Heights. Burgoyne heeded Fraser's advice and instead ordered his men to prepare defensive entrenchments.

A messenger arrived on September 21 with word from New York City that Maj. Gen. Sir Henry Clinton was planning to move north up the Hudson River with an army to reinforce Burgoyne's embattled command. The message emboldened Burgoyne, who ordered his men to hasten their construction of a line of defenses that included five interconnected redoubts at strategic points stretching from Freeman's Farm in the west to the Hudson River in the east. Burgoyne would await the arrival of General Clinton and his reinforcements before going over on the offensive.

The expedition upon which Burgoyne's existence depended did not depart until October 3. Clinton's command consisted of 3,100 men apportioned in three divisions. Clinton reached King's Ferry, six miles below a pair of American forts guarding the Hudson Highlands, on October

5. There, he divided his army into two wings. On the eastern shore at Verplanck's Point he dispatched a 1,000-man force to move northeast and cut off rebel reinforcements from aiding Clinton's intended targets: Forts Montgomery and Clinton. In order to assault the American forts, Clinton debarked the remaining two-thirds of his command at Stony Point, the landing on the western shore of the river. Once ashore, the 2,100 British and Hessians troops marched north to reach the American strongholds. Although the distance to the forts was just six miles, the terrain was steep and the trails wound their way through dense forests.

The British crossed Dunderburg Mountain without incident. On the far (north side) of the mountain at Doodletown Clinton split his command into two columns to maximize surprise and threaten both forts simultaneously. Lieutenant Colonel Archibald Campbell led 900 men west around Bear Mountain and across Popolopen Creek to get behind the enemy and attack Fort Montgomery from the rear, or western side. Clinton remained with Maj. Gen. John Vaughan, who led the other assault force of 1,200 men along the trail northward to attack Fort Clinton. That afternoon American skirmishers opened fire on both British columns as they approached their respective targets, triggering the battle for the Hudson Highlands.

American Perspective: Waiting within the American fortifications on Bemis Heights was the bloodied Continental Army led by Maj. Gen. Horatio Gates. Not an audacious commander, Gates was content to await General Burgoyne's next move. While Gates marked time on Bemis Heights, Patriot forces assigned to defensive positions guarding the entrance to the Hudson Highlands worked to complete two forts on the Hudson River 100 miles south of Albany, New York. Their commander was Brig. Gen. George Clinton (not to be confused with the British commander with the same last name). The forts over which the American Clinton (who was also the governor of New York) labored were named Montgomery, in honor of fallen Patriot Gen. Richard Montgomery, and Clinton, after himself as commander of the forces in that region. Built on opposite banks of Popolopen Creek, which emptied into the Hudson River on its western shore at a strategic bend, eight miles south of West Point, the bastions were key to the strategic defense of the Hudson Highlands.

Fort Montgomery guarded the northern bank of the creek and Fort Clinton the southern bank. To the east of both forts flowed the majestic Hudson River. All told, the Americans fielded 600 men and 20 pieces of heavy artillery. The Patriots strung a heavy iron chain across the river and seeded the water with log obstacles to disrupt any maritime assault upon the

American forts. Patrolling the Hudson were two Americans warships, *Montgomery* and *Congress*, supported by a handful of smaller vessels.

Major General Israel Putnam maintained a small mobile army on the opposite shore, but Putnam's force had been thinned to only 1,500 men because of the reinforcements he had sent northward to join Gates at Bemis Heights. On October 6 Putnam moved his command north when the British suddenly appeared in the Hudson River and landed troops at Verplanck's Point, threatening his position. Putnam's move left the defenders of Forts Montgomery and Clinton in a vulnerable situation.

When he learned of the British threat against the Hudson Highlands, General Clinton (who had been away tending to his responsibilities as governor) returned immediately to the forts. He physically commanded from the ramparts of Fort Clinton (some sources claim Fort Montgomery). His brother, Brig. Gen. James Clinton, commanded the men holding Fort Montgomery. Each Clinton dispatched a 100-man skirmishing party in front of the respective paths leading to each fort, where each group engaged in running skirmishes with the approaching enemy. It was late in the afternoon by the time the British arrived outside the forts.

Terrain: The terrain surrounding Forts Montgomery and Clinton was flat or gently rolling for a relatively short distance before dropping steeply to the river. It was also thickly wooded beginning some distance from the ramparts. Fort Clinton was constructed on the south side of Popolopen Creek on a rocky ridge overlooking the Hudson River below, oriented to cover a 400-yard wide plain before the drop to the waterway. Fort Montgomery also overlooked the Hudson River but was situated on the northern shore of Popolopen Creek, which ran west from the Hudson. At 1,400 feet, it was higher in elevation than Fort Clinton, which was only 123 feet.

The Fighting: After a perfunctory request that the defenders capitulate (which was rejected), the twin assaults began. There was no element of surprise or effort at finesse. The British attacked nearly simultaneously with the sun setting behind Lt. Col. Archibald Campbell's columns. Sir James Wallace's British river fleet also arrived and opened fire on the American vessels and forts, providing the British land forces with supporting fire.

Fort Montgomery fell first. Campbell's command of British regulars, New York loyalists, and hired Hessians stormed the bastion. Campbell's men seem to have made it easily over Fort Montgomery's ramparts, but he was killed early in the effort. Infuriated, the attacking infantry initially refused to give quarter to the stunned rebel defenders. Survivors fled north or across the Hudson with the help of several small vessels. Well placed fire by the American ship *Montgomery* aided their rush to safety.

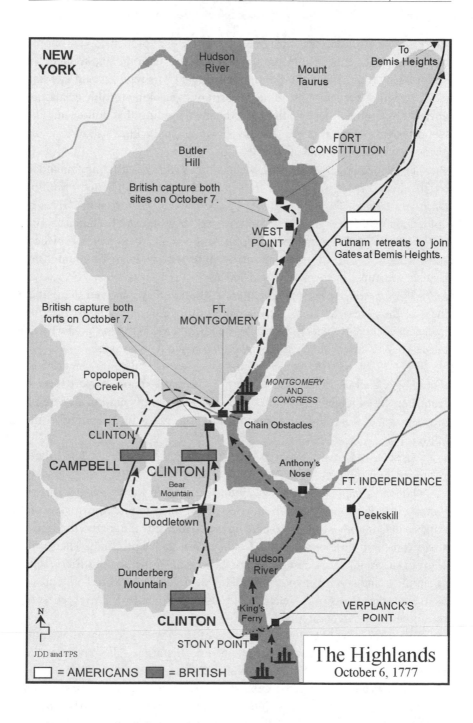

NEW YORK

Hudson River

Mount Taurus

To Bemis Heights

FORT CONSTITUTION

Butler Hill

British capture both sites on October 7.

WEST POINT

Putnam retreats to join Gates at Bemis Heights.

British capture both forts on October 7.

FT. MONTGOMERY

Popolopen Creek

MONTGOMERY AND CONGRESS

FT. CLINTON

Chain Obstacles

CAMPBELL   CLINTON

Bear Mountain

Anthony's Nose

FT. INDEPENDENCE

Doodletown

Peekskill

Dunderberg Mountain

Hudson River

VERPLANCK'S POINT

CLINTON

King's Ferry

STONY POINT

N

JDD and TPS

☐ = AMERICANS   ▨ = BRITISH

The Highlands
October 6, 1777

Fort Clinton's defenders offered a better account of themselves, but the outcome was the same. Sir Henry Clinton ordered his command to launch a direct attack (there was little room to maneuver). His regulars and Hessian allies swept forward through a line of obstructions, taking terrible casualties during the approach and in the close-quarter fighting that followed. The weight of British metal carried the day, however, and within a short time the garrison was dead, wounded, captured, or fleeing.

The sudden and overwhelming land attacks were devastating, but aided by the heavy maritime assault they proved irresistible. British warhips *Diligent, Crane, Dependence, Spitfire, Preston, Tartar,* and *Mercury* unloaded tons of shot and shell into the forts. *Dependence* fired nearly 100 rounds from its 24-pounders and more rounds from its smaller pieces, showering both Fort Clinton and enemy ships with its iron. To counter the British warships, the Americans relied upon the *Montgomery, Congress, Lady Washington, Shark,* and *Camden.* Although they survived the battle, most of the American ships were unable to move upriver against the tide later that evening. *Camden* was run aground and captured; *Montgomery* was burned by her crew. Only *Lady Washington* made it away safely.

By 7:30 or 8:00 p.m. the fighting was over. Only 300 Americans, including Generals James and Governor George Clinton, escaped, most from Fort Montgomery. By 10:00 p.m., the deafening sound of exploding naval magazines and burning Patriot hulks offered a fitful ending to the battle.

Casualties: British: 190 killed and wounded; American: 350 killed, wounded, and captured.

Outcome / Impact: Sir Henry Clinton's offensive was a decisive British victory. The Patriots were outnumbered about three to one; this makes the American Clinton's decision to take up quarters inside the forts with such a small force and little or no hope of outside assistance puzzling. The result was not surprising: 50% casualties and the loss of 67 pieces of artillery, tons of supplies, and several naval vessels. However, the battle would only prove useful to the British if General Burgoyne's embattled army received reinforcements and re-supply.

On the morning of October 7, the fate of Burgoyne's campaign was still a matter of some suspense to Sir Henry and his army. The day after the Hudson Highlands fight, Sir James Wallace's naval force broke through the chain barriers and Sir Henry succeeded in moving as far as Fort Constitution and West Point, New York. Clinton, however, was still nearly 100 miles from Burgoyne and had not been in communication with that officer for nearly two weeks. Clinton had no way of knowing his efforts against Forts

Montgomery and Clinton had been for naught. Impatient, Burgoyne moved against the Americans at Bemis Heights on October 7. His decisive defeat there led directly to his surrender at Saratoga.

Today: Fort Montgomery was built in what is today Highland Falls, New York. The British tried to blow it up when they left, and nature did the rest of the work. The site was rediscovered in the early 1900s, and extensive archaeological excavations were conducted in the 1960s and 1970s. Local citizens established the Fort Montgomery Battle Site Association in 1997 and the 14-acre site was designated a National Landmark.

Further Reading: Cook, Fred J., *Dawn Over Saratoga: The Turning Point of the Revolutionary War* (Doubleday, 1973); Ellis, Davis M. *The Saratoga Campaign* (McGraw, 1969); Luzader, John. *Saratoga: A Military History of the Decisive Campaign of the American Revolution* (Savas Beatie, 2007).

Bemis Heights, Battle of (also known as the 2nd Battle of Freeman's Farm), Saratoga Campaign

Date: October 7, 1777.

Region: Northern Colonies, New York.

Commanders: British: Major General John Burgoyne, Brigadier General Simon Fraser, and Major General Friedrich von Riedesel; American: Major General Horatio Gates, Brigadier General Benedict Arnold, Brigadier General Ebenezer Learned, Brigadier General Enoch Poor, and Colonel Daniel Morgan.

Time of Day / Length of Action: Intermittent fighting, beginning late morning and lasting all day.

Weather Conditions: Clear and pleasant.

Opposing Forces: British: 5,000; American: 11,000.

British Perspective: Since the Battle of Freeman's Farm on September 19, 1777, Maj. Gen. John Burgoyne had strengthened his defensive lines in positions extending from Freeman's Farm in the west to the Hudson River in the east. To the south were the Americans and their fortifications atop Bemis Heights. Burgoyne had his men throw up defensive lines to ward off any American aggression until reinforcements led by Gen. Sir Henry Clinton arrived to strengthen Burgoyne's dwindling army. Burgoyne's excursion out of Canada through New York had started that June, but his army had steadily lost men and materiel.

By the morning of October 7 "Gentleman Johnny" could only field about 5,000 men, which meant his army had lost to all causes (sickness, death, wounds, desertion, and capture) nearly the same number he now had in the ranks. Eager to engage and destroy the Americans, Burgoyne had waited nearly three weeks for the promised arrival of Clinton's reinforcements. (He did not yet know that Clinton had abandoned the idea of marching to join forces with him in New York.) Short of supplies and with many men having taken ill, Burgoyne felt compelled to wait no longer and determined to take the offensive.

On October 4 Burgoyne suggested a turning movement that was spurned by his generals. Von Riedesel suggested a general retreat. Burgoyne decided to make another reconnaissance-in-force, much as he had done on September 18, 1777. The move was designed to push south by southwest and probe the enemy defenses. His senior generals disagreed with the idea, but Burgoyne decided he had to move, break through the American lines, defeat or scatter his enemy, and move south to Albany.

Burgoyne initiated his plan on the morning of October 7 with an advance divided in three columns and 10 guns under Brig. Gen. Simon Fraser: light infantry under Lord Balcarres on the right, Maj. Gen. Friedrich von Riedesel's Hessian jägers and Brunswick infantry in the center, and British grenadiers under Maj. John Dyke Acland on the left. Leading the main force in a wide arc to the west and south was Major Fraser's ranger company and about 600 Tories and Indians (which marched too far west and did not play a major role in the fight). Just as he had at the Battle of Freeman's Farm on September 19, Burgoyne intended to maneuver his columns depending upon how the Americans were deployed and how they reacted to his movement.

General Fraser led his three columns forward from their entrenchments around Freeman's Farm to Barber's wheatfield, but no Americans were spotted. He stopped to align his regiments in front of a branch of Mill Creek, his front spanning 1,000 yards. While Fraser reorganized and tried to identify the enemy line, non-combatants with his command harvested wheat (which at least one writer claims was a major reason for the move south; Burgoyne's animals were starving). On the far creek bank was a heavy forest. Unbeknownst to the British, hidden within the trees were several thousand American soldiers preparing for battle.

American Perspective: Following the Battle of Freeman's Farm, the Americans spent the subsequent weeks strengthening their defenses in anticipation of Burgoyne's offensive. Additional reinforcements arrived during this time frame. By October 7 the army led by Maj. Gen. Horatio Gates numbered nearly 11,000 men. Passive to a fault, Gates kept his army hemmed inside the Bemis Heights entrenchments along the high ground just west of the Hudson River. Some 3,000 troops and the majority of his artillery occupied positions overlooking the river. On the north-northwestern portion of the line was Gen. Benjamin Lincoln's division, which consisted of brigades led by Gens. Ebenezer Learned and Enoch Poor, Col. Henry Dearborn's light infantry battalion, and Col. Daniel Morgan's riflemen.

This area was built around Nielson's farm, a critical piece of terrain that dominated the American position. If the British captured this area, their artillery could force the Americans to flee as they had at Fort Ticonderoga. Augmented by newly arrived militia units, Lincoln's division numbered 3,800 men with another 1,200 militia available for immediate support. Lincoln's position extended from the fortifications at Bemis Heights into the forest and high ground to the northwest. On the American left (west) were 600 light infantrymen commanded by Cols. Daniel Morgan and Henry Dearborn. These men had borne the brunt of the fighting at Freeman's Farm on September 19 and were renowned for their prowess as riflemen.

Another 1,200 New York militia under Brig. Gen. Abraham Ten Broeck were stationed behind Lincoln's division as reserves. When Gates was informed the British were moving south from Freeman's Farm on the morning of October 7, Gates ordered Lincoln's division to move forward and meet them.

Terrain: The American defenses on Bemis Heights were constructed along a plateau just west of the Hudson River and south of Mill Creek. It was a strong position that effectively blocked British movement south to Albany, New York. The dense forest surrounding Bemis Heights provided the Americans with opportunities to exploit flexible tactics. The high ground was entrenched on the north, west, and east sides, while the south remained open. Each fortified face extended approximately three-quarters of a mile, with artillery redoubts built into the center of each line. In the northwestern corner of Bemis Heights was Nielson's Farm, a piece of land owned by a Patriot supporter. The fortified area here was dubbed "Fort Nielson."

The main fighting on October 7 took place northwest of Bemis Heights on terrain similar to Freeman's Farm. The British once again fought in an open field (Barber's wheatfield) north of the Americans about three-quarters of a mile southwest of the main British position at Freeman's Farm. The field

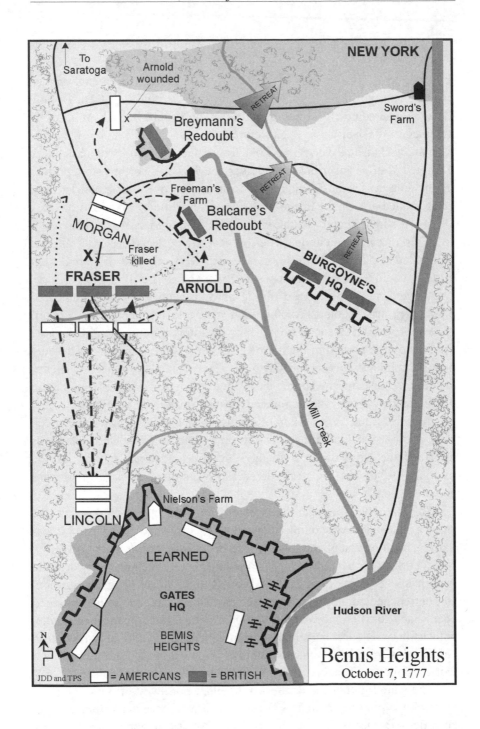

To
Saratoga

Arnold
wounded

NEW YORK

RETREAT

Sword's
Farm

Breymann's
Redoubt

Freeman's
Farm

RETREAT

MORGAN

Balcarre's
Redoubt

Fraser
killed

RETREAT

FRASER

BURGOYNE'S
HQ.

ARNOLD

Mill Creek

Nielson's Farm

LINCOLN

LEARNED

GATES
HQ

Hudson River

BEMIS
HEIGHTS

N

JDD and TPS   ☐ = AMERICANS   ▨ = BRITISH

Bemis Heights
October 7, 1777

of fire was good for both small arms and artillery. The Americans once again enjoyed the protection of the dense forest northwest of Fort Nielson, which also flanked the British position, leaving covered avenues of approach for the Americans to exploit.

The Fighting: Showing more initiative than usual, Gates ordered Colonels Morgan and Dearborn to advance through the woods and attack Burgoyne's right or western flank (Balcarres's light infantry) while General Poor's brigade did the same and assailed the British left or eastern flank (Acland's grenadiers). General Learned's men would hold the center (opposite von Riedesel's Hessians and Brunswickers).

The battle began when Acland's artillery and grenadiers on the British left spotted Poor's 800 men in the woods below them and opened fire. Poor's men (New York Continental regiments under Nathan Hale, Joseph Cilley, and Alexander Scammell, plus New York and Connecticut militia) had formed at the base of a slight elevation. Firing downhill is always difficult, and the British lead sailed above American heads. Acland ordered a bayonet charge, but before it could be delivered Poor's men raked his line with a deadly fire and launched their own attack. Acland and his men were cut to pieces, with Acland himself shot through both legs and captured. Morgan and Dearborn had similar success on the other side of the line against the British right flank, where the American riflemen attacked Balcarres's flank and rear. At one point the British were caught changing front when a volley ripped into them. Balcarres's command collapsed and fled toward the rear.

Fraser's center column under von Riedesel was now flanked on both sides. A courier from Burgoyne carrying an order to retreat was killed and the German general never received word to fall back. General Learned's column pressed forward against the British center. General Benedict Arnold, who had been dismissed by Gates after an argument following the first fight at Freeman's Farm, had remained with the army without a formal command. About this time the aggressive Arnold rode up on his own hook to assist Learned in the attack.

Arnold was instrumental in directing the combat as he rode through the American column urging the men forward. General Fraser tried valiantly to rally his men, to little avail. While he was working with the 24th Regiment to establish a foundation for order, a marksman named Timothy Murphy was ordered to shoot the mounted officer. His third shot mortally struck Fraser. The British and Hessians were well-disciplined veterans, but the pressure from both sides and the front forced them back. They finally reorganized well to the rear at Freeman's Farm around two entrenchments known as Balcarres's Redoubt and Breymann's Redoubt, and two fortified cabins in between. The fight near Mill Creek had lasted about one hour. Arnold realized the opportunity now existed to follow up the British defeat with a decisive battlefield victory. Ignoring Gates's order to return to camp—unlike Gates, Arnold possessed a killer's instinct—he urged the generals to press their advantage.

The second part of the battle began with an American assault on Balcarres's Redoubt on Freeman's Farm. Although the Americans pierced the line of abatis, they were unable to overwhelm the defenders. When the initial assault failed and settled into a longer range musketry duel, Arnold used Learned's arriving brigade to clear the reinforced cabins between the redoubts, which exposed the southern (left) flank of Breymann's Redoubt.

The Hessians inside held out as long as they could, but the redoubt, though well constructed, was not designed to withstand repeated and overpowering assaults from several directions. Arnold was shot down in the struggle, his leg broken by a musket ball. Heinrich Breymann stood his ground but was mortally wounded doing so. (According to some sources he killed some of his own men who tried to fall back, but his soldiers turned on him for his brutality.) The survivors inside the fortification surrendered. Darkness was falling, Arnold was down, and the battle sputtered to a close. Although Gates is recognized as the winning general of this stunning victory, he was not on the battlefield during the fighting. Arnold deserves the lion's share of the credit for the decisive success.

Casualties: British: 600 killed, wounded, and captured; American: 150 killed and wounded.

Outcome / Impact: The initial defeat near the creek and capture of Breymann's Redoubt rendered Burgoyne's entire position untenable. During the following night he ordered a retreat north to Saratoga. Fall weather was closing in and the roads were muddy and difficult to traverse. The retreat was a miserable affair. The British lacked sufficient food, forage, and all manner of supplies to sustain a protracted withdrawal. Burgoyne opened negotiations with the Americans to surrender. On October 17 Gates accepted his surrender, which was formalized in what is known as the Saratoga Articles of Convention. Gates agreed if the British laid down their arms and returned to England they would be free to retain their colors and go home as free men. However, the Continental Congress disagreed with these generous provisions and Burgoyne's army was sent to prison camps.

The victory at Bemis Heights and subsequent surrender at Saratoga is generally looked upon as a major turning point in the American Revolution. The victory prompted France to recognize the American colonies as an independent nation, to declare war on England, and to commit money, ships, arms, and men to the rebellion. Without this support, future victories, including the 1781 Yorktown Campaign, would not have been possible.

Today: Saratoga National Historical Park on the upper Hudson river offers an outstanding visitor center, living history programs, and other cultural and historical activities.

Further Reading: Cook, Fred J., *Dawn Over Saratoga: The Turning Point of the Revolutionary War* (Doubleday, 1973); Ellis, Davis M. *The Saratoga Campaign* (McGraw, 1969); Ketchum, Richard, *Saratoga: Turning Point of America's Revolutionary War* (New York: Henry Hold, 1997); Luzader, John. *Saratoga: A Military History of the Decisive Campaign of the American Revolution* (Savas Beatie, 2007).

Forts Mercer and Mifflin, Battles of (also known as the Siege of Philadelphia), Philadelphia Campaign

Date: October - December 1777.

Region: Northern Colonies, Pennsylvania.

Commanders: British: Lieutenant General William Howe, Admiral Earl Richard Howe, Lieutenant General Earl Charles Cornwallis, Lieutenant General Baron Wilhelm von Knyphausen, and Colonel Carl von Donop; American: General George Washington, Commodore John Hazelwood, Colonel Christopher Greene, Colonel Israel Angell, and Lieutenant Colonel Samuel Smith.

Time of Day / Length of Action: October 21: 4:00 p.m. to 4:30 p.m.

Weather Conditions: October 21: Pleasant and fair; winter weather set in during the course of the siege.

Opposing Forces: British: 2,000; American: 750.

British Perspective: After defeating the American army at Germantown (October 4, 1777), General Howe focused his efforts on clearing American forces away from the Delaware River. The once pristine Philadelphia was transformed into a giant military barracks for the British army of occupation. Tory allies, prostitutes, and myriad opportunistic camp followers added to the burdensome task required of British officers to meet both the needs of the army and the city. Howe decided to pull his forces stationed at Germantown into the city to reduce burdensome logistics and free up soldiers to clear out the enemy from Forts Mercer and Mifflin. As long as the British fleet could not traverse the Delaware River, Howe faced difficulty supplying his army.

On October 11, British engineers established a bridge across the Schuykill River at Webb's Ferry three miles below Philadelphia and emplaced siege batteries on the marshy terrain of Province Island. The batteries opened fire on Fort Mifflin and American naval vessels on the Delaware. During the next three weeks the British bombarded American defensive positions guarding the river entrance to Philadelphia while the Americans launched a series of small raids against the British artillerymen. As the weeks passed Howe grew increasingly anxious. Ice was beginning to form on the river and chilling news arrived from Saratoga, New York, reporting the surrender of General Burgoyne's army.

American Perspective: After retreating from the Germantown fiasco, General George Washington focused on reorganizing his army and bolstering the forts guarding the entrance to Philadelphia. Washington dispatched several regiments to join the inadequately manned positions at Forts Mifflin and Mercer. The forts were established four miles below Philadelphia in a strategic bend in the Delaware River. Fort Mifflin was a large 28-gun log palisade constructed on Mud Island in the center of the river. The post was manned by 350 men under Lt. Col. Samuel Smith. One mile east of Fort Mifflin on the New Jersey shore was Fort Mercer, a smaller stronghold manned by 400 men under Col. Christopher Greene. Fort Mercer was armed with 14 guns aimed through embrasures. The fortress supported Fort Mifflin and guarded the main river channel, which passed between the two forts and was strewn with obstacles (chevaux-de-frise interconnected with piles and chains). Washington sent French engineer Capt. Mauduit du Plessis to improve these defenses, and his skills proved invaluable.

While the British fleet dominated the seas, its ability to reach Philadelphia via the Delaware River was more of a challenge. The narrow channel filled with a host of natural and man-made obstacles made it doubly dangerous for warships to operate there. In order to maximize his riverine defenses, Washington reinforced Commodore John Hazelwood with additional sailors. Hazelwood commanded an ad-hoc mix of Continental and Pennsylvania sailing ships. His little "mosquito navy" consisted of 48 boats, most of which were small single-masted lightly armed vessels. They were no match for the British navy, and the only warship worthy of the name and capable of waging a real sea battle, the 32-gun frigate *Delaware*, was lost on September 27 when it was accidentally grounded and lost to the British near Philadelphia. Hazelwood's flotilla was posted north of Fort Mercer, where it provided maritime patrols in an effort to prevent British excursions from molesting the forts and traversing the channel toward the city. After the

British took Philadelphia, the Americans knew the British navy could not be far behind.

Terrain: The contested area consisted of a broad basin four miles below the heart of Philadelphia where the Schuykill River empties into the Delaware River. The latter river formed the natural boundary between Pennsylvania on the western shore and New Jersey on the eastern shore. The basin measures two miles east to west and the Delaware River empties from north to south. The basin is separated into two narrow channels by a series of small islands (Hog, Mud, Billings, and League Islands) in the middle of the river. The eastern side of the basin contains several small islands (including Province Island) and its shores are extremely marshy. Banks of red clay dominate the western shore and the terrain is much firmer there than on the eastern side. Fort Mifflin was erected on Mud Island, near the center of the river and basin and three-quarters of a mile east of Province Island. Fort Mercer was erected on the eastern shore of the river one mile east of Fort Mifflin. The Americans also placed numerous obstacles in the main river channel east of Mud and Hog Islands.

The Fighting: On October 11, the British established artillery positions on the west bank of the Delaware River opposite Fort Mifflin at Province Island. British and American artillerists spent the next five weeks pummeling one another. Both sides attempted small-scale night raids against the other, though neither achieved notable success.

On October 22 Howe launched a full-scale maritime and land assault against Fort Mercer. The day before, Col. Carl von Donop led a 2,000-man Hessian infantry force across the Delaware at Philadelphia, and marched it south along the New Jersey shore. Just outside the fort, von Donop split his command into two separate columns and attacked simultaneously from the north and south.

In the river south of the fort, meanwhile, British ships of the line *Augusta* and *Merlin* opened fire on Fort Mercer and battled a dozen small Patriot vessels. The defenders in Fort Mercer and on the naval vessels beat back the combined British land-water assault after about thirty minutes. Pummeled by artillery and musket fire, the Hessians reached the shadows of the walls before falling back in disorder. The brave but obvious effort cost them 400 killed, wounded, and captured. Among the mortally injured was Colonel von Donop, who lingered for three days before expiring. The surviving Hessians made their escape back to Philadelphia. Neither *Augusta* nor *Merlin* was as fortunate; the former was destroyed by artillery fire, while the latter was so crippled it was scuttled by its own crew.

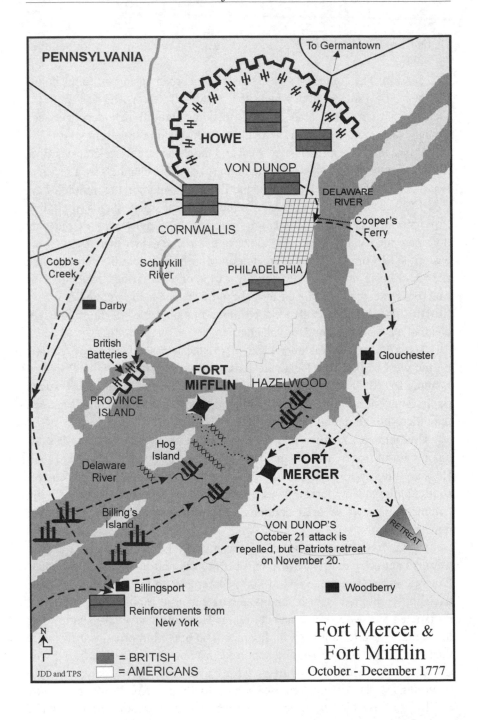

PENNSYLVANIA

To Germantown

HOWE

VON DUNOP

DELAWARE RIVER

Cooper's Ferry

CORNWALLIS

Cobb's Creek

Schuykill River

PHILADELPHIA

Darby

British Batteries

FORT MIFFLIN

HAZELWOOD

Glouchester

PROVINCE ISLAND

Hog Island

FORT MERCER

Delaware River

Billing's Island

RETREAT

VON DUNOP'S October 21 attack is repelled, but Patriots retreat on November 20.

Billingsport

Woodberry

Reinforcements from New York

N

JDD and TPS

= BRITISH
= AMERICANS

Fort Mercer & Fort Mifflin

October - December 1777

Rebuffed in their efforts to carry Fort Mercer, the British turned their attention to Fort Mifflin. On November 10 they initiated a six-day bombardment of the larger bastion, forcing the Americans manning it to flee to the protection of Fort Mercer. Emboldened by this success, Howe dispatched Cornwallis with 5,000 troops to launch another assault against Fort Mercer. This time the British moved south along the Pennsylvania side of the river and crossed it below Fort Mercer. Cornwallis coordinated an assault with the British fleet, and together the combined arms moved northward from Billingsport, New Jersey. With little hope of defending against such overwhelming odds, Colonel Greene and Commodore Hazelwood destroyed the battered American forts and scuttled the remaining ships. On November 20 the quasi-American siege of Philadelphia was lifted.

Casualties: British: 400 killed, wounded, and captured (and two ships of the line); American: 14 killed, 21 wounded (48 sailing vessels, two forts, and numerous artillery pieces and miscellaneous equipment).

Outcome / Impact: Despite the October 22 victory at Fort Mercer, the loss of the campaign and lifting of the threat against Philadelphia soured the mood of the American army. The lifting of the siege bolstered British morale and weakened American resolve. Had the Americans held their positions on the river through that winter, the British may not have been able to remain in Philadelphia. Once the British fleet was able to move freely on the river, however, the army was rejuvenated with fresh supplies and enjoyed an open line of communications. The harsh winter weather prevented large-scale warfare for several months. Howe maintained his headquarters in Philadelphia, while Washington moved his army west and established a winter camp at Valley Forge, Pennsylvania.

Today: Fort Mifflin was rebuilt in the 18th century and retained as part of the US coastal defense system well into the 20th century. Today it is a national monument adjacent to the Philadelphia International Airport and features an outstanding tour and living history programs.

Further Reading: Buchanan, John, *The Road to Valley Forge: How Washington Built the Army that Won the Revolution* (Wiley, 2004); Reed, John F., *Campaign to Valley Forge: July 1, 1777 – December 19, 1777* (Pioneer Press, 1980); Taaffee, Stephen R., *The Philadelphia Campaign, 1777-1778* (University of Kansas, 2003).

Whitemarsh (Edge Hill), Battle of (Philadelphia Campaign)

Date: December 5-7, 1777.
Region: Northern Colonies, Pennsylvania.
Commanders: British: Lieutenant General Sir William Howe, Lieutenant General Baron Wilhelm von Knyphausen, Major General Charles Grey, and Lieutenant Colonel Robert Abercrombie; American: General George Washington, Major General Nathanael Greene, Major General John Sullivan, Brigadier General James Irvine, Colonel Daniel Morgan, and Colonel Mordecai Gist.
Time of Day / Length of Action: Various skirmishes over three days.
Weather Conditions: Cold (20s at night, 40s during the day).
Opposing Forces: British: 13,000; American: 11,000.

British Perspective: After defeating the Patriot army at Germantown (October 4, 1777) and clearing the Delaware River of American forces, General Howe focused his efforts on strengthening his position in and around Philadelphia. The capture of the important colonial city was one of his major strategic goals for the year. The other was the destruction of Washington's field army. While the British enjoyed favorable conditions with excellent shelter and adequate provisions, they were harassed by spies, scouts, and raids. During November the Americans moved their lines within thirteen miles northwest of Philadelphia. The close proximity to the city triggered clashes with advance enemy elements. In retaliation the British pillaged and burned many homes, including some by accident belonging to Tory allies.

The raids, skirmishes, spying, and house burning took a heavy toll on British soldiers and local citizens, and it quickly became apparent that something had to be done about the encroaching Americans. Howe decided to move out and surprise the enemy with a winter battle. Under the cover of darkness about midnight on December 4, the bulk of the British army quietly marched out of Philadelphia in two columns. Cornwallis led the right wing along the Germantown Pike, while Knyphausen led the other wing along Ridge Road. Both columns moved northwest toward Whitemarsh, where Howe planned to confront the Americans.

American Perspective: After retreating from the fight at Germantown, General Washington spent the remainder of October reorganizing and reequipping his army. On November 2 he moved onto a small series of hills at Whitemarsh, thirteen miles northwest of Philadelphia. From that position he could defend his important supply center at Reading and remain close enough to Howe to generate anxiety. Washington ordered his men to construct a long front of interconnected fortified defensive positions along the hills named Camp, Militia, Edge, and Fort. General Nathanael Greene commanded the left wing from Camp Hill in the east, while Gen. John Sullivan commanded the right wing along Fort and Militia Hills in the west. While in these positions Forts Mifflin and Mercer, two American strongholds four miles below Philadelphia on the Delaware River, were lost to a British offensive. After their fall Washington consolidated his entire army at Whitemarsh.

The final weeks of November were especially hard on the American army. Winter weather set in, provisions were scarce, morale was ebbing, and desertions increased. The aggressive Washington longed for a confrontation with Howe, but he wanted to fight a defensive battle from within his strong positions on the hills. In an effort to lure the British into the field, he sent patrols to probe and harass the enemy lines. Washington got his wish when friendly locals told him Howe had mobilized for an offensive and was moving out of the city. Skirmishing increased between Whitemarsh and Philadelphia. At 3:00 a.m. on December 5 American signal guns rattled the darkness: the British were approaching.

Terrain: The battlefield is northwest of Philadelphia in the hilly region at Whitemarsh. The hills, from east to west, were as follows: Camp Hill, Fort Hill, Edge Hill, and Militia Hill. Sandy Run Creek ran parallel to the American lines front (south) of these hills. The British established their primary line of battle on Chestnut Hill, three miles south of the American line. Bethlehem Pike cut between Militia and Fort hills along the western end of the battlefield, running south toward Chestnut Hill. On the eastern end of the field, Limekiln Pike bisected the lines from north to south, running roughly parallel to Bethlehem Pike. In 1777, the region was dominated by thickly forested hills interspersed by farm fields in the valleys between them.

The Fighting: Howe's army reached Chestnut Hill, about three miles south of the American lines, shortly after dawn on December 5. An advance British infantry unit led by Lt. Col. Robert Abercrombie (Cornwallis was with the column) advanced north along Bethlehem Pike toward the American campfires. The supposedly stealthy move through the valley between the hills triggered a clash with 600 Pennsylvania militiamen led by Brig. Gen. James Irvine, whom Washington had sent out to meet the British. A sharp but short engagement ensued that killed and wounded many rebels including Irvine, who was knocked from his horse by one ball, wounded in the hand by another, and taken prisoner. Several men were captured. British

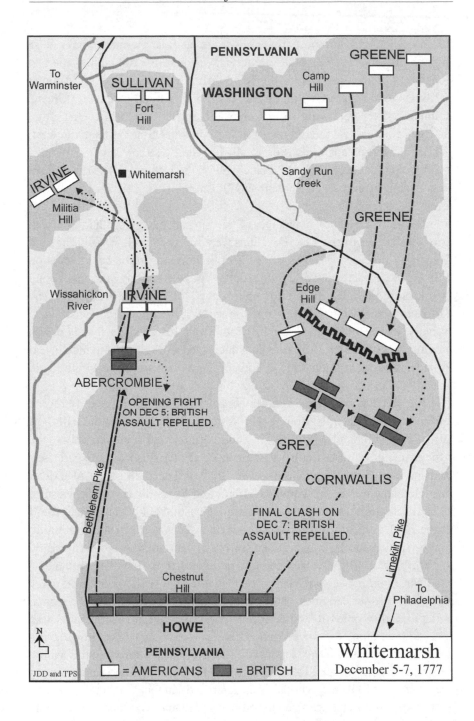

PENNSYLVANIA

GREENE

To Warminster

SULLIVAN

Fort Hill

WASHINGTON

Camp Hill

Whitemarsh

Sandy Run Creek

IRVINE

Militia Hill

GREENE

Wissahickon River

IRVINE

Edge Hill

ABERCROMBIE

OPENING FIGHT ON DEC 5: BRITISH ASSAULT REPELLED.

GREY

CORNWALLIS

Bethlehem Pike

FINAL CLASH ON DEC 7: BRITISH ASSAULT REPELLED.

Limekiln Pike

Chestnut Hill

To Philadelphia

HOWE

N

PENNSYLVANIA

JDD and TPS

☐ = AMERICANS   ▨ = BRITISH

Whitemarsh
December 5-7, 1777

losses were light. Cornwallis secured the ground and camped around St. Thomas Episcopal Church, from whose tower Howe surveyed the enemy line later that morning. When an effort to shell Washington's line failed (the range was too great), Howe decided to attack the American left or eastern flank. Howe's effort on December 6 to get in position to attack the American flank failed when it was determined that Washington held higher ground and could see Howe's every move.

On December 7 Howe moved men into position opposite Washington's center and left on Edge Hill. This sector of the American line was defended by riflemen under Cols. Daniel Morgan and Mordecai Gist. Washington sent them forward to disrupt the scheming British. Fighting "Indian-style" from behind trees and rocks, the riflemen used guerilla tactics to advantage for much of the day to stymie the redcoats. When Cornwallis finally advanced with the 33rd Foot, the Americans withdrew to their own lines.

Shortly after Cornwallis pushed Morgan and Gist north, Howe probed the American center to no avail. He could not find a good way to strike at Washington with advantage. Anxious to attack but instructed to wait, Maj. Gen. Charles Grey decided to advance on his own. A combination of light infantry and rangers attacked, triggering renewed fighting on Edge Hill. Casualties were relatively light and at its climax an American cavalry charge and additional Continental reinforcements disordered the attackers and bolstered Washington's already strong line. The British retreated back to their lines. Reinforcements in the form of two Hessian regiments arrived to further strengthen Howe.

Although Washington anticipated another assault on the morning of the 8th, Howe had had enough. The weather was freezing, his supplies were exhausted, and warm quarters awaited him in Philadelphia just one day's march distant. The Americans pursued the British rearguard, but no further fighting of significance transpired.

Casualties: British: 75 killed, wounded, and captured; American: 86 killed and wounded, and 15 captured (including General Irvine).

Outcome / Impact: The three-day British expedition to Whitemarsh achieved nothing but the additional loss of life and property. The liberal pillaging conducted by the British and Hessians outside the city turned many of the sympathetic Tories into enemies of the Crown. Howe went into winter quarters in comfortable and secure Philadelphia, leaving the Americans out on the frozen windswept countryside. Knowing Howe would not fight him, Washington marched his army southwest away from the city.

Washington's army went into winter quarters on December 19 at Valley Forge. Twenty-five miles southeast of Philadelphia, the encampment was situated on a high plateau surrounded by natural obstacles that provided excellent protection from enemy incursions. The Schuylkill River provided an ample supply of water, but food, clothing, and medicine were in short supply. Many of the American soldiers sought refuge in their homes, and the Continental ranks dwindled to just 6,000 hardy souls that winter at Valley Forge. The men lived in small log huts, where illness, filth, and the challenges of winter made the encampment a long and difficult experience. Several thousand soldiers were lost to dysentery and typhus.

Today: The Whitemarsh American encampment is reenacted each year. Interested readers can visit 3,600-acre Valley Forge National Historical Park in King of Prussia, Pennsylvania, just outside Philadelphia.

Further Reading: Buchanan, John, *The Road to Valley Forge: How Washington Built the Army that Won the Revolution* (Wiley, 2004); Reed, John F., *Campaign to Valley Forge: July 1, 1777 – December 19, 1777* (Pioneer Press, 1980); Taaffee, Stephen R., *The Philadelphia Campaign, 1777-1778* (University of Kansas, 2003).

British Isles, Battles of the (American Naval Campaign: Europe)

Date: April 1778 – June 1780.
Region: Atlantic Ocean (European Theater, naval battles off the coast of the British Isles).
Commanders: British: various; American: Captain John Paul Jones.
Time of Day / Length of Action: NA.
Weather Conditions: varied.
Opposing Forces: British: various; American: various.

British Perspective: France's decision to support American independence and its declaration of war against England forced the British to expend considerable resources to defend European waters. Problems between the two nations had been simmering since the end of the Seven Years' War, and in 1778 France believed a new war with England was likely to weaken its longtime enemy and gain the French overseas possessions.

On July 28, 1778, French and British fleets clashed at the First Battle of Ushant, about 100 miles west of a small island of the same name off the northwest corner of France. The British fleet, the vanguard of an amphibious invasion of France, was comprised of 30 warships commanded by Admiral Augustus Keppel. Arrayed against him were 32 French warships under

Admiral Louis d' Orvilliers. The battle pitted the finest the world's two great sea powers could muster, though the combat seems clumsily waged in shifting winds and rain squalls. Both sides lost heavily. French casualties totaled 674, while British losses amounted to 506. The British viewed the battle as a defeat (Keppel was court-martialed, though cleared) because the amphibious assault was turned away.

France's entry made it easier for other nations hungry to nibble at England's empire to follow suit. Spain declared war on England in 1779 and the Dutch followed suit in 1780. The American Revolution, or at least the ripple effects of the war in the colonies, was now a global affair. The French joined with Spain to plan an ambitious offensive against the British home isles, but after careful planning the invasion was never launched. The British were now fighting four countries (Spain, France, Holland, and America), and their military capabilities were stretched thin. Her enemies exploited the Crown's attenuated condition by grabbing territory and resources around the world wherever and whenever they could, which in turn kept the British fleet and military resources busy and away from the American colonies.

American Perspective: By 1777 the nascent Continental fleet was barely worthy of the name. The colonists had few resources with which to construct and maintain a credible fleet and no one harbored illusions that anything the Americans could float would counter the British head-to-head. Aggravating efforts to build a navy were the individual states themselves, which focused maritime resources on maintaining their own respective state navies. These "mosquito fleets," comprised of converted merchant ships and prize vessels, were dedicated to the defense of their respective shores.

Though limited in number, the few ships of the Continental fleet remained engaged throughout the war in varying degrees of service. In June of 1777 Capt. John Paul Jones was given command of *Ranger*, which he sailed to France. Jones's mission was to inform French authorities that General Burgoyne had surrendered his army at Saratoga—a critical victory that helped convince the French to ally with America. Jones took several prize vessels en route to European shores, and while in France devised a plan to raid shipping around the British Isles. Jones set sail on April 11, 1778, and in the Irish Sea off the west coast of England captured several merchant ships. Following successful small raids on English soil, Jones captured the 20-gun HMS *Drake* in America's first conventional naval battle.

While the American naval campaign was nothing more than a hit and run affair through British home waters, the news of Jones's success bolstered morale back home. *Ranger* returned to America under a different captain. Jones remained in France to work with Ambassador Benjamin Franklin and assist French authorities in refitting an old ship into a man-of-war. The converted 40-gun warship was called *Bonhomme Richard* in honor of Benjamin Franklin. With additional assistance from the French government, Jones built a small squadron around *Bonhomme Richard* and put to sea on August 14, 1779. Jones's fleet captured several ships. On September 23 he engaged in what is probably the best-known ship-to-ship battle of the revolution when *Bonhomme Richard* defeated HMS *Serapis* in the North Sea. In June of 1780, Louis XVI presented Jones with a sword engraved with the phrase "To the valiant avenger of the rights of the sea."

Terrain: The British Isles and the waters in which John Paul Jones conducted his campaign lie in the North Atlantic surrounding Ireland in the west, Scotland in the north, and England in the east. Jones sailed about 1,700 miles on his first cruise into the Irish Sea. He left Brest, France, in the Bay of Biscay and sailed up Ireland's east coast, eventually stopping on the west coast of England (Battle of Whitehaven) before continuing northward around Ireland (Battle with *Drake*). He sailed along the west coast of that country before returning to port at Brest. Jones's second voyage began at Lorient, France, another Biscay port. This time he made a broad arc around the west coast of Ireland, moving north by northeast to the coast of Scotland, and south along the east coast of that country. He continued sailing in a southerly direction to the east coast of England (battle with *Serapis*) before seeking a safe port in Holland.

The Fighting: (Raids on Whitehaven, England, and St. Mary's Island, Scotland) During his cruise around the eastern shores of England, Captain Jones personally led a little-known raid on a British fort at Whitehaven on April 22, 1778. The daring amphibious assault conducted at dawn succeeded in surprising the small garrison and taking the stronghold without firing a shot. Jones knew he would not be able to hold the fort, but that was never his intent. Instead, he spiked 36 heavy cannons and destroyed several British ships in the nearby harbor before sailing away. The next day Jones and his men raided Scotland's St. Mary's Island, where they unsuccessfully attempted to kidnap the Earl of Selkirk. Jones had hoped to use the valuable hostage to negotiate the exchange of American sailors held by the British in England. When the plan failed he continued his cruise around the eastern coast of England.

(*Ranger* vs. *Drake*) The British dispatched several warships to capture the irksome rebel raiders terrorizing the British home islands. On April 24, 1778, British man-of-war *Drake* approached the *Ranger* off Carrickfergus, Ireland. Rather foolishly, the British captain sent a boat out to inquire the nationality of *Ranger*; Jones promptly captured it. Cleared for action, *Drake* eased closer to *Ranger* and hailed the ship. Jones (or his first officer,

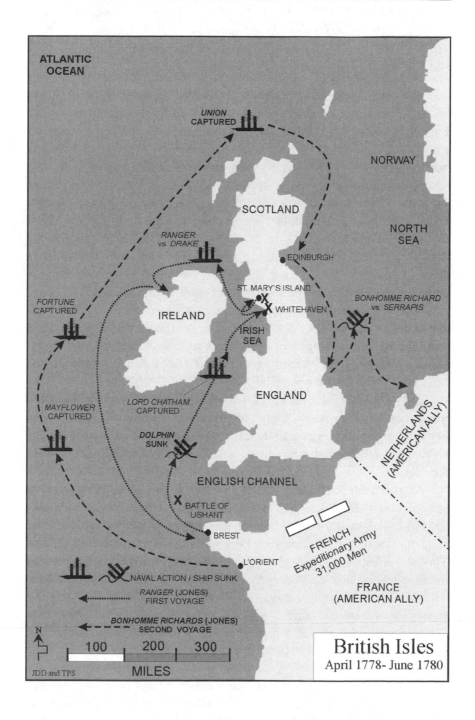

British Isles
April 1778- June 1780

depending upon the source) responded, "This is the American Continental ship *Ranger*, we wait for you, and beg you will come on. The sun is little more than an hour high, and it is time to begin!" After taunting the enemy Jones initiated the battle by sending a broadside into the British ship. About one hour later *Drake* struck her colors and surrendered. Jones lost only two killed and six wounded, while the British suffered 45 killed and wounded. Jones was hailed a hero when he returned to France with his prizes, which he had to sell to feed and pay his near-mutinous crew.

(*Bonhomme Richard* vs. *Serapis*) Jones's small fleet captured more than a dozen prize ships en route to a designated rendezvous site off the coasts of England and Scotland. Several of his ships failed to arrive. While waiting for them at Flamborough Head on September 23, 1779, the 44-gun British frigate *Serapis* and 22-gun *Countess of Scarborough* cruised into range escorting a fleet of 40 merchant ships. Jones attacked the British at sunset under a rising full moon. The dramatic and bitterly contested duel consumed four hours. The struggle between *Bonhomme Richard* and *Serapis* (and to a lesser degree, *Countess of Scarborough*) was as much brawl as masterful seamanship. The two ships repeatedly unloaded broadsides into each other's hulls, cutting rigging, puncturing sails, and killing and maiming sailors. When one of the shots dropped the American flag, British commander Capt. Richard Pearson asked Jones if he intended to surrender. Jones, in one of the war's most famous phrases, supposedly replied, "Surrender? I have not yet begun to fight!" According to Jones, however, his answer was a bit less artful: "That point didn't occur to me, but I am determined to make you ask for quarter!"

As the battle dragged on *Bonhomme Richard* lost both rigging and rudder, but when *Serapis* moved alongside to deliver a final blow, she strayed too close and her jib boom became entangled with the American ship. Jones's men threw grappling hooks onto *Serapis* and lashed her fast. This act effectively removed *Countess of Scarborough* from the action because her captain did not want to risk hitting *Serapis*. Hand grenades were tossed into the *Serapis's* hold, slaughtering dozens of British sailors. Hundreds of captured British sailors held prisoner aboard *Bonhomme Richard* were released with Jones's permission, but most were set to work manning pumps to keep the badly hulled ship from sinking. The battle was but half finished.

With the ships lashed together, Jones led a boarding party onto *Serapis*, where the combatants fought hand-to-hand above and below decks. About 10:30 p.m. Pearson finally surrendered his ship and crew to Jones. *Countess of Scarborough* surrendered to another of Jones's ships a short time later.

Hulled and listing, the badly damaged *Bonhomme Richard* was clearly mortally wounded. With her decks awash with blood and mangled bodies, *Bonhomme Richard* lingered for two days before losing her battle with the sea. Half of Jones's crew of 240 was dead or wounded. Jones took *Serapis* as his new flagship.

Casualties: (*Ranger* vs. *Drake*): British: 42 killed and wounded; American: eight killed and wounded; (*Bonhomme Richard* vs. *Serapis*): British: 600 killed, wounded, and captured; American: 120 killed and wounded.

Outcome / Impact: John Paul Jones's expedition into British home waters had no impact on the overall outcome of the war, though his raid interfered with British shipping and caused considerable consternation. His exploits inflicted several million dollars of damage to British shipping, and the embarrassment he caused his enemy helped boost American morale. Jones's attack on the fort at Whitehaven was the only time Americans set foot on English soil during the Revolutionary War.

In addition to the expeditions of John Paul Jones and the French naval battles fought around the British Isles, other European sea battles played a role in tying up British military resources in waters far from American shores. Because the colonial war was now a global conflict, one of the possessions England was forced to heavily guard was Gibraltar, the strategic guardian of the entrance of the Mediterranean Sea. On October 20, 1782, an allied Franco-Spanish fleet made up of 46 ships of the line fought for control of Gibraltar against 35 British warships under Admiral Sir Richard Howe. The four-hour Battle of Cape Spartel off the coast of Morocco ended in British success, with each side suffering about 600 casualties.

Further Reading: Dupuy, Trevor Nevitt, *The Military History of Revolutionary War Naval Battles* (Franklin Watts, Inc., 1970); Allen, Gardner, *A Naval History of the American Revolution* (Houghton, 1913).

Caribbean, Battles of the (Naval Campaign: Caribbean)

Date: February 1778-April 1782.
Region: Atlantic Ocean (Naval and land battles fought in the Caribbean Sea).
Commanders: British: Various; American and French: Various.
Time of Day / Length of Action: NA.

Weather Conditions: NA.
Opposing Forces: Various.

British Perspective: Throughout the American Revolution, England faced serious challenges to its substantial interests in the Caribbean. Beginning on March 3, 1776, when Americans seized British forts at Nassau in the Bahamas, the Crown was forced to commit men and resources to the defense of its West Indies colonies. The nascent American navy was too small to maintain control of territory beyond its borders or directly threaten England at sea, so colonial naval threats did not overly preoccupy England's military commanders. All of this changed in 1778 when the French recognized America and joined the war. The move forced the British to commit fleets and permanent garrisons to the West Indies lest they lose their island colonies to the French. In 1779 and 1780, Spain and Holland, respectively, joined the war as American allies. Both were naval powers. The threat to British sovereignty in the West Indies was at a crisis point.

From 1778 to 1782 the British continuously reinforced their Caribbean forts, committed a permanent military presence in the islands, and posted large numbers of warships there to guard island territories. Occasional enemy raids into the region from 1778 through 1780 were successfully defended. However, in 1781 and 1782, as the war in America drew to a close, France and Spain attacked the weakened but still powerful British with their full strength. As the French and Spanish discovered, the British navy still ruled the seas. When the fighting was over England's possessions were still under the Union Jack.

American Perspective: The small Continental Navy launched successful small-scale raids of British possessions in the Caribbean, but the risk to the enemy was irksome at best. The tiny American squadrons faced great peril as the British steadily increased the military strength of her island colonies. By 1780 the shattered American fleet consisted primarily of borrowed vessels and tiny state-run squadrons that could do little more than capture foreign merchant vessels as prizes. However, American allies actively engaged British interests with increasing frequency and strength, and from an American perspective, every action that forced the British to employ resources away from the colonies was a success. After the surrender of Cornwallis at Yorktown in October 1781, America's allies moved the thrust of their war with Great Britain to distant shores. In the Caribbean, French and Spanish fleets attacked the British, though without lasting success.

Terrain: The Caribbean consists of the Caribbean Sea, which is a part of the North Atlantic Ocean and the islands located therein, including Antigua,

Barbuda, Bahamas, Cuba, Dominica, Dominican Republic, Grenada, Haiti, Trinidad, Tobago, Jamaica, St. Lucia, St. Kitts, Nevis, and St. Vincent. These primary islands are commonly known as the West Indies. In the 18th Century, several empires wrestled for control of these islands, including France, Great Britain, Spain, and Holland. The islands were prized for their resources and for their strategic location as ports and colonies. The name Caribbean is derived from the Carib people who originally inhabited the area at the time of its discovery by Spanish explorers in the 15th Century.

The sea is roughly 1,500 miles (east to west) by 1,400 miles (north to south), or roughly 1,050,000 square miles. Its major shipping lane was the Windward Passage between Haiti and Cuba. Its boundary to the north and east is the West Indies, South America to the south, and Central America to the west. The Gulf of Mexico lies to the northwest, connecting with the Caribbean Sea via a 120-mile wide corridor between Cuba and the Yucatan Peninsula of Mexico. The sea was generally easy to navigate, offered mild tides, and tropical weather. The equatorial currents provided excellent sailing via a predominantly northwestern flow. However, hurricanes also followed this track from June to November.

The Fighting: *2nd Raid on Nassau*: In January of 1778, the Americans conducted several operations in Caribbean waters. The frigate *Providence* returned to the Bahamas and helped capture British forts in Nassau on January 27, seize 1,600 pounds of gunpowder, and free 30 American prisoners of war being held on the island. The effort also recaptured five American ships and captured a 16-gun British sloop. This raid was nearly a replay of a previous assault in 1776, only much more successful. After returning to America, *Providence* captured prize ships along the coast of New England until she was destroyed at the Battle of Penobscot Bay (August 14, 1779).

Randolph vs. *Yarmouth*: On February 12, 1778, the American frigate *Randolph* and four South Carolina ships commanded by Capt. Nicholas Biddle cruised into the Caribbean Sea in search of prize vessels. Instead of easy prizes, however, on March 7, 1778, the little American squadron ran squarely into *Yarmouth*, a 64-gun British ship-of-the-line. *Yarmouth* was twice its size and boasted twice as many guns, but the faster *Randolph* heroically (some might say foolishly) closed for battle. Captain Biddle fired first and the British quickly returned fire. Although Biddle's shots ripped apart *Yarmouth's* rigging and sails, *Randolph* exploded and sank with 311 men, including the promising young Captain Biddle. In all likelihood a lucky shot had penetrated *Randolph's* magazine. Biddle's well-handled guns,

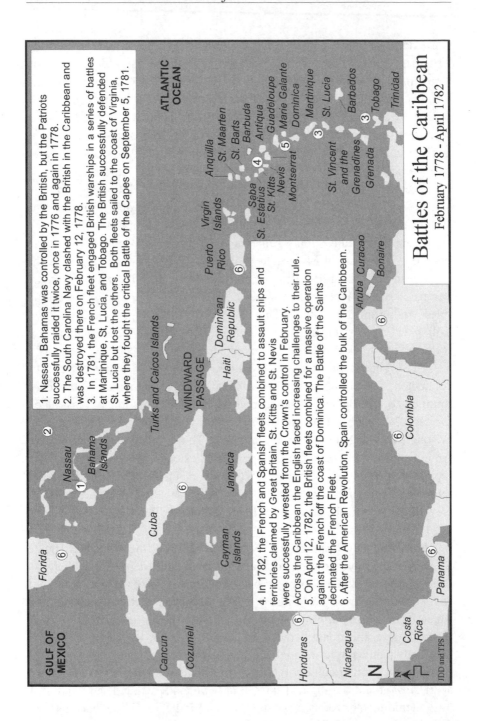

1. Nassau, Bahamas was controlled by the British, but the Patriots successfully raided it twice, once in 1776 and again in 1778.
2. The South Carolina Navy clashed with the British in the Caribbean and was destroyed there on February 12, 1778.
3. In 1781, the French fleet engaged British warships in a series of battles at Martinique, St, Lucia, and Tobago. The British successfully defended St. Lucia but lost the others. Both fleets sailed to the coast of Virginia, where they fought the critical Battle of the Capes on September 5, 1781.

4. In 1782, the French and Spanish fleets combined to assault ships and territories claimed by Great Britain. St. Kitts and St. Nevis were successfully wrested from the Crown's control in February. Across the Caribbean the English faced increasing challenges to their rule.
5. On April 12, 1782, the British fleets combined for a massive operation against the French off the coast of Dominica. The Battle of the Saints decimated the French Fleet.
6. After the American Revolution, Spain controlled the bulk of the Caribbean.

Battles of the Caribbean
February 1778 - April 1782

JDD and TPS

however, heavily damaged *Yarmouth*, which had to put in for repairs in Jamaica before sailing for Portsmouth. She never saw combat service again.

Battles of Martinique, St. Lucia, and Tobago: In 1781, a French fleet led by Admiral François Joseph Paul Comte de Grasse sailed for the island of Martinique, where it clashed with a British fleet commanded by Rear Admiral Samuel Hood. The British valiantly attempted to keep the French from reaching their port at Fort de France, but were unsuccessful. De Grasse tried to land 1,200 marines to take the island of St. Lucia, but the British succeeded in knocking back the effort. Stymied, the French fleet moved on to Tobago, which was seized on July 26, 1781. De Grasse next sailed his French warships to Haiti, where they joined forces with another squadron commanded by Rear Admiral Comte de Guichen. Together they sailed for the coast of Virginia to assist Washington's Franco-American army against Cornwallis. On September 5, the French fleet engaged a British fleet commanded by Rear Admiral Thomas Graves at the Battle of the Capes. The combat was the decisive naval battle of the American Revolution. The French victory drove away Graves's fleet and secured the Chesapeake Bay for the Allied siege of Yorktown, Virginia, which ultimately forced the surrender of Cornwallis's army and the end of the war.

Battles of St. Kitts and Nevis: In late 1781 and 1782, with the war virtually over in America and treaty negotiations underway, the French and Spanish continued fighting the British. On November 5, 1781, a strong French fleet of 29 ships under de Grasse returned to the Caribbean and successfully captured the islands of St. Kitts and Nevis. On January 25, 1782, Admiral Samuel Hood's inferior force recaptured the harbor and waged what is largely recognized as the finest example of British military seamanship of the war, but the British post on St. Kitts surrendered to the French on February 12. The French rolled up the islands and after two months of campaigning the British had nearly lost control of the Caribbean.

Battle of the Saints / Iles de Saintes: After de Grasse's victory at St. Kitts and Nevis, he planned to join his warships with the Spanish fleet and, in a massive joint operation, attack British-held Jamaica. The British were equally determined to prevent a link up of their two main enemies and attacked the French before they could get into position to strike. Admirals George Rodney and Samuel Hood combined their fleets and the large British armada struck the French on April 12, 1782, near the Dominican coast at Iles de Saintes. Known as the Battle of the Saints, 36 British ships of the line squared off against a French fleet of 33 warships. The French were out maneuvered and outfought and many of de Grasse's ships ran out of ammunition. Badly beaten, the French fleet was captured or destroyed and 6,000 men lost their lives. Admiral de Grasse surrendered *Le Ville de Paris*, his 130-gun flagship and the pride of his fleet. The surviving French warships sought shelter at their port in Haiti. The bloody battle ended French efforts against the British in the Caribbean. It also marked the end of major naval combat during the American Revolution.

Casualties: Known casualty data has been included in the narrative above.

Outcome / Impact: The impact of these battles was primarily realized in their collateral assistance rendered to the American cause by forcing the British to focus on areas beyond the colonies. The battles also provided for a division of the island colonies in the Caribbean.

Further Reading: Dupuy, Trevor Nevitt, *The Military History of Revolutionary War Naval Battles* (Franklin Watts, Inc., 1970); Allen, Gardner, *A Naval History of the American Revolution* (Houghton, 1913).

Monmouth Court House, Battle of (Philadelphia Campaign)

Date: June 28, 1778.
Region: Northern Colonies, New Jersey.
Commanders: British: Lieutenant General Sir Henry Clinton, Major General Earl Charles Cornwallis, Lieutenant General Baron Wilhelm von Knyphausen; American: General George Washington, Major General Nathanael Greene, Major General William (Lord Stirling) Alexander, Major General Charles Lee, and Major General Marquis de Lafayette.
Time of Day / Length of Action: All day (10:00 a.m. to 6:00 p.m.).
Weather Conditions: Very hot and humid.
Opposing Forces: British: 10,000; American: 12,000.

British Perspective: General Howe successfully outmaneuvered and defeated the Americans during the fall of 1777 in a series of engagements culminating in the capture of the Patriot capital at Philadelphia. Howe had hoped the city's fall would dramatically tilt the war in the Crown's favor. It did not, largely for reasons he could not have foreseen. The British commander-in-chief in America was also unhappy with the failure of his superiors to reinforce his command or heed his advice about how to prosecute the war. Other than a handful of smaller satellite actions in the region, he made no further effort during the winter of 1777-1778 to seriously molest the American army encamped at Valley Forge.

Unlike the fall of Philadelphia, the nearly simultaneous American victory at Saratoga, New York, resulted in the surrender of General Burgoyne's large British army and far reaching repercussions. France used the Patriot triumph to formally endorse the American war effort, believing it a viable means of enlarging France's empire at Britain's expense. An alliance between France and America was announced in February of 1778. Howe resigned from his command in Philadelphia and Gen. Sir Henry Clinton succeeded him as commander of the British Army in America. France's entry into the colonial war made the Crown's already vexing rebellion several times more complex.

Clinton received orders in May 1778. The entry of the French, coupled with American victories, forced the Crown to change its colonial war strategy. France was now Britain's primary concern and holding Philadelphia was no longer worthwhile. The British military machine and its deployment would have to be dramatically reorganized. Until further notice, Clinton's effort in the North was to be defensive. He was ordered to abandon Philadelphia and retreat to New York City (which he could also abandon if he believed absolutely necessary). Once there, Clinton was to dispatch 5,000 soldiers to the West Indies for offensive operations against the French, and 3,000 more for operations in the Southern colonies. Much of this change in deployment was the result of intelligence that France had dispatched an eleven-warship squadron and 4,000 soldiers for the Americas under Comte d'Estaing. British authorities could only speculate as to d'Estaing's exact destination. If anyone doubted that open war between France and England was imminent, events of June 17 changed that. On that day off the coast of England, British ships attacked two French frigates, initiating a full-fledged state of war between the longtime antagonists.

In accordance with his orders, Clinton planned his move to New York City. He had two choices: move by land or by sea. The latter route entailed loading his men on transports down the Delaware River, through the bay, and up the Atlantic coast to New York City. Clinton did not have enough ships to shift his entire army at once. Fearful of French intervention at sea if he spent weeks shuttling his command by ship, he compromised. On June 18 several thousand Tories, heavy equipment, and tons of supplies were put on ships for New York City. The balance of his army, about 10,000 of all arms and 1,500 wagons, marched out of Philadelphia for the land journey across New Jersey.

The army moved slowly, crossed the river, and marched east by northeast roughly parallel to the Delaware through Haddonfield, Moorestown, Mount Holly, Bordentown, and Allentown. The weather was hot and the roads heavy with dust and sand. Enemy militia used the heavy woods as cover to nip at the rear of the column while small enemy bands picked at Clinton's flanks. Clinton knew his strung out army was ripe for attack and that its loss would seriously imperil the British war effort in America. After rumors arrived that Horatio Gates's American army, fresh from its Saratoga victory, was moving south to intercept his march, Clinton changed his plans and moved in a more easterly direction for the coast. He would make the balance of the journey by ship from Sandy Hook. His new route, however, meant he had to march his entire army on a single road. On June 26 the head of the army reached Monmouth, New Jersey. The day's 20-mile journey under a 100+ degree sun was so unbearable it killed many of his heavily uniformed and overburdened soldiers.

Clinton aligned his army to receive an attack, launch his own, or continue the retreat. His intent was to march toward the coast at daybreak on June 28. He did not know that a large force of the enemy had gathered just five miles west of his position, or that the bulk of the American army was only three miles behind it. Lieutenant General Baron Wilhelm von Knyphausen led about one-half of Clinton's army out of Monmouth before daybreak on the 28th; Maj. Gen. Earl Charles Cornwallis and Clinton remained in camp and left about four hours later. A rearguard of about 1,500 men remained in Monmouth.

American Perspective: General Washington's army suffered through the long and arduous 1777-1778 winter twenty miles northwest of Philadelphia at Valley Forge, Pennsylvania. During those months a Prussian military professional, Baron Friedrich Wilhelm von Steuben, helped Washington and his officers reorganize and train the Americans. Von Steuben instructed the soldiers in European formations, drills, maintenance of arms, and the employment of the bayonet. It was a new Patriot army that readied itself for the 1778 campaign. Spring brought better living conditions and welcome news in the form of an alliance with France. Morale skyrocketed and American resolve stiffened; it was unlikely France would ever make peace with England unless the independence of the United States was formally acknowledged.

The Continental Congress bolstered Washington's staff with the addition of Maj. Gen. Charles Lee and Maj. Gen. Marquis de Lafayette. Lee gained his freedom during a prisoner exchange after being held for eighteen months. He enjoyed an elevated reputation not entirely deserved, and was cautious in battle. The young and brash Lafayette was more willing to eagerly commit troops to fight the enemy. Despite his youth, Lafayette's bravery and invaluable leadership and command skills had earned Washington's confidence.

When it became obvious in late May that Clinton was preparing his army in Philadelphia for a major operation, Washington readied his own 12,000 men for action. When the British moved out of Philadelphia Washington triumphantly reentered the city, leaving Benedict Arnold in command there. Washington dispatched various small commands northeast and east to shadow, harass, and delay the British move across New Jersey. Washington guessed (correctly) that Clinton would march along a more southerly route toward New York and so planned accordingly. General Lee cautioned against engaging the British during a famous June 24 council of war. His belief was that France's entry into the war guaranteed victory, so why risk a decisive battle? He also doubted American troops could stand in the field against the British. Lee was not entirely alone in his belief. Lafayette argued otherwise, as did several other officers. The council broke up, as most councils do, without agreeing to seek a major battle (though the officers agreed to send a 1,500-man command under Col. Charles Scott to operate against Clinton's exposed left flank).

The main American columns traversed a more northerly trek across New Jersey through Coryell's Ferry, Hopewell, Kingston, and Princeton. Both the American and British routes intersected at Monmouth (present-day Freehold), New Jersey. When Clinton's destination at Monmouth became clear, Washington wisely reinforced Scott's command but had to put an officer in charge with sufficient rank to lead 4,000 men. He preferred and sent Lafayette to Englishtown (near Monmouth), but military protocol and political considerations convinced Lee (the army's second-in-command) to seek the role. Washington compromised. He allowed Lee to assume command with the understanding that he was not to interfere with Lafayette if an action was underway when Lee arrived on scene.

June 27 dawned with difficulties for Washington. His army was dispersed and tired, his scouting system was not working well, his supply wagons were miles from where they were needed, and the roads were bad. His opportunity to bag Clinton seemed to be slipping through his fingers. Washington ordered the bulk of his army to march for Englishtown to support Lafayette (Lee), sending orders ahead that Lee should attack Clinton's vulnerable left flank as soon as the British continued their retreat. The stage was set for one of the most potentially important battles of the American Revolution.

Terrain: Monmouth unfolded on the north and west side of Freehold, New Jersey (Monmouth County Court House). The terrain is dominated by gently rolling farmland rising from east to west. The highest elevation is 160 feet on Comb's Hill in the southwestern corner of the battlefield. The most severe fighting, which included the large artillery duel, took place west of town where the Americans occupied positions along the heights above three branches of Wemrock Creek. The British attacked from east to west from positions on the lower terrain east of the American army. Natural barriers were formed by branches of Wemrock Creek (then known as Middle Ravine and West Ravine).

The Fighting: General Lee confirmed his cautious nature (but not his exalted field prowess) early on June 28. About 9:00 a.m. he moved his 5,000 men east toward the Middletown Road in a confusing series of fits and starts that triggered an engagement with Clinton's rear guard of 1,500 men. Unfortunately, Lee moved that morning without a firm plan—and it showed. Brigadier General "Mad" Anthony Wayne's brigade was the first to make contact with the British north of Monmouth. The spreading fight alerted Clinton to the proximity of a significant American column in his rear. Knyphausen was ordered to watch his left flank and continue marching. Clinton, meanwhile, turned Cornwallis's powerful wing of 14 battalions and the 16th Light Dragoons around to meet and crush Lee's vanguard before the rest of the American army could reach the field.

Clinton arranged Cornwallis's arriving infantry into a pair of strong lines of battle facing west. With his right he moved forward against Lee's left. What happened thereafter is difficult to piece together because the sources conflict on nearly every count. What is clear is that Lee rapidly lost control of the situation and his command began retiring to the southwest and then west along the causeway crossing Middle Ravine. Clinton's infantry rapidly pursued the fleeing Americans. Some attempts were made to establish hasty defensive positions during the withdrawal, but much of Lee's command moved as a disorganized mob. General Washington arrived on the field about noon only to learn to his shock that Lee's command was in retreat. When he reached the West Ravine his own astonished eyes confirmed the reports. According to some accounts, an angry exchange between Washington and Lee took place with the former questioning the latter about his commitment to fighting the enemy.

Washington brought order to the chaos and organized a new line to slow down the British until the rest of his army could come up. Exactly where the line was drawn depends upon the source. Most suggest it was between the Middle and West ravines north of Wemrock Brook. The arriving units

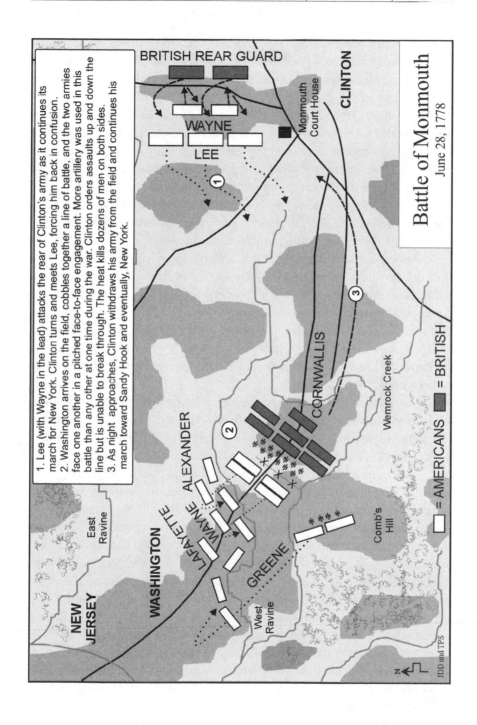

Battle of Monmouth
June 28, 1778

1. Lee (with Wayne in the lead) attacks the rear of Clinton's army as it continues its march for New York. Clinton turns and meets Lee, forcing him back in confusion.
2. Washington arrives on the field, cobbles together a line of battle, and the two armies face one another in a pitched face-to-face engagement. More artillery was used in this battle than any other at one time during the war. Clinton orders assaults up and down the line but is unable to break through. The heat kills dozens of men on both sides.
3. As night approaches, Clinton withdraws his army from the field and continues his march toward Sandy Hook and eventually, New York.

BRITISH REAR GUARD

CLINTON

WAYNE

LEE

Monmouth Court House

ALEXANDER

CORNWALLIS

Wemrock Creek

LAFAYETTE

WAYNE

GREENE

WASHINGTON

Comb's Hill

NEW JERSEY

East Ravine

West Ravine

N

= AMERICANS   = BRITISH

JDD and TPS

formed a main line of defense behind West Ravine. Artillery was rushed forward under Knox, Washington's gunner, and Nathanael Greene unlimbered at least four pieces on a prominent bit of high ground below the stream known as Comb's Hill. Supported by a brigade of infantry, Greene's artillery enfiladed the advancing enemy. This fire, coupled with small arms and supported by other artillery pieces from the front temporarily stabilized the holding position. Clinton had also brought up a large number of artillery pieces, and the duel that followed (and continued later in the day) was one of the most intense of the war. The fighting was long and hard, often at close quarters and, according to some accounts, hand-to-hand. A mounted attack against Washington's left, together with a final British push by mounted infantry and grenadiers, folded and broke the holding line.

Washington's final line of battle was well chosen with the help of a local officer who knew the ground. Marshy terrain in front of the high ground made attacking there problematic, while woods in the back allowed the Americans to maneuver troops unseen. Anthony Wayne deployed his brigade slightly in advance of the line in the center, while Alexander (Stirling) held the left and Greene the right. Lafayette was in charge of a semi-second line (perhaps best described as a reserve) behind and between Alexander and Greene.

By this time it was mid-afternoon. Clinton aligned his exhausted soldiers and attacked again, confident that one more push would win the day. His light infantry and the 42nd ("Black Watch") Regiment of Foot struck Alexander (Washington's left). Strong leadership and the steadfastness of the newly-trained American riflemen blunted the assaults of some of the world's finest infantry. A counterattack threw back the redcoats and ended the danger on the northern end of Washington's line.

As the fighting raged on in the north, Cornwallis organized an attack in the south against Greene's front (Washington's right flank). The Earl oversaw the assault himself. His attacking column was comprised of perhaps the best soldiers in Clinton's army. In precise rows they advanced as if on parade, but Greene's Continentals shot them from the front, and the artillery on Comb's Hill ripped into their flank. Unable to break through and having suffered heavy losses, Cornwallis gave up. A series of heavy attacks was launched against Wayne's men in the center of the line even before Cornwallis had finished, but those were also bloodily repulsed. Washington withdrew Wayne's command when the British formed for a fourth attack, this one threatening to overlap both of Wayne's flanks.

With Wayne's men now on a line with Alexander and Greene, Washington straightened his front and awaited Clinton's next assault. It never came. It was now about 5:30 p.m., and even though plenty of daylight remained, the fighting was largely over. Although the battle had thus far been a tactical draw, both sides were losing the battle against the heat, which had prostrated hundreds of men and killed scores. Displaying his penchant for aggressive tactics, but failing to fully appreciate the enervated state of his army, Washington ordered a counterattack. Although the men attempted to carry out the order, they were only able to march a short distance before collapsing in exhaustion. Clinton, meanwhile, withdrew his army about one mile east, rested until midnight, and continued his retreat in the wake of Knyphausen's wing. By June 30 his entire army was on the coast at Sandy Hook. He and his men reached New York City on July 5.

Casualties: British: 147 killed, 170 wounded, and 60 more who died from heat stroke; American: 72 killed, 161 wounded, and 130 missing (37 died from heat stroke). Many authorities question these traditional casualty figures. Almost certainly both sides lost substantially more, especially in wounded. American soldiers buried between 217 and 249 enemy dead. One credible source puts Clinton's losses at 1,200 from all causes. In addition, more than 400 German deserters surrendered in Philadelphia one week later.

Outcome / Impact: The battle of Monmouth ended in a tactical draw, with Washington's army holding the field the following morning. It was the last major engagement in the Northern colonies during the American Revolution, the longest battle of the war, and witnessed the largest artillery duel. The American army had proven it could stand up against an entire British army in a pitched battle. The years of experience, coupled with the training it received at Valley Forge, had finally paid off.

Clinton conducted a difficult retreat reasonably well, though his entire career in the war was marked by bad luck. He was a good general with a solid grasp of the realities of the American conflict, plagued by weak political connections, surrounded by a fractious command structure, and hampered by his own difficult personality.

The battle ended Charles Lee's military career. Washington did not intend to officially investigate Lee's poor performance, but Lee insisted upon an immediate court of inquiry in a series of letters that personally attacked Washington. The commander in chief ordered Lee's arrest and launched a courts-martial. General Alexander presided over the hearing. Lee was found guilty on all counts and suspended from command for one year. His withering personal attacks against Washington made it impossible for anyone in a position of authority to support him.

During the battle an American heroine known popularly as "Molly Pitcher" (likely Mary Ludwig Hays) rendered her famous service to the nation by carrying water for the troops and manning an American field piece when her husband, an artilleryman, was wounded.

Today: Monmouth Battlefield State Park honors the memory of the combatants and preserves the rural area as it looked in the summer of 1778. The area offers recreational opportunities such as hiking and horseback riding, and picnic areas are also available. A Revolutionary-era farmhouse and a visitor center on Comb's Hill provide interpretive programs and archaeological artifacts. A reenactment is held annually each June.

Further Reading: Stryker, William S., *The Battle of Monmouth* (Princeton University Press, 1927); Ward, Christopher, *The War of the Revolution,* 2 vols. (Macmillian Company, 1952); Willcox, William B., *Portrait of a General: Sir Henry Clinton in the War of Independence* (Knopf, 1964).

Wyoming, Battle of (also known as the Massacre of Wyoming), Sullivan's Campaign

Date: July 3, 1778.

Region: Northern Colonies, Pennsylvania.

Commanders: British: Major John Butler; Tory: Sir John Johnson; Indian: Chief "Captain" Joseph Brant; American: Colonel Zebulon Butler and Colonel Nathan Denison.

Time of Day / Length of Action: Late afternoon (6:00 to 6:30 p.m); 30 minutes of fighting followed by twelve hours of torture and murder.

Weather Conditions: Hot and humid.

Opposing Forces: British: 700; American: 375.

British Perspective: After losing the battles of Fort Stanwix and Oriskany, most of Col. Barry St. Leger's forces retreated to Canada; others wintered at Fort Niagara in the wilds of western New York. This disheartened and revenge-seeking force was composed of opportunistic Tories, embittered British soldiers, and Indians. In May and June of 1778, these men organized into raiding parties under the overall (though loose) command of British Maj. John Butler, Tory leader Sir John Johnson, and Indian Chief "Captain" Joseph Brant. Although these men conducted a series of raids under the guise of military operations, their deeds reflected the actions of barbaric mobs. Their focus was the American settlements in the western valleys of New York and Pennsylvania.

The largest raiding party departed Fort Niagara in June and marched for the settlements and outposts of Wyoming Valley (present-day Wilkes-Barre, Pennsylvania). The 700-man raiding "army" contained British rangers, Tories, and Indian warriors of the Mohawk, Onondaga, Cayuga, Oneida, Tuscarora, and Seneca tribes. These Indians of the Iroquois Nation were notoriously ruthless and were feared by American settlers.

The raid into the Wyoming Valley caught the settlers unaware, allowing the British to capture American outposts in the northern part of the valley at Forts Wintermoot and Jenkins with little effort. Major Butler sent a detachment south to the main American garrison at Forty Fort and extended an offer of surrender. The Americans refused, leaving Butler to wait for the arrival of an American relief force. On July 3 the American column was detected and Butler ordered the destruction of the American forts and planned an ambush against the advancing enemy relief column.

American Perspective: Colonel George Rogers Clark was conducting his offensive into the Northwestern Territory when the combined British and Indian expedition struck the American settlements in the northeastern frontier lands of New York and Pennsylvania. Word spread quickly throughout western Pennsylvania in May and June of 1778 that Indians were with the raiding British and Tories. Settlers had fought long and hard to keep the Indians at bay in Pennsylvania's Wyoming Valley. These summer 1778 raids were different because they were more organized and included not just Indians but experienced British and Tory soldiers.

In late June 1778, Col. Nathan Denison, the local commander of forts and settlements in western Pennsylvania, learned from scouts that a large British and Indian raiding party was assembling in Pittston near Fort Wintermoot. The Americans utilized a network of scouts and forts to protect the frontier settlements, and the alarm echoed throughout the Wyoming Valley. Settlers moved quickly into the forts and militiamen reported for duty, just as they had done so many times before. At Forty Fort, Colonel Denison and the more experienced Col. Zebulon Butler (no relation to British Maj. John Butler) decided to venture north and meet the enemy before they could reach their homes, crops, and loved ones. While debating the merits of an offensive campaign, a detachment of the enemy arrived with several prisoners captured at Fort Wintermoot. The British demanded an immediate surrender, which the Americans refused.

Terrain: In 1778 this area of Pennsylvania was wilderness forest sprinkled with several small settlements and farms interspersed along the fertile river valleys. The Wyoming Valley is a large fertile plain surrounded by rolling hills that dominate the countryside. The valley covers 25 miles of the north branch of the Susquehanna River. Within this valley was a chain of forts approximately three miles apart, south to north as follows: Wilkes-Barre, Forty Fort, and Forts Wintermoot, Jenkins, and Pittston.

The Fighting: On the afternoon of July 3, American Colonels Butler and Denison led 375 Americans northward from Forty Fort into the Wyoming Valley, across Abraham's Creek, and on to Swetland's Hill. The army moved cautiously as it advanced through the forested hills. Around 4:00 p.m. advanced scouts returned to report the enemy had burned American forts and was retreating from the area. Butler and Denison continued moving north to Exeter Flats, near Fort Wintermoot.

With the afternoon sun going down behind the hills, the British replaced their red uniform coats with dark clothing and hid in the shadows of a thick forest across a plain from the smoldering hulk that was once Fort Wintermoot. As the Americans approached the ambush was sprung, with musket fire erupting from a line of British rangers posted in a field. The Americans were reasonably well trained and advanced with traditional volley fire. Without warning, Indians sprang up from the woods on the American right (east) and attacked the surprised column. Although the attack was beaten back, the Americans took heavy casualties. Without pause more Indians attacked the American left (west) as the British regulars began retreating from the field. The Americans held off the attacks, but their renewed advance carried the column deeper into a trap where more Indians were waiting to attack them while hidden in the forest. With their left flank under assault, the American ranks were rolled up and surrounded by a British and Indian force twice their strength. Butler and Denison attempted to retreat, but their little army was surrounded, confused, and at the mercy of their foe. Only Colonel Butler and 15 Americans escaped the ambush; the others were killed, wounded, or forced to surrender.

The events that followed that evening were nothing less than a large-scale massacre. For the next twelve hours, the British allowed their Indian allies to torture and kill their prisoners. In a humiliating ceremony the following day (July 4), Major Butler forced Denison to sign a formal declaration of surrender. The terms stipulated the Americans would lay down their arms and destroy their remaining forts.

Casualties: British and Tory: five killed, eight wounded; Indian: 80 reported casualties; American: 301 soldiers killed (227 scalped), 300 settlers including women and children were carried away and/or killed, 1,000 homes were burned, and large numbers of livestock killed or carried away.

Outcome / Impact: The British-Indian victory led to the systematic destruction of homes throughout the Wyoming Valley. Surviving settlers

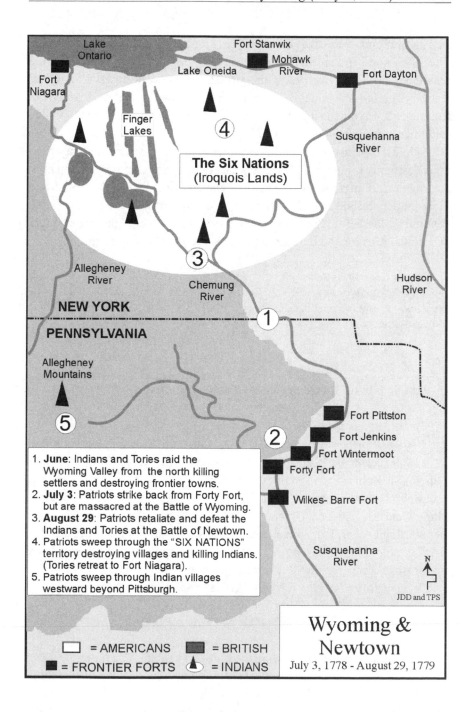

Wyoming & Newtown
July 3, 1778 - August 29, 1779

fled the area and news of the disaster spread through the western settlements. The British and Indian marauders terrorized the entire region through the remainder of 1778. Even after the British retreated northward to winter quarters, the Indians remained and continued raiding operations. American frontiersmen avoided the Wyoming, Cherry, and Lackawanna Valley settlements until the summer of 1779.

While the British and their Indian allies achieved a sense of victory from their destructive raids, the temporary success only intensified sentiment to destroy the Indian presence in America. The growing disdain for British and Tory soldiers rallied more Americans to the cause of liberty. The cry of the Wyoming Massacre echoes through history as a reminder of the brutal nature of partisan warfare and the hatred that fans the flames of retribution.

Further Reading: Tomlinson, Everett, *In days of peril: A Boy's Story of the Massacre in the Wyoming Valley in 1778* (A. L. Burt, 1901); Ward, Christopher, *The War of the Revolution*, 2 vols. (Macmillian Company, 1952); n.a., *The Massacre of Wyoming* (Wilkes-Barre, PA, 1895).

Rhode Island, Battle of (Rhode Island Campaign)

Date: August 29, 1778.
Region: Northern Colonies, Rhode Island.
Commanders: British: Lieutenant General Sir Henry Clinton, Major General Sir Robert Pigot, Major General Frederich Wilhelm von Lossberg, and Major General Francis Smith; American: Major General John Sullivan, Major General Nathanael Greene, Brigadier General John Glover, Brigadier General John Tyler, Brigadier General James Varnum, Colonel Christopher Greene, Colonel Ezekiel Cornell, Colonel John Laurens, and Colonel Henry Livingstone; French:Admiral Comte d'Estaing.
Time of Day / Length of Action: All day (pre-dawn to 4:00 p.m.).
Weather Conditions: Clear and extremely hot.
Opposing Forces: British: 7,000; American: 5,000.

British Perspective: Following the Battle of Monmouth (June 28, 1778), General Sir Henry Clinton continued his withdrawal to New York, marching his army to the Atlantic shore at Sandy Hook, New Jersey. A French fleet of twelve powerful warships commanded by Admiral Comte d'Estaing arrived off the bar before Clinton could finish his journey by sea. Hesitant about sailing into unfamiliar waters (he could not get safely over the bar), the French admiral lingered for eleven days before sailing away to the north. Admiral Richard Howe's fleet safely ferried the British army to New York City.

With France now allied with the Americans, the Crown ordered Clinton to abandon his offensive strategy in the Northern department in favor of a defensive approach. A new offensive would be opened in the Carolinas. The French fleet lurking offshore offered the Americans a broader array of offensive opportunities than they had previously enjoyed. During the first week of August, British intelligence reported American troops massing near Providence, Rhode Island, for an attack against Newport, and that the French fleet was supporting the operation. Clinton organized a relief operation and set sail with a strong fleet and 5,000 reinforcements.

The commander of the British garrison at Newport was Maj. Gen. Sir Robert Pigot. His men were protected by the sea on two sides, a narrow inland channel on the third, and strong entrenchments covering the land approaches on the fourth side. Pigot's troops included British, Hessians, and Loyalists, about 3,000 men.

American Perspective: General Washington abandoned his pursuit of Clinton's field army when his plan to interrupt the British march to the sea failed at Monmouth (June 28, 1778). Instead, Washington focused on realigning his army to prepare to exploit opportunities pending arrival of the French fleet. Admiral Comte d'Estaing's French squadron arrived off the New Jersey shore on July 9, where it was unable to molest the British naval effort waiting to ferry Clinton's army to New York City. Washington persuaded the French admiral to sail north to support an American plan to assault and capture Newport, Rhode Island. His ships would be needed to protect and support General John Sullivan's land force, and d'Estaing's 4,000 men available for land operations could easily be put to good use.

Meanwhile, the Continental Congress returned to newly recaptured Philadelphia and Washington moved his headquarters to West Point, New York. From this position he could defend the Hudson River Valley from another British expedition he was all but certain was coming. By defending in the north and simultaneously moving against the British garrison in Rhode Island in the south, Washington hoped the combined French-American operation would score a military and political victory sufficient to humiliate the British and weaken their will to fight on. The ranks of the Rhode Island militia swelled with the prospect of removing the British antagonists occupying their homeland.

Washington requested 5,000 militia from New England to bolster Sullivan's operation and dispatched Lafayette with two veteran Continental brigades, together with Nathanael Greene, to assist. By the time the operation was set to begin Sullivan had 10,000 men in his army, which was divided into two grand divisions, one each under Lafayette and Greene. Their mission was straightforward: move from Providence to the island holding Newport and, in conjunction with the French naval and ground resources, cut off and capture the British garrison. Success would effectively remove British troops from Rhode Island soil. Implementing the plan, however, would prove much more difficult than it looked on paper.

The French fleet anchored in Narragansett Bay opposite the western shore of Newport. The plan of attack formulated by General Sullivan for August 10 consisted of a two-pronged move designed to trap the British within the confines of Newport. Sullivan would march from the mainland at Tiverton in the east, cross the Sakonnet River, and march south down the length of the island toward the fortified enemy position while the French moved toward Newport in a similar manner from the west. A preliminary move on August 5 demonstrated how skittish the defenders were when the French thrust a pair of fast frigates into the Sakonnet Channel. In one of the strangest episodes of the war, the British reacted by destroying their own fleet—eight warships and a variety of transports. Some were run aground and set afire; others were sunk to block passage to the French. On August 8, d'Estaing ran his fleet up the Middle Passage to support Sullivan's operation. The next day Sullivan crossed his army onto the northern end of the island after British forces there fell back south to avoid being trapped by the French. As more than one writer has pointed out, it was at this juncture Franco-American fortunes took a sudden and unexpected turn for the worse.

Terrain: The battle occurred on the Island of Rhode Island (also known as Aquidneck Island) in Narragansett Bay, Rhode Island. The 44-square mile island is 15 miles long north to south. It is four miles across at its widest point in the south, and two miles wide in the north, where its primary connection to the mainland is across a narrow passage of the Sakonnet River to Tiverton. Newport offered an excellent harbor on the extreme southwestern tip of the island, which extends into Rhode Island Sound and the Atlantic Ocean beyond it. In 1778 there were two main roads (East Road and West Road) running the length of the island (north and south) connecting Newport with Portsmouth and the passage to the mainland at Tiverton (in the northeast). The hilly terrain on the northern end of the island descends in a gentle slope to the southern side of the island. Newport was built on the island's lowest point in the southwestern corner. The primary fighting occurred in the north on three dominant hills: Turkey Hill in the west, Quaker Hill in the east, and Butts Hill in the north.

The Fighting: When Clinton learned of the plan to capture Newport, he dispatched a fleet under Admiral William Howe on August 1 to confront the French. Unfavorable wind delayed his arrival until the 9th. When Admiral d'Estaing learned of Howe's arrival he abandoned his part of the land operation and made for open water to crush or disperse the enemy fleet. It was a dangerous gamble even though the French fleet was fully one-third larger than Howe's. The French had already landed hundreds of sick soldiers on Conanicut Island. Together with Sullivan's command, they would be cut off and captured if d'Estaing suffered a reverse. Sullivan, however, marched to the southern end of the island on August 15 opposite Pigot's heavy entrenchments and prepared for what he hoped would be a short siege.

What was shaping up to be one of the potentially great sea battles of history failed to materialize. A giant gale blew up on the night of August 11, separating the fleets and the individual ships of each. Several large French warships (especially d'Estaing's own flagship *Languedoc*, which lost all three masts) were heavily damaged. A few brief small combats were waged to no one's advantage. The British ships, already long overdue for repairs, were now no longer seaworthy, which prompted Howe to sail for New York.

Sullivan, meanwhile, laboring under the impression the French would be assisting his campaign, undertook traditional siege approaches. On August 20 d'Estaing returned to announce he was sailing for Boston to repair his ships—and then left. The news crushed American morale and tens of hundreds of militia melted away from the army, cleaving it nearly in half. Substantially weakened and now alone on the island, Sullivan's command was ripe for capture, especially if British warships reappeared. Although Sullivan boasted he would continue the siege, on the 28th of August he marched his army north to escape to the mainland. Pigot promptly pursued the Americans with his British and Hessian troops covering both roads. The move forced Sullivan to deploy his men in a two-mile defensive line on the high ground seven miles north of Newport.

The American left wing (which would have been under the command of Lafayette, but he had ridden to Boston to try and persuade d'Estaing to return the fleet to Newport) was comprised of Gen. John Glover's brigade, Gen. John Tyler's Connecticut militia, and a brigade led by Col. Christopher Greene. These troops guarded the East Road and Quaker Hill. On the right was Nathanael Greene's wing, with Brig. Gen. James Varnum's brigade and a regiment led by Col. Henry Livingstone defending the West Road and Turkey Hill. In the center connecting the two wings was Col. Ezekiel

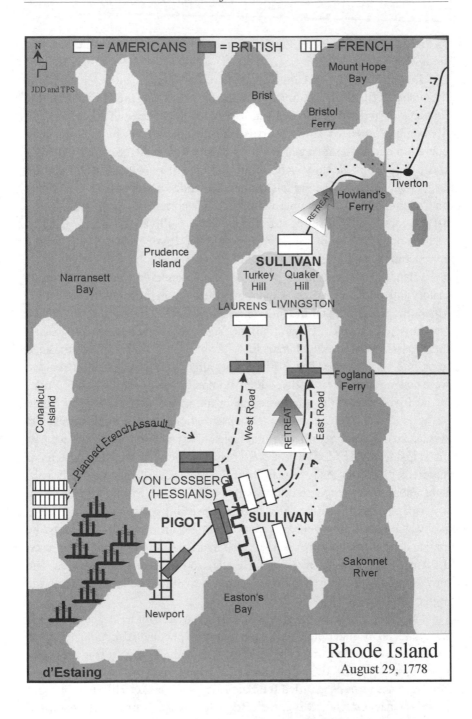

N

JDD and TPS

☐ = AMERICANS   ▨ = BRITISH   ⊞ = FRENCH

Mount Hope Bay

Brist

Bristol Ferry

Tiverton

Howland's Ferry

RETREAT

Prudence Island

SULLIVAN

Narransett Bay

Turkey Hill   Quaker Hill

LAURENS LIVINGSTON

Conanicut Island

Planned French Assault

West Road

East Road

Fogland Ferry

RETREAT

VON LOSSBERG (HESSIANS)

PIGOT

SULLIVAN

Sakonnet River

Easton's Bay

Newport

d'Estaing

Rhode Island
August 29, 1778

Cornell's brigade of Rhode Island militia. Sullivan deployed skirmishers on both main roads under Col. John Laurens in the west and Colonel Livingstone in the east.

Pigot's pursuit moved rapidly in three columns up the main roads. The left column on the West Road under Maj. Gen. Frederich Wilhelm von Lossberg (Hessian Jägers, two Ansbach regiments, Hessian Regiment Huyn, Fanning's Provincial New York Regiment, and later Brown's Provincial Regiment) made contact with Greene. The other columns moving against Sullivan's left up the East Road were led by Maj. Gen. Francis Smith (22nd and 43rd regiments and the flank companies of the 38th and 54th regiments). General Richard Prescott, who had been exchanged for General Sullivan in September 1776, also moved north near the East Road leading the 38th and 54th regiments. Pigot found advanced enemy skirmishers about midnight three miles ahead of Sullivan's main line. An effort to break through failed when Sullivan reinforced them. A more serious attempt opened both roads.

Early on the 29th Greene urged Sullivan to attack von Lossberg before his supporting troops were up, but Sullivan was not as bold as Nathanael Greene and so declined to do so. Attacks against Sullivan's left were thrown back. Von Lossberg had more success against the American right wing, where he captured some advance works and began an artillery duel with Sullivan. Several British warships made their appearance and began enfilading Sullivan's right, but the troops remained in place and threw back Pigot's attackers. The ships moved out of range when Greene turned his heavier guns against them. A new regiment of black troops from Rhode Island played a prominent role in the repulse of von Lossberg's Hessians. The long hot summer day wore down the exhausted combatants, many of whom on both sides died of sunstroke.

The balance of the day was spent fitfully firing muskets at long range. When darkness arrived Sullivan continued his withdrawal, loading his men and equipment into boats and rowing across the narrow strait to Tiverton. Those militiamen still in the ranks were dismissed and Sullivan returned with about 1,200 Continentals to Providence.

Casualties: British: 38 killed, 210 wounded, and 12 missing; American: 30 killed, 137 wounded, and 44 missing.

Outcome / Impact: The Franco-American expedition, so carefully planned and promising much success, ended in humiliating disappointment. It had no strategic consequences of note, though it threatened to break apart the new working relationship between the French and Americans. Sullivan believed d'Estaing deserted him in his hour of need, and news being what it was at that time, many of the colonists seemed to agree. General Washington eventually got involved to smooth emotions and settle the matter. After the failed fiasco at Newport Sullivan returned to Providence, guarded American interests in the state, and went into winter quarters there. The British victory allowed them to maintain control of Newport and its splendid harbor. Clinton reinforced Newport with 4,000 additional troops on September 1, swelling the total in Rhode Island to about 11,000.

Today: Little remains today to tell the story of this campaign. Fort Barton, which served as a staging area for the island's invasion, can be toured, and a memorial honors the service of black soldiers in the battle.

Further Reading: Angell, Israel (Edward Field, ed.), *Diary of Colonel Israel Angell Commanding the Second Rhode Island Continental Regiment during the American Revolution 1778-1781* (Preston and Rounds, 1899); Walker, Anthony, *So Few The Brave: Rhode Island Continentals 1775-1783* (Seafield Press, 1981); Ward, Christopher, *The War of the Revolution,* 2 vols. (Macmillian Company, 1952).

Savannah, Battle of (Southern Campaign)

Date: December 29, 1778.
Region: Southern Colonies, Georgia.
Commanders: British: Lieutenant Colonel Archibald Campbell, Major General Augustine Prevost, Commodore Hyde Parker, and Sir James Baird; American: Major General Robert Howe, Brigadier General Isaac Huger, and Lieutenant Colonel Samuel Elbert.
Time of Day / Length of Action: Afternoon (2:00 p.m. to 3:00 p.m.).
Weather Conditions: Cool and clear.
Opposing Forces: British: 3,500; American: 850.

British Perspective: With a stalemate in the Northern Department, General Clinton reluctantly transferred 5,000 soldiers to the West Indies to bolster the defense of the British Islands against the French and dispatched Lt. Col. Archibald Campbell with 3,500 troops to join Maj. Gen. Augustine Prevost in British-occupied East Florida (which was claimed by Spain). General Prevost, who had been launching raids into Georgia, also controlled a large contingent of Tory militia.

On February 17, 1777, these soldiers (known as the "Florida Rangers") had attacked Fort McIntosh near present-day Atkinson, Georgia. Fort

McIntosh was a small but strategically important American outpost located between the Satilla and Altamaha rivers. Its commander, Capt. Richard Winn, together with 60 Patriot soldiers defended the post for two days against several hundred Indians and British provincials led by Col. Thomas Brown. The Patriots ultimately surrendered the fort in the face of overwhelming odds. The citizens of coastal Georgia realized the gravity of the growing threat directed against them.

The brave but ill-prepared Georgians struck back with three successive raids (1st, 2nd, and 3rd Florida Expeditions) into East Florida. However, the Florida Rangers successfully repelled each American expedition. While the difficult swamps of coastal Florida played a role in the American setbacks, the Tory Florida Rangers soundly defeated the Americans in the battles of Alligator Creek and Trout River. The Tories— and especially Col. Thomas Brown—excelled in launching raids. During 1777 and 1778, these same Tories also captured Fort Howe, another American outpost in coastal Georgia. This fighting had no real impact on the war as a whole, but they set the stage for a bitter contest for southern Georgia and East Florida, a campaign that would ultimately focus on the key port city of Savannah. The arrival of Campbell's reinforcements provided General Prevost with an army large enough to launch a campaign into Georgia. The state's citizens were about to pay dearly for sending raiding parties into Florida.

Anticipating the arrival of Campbell's reinforcements, General Prevost had been moving his command north from Florida toward Sunbury, Georgia, 40 miles below Savannah. He advanced in two columns, one led by Lt. Col. L. V. Fuser with 400 men and the other with 500 men under the general's brother, Lt. Col. Mark Prevost. The columns moved northward on parallel routes, Fuser by boat and Prevost by land. The overall goal was to defeat the rebel outposts at Sunbury and Fort Morris.

On November 22, 1778, Colonel Prevost made contact with the enemy below Sunbury. Although he had a superior force, he was not in contact with Colonel Fuser's command and decided to withdraw. Fuser's force, meanwhile, arrived by water at Fort Morris three days later and disembarked. The determined men defending the fort refused to be intimidated by a few hundred soldiers in small boats. In a replay of the Sunbury fiasco, Fuser also withdrew. He was unsure of where the land column was and did not have the stomach to assault on his own.

The British squadron en route to Florida carrying Colonel Campbell's men, meanwhile, faced difficult seas. On December 23 the ships finally arrived at Tybee Island just off shore from Savannah, Georgia. Colonel Campbell gathered information about the port's defenses and surmised he could conquer the city without General Prevost. Campbell, an aggressive veteran of many fields of battle, decided to conduct an offensive with his forces at hand.

On December 27, Commodore Hyde Parker maneuvered his squadron into the mouth of the Savannah River. On the morning of the 29th Campbell launched his invasion of Georgia. He disembarked his command at Girardeau's plantation. A battalion of the 71st Foot and the New York Volunteers moved quickly to secure the beachhead against 50 South Carolina Continentals. A brief skirmish killed three British and wounded five more, but the Americans were easily thrown back. Once ashore, the British moved along a wide arc on the only roads that led southward around rice fields and then northwest to face the defenders of Savannah.

American Perspective: Major General Robert Howe was the commander of the Southern Department in 1778. While Georgia had a militia and a small navy, there was a lack of unity and the lack of a direct threat from the British. As a result, the area around Georgia's chief port of Savannah was not on a war footing when the enemy arrived. The British had a foothold in Florida, but the troops there consisted primarily of Indians and Tories seeking refuge in the nearest British post. Three separate expeditions had been launched against the Florida-based British, but each succumbed to the climate, swampy terrain, and Tory resistance. In late 1778 the Georgians decided to leave the enemy to the south alone. Occasional enemy raids threatened coastal Georgia towns, and the local militiamen did what they could to maintain a vigilant defense to provide a barrier between the port city and the enemy in Florida.

On November 22, just south of Sunbury, Georgia, Cols. John White and James Screven rallied their troops when word spread through the area the British were advancing northward. These officers could only muster a 120-man composite force of Continentals and militia and so retreated. Another British column at nearby Fort Morris arrived by boat on the 25th of November. The enemy troops disembarked and approached the fort. Patriot commander Col. John McIntosh led a contingent of 200 determined men. When the British commander demanded they surrender McIntosh told him to try and take it. To his surprise, the British retreated.

On the morning of December 29, British warships crossed the bar and moved inland via the Savannah River. The fleet halted three miles east of Savannah at Girardeau's plantation, where 3,500 troops disembarked. Once ashore, the British moved along a wide arc on the only roads that led southward around rice fields and then northwest to face the defenders of Savannah.

With 200 men defending Sunbury, Howe was left with only about 850 men (some sources claim as many as 1,200) to defend Savannah. It would not be nearly enough. Because the city's fortifications had been allowed to decay, Howe defended the port at a strategic point on the main road between Savannah and the coastal plantations southeast of the city. He divided his army into two wings and positioned them in a semi-circle on the outskirts of the city facing the enemy, who were approaching from the southeast. Brigadier General Isaac Huger commanded the right wing of Continentals and other troops, while Lt. Col. Samuel Elbert commanded Georgia militia troops on the left. Patriot artillery was unlimbered to support both wings. The flanks were protected by river marshes on the left, a wooded swamp on the right, and 200 yards to the front a marshy creek divided the combatants. The lone bridge crossing the creek between the armies was destroyed. Within these defensive positions the Americans, outnumbered about 4-to-1, waited for the British to attack.

Terrain: Savannah lies on the southern bank of the Savannah River seventeen miles inland from the Atlantic Ocean. The river averaged a depth of 30 feet and emptied from the highlands in the northwest to the coastal plain and Savannah in the southeast. In the 1770s the lowlands of Georgia along the river were comprised primarily of rice plantations. Savannah served as the heart of this thriving agricultural and mercantile center. The region consisted of shifting sands and salt marshes, though most of the city was constructed on solid terrain. Approaches to the city from the south, east, and west were canalized on narrow spits of land surrounded by marshes, creeks, and tidal flats.

The Fighting: As Colonel Campbell led his British toward Savannah he dispatched scouts to conduct a reconnaissance. A slave showed the British scouts how to traverse the swamp through a footpath around the American right flank. Campbell marched his light infantry and Highlanders into position directly opposite the Americans center and left to leave the impression he would assault that position. A detachment of light infantry under Sir James Baird, together with the New York Volunteers, followed the footpath around the western flank of Howe's position. While Baird marched Campbell made demonstrations with field artillery and skirmishers to hold his enemy's attention and distract them from his heavy left hook.

Baird's men found and successfully attacked the American right flank and rear and collapsed it, at which time Campbell rolled forward his light field artillery and ordered his main line to attack. The tactical plan was brilliant and well executed. The next act in the fighting was described by Campbell in his after-action report: "I commanded the line to move forward

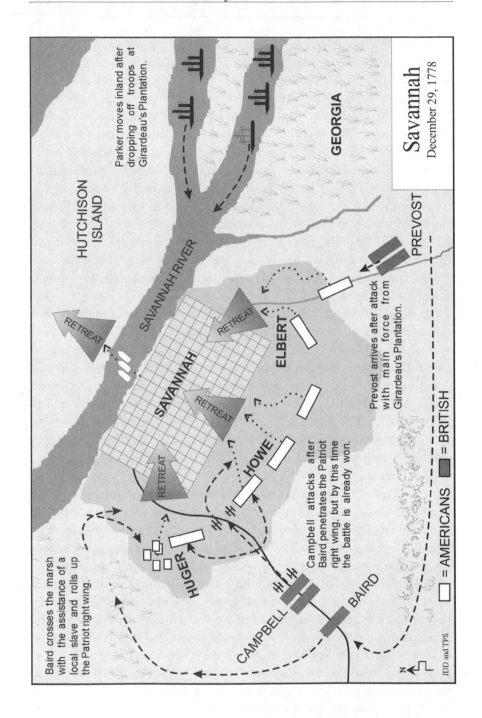

Parker moves inland after dropping off troops at Girardeau's Plantation.

HUTCHISON ISLAND

SAVANNAH RIVER

GEORGIA

RETREAT

RETREAT

RETREAT

RETREAT

SAVANNAH

ELBERT

HOWE

HUGER

CAMPBELL

BAIRD

PREVOST

Baird crosses the marsh with the assistance of a local slave and rolls up the Patriot right wing.

Campbell attacks after Baird penetrates the Patriot right wing, but by this time the battle is already won.

Prevost arrives after attack with main force from Girardeau's Plantation.

Savannah
December 29, 1778

☐ = AMERICANS ■ = BRITISH

N

JDD and TPS

briskly. The well aimed fire of the artillery, and the rapid advance of the troops caused the Enemy to disperse instantly. As the Light Infantry under Sir James Baird came out of the Swamp, the scattered remains of the Carolina and Georgia Brigades ran across his front, and he dashed forward on their flank, and with his usual gallantry terminated the Fate of the Day with a brilliant success." Howe quickly realized his plight and did his best to effect a withdrawal across narrow Musgrove causeway. With the British in his rear, on one of his flanks, and now piercing what had been his front, his army dissolved into a desperate mob seeking escape by any means. The defense of Savannah ended after less than one hour of light artillery fighting and a few minutes of small arms exchange.

Casualties: British: three killed and 10 wounded; American: 83 killed and wounded and 453 captured. It is worth noting that only about half of Campbell's men (Baird's flanking column) were actually engaged against perhaps 150 defenders.

Outcome / Impact: The loss of Savannah was a tremendous blow to American morale and the economy of the Southern Theater. While General Howe escaped from the battlefield, American losses were staggering. In addition to the killed and wounded the British captured 48 cannons, 23 mortars, 94 barrels of powder, vast quantities of food, materiel, several ships, and the city itself. The fall of this port city was one of the more significant battlefield losses of the war for the Patriots. Howe was cleared by a court of inquiry, but his failure to demonstrate much initiative or choose his options wisely ended his military career. Campbell, by contrast, demonstrated his tactical brilliance.

During the next few weeks General Prevost and his troops pushed northward and captured Fort Morris at Sunbury and other pockets of Patriot resistors. This resulted in the loss of 212 Patriots and 40 more cannons. One month to the day after Savannah fell Campbell captured Augusta, Georgia. The victorious British spread out to secure more terrain and quell the rebellion in southwest Georgia. Tory leaders were utilized to rally Loyalist support across the state. The loss of Savannah, Augusta, and strong Tory support marked the beginning of British occupation of the state, which would continue until almost the end of the war.

Today: Little physical evidence remains of the fighting in Savannah because of modern construction. However, the Coastal Heritage Society interprets and preserves Savannah history and has joined with the city of Savannah to expand historical interpretation and preservation efforts that include the Revolutionary War.

Further Reading: Lumpkin, Henry, *From Savannah to Yorktown: The American Revolution in the South* (Paragon House, 1981); Walcott, Charles H., *Sir Archibald Campbell of Inverneill; Sometime Prisoner of War in the Jail at Concord, Massachusetts* (Concord, 1898).

Kettle Creek, Battle of (Southern Campaign)

Date: February 14, 1779.
Region: Southern Colonies, Georgia.
Commanders: British: Colonel James Boyd; American: Colonels Elijah Clarke, John Dooly, and Andrew Pickens.
Time of Day / Length of Action: Afternoon, one hour.
Weather Conditions: Cool and clear.
Opposing Forces: British: (Tory) 750; American: 340.

British Perspective: After Lt. Col. Archibald Campbell defeated the Patriots in late December 1778 at Savannah, Georgia, the British swept through the region destroying pockets of rebel resistance. Word of the successful British invasion and the successful opening of a Southern front forced local citizens to make difficult choices. The British presence inflamed the passions of Tories (Loyalists) and Whigs (Patriots), and the choices made embroiled the region into a bloody civil war. This irregular and often brutal combat quickly spread into the hinterlands of Georgia and the Carolinas. In order to persuade the local populace to join the Loyalist cause, Tory leader Col. John Hamilton traveled to Augusta with a large mounted force to rally support for the Crown. Lieutenant Colonel Campbell followed Hamilton to Augusta with 1,700 British regulars to occupy the city and extract pro-British support from the local population.

Meanwhile, another Tory leader named Col. James Boyd traveled through the rural hinterlands of northeast Georgia toward Augusta to join the British army. On February 11 (or 12, depending upon the source), while Colonel Boyd swept through Wilkes County, a 100-man Patriot patrol attacked his column as it crossed Van[n]'s Creek (Cherokee Ford). Boyd's force numbered 750 men, however, and easily brushed aside the Patriots. Boyd knew anti-British sentiment was rampant in the area, and he adopted more protective measures as his column continued southward. On the 14th of February Boyd's column established a campsite in a draw along Kettle Creek. A strong security force was deployed on the high ground surrounding the camp. With 150 men out foraging, the Tory force in and around the camp numbered about 600 men.

American Perspective: The loss of Savannah at the end of 1779 was a tremendous blow to the morale and economy of Georgia. The British pushed inland and rallied available Loyalists to fight alongside them to crush the rebellion in the South. With the arrival of a strong Tory presence in Augusta under Col. John Hamilton, a North Carolinian and veteran of the famous Scottish battle at Culloden in 1745, the Patriots in the region rallied to counter the enemy threat.

South Carolinian Col. Andrew Pickens and about 200 men traveled from South Carolina's District Ninety Six into northeast Georgia to join forces with those of Cols. Elijah Clarke and John Dooly. Pickens assumed command of the combined column. As the Tories moved from Augusta into the rural backwoods of Georgia, Patriot patrols attacked them whenever possible. Pickens and his men were picking and prodding elements from Colonel Hamilton's British force at Carr's Fort along Beaverdam Creek when Pickens learned of Boyd's larger and potentially more lucrative column of Tories. The South Carolinian abandoned his effort and decided to go after Boyd. On or about February 11 a large Patriot patrol briefly clashed with Boyd as his command crossed the Savannah River north of Cherokee Ford at Van[n]'s Creek. The extent of the casualties and specifics vary, but the short combat alerted the Tories that rebels were nearby and in strength.

On February 13, in Wilkes County, Georgia, Pickens learned that Colonel Boyd's Tory column had made camp in a wooded draw along Kettle Creek, eight miles southwest of present-day Washington, Georgia. Pickens decided to attack the enemy encampment and organized his men for an assault. The Georgia and South Carolina militia numbered a combined 340 men. The small army was divided into three units and deployed into a line of battle with Colonel Pickens holding the center, Colonel Dooly the right, and Colonel Elijah Clarke on the left. Moving together in a three-pronged assault, the Patriot line approached the Tory encampment.

Terrain: The rural area surrounding Washington, Georgia, is hilly and interspersed with swift moving creeks that drain southeast into the Savannah River. The battlefield consists of a single dominant hill (known today as War Hill) and Kettle Creek below. The low-lying areas around the creek are marshy and contain patches of thick cane and brambles.

The Fighting: Gunfire erupted as the militiamen advanced toward the Tory camp and Boyd's sentinels detected them. Boyd ordered his men to move out of the draw and occupy positions on the rocky high ground. While Pickens seems to have advanced the center of the line toward the Tory defenders with little difficulty, the flank columns under Dooly and Clarke were slowed by marshy terrain. Pickens's men advanced to a fence near the top of a hill occupied by the Tories while the defenders poured a steady and accurate fire into their ranks. Alone and vulnerable, Pickens faced a difficult challenge: the resistance in front was heavy, and both of his flanks were unprotected because his fellow officers could not maneuver their way through the thick cane and marshes. The fighting continued for some time until Pickens finally fell back.

After repulsing the attack, Colonel Boyd ordered his men to retreat to their campsite at Kettle Creek. About this time a rebel marksman mortally wounded the luckless colonel, changing the course of the battle. Just as Boyd was felled, the American flank columns slogged their way through the swampy terrain and gained the high ground. Pickens also moved forward and together the entire Patriot force rushed the enemy. How soon the Tory defending line collapsed is open to speculation, but collapse it eventually did. The sudden loss of their commander had thrown the Tories into confusion. Pickens and his men pushed and chased the Tories back toward Kettle Creek, the sight of hundreds of screaming enemy soldiers descending upon them on a broad front sending them into a terrified panic. While most of the Tories managed to escape what very nearly became a terrible killing zone, Colonel Clarke's men moved around the creek and boxed in some of the slower Loyalists, most of whom surrendered.

Casualties: British (Tories): 21 killed and 22 captured (sources claim as high as 70 killed and 70 wounded); American: seven killed and 14 wounded.

Outcome / Impact: Although a small affair, the death of Colonel Boyd and the rout of his Tory army at Kettle Creek was a setback for the British. The Patriot victors were viewed as heroes in the local communities and the Tory cause lost most of its regional support. Kettle Creek also rallied large numbers of Patriots to the cause of independence and helped trigger the British evacuation of Augusta.

The treatment of some of the captured Tories, however, put a different spin on the war. Many were tried and sentenced to hang for "war crimes." When the British promised to retaliate most of the prisoners were pardoned; five, though, were executed. Although the trials and hangings quelled the enthusiasm of many pro-Loyalists throughout Georgia and South Carolina, it signaled that under certain circumstances no quarter would be given. It was into this desperate environment that Gen. Charles Cornwallis and Col. Banastre Tarleton stepped.

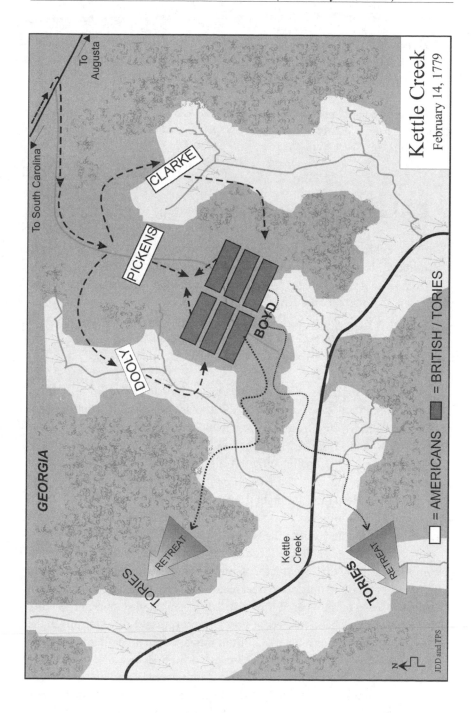

Kettle Creek
February 14, 1779

Today: About twelve acres of land are preserved with a monument, historical marker, and a handful of marked graves. Walking tours can be arranged through the Washington-Wilkes Chamber of Commerce.

Further Reading: Lumpkin, Henry, *From Savannah to Yorktown: The American Revolution in the South* (Paragon House, 1981); Ward, Christopher, *The War of the Revolution*, 2 vols. (New York, 1952).

Fort Sackville, Battle of (Illinois Campaign)

Date: February 23-25, 1779.
Region: Northwest Territory (claimed by several states).
Commanders: British: Lieutenant-Governor Henry Hamilton; American: Colonel George Rogers Clark.
Time of Day / Length of Action: Sporadic fighting for two days.
Weather Conditions: Brutally cold and frequent snowfall.
Opposing Forces: British: 80; Indian: 420; American: 180.

British Perspective: Throughout the American Revolution British authorities maintained a presence in the trans-Appalachian frontier. This region had been wrested from the French during the French and Indian War (1754-1760), but English settlements there were forbidden by the Proclamation of 1763, which granted all land west of the Appalachian Mountains to the Indians. The British continued to maintain outposts and forts in the frontier along the major rivers, where they traded with French trappers and local Indians. These outposts also served as launching points for Indian raiding parties into the western wilds of Virginia.

In 1778 Virginia included large tracks of untamed wilderness in what are today the states of Kentucky, Ohio, Indiana, Michigan, Wisconsin, Illinois, and part of Minnesota. This area, often referred to as the Northwest Territory, was administered by British Lieutenant-Governor Henry Hamilton. From his headquarters at Fort Detroit (present-day Detroit) in the northwest corner of Lake Erie, Hamilton managed an area stretching from Lake Erie in the north to the Mississippi River in the west, and to the Ohio River in the south. Within this vast territory dominated by Indians the British had two key trading posts along the Mississippi River at Kaskaskia and Cahokia (near present-day St. Louis), and Vincennes on the Wabash River. The British had long maintained trading interests with the Indians in this region while tolerating the presence of small numbers of French inhabitants. Although the British maintained small garrisons at these distant posts, their purpose was predominantly administrative with overtones of local security, rather than for any larger military purpose.

During the spring and summer of 1778, Governor Hamilton learned of an American military expedition moving through the southern wilderness along the major waterways in his territory. Hamilton left Fort Detroit on October 7 and headed south in command of a 500-man detachment to meet and eliminate the American threat on the frontier. Hamilton's 600-mile journey was conducted primarily by boats down the Maumee and Wabash rivers. By December the British were in position to strike. The American outpost at Vincennes, whose largely French inhabitants had switched allegiance to Virginia, was but lightly defended. The combined British-Indian army of 500 quickly retook the dilapidated post, which Hamilton renamed Fort Sackville.

After the victory at Vincennes, many of the French reaffirmed their loyalty to the Crown, as did leaders of the Shawnee, Delaware, Wyandot, Ottawa, Chippewa, Miami, and Kickapoo Indian tribes. Hamilton oversaw improvements to Fort Sackville. In addition to the emplacement of artillery, he strengthened its fortifications and established his headquarters in the fort. However, his Indian allies left him, as did about half his militia. The governor sent out small patrols to find the Americans and determine what they were up to. However, the cold weather made military operations impractical and the British settled into winter quarters. Hamilton spent the cold weeks reorganizing his command for spring operations, when he intended to attack the Americans occupying former British strongholds along the Mississippi River. Once the British outposts were recaptured he intended to launch a large-scale joint campaign south of the Ohio River with his Indian allies to drive American settlers from western Virginia and the entire trans-Appalachian frontier. Governor Hamilton was confident Fort Sackville was secure and the Americans would wait for warm weather before continuing their expedition.

American Perspective: The Clarks were early settlers of western Virginia's frontier, and had long served as surveyors and militiamen throughout the trans-Appalachian region. Colonel George Rogers Clark was a young 25-year-old Virginia militia officer and renowned Indian fighter. He was also the brother of William Clark, who would one day travel with Meriwether Lewis on the famous Lewis and Clark Expedition. In 1778 Colonel Clark traveled to Williamsburg, Virginia, to seek permission from the state's Governor Patrick Henry to lead an expedition against the British and their Indian allies in the Northwest Territory. It was important for America to have control over the Indians and policy set there, argued Clark, to prevent the British from using the Indians to attack settlements. Thomas Jefferson and other prominent leaders agreed with Clark, and Henry gave the young officer command of 175 volunteers for a secret mission to break British control over the frontier.

The 900-mile journey began in May of 1778 from Fort Pitt (Pittsburgh, Pennsylvania), from which they moved in a southwesterly direction through the heart of Indian lands along the Ohio River and an overland route to the British outposts on the Mississippi River. Clark's mission was multifaceted and extremely risky. His job was to remove the British threat and simultaneously convince the French and Indians to abandon their support of the Crown. Given its difficulty the campaign went smoothly. Neither the Indians nor the British were expecting an expedition like this.

Moving overland through the dark of night, the Americans captured both British outposts swiftly, and with little opposition. Kaskaskia fell on July 4 and Cahokia two days later. Not a shot was fired to affect their capture and Clark's own memoir lauds diplomatic as much as military skill for the successes. Clark's ability to curry favor with potential enemies helped win over the Spaniards, who controlled the area west of the Mississippi, and many of the local Frenchmen joined their cause. Several influential French traveled to Vincennes to convince their friends there to embrace the American cause. This initiative removed the military threat at Vincennes, where the locals warmly received Clark's expedition.

North of Vincennes, however, French inhabitants remained loyal to the British. Clark left Capt. Leonard Helms with a small detachment to defend Vincennes while he continued his mission into the wilderness. When word arrived in Detroit later that summer of Clark's audacious incursion into British territory, Governor Hamilton left with a strong column of troops for Vincennes. On December 17 Hamilton and his 500 infantry overwhelmed the small force of American defenders at Vincennes.

It was not until late January of 1779 that Colonel Clark was informed by local settlers of Governor Hamilton's disposition at Fort Sackville and his plans to launch a spring invasion against the American column. Clark was not about to wait for his enemy. He immediately organized a raid to assault Fort Sackville. After a harrowing 18-day journey through ice and snow the Americans and their French sympathizers arrived on the outskirts of Vincennes (Sackville). French locals provided the Americans with food, shelter, and dry gunpowder while Colonel Clark made final plans for capturing the stronghold.

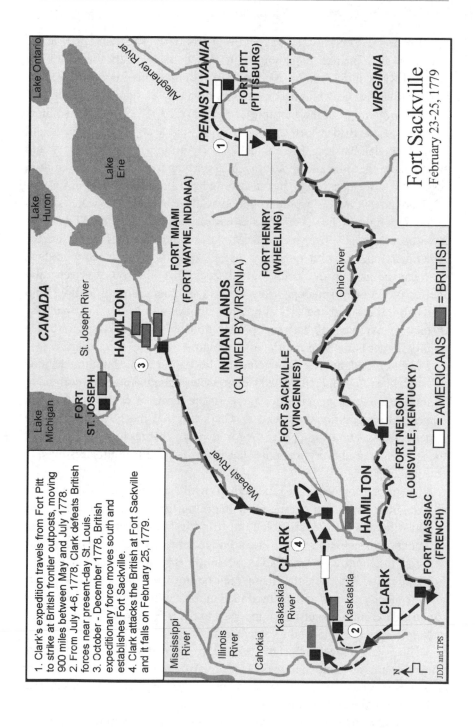

Fort Sackville
February 23-25, 1779

1. Clark's expedition travels from Fort Pitt to strike at British frontier outposts, moving 900 miles between May and July 1778.
2. From July 4-6, 1778, Clark defeats British forces near present-day St. Louis.
3. October - December 1778, British expeditionary force moves south and establishes Fort Sackville.
4. Clark attacks the British at Fort Sackville and it falls on February 25, 1779.

= AMERICANS   = BRITISH

CANADA

VIRGINIA

PENNSYLVANIA

INDIAN LANDS
(CLAIMED BY VIRGINIA)

Lake Ontario

Lake Erie

Lake Huron

Lake Michigan

Allegheny River

St. Joseph River

Ohio River

Wabash River

Mississippi River

Illinois River

Kaskaskia River

FORT PITT
(PITTSBURG)

FORT HENRY
(WHEELING)

FORT MIAMI
(FORT WAYNE, INDIANA)

HAMILTON

FORT ST. JOSEPH

FORT SACKVILLE
(VINCENNES)

FORT NELSON
(LOUISVILLE, KENTUCKY)

HAMILTON

FORT MASSIAC
(FRENCH)

Kaskaskia

Cahokia

CLARK

CLARK

JDD and TPS

N

Terrain: Fort Sackville was a strong frontier fort constructed of log palisades and fortified blockhouses. It was located on the banks of the Wabash River in the southwest corner of Indiana. This important frontier trading town has grown to become the modern city of Vincennes, Indiana.

The Fighting: On the morning of February 23, 1779, Clark's soldiers surrounded the British fort, taking cover in a series of light trenches and behind wooden barriers. The colonel cleverly arranged his men, flags, and fire to make his command appear much larger than it actually was. Hamilton responded to the quasi-siege by unleashing fire from two swivel guns, a pair of 3-pounders, and a single 6-pounder. The Americans were skilled wilderness fighters, however, and successfully eluded what could otherwise have been a deadly fire. In the face of this loud but ineffective fire the Americans opened with musketry that picked off a few enemy soldiers between the gaps in the fort's log palisades; this fire, too, was generally ineffective. As the American sharpshooters smothered the stronghold with lead balls others marched back and forth in the woods waving flags in a false display of overwhelming strength. Hamilton only had 35 regulars and a slightly larger number of militia left with him.

After exchanging fire throughout the day on the 24th, Hamilton decided he had had enough and contacted Colonel Clark about a possible surrender. When the combatants could not agree on the terms of capitulation (Clark demanded unconditional surrender), Clark advised the governor that the Americans were tunneling under the fort to place charges that would destroy the stronghold and everyone in it. The ruse failed and Hamilton resolved to continue fighting.

During a lull in the siege (and perhaps while surrender discussions were still ongoing) an Indian raiding party returning from American settlements south of the Ohio River stumbled into Clark's lines; many were killed or wounded. In retaliation for killing frontier settlers Clark had five Indian captives executed with tomahawks while the British watched from inside Fort Sackville. After scalping them, their bodies were thrown into the river and the bloody clumps of hair suspended in front of the fort's front gate. The ritualized executions sent a clear message to the British, who had incited the Indian to violence against the settlements.

The psychological impact of the killings, coupled with the belief that the American army was much larger than his own, convinced Hamilton to accept defeat. He executed the documents on February 24 and formally surrendered at 10:00 a.m. the next morning.

Casualties: British: one killed, 10 wounded, and 80 captured; Indian: 22 killed; American: two killed and two wounded.

Outcome / Impact: On March 7, 1779, Hamilton and his officers were sent to Williamsburg, Virginia, as prisoners of war. Colonel Clark and his soldiers spent the next few years maintaining an important American presence in the frontier constructing key forts at strategic points along the inland rivers.

Clark wanted to crush Fort Detroit, but the vast distances to be covered and pro-British sentiment in the region made the quest impossible. However, the American expedition Clark led achieved a great deal of related success, and its impact reverberated throughout the frontier for many years. Clark's accomplishments led to a substantial reduction in the frequency of Indian attacks against settlers south of the Ohio River, and coincided well with the entry of France in the war as an ally.

Today: George Rogers Clark National Historical Park, Vincennes, Indiana, provides visitors with a wealth of information regarding these historic 1779 events. A memorial at the site of Fort Sackville commemorates the capture of the fort.

Further Reading: Barnhart, John D., ed., *Henry Hamilton and George Rogers Clark in the American Revolution with the Unpublished Journal of Lieut. Gov. Henry Hamilton* (Crawfordsville, Indiana, 1951); English, William Hayden, *Conquest of the Country Northwest of the River Ohio 1778-1783 and Life of Gen. George Rogers Clark* (Bowen-Merrill Company, 1897).

Brier [Briar] Creek, Battle of (Southern Campaign)

Date: March 3, 1779.

Region: Southern Colonies, Georgia.

Commanders: British: Major General Augustine Prevost, Lieutenant Colonel Mark Prevost; American: Major General Benjamin Lincoln, Brigadier General John Ashe, Brigadier General Samuel Elbert, and Colonel Leonard Marbury.

Time of Day / Length of Action: Early morning to 2:00 p.m.

Weather Conditions: Clear and cool.

Opposing Forces: British (Tory): 1,500; American: 1,800.

British Perspective: After securing Savannah, Georgia, and the entire southeastern region of that state, the British moved inland in January 1779 under the command of Maj. Gen. Augustine Prevost. This Swiss-born officer had moved north from Florida late in 1778 with the authority to assume control of British southern forces. Prevost launched a surprise amphibious assault on February 3 against the Patriots at Port Royal Island. The expeditionary force was too small to threaten Charleston's defenses, and Prevost retreated from his beachhead. Seeking Tory support for his invasion, Prevost dispatched Lt. Col. Archibald Campbell and 1,700 men to Augusta, Georgia, while Prevost remained to defend Savannah. About 3,500 troops were shifted along the bank of the Savannah River at Ebenezer, Georgia, to counter a smaller Patriot army positioned at Purysburg, South Carolina. In addition to the disappointment at Port Royal, on February 14 the Tory allies lost a battle at Kettle Creek, just north of Augusta.

The rising anti-British sentiment and swelling contingent of Patriot militia around Augusta convinced the British to change their strategy. Leaving a garrison force of British and Tories to occupy Augusta, Colonel Campbell marched the bulk of his force southward to link up with Prevost's army at Hudson's Ferry, 45 miles below Augusta. This location midway between Savannah and Augusta also provided the British with a viable crossing point into South Carolina. With Georgia firmly under British control and the Americans in South Carolina, the Savannah River served as the dividing line between the two opposing sides. A large American column warily followed behind Colonel Campbell's force as it marched southward through Georgia roughly parallel to the western bank of the Savannah River.

Campbell arrived near Prevost's headquarters at Hudson's Ferry, 15 miles south of Freeman's Bridge on Brier Creek. Along the way British soldiers destroyed the old bridge and established a blocking position on the road south of the waterway. The Americans following the British column established a camp north of Brier Creek. A reconnaissance of the rebel force convinced Prevost it could be attacked with advantage. His plan called for gathering reinforcements at Hudson's Ferry, where one column would move up below the creek to divert rebel attention from a second more powerful column that would make a flanking march to strike the enemy from the rear.

American Perspective: After Gen. Robert Howe's failed defensive effort at Savannah in December 1778 (a court of inquiry cleared him of blame), he was replaced as commander of the Southern Department by Maj. Gen. Benjamin Lincoln. With the British in control of Georgia, Lincoln was eager to find a way to strike a blow against them. His options were limited. At his disposal were only 6,500 troops, and with them he had to defend Charleston in the southeast and Augusta (now in enemy hands) on the far side of the Savannah River to the northwest. Leaving the city of Savannah in enemy hands was unthinkable, however, and Lincoln set out to take back the port city. After meeting with his field commanders to discuss offensive strategy and sending an urgent request for naval support to French allies in the West Indies, Lincoln decided to move against the British.

Important but small victories against the British at Port Royal, South Carolina, and a Tory force at Kettle Creek in Georgia boosted American morale as Lincoln focused his initial efforts toward Augusta. He ordered Brig. Gen. John Ashe and 1,400 men to join up with 1,200 soldiers opposite the city under Brig. Gen. Andrew Williamson. The conjunction of these columns on February 13 put a powerful force within striking distance of British-held Augusta. Lincoln's noose was tightening. Recognizing the danger of the gathering enemy, the British left a small occupation force in the city and marched the bulk of their army southward toward the main army behind Brier Creek. Williamson and a small force remained behind on the outskirts of Augusta while Ashe led 1,800 troops in pursuit along the marshy banks of the Savannah River.

Ashe followed closely but was careful to maintain a respectful distance to avoid being ambushed. On February 27 his command arrived at Brier Creek and joined the 200 mounted men already there under Col. Leonard Marbury, who informed Ashe the bridge had been destroyed and the British were operating south of the creek. Ashe's 1,800-man command consisted of a brigade under Brig. Gen. Bryan, light infantry under Lt. Col. Lytle, 100 Georgia Continentals under Col. Samuel Elbert, and Marbury's troopers. Ashe divided his small force into several detachments and deployed them to defend key crossing points along the waterway. Marbury's mounted outfit was tasked with protecting the rear of the American defenses at Paris's Mill, 15 miles northwest of the burned bridge. Ashe established the bulk of his command in a camp north of the burned bridge between Brier Creek and the mill site. As defensive postures go, his arrangement was ill-advised. Ashe was now boxed into the triangle formed by the confluence of the creek and the Savannah River, and the bridge over the creek was destroyed. Worse, his new deployment did not allow him to keep close tabs on the British. Ashe met with Lincoln, who ordered him to hold his position until additional forces could join him and attack the British south of the creek.

Terrain: The battlefield is located in rural Screven County eleven miles northeast of Sylvania, Georgia. Brier Creek flows from northeast to southwest and empties into the Savannah River. This area is dominated by low marshy ground surrounding numerous creeks that empty into the Savannah east of the battlefield. The Savannah River flows southeast from Augusta down to Savannah and the Atlantic Ocean. The battle occurred on the Old Augusta Road between Brier Creek on the west and the Savannah River to the east.

The Fighting: General Prevost's plan of attack was a good one. A battalion of the 71st Regiment under Major McPherson, together with some Tories and two field pieces moved north closer to Brier Creek while Col. Mark Prevost (the commanding general's younger brother) marched about 1,000 men from near Hudson's Ferry on a parallel road around the American army from the west to attack Ashe's rear at Paris's Mill. If all went according to plan, McPherson would occupy Ashe's attention while Prevost rolled up the enemy all the way down to the creek.

Colonel Prevost's column, composed of another battalion of the 71st, some light infantry, grenadiers from the 60th Regiment, light cavalry, and militia crossed the creek fifteen miles above (west) of Ashe's position on the night of March 2. By the morning of March 3 he was behind Ashe's position. Prevost's brilliantly executed flanking maneuver covered 50 miles from the point of departure to the battlefield. Rebel horse had spotted the move the day before, but sources disagree as to whether Marbury's messenger was captured before Ashe could be notified. Although the bridge across the creek at Paris's Mill was also destroyed, Prevost charged his cavalry and light infantry across the shallow waterway and quickly dispersed Colonel Marbury's mounted rearguard, which fled in panic east toward Burton's Ferry. After his command was reorganized, Prevost led his men southeast toward the main American camp.

Ashe had just returned to camp on the morning of March 3 and was constructing a new bridge across Brier Creek when word reached him about the British attack at Paris's Mill. About 1:00 p.m. Prevost's soldiers appeared before the American camp and deployed only 150 yards distant. The failure to prepare for the attack suggests Ashe did not fully understand (or know of) the threat facing him. Elbert's Continentals formed in front and engaged the British, but once the firing began the militia threw down their arms and retreated into the swamps. According to some witnesses, Ashe attempted to rally them to no avail, leaving Elbert in effective tactical command on the field. The British onslaught was as rapid as it was effective. Colonel Prevost's well-disciplined soldiers moved forward in precise formations and emptied musket and artillery fire into the disorganized American ranks. Somehow Elbert and other officers managed to align those who remained into three distinct bodies with a left, right, and center line.

Surprised, outnumbered, and outclassed, Elbert and those few hundred remaining were unable to stand more than a few minutes before a gap opened in the center of the line, though whether from the effects of enemy fire or

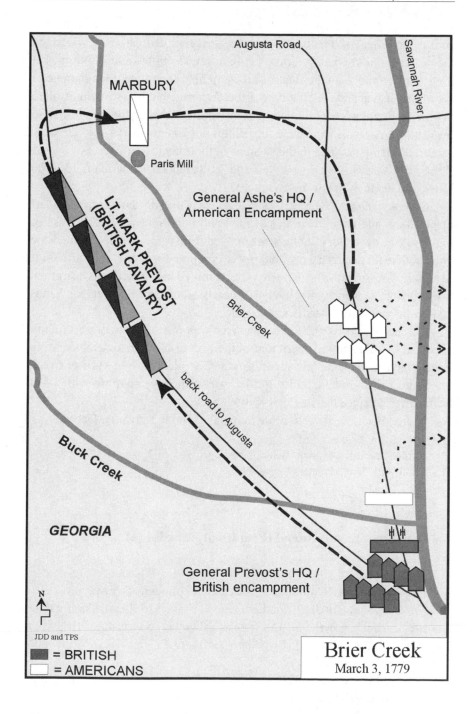

Brier Creek
March 3, 1779

confusing orders is unclear. Advancing veteran British troops wedged themselves into the gap. A brutal battle ensued with bayonets and musket butts. Patriot troops on the flanks of the gap held for a time, though most of the militia had abandoned the field. Elbert's heroic but tragic stand resulted in almost the complete annihilation of his soldiers, many of whom fought to the death. A dozen officers including Elbert, together with 162 soldiers were captured. Many drowned in the swamps in their panic to escape.

Casualties: British: five killed and 11 wounded; American: 150-200 killed and another 200 or more captured.

Outcome / Impact: General Ashe lost nearly one-third of his army, all of his artillery, and large quantities of food and other resources. The court of inquiry Ashe called for after he was removed from command determined "he did not take all necessary precautions" to prepare for battle, a charitable if damning assessment. The British victory forced the Americans to retreat toward Augusta, which effectively left nearly all of Georgia in enemy hands and/or vulnerable to British exploitation.

Colonel Prevost's flanking maneuver was one of the most brilliantly executed (if little known) operations of the war. In addition to demonstrating British tactical and strategic superiority in Georgia, the fight at Brier Creek improved British morale and solidified wavering Tory support, which had been suffering since the fiasco at Kettle Creek.

Today: Brier Creek Battle Site may be visited in Sylvania, Georgia.

Further Reading: Lumpkin, Henry, *From Savannah to Yorktown: The American Revolution in the South* (Paragon House, 1981).

Penobscot Bay, Battle of (Penobscot Expedition)

Date: June 17, 1779 – August 13, 1779.

Region: Northern Colonies, Massachusetts (modern-day Maine).

Commanders: British: Brigadier General Francis McLean, Commodore George Collier; American: Commodore Dudley Saltonstall, Brigadier General Solomon Lovell, Brigadier General Peleg Wadsworth, and Lieutenant Colonel Paul Revere.

Time of Day / Length of Action: Two months.

Weather Conditions: Warm summer weather.

Opposing Forces: British: 800 (including Marines); Navy: 10 ships; American: 1,000 Massachusetts militia and 40 ships.

British Perspective: By the summer of 1779 a military standoff of sorts had settled into the war's Northern theater. Burgoyne's defeat and surrender the previous autumn had set back British efforts there, as had the failure to defeat Washington's main field army. Lowering their expectations, the British sought targets of opportunity to exploit with minimal risk. One was conducted by the former Royal Governor of New York, Brig. Gen. William Tryon. He led a 2,600-man force in an opportunistic raid against the coastal towns of New Haven, Fairfield, Norwalk, and Green's Farm, Connecticut. With only several hundred militiamen opposing him, Tryon easily brushed them aside and devastated the vulnerable towns before moving back to his base at New York. In the northern coastal region of Massachusetts (modern-day Maine), the British looked to Penobscot Bay as an excellent logistical base for future operations in New England and a good post for their loyal Tory allies. On June 17, 1779, three British sloops of war anchored in Penobscot Bay and disgorged 800 men unopposed on the peninsula of Bagaduce (known today as Castine).

The British spent the next five weeks establishing fortifications to defend the bay. Earthen bunkers and trench lines were constructed on the tip of Bagaduce Peninsula and Nautilus Island, which jutted south into the seaward approach to the bay. The main bastion of the British defense was Fort George, established near the center of Bagaduce Peninsula. Artillery was emplaced within the land fortifications. The three ships *Albany*, *North*, and *Nautilus*, each boasting 18 guns, were stationed on the eastern shore of the peninsula for protection and to surprise any would-be liberation force.

On July 28 British authorities received information that an American naval squadron was moving from Boston to attack the British in Penobscot Bay. To counter this effort, the British navy dispatched seven more warships. Led by Commodore Collier, the British squadron was comprised of *Raisonable* (64 guns), *Blonde* and *Virginia* (32 guns each), *Greyhound* (28 guns), *Camilla* and *Galatea* (20 guns each), and *Otter* (14 guns).

American Perspective: On June 17, 1779, war arrived suddenly in the rustic fishing villages lining scenic Penobscot Bay when a sizeable British invasion force appeared. During the next eight weeks local inhabitants faced an occupation army that confiscated livestock and other property while building fortifications in strategic locations. With no organized militia the locals raced to Boston to report the incident to Massachusetts authorities.

A land-sea expeditionary force was formed from volunteer militia organizations and the few Continental troops available. Command of the ground force was given to Brig. Gen. Solomon Lovell and his deputy commander, Brig. Gen. Peleg Wadsworth. Lieutenant Colonel Paul Revere was selected to lead the artillery. About 1,000 soldiers and marines rallied to confront the enemy invasion. Commodore Dudley Saltonstall of the Continental navy organized an ad-hoc fleet for the operation comprised of 40 ships of war and transportation vessels. Commodore Saltonstall's flagship, the 32-gun frigate *Warren*, was accompanied by the 14-gun *Diligent* and 12-gun *Providence*. The Massachusetts State Navy provided the bulk of the ships: the brigs *Hazard*, *Active*, and *Tyrannicide* (14 guns each), two captured British ships, *Diligent* and *Active*, and twelve various armed privateers. The New Hampshire State Navy provided Saltonstall's fleet with the 20-gun *Hampden*, with 20 other ships available to transport troops for a ground assault. The Americans arrived in Penobscot Bay on the afternoon of July 25, 1779.

Terrain: Penobscot Bay is 40 miles long (north to south), 15 miles wide (east to west), and sprinkled with more than 200 small islands. In 1779 the coastal area was heavily forested. The dominant terrain was on Bagaduce Peninsula, which rises quickly to an elevation of 300 feet.

The Fighting: The battle began when British warships spotted American vessels on July 25 and opened fire. High winds made combat too difficult, however, and the initial exchange ended in a draw with neither side losing any ships. The next day the Americans launched an amphibious assault against the British defenses on Nautilus Island and captured the isolated fort with little difficulty. Two days later American warships pounded British positions on the mainland at Bagaduce Peninsula and landed a sizeable amphibious assault force on the southwestern shore with the purpose of establishing a beachhead and opening a siege of Fort George.

The Americans were organized into three 200-man divisions, the left and center columns comprised of militia and the right of Continental marines. Confronted with steep terrain and an entrenched enemy, the marines suffered heavily under a well-delivered veteran fire. About 30 minutes after the fighting began, however, the marines managed to defeat advanced enemy elements and drive them back toward the main line. This small tactical victory allowed Lieutenant Colonel Revere to move his artillery into a supporting position. After securing a toehold on the peninsula, the Americans began digging entrenchments and establishing their own siege line to threaten Fort George.

That same evening Lovell launched a night attack against Fort George. As Lovell quickly discovered, however, the British fortification was too strongly defended and the attempt was driven back quickly with some loss. A two-week stalemate ensued. On August 11 the British launched a counterattack that triggered an early stampede for the rear. Although the

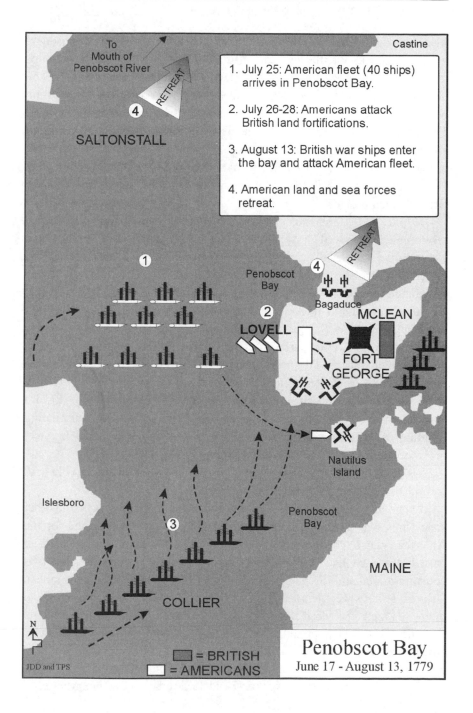

To Mouth of Penobscot River

RETREAT

4

SALTONSTALL

Castine

1. July 25: American fleet (40 ships) arrives in Penobscot Bay.

2. July 26-28: Americans attack British land fortifications.

3. August 13: British war ships enter the bay and attack American fleet.

4. American land and sea forces retreat.

1

Penobscot Bay

4

RETREAT

Bagaduce

MCLEAN

LOVELL

2

FORT GEORGE

Nautilus Island

Penobscot Bay

Islesboro

3

MAINE

COLLIER

N

JDD and TPS

= BRITISH
= AMERICANS

Penobscot Bay
June 17 - August 13, 1779

British assault was eventually halted and thrown back, Patriot commanders were worried about the level of militia resolve. Three British warships moved into a supporting position near Bagaduce Harbor east of the peninsula and Fort George. The naval move threatened Lovell's position with an enfilading fire that made an assault against Fort George too risky. The disorganized American commanders spent the next three weeks arguing about the best course of action to pursue. Lovell's infantry and artillery was bogged down in a quasi-siege that required naval assistance, but Commodore Saltonstall refused to engage or even attempt to drive off the British warships.

While the American officers bickered over strategy, British reinforcements arrived on August 13 in the form of seven large ships of war. Commodore Saltonstall quickly formed his armada into a crescent formation to keep the British from entering the bay, but his ragtag fleet was severely outgunned and outclassed. Backed by overwhelming strength, the British armada slammed into the American fleet and easily dispersed it, sinking and capturing many of Saltonstall's ships. While some American captains pitched munitions overboard, grounded their vessels, and set them afire, others bravely retrieved the ground troops on Bagaduce Peninsula and sailed northward to seek shelter in the Penobscot River. What was left of the fleet spent the next several days hugging the coast in a flight to safety toward Boston; many were sunk or damaged along the way. The humiliating running sea fight was one of the worst (and yet little known) naval disasters in American history, especially if measured by ships lost.

Casualties: British: 16 killed and 35 wounded; American: 35 killed, 30 wounded, 500 captured, and 40 ships destroyed.

Outcome / Impact: The destruction of the Massachusetts navy and other state ships was an unmitigated financial and military catastrophe for the American cause. The British achieved not only the establishment of their base but a complete sea and land victory. Commodore Saltonstall was court-martialed and discharged for his inept leadership. Despite American failures, lessons were learned from the fiasco. Those smart enough to heed them realized the need to forge strong bonds under a professional Continental military organization instead of forming ad-hoc military adventures. The British maintained their stronghold in Penobscot Bay and on Bagaduce Peninsula through the remainder of the war.

Today: Historic Fort George can be visited today in Castine, Maine.

Further Reading: Allen, Gardner W., *A Naval History of the American Revolution* (Houghton, 1913).

Stono Ferry, Battle of (Southern Campaign)

Date: June 20, 1779.
Region: Southern Colonies, South Carolina.
Commanders: British: Major General Augustine Prevost and Lieutenant Colonel John Maitland; American: Major General Benjamin Lincoln and Brigadier General William Moultrie.
Time of Day / Length of Action: Afternoon, one hour.
Weather Conditions: Hot and humid.
Opposing Forces: British: 500 of a 2,000-man army; American: 1,000 of a 5,000-man army.

British Perspective: After soundly defeating the American force at Brier Creek, Georgia (March 3, 1779), British forces reassembled at Savannah. General Augustine Prevost wanted to move north and take Charleston, South Carolina, but a previous expedition had been turned back at Port Royal on February 3, 1779. Bolstered by local Tory and Indian support, Prevost decided to launch another considerably larger effort to capture the coastal city. His army consisted of 2,000 British Regulars, Tories, and Indians.

On the morning of May 11 Prevost crossed the Ashley River just west of Charleston and marched his men toward the enemy defenses at Charleston Neck. When he reached the outer ranges of American artillery, he sent an ultimatum for the enemy to surrender the city. His response arrived in the form of an artillery barrage and a detachment of Patriot cavalry. Unmoved, Prevost repeated his demands and throughout the evening communications were exchanged in an attempt to avoid bloodshed. That night, however, Prevost received reports that General Lincoln was marching to Charleston with 4,000 American troops to bolster its defense. Frustrated by the news, he moved his men back a short distance though remained close enough to constitute a threat to the safety of the city.

When the American reinforcements arrived, Prevost realized he had been outsmarted and was himself in danger of being attacked and overwhelmed. He decided to withdraw with the bulk of his command, but left behind about 900 men under Col. John Maitland to watch Lincoln and threaten the city. Maitland's command was a composite of Maitland's own 1st Battalion of the 71st Foot (Fraser's Highlanders), the Hessian Regiment von Trumbach, Provincial Loyalists, and a battery of artillery.

For the next month the combatants sat on their hands in something of a stalemate. Maitland's primary responsibility was covering Stono Ferry, which served as both the British front and rear guard, with a series of fortified positions enhanced with abatis obstacles. One that would play a key role in the battle was separated from Johns Island by a small inlet. On June 20 the Americans moved out to attack Stono Ferry (near present-day Rantowles). Defending it was the Hessian Regiment von Trumbach and a battalion of Scottish Highlanders, all told about 500 men, with the balance of Maitland's force across the river on Johns Island.

American Perspective: After the debacle at Brier Creek, Georgia, General Lincoln concentrated his army around Augusta while the British reassembled at Savannah. Lincoln's decision left only a small force of several hundred men under General Moultrie to protect Charleston, a wholly inadequate force for such an important task. When Lincoln learned a sizable British army was moving against him, he left Augusta and marched quickly to reach Moultrie. Although Prevost reached the outskirts of Charleston on May 11, Moultrie was able to bluff and delay his opponent until Lincoln's reinforcements arrived to stabilize the situation. With nearly 5,000 American troops on hand, Prevost knew offensive operations were no longer feasible and he established a defensive position south of the primary American position.

Even though the cautious Lincoln had a much larger army under his command (6,500) than his adversary, he was unsure whether additional forces were moving to reinforce Prevost. Unbeknownst to the American commander, Prevost knew his opportunity (if it ever existed) had passed, and had withdrawn part of his command to Savannah, leaving behind a credible rear guard under Maitland. The next month passed uneventfully until June 20, when Lincoln decided to sally forth with about 1,200 men and attack the British rear guard posted at Stono Ferry.

Lincoln led the main column, crossing the Ashley River shortly after midnight on June 20 and marching eight and one-half miles. (There is some dispute as to who was in command of this force. Some usually reliable secondary accounts claim General Moultrie led the assaulting column. Several credible contemporary sources, however, state clearly that General Lincoln led the offensive while Moultrie played a secondary role.) Lincoln's intention was to reach James Island in the early morning hours with enough time to prepare for an attack at dawn. Moultrie, meanwhile, guided a diversionary effort against Johns Island to the west on the far side of the Stono River. His role was to feint against Maitland and keep him from detaching troops against Lincoln, or attack if the opportunity offered. The main column under Lincoln was organized into two main wings, the right composed of militia troops from both the Carolinas under Gen. Jethro

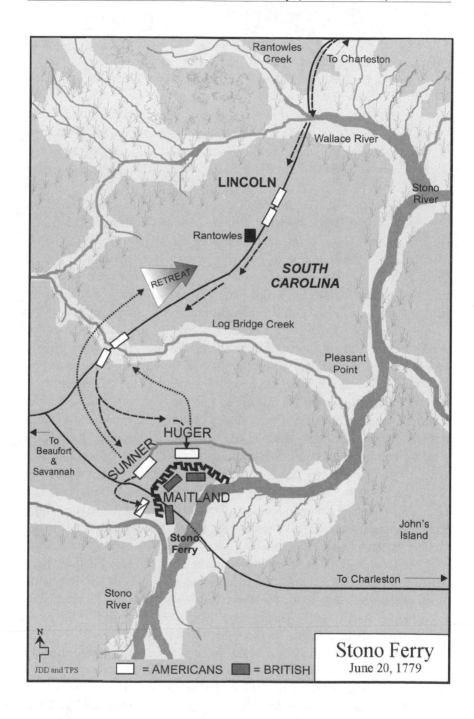

Stono Ferry
June 20, 1779

= AMERICANS   = BRITISH

Sumner and the left of Continentals under Gen. Isaac Huger. Virginia militia, some light infantry, and a small cavalry detachment hovered about on the wings or behind the column. Eight light artillery pieces accompanied Lincoln.

Terrain: The battlefield is located near the present-day town of Rantowles, South Carolina. In 1779, the Stono ferry and Rantowles Bridge provided local citizens with the ability to cross a small branch of the Stono River (known today as Wallace River) and the Stono River itself. Rantowles community is 15 miles west of Charleston with an elevation of 15 feet. Several large coastal islands—John, James, and Edisto—surrounded by marshes and tidal flats dominate the area south of Charleston. The Stono River is an important tributary that drains into the Atlantic Ocean just south of Charleston, flowing west to east just below John and James islands. Troops marching between towns and cities in the area were forced to traverse numerous waterways along narrow spits of land surrounded by marshes, creeks, and tidal flats. It was a difficult area to maneuver an army.

The Fighting: As the small American column approached from the north, the one-armed Colonel Maitland (who had lost his limb during the French and Indian War) had his 1st Battalion of Highland Scots acting as an outpost. One of Lincoln's light infantry companies posted on the flanks of the column stumbled into the outpost and triggered the fight. Lincoln had lost the element of surprise. The Scotsmen stood their ground and Lincoln fed troops into the action, the musketry intensifying as more Americans joined the firing line. The Highlanders did not fall back until most had been killed or wounded. Fewer than a dozen traversed the several hundred yards to the main British line held by the von Trumbach Hessian regiment. The stand of the Scotsmen bought Maitland the time he needed to prepare for the attack, especially along the western sector of his light fieldworks where the Americans now focused their attack.

The action became general at this point, and Lincoln brought up artillery to add to his firepower. The fighting had consumed about one hour when the Hessians began falling back. The surviving Scots from the 71st seemed to have helped steady the Hessians, who returned to their duty. Unable to breach the main line, the Americans fell back.

By this time reinforcements began arriving from Johns Island. Having already suffered significant casualties, and with no sign or word from Moultrie, Lincoln ordered a tactical retreat and covered it with his cavalry and light infantry. Maitland held his position and gathered his dead and wounded. Three days later he retreated southwest to Port Royal Island. Lincoln did not molest the withdrawal.

Casualties: British: 26 killed, 163 wounded, and one missing; American: 146 killed and wounded (including 24 officers), and 155 missing. No prisoners were reported.

Outcome / Impact: The battle was poorly planned and executed by Lincoln and had no strategic effect on the Southern Campaign. Maitland had already decided on June 15—five days before Lincoln attacked—to withdraw to Port Royal Island (Beaufort, South Carolina). According to one source, only a lack of shipping prevented an earlier withdrawal. Whether Lincoln's attack hastened the movement is in doubt. The moves and countermoves of the spring and summer of 1779 frustrated both sides, neither of whom seemed well positioned to assume the upper hand in the South. The British held Savannah and the bulk of Georgia while the Americans looked to the sea for assistance from the French.

Today: The battlefield has nearly been completely lost. The owners of The Links, a golf course at Stono Ferry, acknowledge their 12th, 13th, and 14th fairways were once the scene of the 1779 Revolutionary War battle. Locals can still point out the site of the old ferry crossing as well as some Civil War-related sites.

Further Reading: Lincoln, Benjamin Papers, Massachusetts Historical Society; Lumpkin, Henry, *From Savannah to Yorktown: The American Revolution in the South* (Paragon House, 1981); Mattern, David, *Benjamin Lincoln and the American Revolution* (University of South Carolina Press, 1998).

Stony Point, Battle of (New York Campaign)

Date: July 16, 1779.

Region: Northern Colonies, New York.

Commanders: British: Lieutenant General Sir Henry Clinton, Lieutenant Colonel Henry Johnson; American: General George Washington, Brigadier General Anthony Wayne, Colonel Richard Butler, Lieutenant Colonel Francois de Fleury, and Major Hardy Murfee.

Time of Day / Length of Action: 12:30 a.m. to 1:00 a.m.

Weather Conditions: Warm summer night (dark, no moonlight).

Opposing Forces: British: 624; American: 1,350.

British Perspective: During the summer of 1779, the Northern Theater of war was grounded in stalemate, the major fighting having shifted into the

Southern colonies. To protect the main British garrison stationed in New York City and dissuade Washington from moving his army down the Hudson River from his encampment at West Point, Gen. Sir Henry Clinton established and maintained an outer network of defenses. An integral part of this defensive network included several strongholds along the river. Two of the strongest were at Stony Point, twenty-four miles north of New York City on a spit of land jutting out from the western side of the river, and Fort Lafayette on Verplank's Point directly across the Hudson on the eastern shore. British warships patrolled the Hudson, with the sloop-of-war *Vulture* stationed between these two strategic river posts.

Stony Point was garrisoned by 625 soldiers (17th Regiment, one company of 71st Highlander grenadiers, Tories from the Loyal Americans, and fifteen field pieces) under the command of Lt. Col. Henry Johnson. Its defenses consisted of two landside lines (inner / upper and outer / lower) and outposts protected by obstructions that made an approach from the west over the cleared terrain difficult. The longer outer line designed to defend the western approaches and cover the ground south toward Haverstraw Bay was swept by six field peices and 300 men. The shorter inner defensive line served as a secondary supporting position that offered increased strength through depth. The inner line was also protected by abatis and was reinforced by seven field pieces and another 300 men.

American Perspective: Once the British changed from an offensive to defensive strategy in the Northern Theater in 1778, the war in New England sputtered to a fitful standstill. General Washington knew a major offensive against the powerful enemy in New York City was out of the question. He also knew it was unlikely General Clinton would conduct a serious aggressive campaign against his army in upstate New York at West Point. With large-scale operations off the table Washington searched for ways to harass and injure the enemy on a smaller scale. A minor British thrust partway up the Hudson River offered Washington an opportunity to embarrass his opponent.

In late May and early June a British expedition moved upriver to Stony Point and Verplank's Point just a dozen miles below West Point. The narrows at that point comprised King's Ferry, a major Hudson crossing point and communications link for the Patriots that also provided access to the Hudson Highlands. The forts on both points were unfinished and fell easily. When it became obvious West Point was not under threat of attack, and that Clinton was working to reinforce and strength the captured forts, Washington decided to send General "Mad" Anthony Wayne and his 1,200-man brigade to capture Stony Point. Based upon intelligence and firsthand observation, Washington ordered his subordinate to use a night assault to overwhelm the bastion.

Wayne's command left Sandy Beach near West Point at noon on a meandering fifteen-mile march that took about eight hours to complete. By 8:00 p.m. the Americans were organizing for the attack on David Springsteel's farm, less than two miles west of the outer line at Stony Point. The attack plan was both elegant and complex. The main assault would be delivered in two prongs, one from the north and the other from the south. Both would have to cross the muddy tidal flat marshes at low tide to reach the British defenses. Because the main attack would be delivered by the southern thrust, General Wayne traveled with that column, which consisted of 700 men. They would strike just above the shoreline near Haverstraw Bay. The northern column of 300 men was led by Col. Richard Butler. In order to provide as much stealth and deception as possible, the main attack columns moved out with unloaded weapons; they would rely solely on fixed bayonets. White swaths of paper were affixed to American headgear for visual recognition. Each column was spearheaded by a Forlorn Hope— twenty men armed with nothing but axes to chop their way through the abatis. On their heels was an advance party of 150 riflemen, who in turn would be followed by the main body (700 in the north, 300 in the south) to drive home the attack and secure the victory. In the center Wayne placed a contingent from Lee's Light Horse under Maj. Hardy Murfee. It was his job to create a diversion sufficient to convince the British the main attack was being delivered up the middle. Only Murfee's men advanced with their muskets loaded and with orders to use them early and often.

Wayne divided his command into two (or possibly three, sources disagree on this point) columns for the approach march and set out toward the fort about 11:30 p.m. When he drew near the outer line of obstructions Major Murfee's 150 men broke off as a center column, halted opposite the center of the British outer line, and formed for battle. The horns of the attack, meanwhile, circled around to the northern and southern edges of the peninsula and waded into the mud and water simultaneously to the extreme ends of the abatis. It was just after midnight.

Terrain: The Stony Point battlefield is twenty-four miles north of Manhattan on the rocky western shore of the Hudson River. The peninsula, which juts into the river from northwest to southeast, is about one-half mile wide by one-half long. The neck of the peninsula was entrenched from north to south, making the rocky high terrain a natural fortress. The peninsula towers above the water 150 feet, making it the dominant terrain along that portion of the Hudson. The terrain one mile west of Stony Point was cut from north to south by a creek surrounded by marshy tidal lowland. Just to the east of this creek is where the British established their defensive works and an outer line of abatis of felled trees. Across the half-mile wide Hudson is another less commanding terrain feature known as Verplank's Point, where a smaller British garrison manned Fort Lafayette.

The Fighting: About 12:15 or 12:30 a.m. on July 16 British sentries signaled that something was amiss by opening fire at dark figures moving on either end of their outer line of obstacles. Within a few minutes the American pioneers in the Forlorn Hope chopped their way through and rushed toward the inner line of obstructions without firing a shot. The confused British sentries were still trying to figure out what was happening when Major Murfee's center column opened a hot fire that was promptly returned by the defenders. General Wayne was struck in the head by a musket ball, but luckily the slug glanced off his skull. The pioneers suffered heavy losses in their efforts to chop through the defenses. Only three of the twenty in advance of the northern wing reached the main inner line. Rushing to organize his men, Lt. Col. Henry Johnson naturally focused his defensive efforts against the flashing musket fire—Murfee's demonstration in the center. Johnson formed six companies (about half his command) and moved forward down the hill to strengthen the British center. Wayne's tactical plan was working perfectly.

Both wings of the attack breached the British abatis and poured into their respective assault areas. French officer Lt. Col. Francois de Fleury was the first soldier to breach the British lines; Henry Knox was second. Almost immediately the embrasures of the upper works flooded with bayonet-wielding Americans. Johnson realized the desperation of his situation and that an organized defense was no longer possible. The bloody close-quarter fight that followed within the British works consumed about fifteen minutes and ended with the surrender of the British garrison. At least one British soldier escaped by swimming out into the Hudson to the warship *Vulture*, which promptly moved downriver to avoid the fort's American-controlled artillery.

Casualties: British: 20 killed, 74 wounded, 472 captured, and 58 missing; American: 15 killed, 83 wounded.

Outcome / Impact: General Wayne's stunning coup-de-main was tactically brilliant but strategically devoid of consequence. Washington could not afford to man the positions with American defenders, and within two days withdrew from Stony Point with as much captured equipment as possible. Captured artillery was put aboard a transport ship that was sunk by

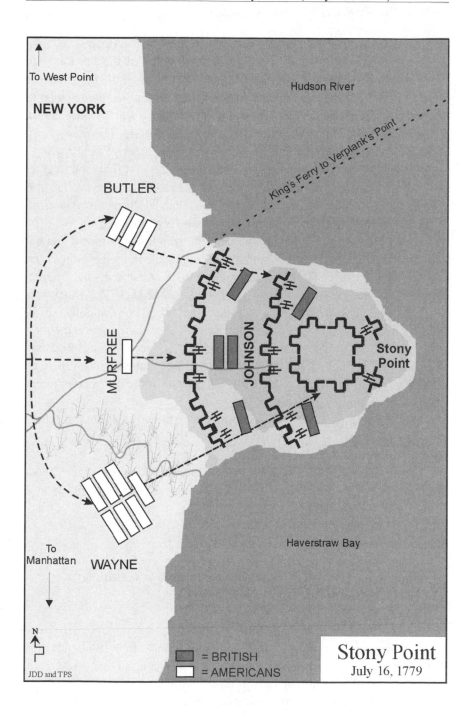

To West Point

NEW YORK

Hudson River

King's Ferry to Verplank's Point

BUTLER

MURFREE

JOHNSON

Stony Point

To Manhattan   WAYNE

Haverstraw Bay

N

JDD and TPS

= BRITISH
= AMERICANS

Stony Point
July 16, 1779

Vulture when the British warship reappeared at a most inopportune time. Clinton ordered Stony Point reoccupied and reinforced the bastion with more extensive works and a more alert garrison. Although the British could have launched an offensive toward West Point, Clinton decided against it. Stony Point–Verplank's Point was the northernmost point on the Hudson River controlled by the British until the war ended in 1783. The Stony Point action was the last significant clash of arms in the Northern Department.

Before the attack cash prizes were offered to the first five men to enter the fort. Lieutenant Colonel Fleury, the first man to breach the works, also captured the British colors. He was given a medal from the American Congress and $500, which he generously shared with his men.

Four weeks after the Stony Point battle Washington authorized another similar assault against a British outpost on a peninsula in the Hudson River. On August 19, Paulus Hook was assaulted by 300 Americans led by Maj. Henry "Light-Horse Harry" Lee (Robert E. Lee's father). The attack was nearly a carbon copy of Wayne's assault against Stony Point and netted 150 British prisoners. Like Stony Point, however, Paulus Hook (across the river from New York City) could not be held by the Americans. And, like Stony Point the Paulus Hook affair raised American morale but was little more than a nuisance to the British. Both sides knew the focus of the war was hundreds of miles south in the Carolinas.

Today: The July 1779 battle is interpreted by the Stony Point Battlefield State Historic Site.

Further Reading: Tucker, Glenn, *Mad Anthony Wayne and the New Nation* (Stackpole Books, 1973); Ward, Christopher, *The War of the Revolution*, 2 vols. (Macmillian Company, 1952).

Newtown, Battle of (Sullivan's Expedition or Campaign)

Date: August 29, 1779.
Region: Northern Colonies, New York.
Commanders: British: Colonel John Butler and Major Walter Butler; Tory: Sir John Johnson; Indian: Chief "Captain" Joseph Brant; American: Major General John Sullivan, Brigadier General James Clinton, Brigadier General Enoch Poor, Brigadier General William Maxwell, and Brigadier General Edward Hand.

Time of Day / Length of Action: Late morning to late afternoon, six hours.
Weather Conditions: Hot and dry.
Opposing Forces: British: 1,100; American: 4,000.

British Perspective: Since May of 1778, the marauding raiders of British Col. John Butler, Tory leader Sir John Johnson, and Indian Chief "Captain" Joseph Brant had conducted several raids throughout the American settlements scattered across western New York and Pennsylvania. As far as the warriors of the Iroquois Nation were concerned, the entire territory belonged not to American settlers but to the confederated tribes of the Mohawk, Onondaga, Cayuga, Oneida, Tuscarora, and Seneca. The Indians were allies of the British, and their destructive raids against American forts and settlements (though viewed as uncivilized by the colonists) were helpful to the Crown in its effort to defeat the revolution. The 15-month campaign waged by the joint British, Tory, and Indian forces was much more successful in military terms than the earlier disastrous operations under Gen. John Burgoyne in the same area in 1777. However, their bloody work at the Battle of Wyoming (July 3, 1778) brought about unwanted consequences when the Americans decided to fight on the same terms: no quarter for the enemy.

During the winter and spring of 1779, the British and Indians moved their headquarters to the southern region of New York along the banks of the Chemung River. Within this fertile region the Indians settled down, established villages, and planted crops. With British assistance, the Indians established the villages Kanadasega, Kendaia, Kanadaque, Hannayaye, Gothseunquean, Chinesee, Koneghsaw, and Newtown. During the summer of 1779 the British and Indians suffered a series of small scale losses when a large American army vengefully struck back in a massive offensive campaign. Sweeping through the Iroquois Nation, the colonists burned villages and destroyed crops. By August 29 they were approaching the village of Newtown where Butler and Joseph Brant had combined their forces to meet the Americans. At Brant's insistence they threw up log barricades to ambush the enemy.

American Perspective: Following the debacle at the Battle of Wyoming, the reign of terror that descended upon the western settlements of New York and Pennsylvania forced American settlers there to seek refuge in eastern cities. The matter was of sufficient importance to involve General George Washington, who conferred during the winter months with Congress and his fellow officers to forge a plan to resolve the deteriorating situation. On July

22, 1779, at Minisinc, New York, Indians and Tories led by Chief Joseph Brant conducted yet another assault on the frontier, surrounding and slaughtering a detachment of 45 colonial militiamen led by Col. Benjamin Tusten.

When the tale of yet another gruesome massacre spread across the frontier, Continental authorities decided to send an expeditionary force into the region to seek out and destroy the joint Indian-British enemy. Although the war was heating up again in the lower colonies, it had reached something of a stalemate in the Northern Theater, which freed colonial forces there to focus on the menace to the frontier. Major General John Sullivan was selected for the task and was given four full brigades (more than 4,000 men). Designed as an offensive campaign, Sullivan was to push the enemy from the region, destroy his capability to wage effective war, and free the area for American settlers to safely reoccupy the land. While Sullivan marched north Col. Daniel Broadhead would lead 600 men into the Allegheny River Valley, sweep west from Pittsburgh, and locate and destroy Indian villages.

General Sullivan marched his three brigades northward through the Susquehanna River Valley while Gen. James Clinton's brigade swept westward across the Mohawk River Valley and traversed the Susquehanna River Valley toward the south. The Wyoming Valley was re-secured in late June. Although it was difficult to maintain a good logistical lifeline, the Americans were steadily achieving the success they had envisioned. On August 11 Generals Clinton and Sullivan linked up at Tioga Point in the Iroquois territory. From there the American army marched northwest through the Indian settlements, devastating everything in their path. On the morning of August 29 the American column was marching along a trail parallel to the Chemung River intent on destroying the village of Newtown.

Terrain: In 1779, this area of southwestern New York (five miles southeast of Elmira) was wilderness forest with several small settlements and farms interspersed along the fertile Chemung River Valley. The gently rolling hills are well drained and crops grew abundantly in the valley. The battlefield was restricted to an area about five miles square within a natural bend in the Chemung River. The trail followed by the Americans ran east to west parallel to the river along its northern bank, between the river to the south and high ground in the north. The river ran west to east and served as a major trading route. The village of Newtown was also located on the river's northern bank west of the battlefield. Two hills that create north-south ridge lines cut across the northern end of the battlefield, and a small creek flows from the north, bisecting the field of battle before emptying in the Chemung River.

The Fighting: The breastwork constructed by Butler and Brant was positioned across one of the north-south ridge lines cutting across the east-west trail leading to Newtown. Within these entrenchments, which were masked by timber and brush, Butler and Brant deployed 300 rangers and 800 Indians. They planned to lure the Americans into a trap by attacking the marching American column with a band of Indians well east of their main line. Virginia infantry skirmishers, however, detected the enemy positions and alerted the main column in time to avoid a tactical blunder.

At 11:00 a.m., Sullivan ordered Gen. Enoch Poor's brigade (part of Sullivan's division) and James Clinton's 1,500-man division to maneuver to the right, scale the high ground there, and crush the enemy's left flank. Artillery attached to the flanking operation was to be emplaced on the high ground to enfilade the fixed enemy position. General Edward Hand, meanwhile, was to push his light infantry brigade west along the route of movement directly into the enemy line, while General Maxwell's infantry brigade and two artillery batteries under Thomas Proctor moved in support with orders to attack the enemy's right once they began falling back.

Poor and Clinton had a hard time getting into position. Their march carried them over difficult and at times swampy ground. A sharp fight broke out as they climbed the steep hill in the face of Indian fire. About 3:00 p.m., before Poor and Clinton were in position, Sullivan ordered Proctor to open fire with his artillery. The cannonade frightened many of the Indians who, according to Butler, were convinced the Americans were behind them and fled as fast as they could run. Hand's infantry advanced against the defenders in a bayonet charge. Some of the defending Indians, Tories, and British put up a stout defense, counterattacking Poor's right flank and nearly overwhelming it. Only reinforcements from Clinton's trailing column saved the embattled New Hampshire troops.

Unable to check the overwhelming forces, and with Hand and Maxwell moving against his right close to the river, Colonel Butler ordered a retreat. In places brutal hand-to-hand fighting erupted on the western side of the earthworks until the Indians were overrun. Sullivan's apathetic pursuit was so cautiously managed that Butler later commented on it.

Casualties: British, Tory, and Indian: approximately 20 from all causes; American: 42 from all causes.

Outcome / Impact: The Patriot victory at Newtown resulted in several inconsequential skirmishes as the British, Tories, and Indians retreated north toward Fort Niagara. The Americans followed in a slow but deliberate pursuit. During the next few weeks the Americans destroyed about 40 Indian villages, burned 160,000 bushels of corn, and ultimately drove the Indians

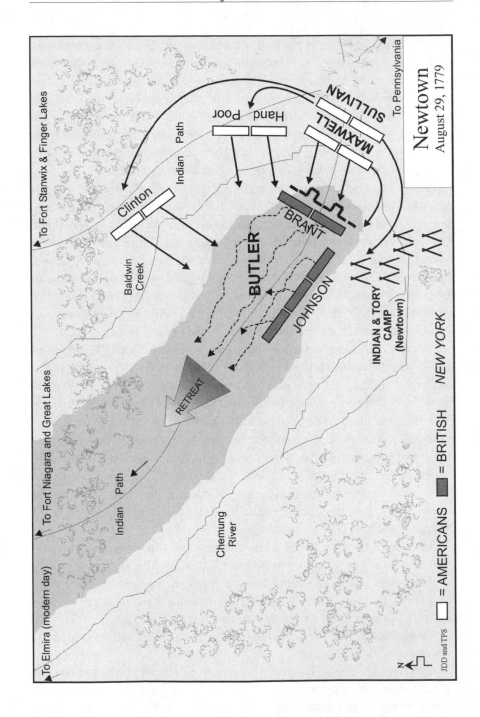

Newtown
August 29, 1779

completely out of the area. The offensive also liberated many white women who were being held captive. The campaign demoralized the Indians, who lost many more men than history will ever record. The Cayuga and Oneida Indians appealed to General Sullivan to reestablish friendly relations, but General Washington had given Sullivan explicit orders not to enter into any treaties. While successful, the expedition took a toll on Sullivan's health, who resigned and returned home once his mission was complete. Washington recalled Sullivan's army east after its expedition ended.

Colonel Daniel Broadhead's expedition into the Allegheny Valley met with little opposition and his force destroyed at least ten Indian villages. Following these punitive expeditions, the American settlers of western Pennsylvania and New York returned to their settlements, while the Iroquois Nation pondered its relationship with the British. Despite the events of 1779, once the settlers returned to the frontier settlements the Indians had little recourse but to continue raiding, though in smaller bands. Frontier skirmishes between the Indians and pioneers continued for many years.

Today: Newtown Battlefield State Park is a multi-purpose recreational area that, among other things, interprets Sullivan's Campaign and the Revolutionary War in that region of the state.

Further Reading: Fischer, Joseph R. *A Well-Executed Failure: The Sullivan Campaign against the Iroquois, July-September 1779.* Columbia: University of South Carolina Press, 1997.

Savannah, Siege of (also known as 2nd Battle of), Southern Campaign

Date: September 16 – October 19, 1779.

Region: Southern Colonies, Georgia.

Commanders: British: Major General Augustine Prevost, Lieutenant Colonel John Maitland, Lieutenant Colonel John Harris Cruger, Lieutenant Colonel Thomas Brown, and Major James Wright; American: Major General Benjamin Lincoln, Brigadier Generals Isaac Huger, Andrew Williamson, and Casimir Pulaski, and Lieutenant Colonels Lachlan McIntosh and Francis Marion; French: Admiral Comte Valerie d'Estaing and Count Arthur Dillon.

Time of Day / Length of Action: 8:00 a.m. to 10:00 a.m.

Weather Conditions: Cool and clear, unremarkable Fall weather.

Opposing Forces: British: 3,000; American: 3,000; (French) 4,000 and 37 warships.

British Perspective: On September 4, 1779, sentinels stationed on the Atlantic coast of Georgia sent word to Gen. Augustine Prevost that the French fleet had arrived at Tybee Island. The news triggered concern within the British high command, which ordered defensive positions immediately improved. General Prevost and the Royal Colonial Governor of Georgia, James Wright, encouraged the locals to assist them in their efforts. While some locals despised the British, many remained loyal Tories and supported English rule. The result was many Loyalists and some 400 slaves helped the British build earthworks and redoubts around Savannah for their army.

Despite demands of surrender and threats from the French and Americans, during the next few weeks the defenders of Savannah worked night and day to improve their defenses. The exhausting effort was tremendously successful. British artillery positions increased from 12 to 100 pieces emplaced within embrasures. Additionally, successful raids were conducted by members of the 71st Highland Regiment against French and American targets of opportunity. However, these hit and run strikes were merely harassing in nature and did not prevent the combined French and American force from inching closer in preparation for a massive strike against Savannah.

On October 4, the French and Americans initiated a massive five-day bombardment of the city. The weeks of diligent preparations proved their worth. The fortifications were built well and few casualties were suffered by the British. The southern approaches to Savannah were defended by a semi-circle of interconnecting redoubts, with the Savannah River offering a significant defensive barrier on the north. Several ships had been sunk in the river at strategic points to prevent the French from moving warships too far inland. Three redoubts and two artillery batteries defended the right wing (south to west) sector, which was commanded by Col. John Maitland. Under Maitland's command were several British regular regiments and Provincial rangers led by Lt. Cols. Thomas Brown and John Hamilton. The left wing (south to east) sector was comprised of two large redoubts filled with artillery batteries and manned by a mixed force of Hessian regiments, British light infantry regiments, and several companies of Loyalists. Major James Wright (son of the Royal governor) led the Loyalist militia, while Lt. Col. John Harris Cruger commanded the Regulars. Within these defensive fortifications the British awaited an assault from the approaching combined French and American armies.

American Perspective: Admiral Comte Valerie d'Estaing and the French fleet returned to America from their campaign in the Caribbean Sea, reaching Charleston, South Carolina, on September 1, 1779. This powerful naval squadron was comprised of 37 warships and 4,000 marines, a powerful force the Americans desperately needed to save the Southern colonies from British domination. General Benjamin Lincoln and Admiral d'Estaing coordinated an expedition to attack the British at Savannah, Georgia. Leaving General Moultrie with 2,000 troops to defend Charleston, General Lincoln marched a 3,000-man army toward Savannah while the French sailed to meet him there. The French warships arrived at Tybee Island, Georgia, on September 1 to establish a maritime blocking force at the mouth of the Savannah River. Lincoln's army arrived at Ebenezer, Georgia, eight days later, when preparations for the siege of Savannah began in earnest. On September 12 Admiral d'Estaing conducted an amphibious landing with French marines south of Savannah at Beaulieu and moved inland, establishing positions at Thunderbolt just southeast of the city.

On September 16 General Lincoln and Admiral d'Estaing (who seemed equally adept as a ground commander) met at Thunderbolt to complete their plans. They issued a demand for surrender to the British. General Prevost delayed and bluffed past the request while his men hurriedly completed their defense works. By September 23 both sides were prepared for battle. However, another two weeks elapsed before the Americans actually threatened their enemy with hostile action. On October 4 Admiral d'Estaing maneuvered warships closer to Savannah and began bombarding the city. Despite five days of heavy shelling from 67 cannons, the effort inflicted little damage. The bulk of the civilians had already evacuated the city, and the British were well protected behind their earthen and palmetto log berms.

On the evening of October 8, Lincoln and d'Estaing finalized a plan of attack against the British fortifications, agreeing to launch the assault the next morning. The attack would be coordinated and delivered across a broad front. Lincoln and d'Estaing would personally lead one column against the western part of Savannah's defenses (the British right flank) while Lt. Col. John Laurens and Count Arthur Dillon each led another column comprising the main thrust of the combined French and American assault. Simultaneously, Brig. Gens. Isaac Huger and Andrew Williamson would press as close to the river as possible against the eastern defenses (the British left flank) in an effort to distract enemy attention away from the main attack. The main attack was planned to fall against the Spring Hill redoubt, which was defended primarily by the Loyalist Militia. The American commanders believed the untrained volunteers would crumble if pressed hard enough. If the feint in the east presented an opportunity, however, Huger and Williamson had orders to exploit it. At 1:00 a.m. on October 9 the combined French and American ground forces assembled and prepared for the early morning attack.

Terrain: The city of Savannah was built on a plateau along the southern bank of the Savannah River seventeen miles inland (west) of the Atlantic Ocean. The river averaged a depth of 30 feet and the city served as one of the most important Atlantic ports. The Savannah River empties from the highlands in the northwest to the coastal plain and Savannah in the southeast. In the 1770s the lowlands of Georgia along the river were comprised primarily of rice plantations and the city served as the heart of this thriving agricultural and mercantile center. The region consisted of salt marshes and shifting sandbars, with Savannah constructed on the most solid terrain in the vicinity. Approaches to the city from the south, east, and west were canalized on narrow spits of land surrounded by marshes, creeks, and tidal flats.

The Fighting: Ideally, the French and Americans desired to attack under cover of the pre-dawn darkness. However, as is common with large-scale attacks, coordination problems delayed the assault until daylight, and the element of surprise was lost. General Huger's force in the east and Count Dillon's force on the far right became mired in rice fields and mud flats, further weakening the Allied offensive. Their predicaments were further complicated when the British spotted the effort and opened a deadly artillery fire. To some degree, however, the hoped-for diversion worked, for as the British focused on Huger's and Williamson's struggling columns the main thrust led by Lincoln and d'Estaing reached its objective and opened the attack against the Spring Hill redoubt.

Soldiers from regiments of the South Carolina Continental Line led by Lt. Cols. Lachlan McIntosh and Francis Marion spearheaded the advance, clambering up the parapet. The struggle that followed was bloody and fought at close quarters. Several of Marion's men were killed as they fought to plant a pair of silk South Carolina flags, one red and one blue, atop the British parapet. As the battle raged, Colonel Maitland rushed in British reinforcements to bolster the position. The allied troops were unable to complete their victory, the British captured the American colors, and behind rows of shiny bayonets won back their redoubt. Forced back into the ditch below the position, the attackers suffered heavily while the British poured a deadly fire into them from above. In an effort to turn the tide of battle, Gen. Casimer Pulaski led a daring cavalry charge. Armed with pistols and sabers, his horsemen galloped toward the redoubt at top speed. The British easily mowed them down with their musket fire. Although the charge was heroic, it

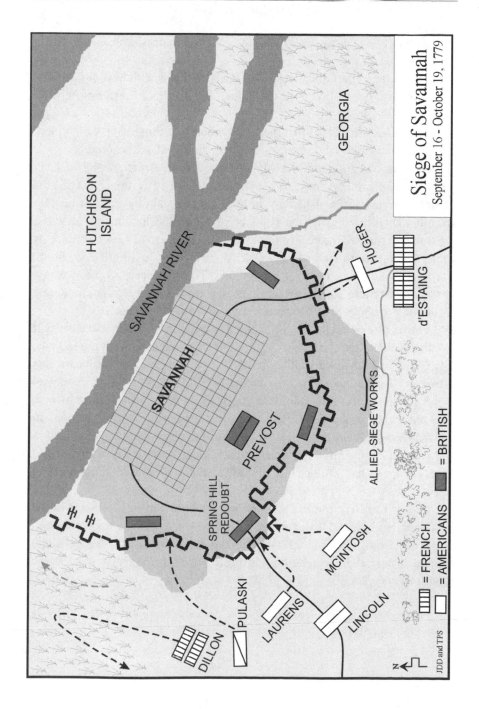

Siege of Savannah
September 16 - October 19, 1779

ended quickly and disastrously with the death of General Pulaski and many of his men.

For the better part of the next hour the Americans withdrew as best they could under a heavy fire from the British fortifications, suffering terribly during the retreat.

Casualties: British: 140 killed and wounded; American: 250 killed, wounded, and captured; French: 828 killed, wounded, and captured.

Outcome / Impact: The siege/attack against Savannah was an unmitigated disaster. Admiral d'Estaing was wounded during attack and his French marines suffered heavily in the effort to capture the Spring Hill redoubt. Displeased with the conduct of General Lincoln's Americans, d'Estaing evacuated the coast and sailed his fleet and men back to France. A chagrined Lincoln marched his defeated army back to Charleston, South Carolina, on the afternoon of his repulse. The unsuccessful siege was a tremendous failure for American interests, especially because the defeat eroded the confidence of their most important ally: the French.

The repulse of a superior Allied force helped the British in many ways. It solidified their control of Georgia and improved relations with the Indians. The Creek and Cherokee rallied to the Crown. The Savannah success also increased Tory support throughout the Southern colonies and prompted General Clinton to send additional troops to the Southern Theater of war. The only setback for the British (who had stripped Florida of troops to defend Georgia), was the loss of St. Augustine when the Spanish moved in and reoccupied the city. The Spanish had declared war against England in June 1779, but had not yet formally allied themselves with the American cause.

Today: Construction has all but eliminated the physical remains of the Savannah battlefield. However, the Coastal Heritage Society interprets and preserves Savannah history. It has joined with the city of Savannah to expand historical interpretation and preservation efforts that include the Revolutionary War.

Further Reading: Lumpkin, Henry. *From Savannah to Yorktown: The American Revolution in the South.* New York: Paragon House, 1981.

Charleston, Siege of (Southern Campaign)

Date: April 18, 1780 – May 12, 1780.

Region: Southern Colonies, South Carolina.

Commanders: British: Lieutenant General Sir Henry Clinton, Lieutenant General Charles Cornwallis, Admiral Mariot Arbuthnot, Major General Augustine Prevost; American: Major General Benjamin Lincoln, Brigadier General Isaac Huger, and Brigadier General William Moultrie.

Time of Day / Length of Action: Siege: Three weeks; Battle of Monck's Corner: 3:00 p.m. to 4:00 p.m.

Weather Conditions: Typical mild, Spring weather.

Opposing Forces: British: 13,500; American: 7,000.

British Perspective: Following Maj. Gen. Augustine Prevost's victory at Savannah (September-October 1779), Lt. Gen. Henry Clinton decided to attack Charleston a second time and invest more resources in the Southern Theater of operations. Clinton was keenly aware of the failed previous attempt to take Charleston on June 28, 1776, and that the earlier operation had consisted of a maritime assault against strong Patriot fortifications erected on Sullivan's Island. With a stalemate in the Northern Theater, Crown authorities decreed the major effort to win the war would be undertaken in the South, where it was believed better opportunities for long-term strategic success could be found. Many believed Loyalist support there would turn decisively in England's favor with a significant victory similar to Prevost's Savannah operations. Charleston was believed to be the key to obtaining that high-profile success.

British naval elements spent the months of December 1779 and January 1780 battling storms and moving through frigid winds to reach Savannah. The fleet was comprised of 90 troop carriers and 14 warships. The stormy seas delayed the effort and at one point dispersed the fleet. The British assault troops did not set foot in Georgia until February 4, 1780. The first units ashore included Lt. Col. Banastre Tarleton's infamous cavalry and the Loyalist Provincials led by Maj. Patrick Ferguson. These men would later play key roles in several battles. They moved their horsemen north to attack and harass Charleston by land. The British Fleet, meanwhile, sailed northward for Charleston. The main army disembarked at Seabrook Island, well south of the city, while the fleet sailed on to Johns Island, just a few miles below Charleston, on February 11, 1780. During the course of the next few weeks the army moved on to James Island and Wappoo Cut, inching closer to Charleston. The fleet followed the troops northward along the inter-coastal waterways, providing supplies to keep the large army fed and equipped. Americans harassed the British during the approach to the outskirts of Charleston, but the large British force simply pushed them aside and continued its offensive.

Moving steadily northward, the British crossed the Ashley River and marched east toward Charleston Neck from the mainland of South Carolina. Clinton's line stretched for about one and one-half miles across the peninsula, its flanks anchored on the Ashley and Charles rivers. On April 2 the British began building formal siege lines in the time-honored European fashion. The British fleet also made its presence off the Charleston bar.

American Perspective: The move against Charleston posed significant and largely insurmountable problems for Maj. Gen. Benjamin Lincoln, the commander of the American Southern Department. He had only 3,600 men available when operations commenced, his few forts were not prepared for action, and his navy was hardly worthy of the name. When the British landed troops at Johns Island on February 11, Lt. Col. Francis Marion, commander of the city's southern defenses, warned his leaders in Charleston of the impending danger and used his small force of mounted "swamp fighters" to harass the British. Nothing Marion could do would stop the scarlet juggernaut. Panic gripped the city when the British army marched inland and threatened it with capture from west of Charleston Neck. Offshore, the huge British fleet threatened the small American navy. Its commander, Commodore Abraham Whipple, scuttled most of his vessels along with a few merchant ships at the mouth of the harbor in the Cooper River to obstruct that waterway. In an effort to mount a credible defense of the city, Lincoln lashed out at the British siege lines on Charleston Neck and opened fire with a long and occasionally effective cannonade.

Lincoln's problems were multiplied when smallpox broke out in Charleston, local militia organizations provided faulty intelligence, and Spain refused to send assistance. Worse still, the French had virtually abandoned the Americans after the fiasco at Savannah. South Carolina's first Patriot Governor, John Rutledge, assumed dictatorial powers to control the growing chaos in Charleston.

On April 6 Brig. Gen. William Woodford arrived in Charleston with 750 reinforcements from Virginia and North Carolina after a 28-day forced march. Unfortunately, there was little additional troops could do to save the city. The British war machine was steadily tightening its vice-like grip on the citadel of the south, and there were not nearly enough Patriot troops in position to stop it. On April 9, fourteen British warships crossed the sandbar,

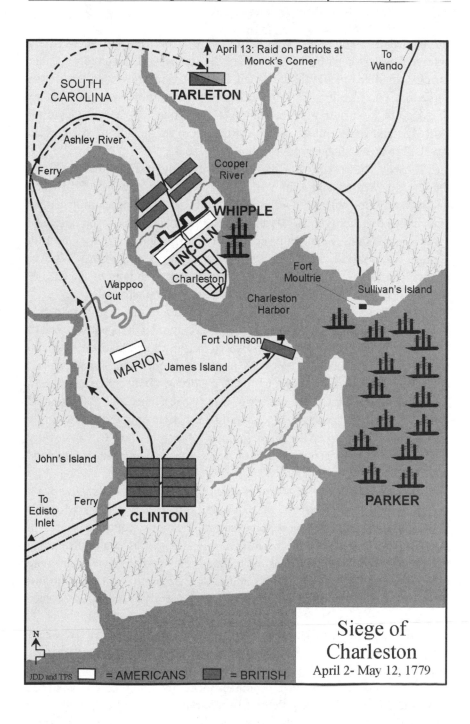

April 13: Raid on Patriots at Monck's Corner

TARLETON

SOUTH CAROLINA

Ashley River

Ferry

Cooper River

WHIPPLE

LINCOLN

Charleston

Wappoo Cut

Fort Moultrie

Sullivan's Island

Charleston Harbor

MARION

James Island

Fort Johnson

John's Island

To Edisto Inlet

Ferry

CLINTON

PARKER

To Wando

N

JDD and TPS   ☐ = AMERICANS   ◼ = BRITISH

Siege of Charleston
April 2– May 12, 1779

exchanged fire with the artillery from Fort Moultrie, and successfully entered Charleston harbor. The next day Clinton asked Lincoln to surrender the city, an offer Lincoln flatly refused. It was obvious, however, that unless something completely unexpected occurred, capitulation was only a matter of time. In an effort to save the state's political apparatus, Governor Rutledge and other public officials were secreted outside Charleston on April 13 to reestablish the government elsewhere.

Terrain: The port city of Charleston sits on a peninsula at the conflux of the Cooper, Wando, and Ashley rivers, all of which empty into Charleston harbor and the Atlantic Ocean. This terrain forms a natural harbor surrounded by marshy lowlands and shifting sand bars. The harbor entrance is narrow and shallow, and at its entrance is a large sand bar that in the 18th century was not passable during low tide; at high tide there were only five channels through which ships could pass safely into and out of the harbor. The peninsula on the land side was flat, sandy, and marshy.

The Fighting: On April 12 Clinton ordered Colonel Tarleton to ride behind and north of Charleston and sever its communications with the rest of South Carolina by land. With Maj. Patrick Ferguson and his men, Tarleton rode out on the night of April 13 toward the important logistical and communications strong point at Monck's Corner, about 30 miles distant. Defending Monck's Corner was Brig. Gen. Isaac Huger and 500 mounted militia. Lincoln had ordered Huger to hold the critical crossroads and supply depot at all costs. On the way to their objective the British cavalry intercepted an American courier with a message detailing the strength and disposition of Huger's troops.

At 3:00 a.m. on April 14 Tarleton launched his troops in a rapid assault that utterly defeated the unsuspecting Americans. Tarleton's Monck's Corner victory cut off Charleston's communications, captured scores of wagons and horses, and burnished his image as an outstanding raider-tactician. Huger and most of his men managed to escape, but more than two dozen were killed and wounded. According to Tarleton, who lost three wounded, Huger had not sent out proper patrols or deployed his men correctly.

After the April 14 fight at the strategic crossroads, the next few weeks around Charleston consisted of artillery duels, small-scale infantry sorties, and traditional siege methodology. Fort Moultrie surrendered on May 6 with the loss of 200 prisoners. Two days later General Clinton again demanded that Lincoln surrender. Negotiations began, but were eventually broken off when each officer blamed the other of violating the agreed-to cease fire. Throughout this period local citizens pleaded with Lincoln to capitulate. On

May 11 British "hot shot" artillery fire triggered a conflagration that consumed many homes. The following day Lincoln surrendered Charleston and his army.

Casualties: British: 78 killed and 189 wounded; American: 89 killed, 138 wounded, and 6,684 soldiers and sailors captured.

Outcome / Impact: The siege of Charleston was one of the most disastrous American defeats of the entire Revolution. Along with the thousands of men who laid down their arms to the British, the Patriots forfeited 154 cannons, tons of gunpowder and food, and yet another major southern port city. The loss was significant and its impact, including a loss of confidence in the Patriot cause, echoed around the world. General Lincoln and most of his senior officers were later exchanged for British officers, but many of the Regular Continental line soldiers and sailors were imprisoned and died miserable deaths aboard British prison ships. Major General Horatio Gates was placed in command of the remnants of the American Southern Department.

The victory convinced General Clinton that his theory the colonies could be rolled up from south to north was viable. In order to conduct this operation, Clinton transferred command of all British forces in the Southern colonies to Lt. Gen. Charles Cornwallis and returned to New York on June 5, 1780. Cornwallis had explicit instructions to secure the Carolinas for the Crown and march north toward Virginia. Clinton, meanwhile, would return to New York and sweep southward from that point, the generals crushing what was left of the rebellion between them.

By June of 1780, the British controlled Georgia from Augusta to Savannah. In South Carolina they established outposts, offered paroles to rebels, and lucrative enlistments to the local Tories. One of Clinton's biggest mistakes was his decision to free those American militiamen who had sworn allegiance to the King. This distasteful demand was intolerable to the Patriot warriors, who returned to the field after their release and continued fighting.

Today: The Monck's Corner field remains in private hands. Little in the way of the siege of Charleston discussed in this entry remains, although historical plaques and markers can be found throughout the city and its surrounding countryside.

Further Reading: Borick, Carl P., *A Gallant Defense: The Siege of Charleston, 1780* (University of South Carolina Press, 2003); Gordon, John W., *South Carolina and the American Revolution: A Battlefield History* (University of South Carolina Press, 2003); Lumpkin, Henry, *From Savannah to Yorktown: The American Revolution in the South* (Paragon House, 1981).

Waxhaws (Buford's Massacre), Battle of (Southern Campaign)

Date: May 29, 1780.
Region: Southern Colonies, South Carolina.
Commanders: British: Lieutenant Colonel Banastre Tarleton; American: Colonel Abraham Buford and Lieutenant Colonel William Washington.
Time of Day / Length of Action: 3:00 p.m. to 4:00 p.m.
Weather Conditions: Mild, unremarkable.
Opposing Forces: British: 270; American: 350.

British Perspective: After the victorious siege of Charleston (April 18 – May 12, 1780) General Cornwallis led a 2,500 man army inland toward Camden, South Carolina, to establish an outpost in the backwoods region between Charleston and the North Carolina border. During the journey Loyalists informed Cornwallis that South Carolina Governor John Rutledge was escaping into North Carolina escorted by 350 Patriots led by Col. Abraham Buford. Rutledge and his escort were at least 10 days ahead of the British, and after a short pursuit Cornwallis realized his infantry did not stand a chance of capturing the rebellious leader. He assigned the task of catching Buford and Rutledge to Lt. Col. Banastre Tarleton, who had a well deserved reputation as a capable and zealous officer who pushed his dragoons hard and fast.

Tarleton left the main column on May 27 with about 275 dragoons, Tory cavalry, and infantry (most mounted double). Riding night and day through punishing heat, Tarleton caught up with the enemy after covering more than 100 miles in just 54 hours. On the afternoon of May 29, he dispatched a detachment to demand surrender. The Americans refused.

American Perspective: General Lincoln's surrender of Charleston on May 12, 1780, threw the American Southern Department into disarray. Although Continental and militia units remained in service, there was no organized plan to quickly and efficiently reassemble a force capable of meeting the British in a pitched action. When units moving south to assist the Charleston defenders learned of Lincoln's surrender, they turned around and marched north to regroup and escape what would surely be a large-scale inland push by Cornwallis. One of these marching units, the 11th Virginia Regiment led by Col. Abraham Buford, was ordered by Isaac Huger to retreat with the survivors of the Monck's Corner fiasco northward to Hillsboro, North Carolina.

Colonel Buford reversed direction and moved his composite force of 350 Virginia Continentals as ordered, but he did not move rapidly enough. Governor John Rutledge was riding in the ranks (the governor was moving north under the protection of another unit). While moving with no sense of urgency through the Waxhaws District (and drawing near the relative safety of North Carolina), Buford learned of Tarleton's pursuit. Governor Rutledge left the column with his small escort. A detachment of British cavalry approached the Virginians from behind on May 29 demanding surrender, an offer Buford adamantly refused. While he and his leaders discussed their options, Tarleton's cavalry and infantry formed for an attack.

Terrain: The battlefield is 185 miles north of Charleston and six miles south of the North Carolina border. In 1780 the site was a crossroads in rural Waxhaws District (Lancaster County). Today, the small town of Buford sits adjacent to the battlefield, named in honor of the Patriot commander. The flat area consists of woods interspersed with farms and pastures.

The Fighting: After some of Tarleton's men attacked his rear guard, Buford turned and organized his men for battle. It was about 3:00 p.m. He aligned his infantry and cavalry into a single line of defense with a small reserve in the rear. Tarleton divided his command into three detachments: on his right were 60 dragoons and 50 light infantry; on the left was Tarleton himself with another 30 dragoons and additional infantry; in the center were the rest of the 17th Dragoons and infantry. Given the flat and lightly wooded terrain upon which Buford had formed, Tarleton's disposition was flexible enough to attack the center and both flanks simultaneously.

When the British dragoons charged, Buford ordered his men hold their fire. He held firm until the enemy was just 10 yards from his line, when his men poured a single volley into the charging enemy. Buford's choice of tactics was unfortunate. Although the volley killed and wounded many enemy horses and a few men, the momentum of the charge carried both beast and rider into the American lines. The tons of galloping horse flesh trampled and crushed the defenders. Tarleton killed a Virginian trying to raise a white surrender flag before his own horse went down, perhaps from the same volley. Once Tarleton's cavalry closed, Buford's Virginians had no chance against an experienced mounted foe, followed up by infantry.

Exactly what happened next will forever be subject to dispute. Some sources claim the British grew angry when they learned Tarleton had been struck down (he had not). The dragoons went to work, cutting and slashing the Patriots with their sabers, wounded and unwounded alike. British infantry added their bayonets to the bloody chaos. The hacking and close-quarter fighting, if as extensive as described, probably lasted for

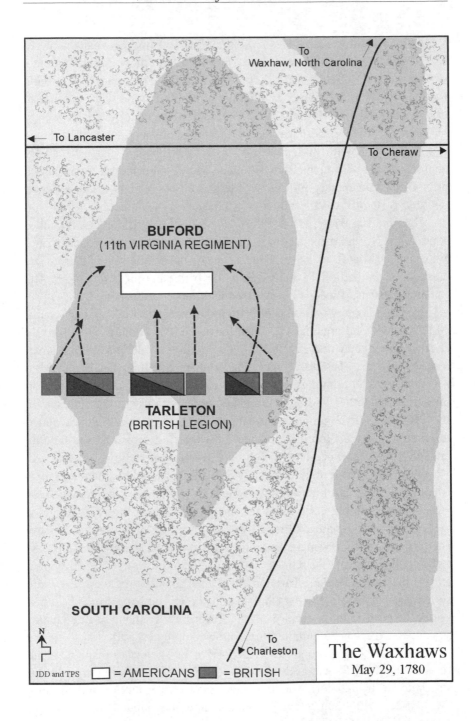

fifteen minutes. Surrender was out of the question as no quarter was offered or accepted. It should be taken into consideration that any cavalry charge followed by a determined bayonet attack—with screaming adrenalin-drenched soldiers shrouded in powder smoke fighting for their lives—would result in horrendous wounds. Depending on one's perspective, Waxhaws was either a well-executed tactical British victory or a bloody crime.

Casualties: British: four killed and 14 wounded; American: 113 killed, 150 wounded, and 53 captured. Colonel Buford and about 30 men escaped, as did about 100 additional infantry at the head of the column who did not turn and form to fight.

Outcome / Impact: Most of the Patriot wounded died, their bodies buried in a mass grave. Governor Rutledge escaped and worked in exile at Hillsboro, North Carolina. The Waxhaws combat was an overwhelming tactical victory for the British, though strategically inconsequential. However, the belief that Tarleton and his dragoons had massacred helpless men had tremendous repercussions. For the remainder of the war Patriots rallied behind the cry of "Tarleton's quarter," meaning show no mercy. Tarleton's methods, unarguably severe, forever earned him the nicknames "Bloody Ban," "Ban the Barbarian," and "Ban the Bloody Scout."

On July 25, 1780, Gen. Horatio Gates assumed command of the American Southern Department with headquarters at Deep Creek, North Carolina, ten miles southeast of Greensboro. General Washington sent Brig. Gen. Johann De Kalb with several regiments of the Maryland and Delaware Continental Line to reinforce Gates. The Patriot army in the South slowly reemerged as the surrounding states dispatched militia units to swell Gates's ranks. Deep within the backwoods of the Southern states, however, militiamen anxious to even the score with Tarleton and his dragoons were already fighting back against the British invaders.

Today: The site of this brutal fight has several granite monuments, one of which dates from before the Civil War. More than 100 Patriot bodies are buried there in a well preserved and marked mass grave. The area is still quite rural and looks much as it did more than two centuries ago.

Further Reading: Gordon, John W., *South Carolina and the American Revolution: A Battlefield History* (University of South Carolina Press, 2003); Lumpkin, Henry, *From Savannah to Yorktown: The American Revolution in the South* (Paragon House, 1981); Tarleton, Banastre, *A History of the Campaigns of 1780 and 1781, in the Southern Provinces of North America* (Cadell, 1787); Wilson, David K., *The Southern Strategy: Britain's Conquest Of South Carolina And Georgia, 1775-1780* (University of South Carolina Press, 2005).

Williamson's Plantation, Battle of (also known as Huck's Defeat), Southern Campaign

Date: July 12, 1780.
Region: Southern Colonies, South Carolina.
Commanders: British: Captain Christian Huck; American: Colonels William Bratton and Edward Lacey.
Time of Day / Length of Action: 6:00 a.m. to 7:00 a.m.
Weather Conditions: Hot and humid.
Opposing Forces: British: (Tories) 115; American: 250.

British Perspective: As the main British army under Lt. Gen. Charles Cornwallis moved across South Carolina toward Camden, cavalry led by Lt. Col. Banastre Tarleton and British provincials led by Lt. Col. Patrick Ferguson fanned out into the backwoods of South Carolina. Across these rural hinterlands the British encouraged men loyal to the Crown to join the army and report on the locations of their Patriot neighbors and all suspected insurgents. As with most backwoods counties of both Carolinas, Georgia, and Virginia, rural York County citizens were divided into three groups: Whigs (Patriots or rebels), Tories (Loyalists or pro-British sympathizers), or neutrals. Animosities and hatred ran deep, and the invading British army did all it could to fan the flames of violence into a brutal civil war pitting neighbor against neighbor and even brother against brother.

Encouraged by their victories in the Southern colonies, the British declared that the capture of Charleston had crushed the rebellion in South Carolina. During the summer of 1780 the British occupation forces moved inland, their Tory allies riding across the state destroying crops, burning homes, and murdering Patriots. On July 11 a composite 115-man British and Tory patrol led by Capt. Christian Huck moved through the Upcountry in search of rebel ringleader Col. William Bratton and his men in the Catawba district. Unable to locate Bratton, the soldiers camped in a field adjacent to Bratton's neighbor at Williamson's Plantation.

American Perspective: Following Buford's Massacre at Waxhaws (May 29, 1780), regional Patriots rallied into bands of hard-hitting partisan rangers. Colonel Francis Marion, known as the "Swamp Fox," is the most readily recognized of these men. Marion harassed the British from his hideout deep in the swamps of coastal South Carolina. His unconventional tactics befuddled the tradition-minded British. Other partisan leaders were also adept at waging this type of warfare, including Cols. William Bratton and Edward Lacey, both of whom led bands of partisans in the Upcountry region of the Carolinas. Their small commands were made up largely of state militia. After the fall of Charleston in 1780, however, the deteriorating circumstances in the Southern Department convinced them it was better to fight in tight-knit bands and conduct hit and run raids.

The Patriots maintained secret camps throughout the countryside and from these locations struck at British and Tory patrols throughout much of the Carolinas. Colonel Thomas Sumter maintained the largest camp in Lancaster County. It was there Colonel Bratton learned of Captain Huck's patrol camped at Williamson's Plantation. Bratton immediately organized a force to strike the enemy. By dawn on July 12 Bratton and 250 mounted soldiers had ridden to Williamson's Plantation and were in position to launch an early morning attack.

Terrain: The battlefield is 50 miles east of Spartanburg just outside Brattonsville, South Carolina. This rural community is comprised of gently rolling wooded foothills interspersed by farms and pastures. The terrain on the battlefield itself is level.

The Fighting: Bratton split his command into two equal patrols. He positioned one on the north side of Williamson house and the other well to the east. The sun was rising in the eastern sky when the twin pincer movement moved against an unsuspecting enemy. Rebel fire ripped into the sleeping British and Tories at short range. Captain Huck attempted to mount a credible defense but his men were caught in a crossfire. Rail fences made it impossible for them to close with Bratton's men and use their deadly bayonets. Huck mounted his horse and was attempting to rally his men when a Patriot unnamed to history shot him through the head. After several minutes the chaotic scene took on a more fluid movement when surviving British and Tory soldiers escaped southward toward the Bratton house. A short but bloody running battle ensued until the Americans overran the enemy and forced the survivors to surrender. According to British reports, only a dozen of their dragoons and another dozen or so Tory militia managed to escape the brilliantly planned and executed dawn surprise attack.

Casualties: British: 62 casualties and 29 captured; American: one killed.

Outcome / Impact: This battle represents the typical civil war-style rural combat waged against the backdrop of the larger revolution. Williamson's Plantation was one of the first fights in which the victors summarily executed captives. The cold-blooded killing instituted a brutal cycle of retribution that continued until the war's end. Both sides were guilty of these atrocities. Unfortunately, brutality became the norm. As the British quickly came to appreciate, the small partisan battles (of which Williamson's

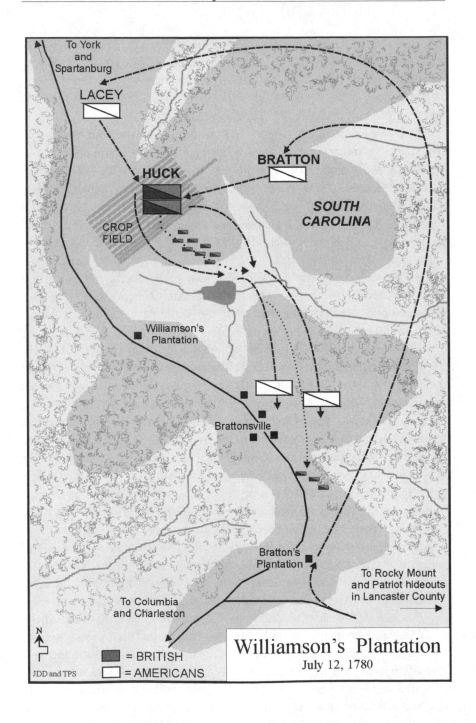

To York
and
Spartanburg

LACEY

HUCK

CROP
FIELD

BRATTON

SOUTH
CAROLINA

Williamson's
Plantation

Brattonsville

Bratton's
Plantation

To Rocky Mount
and Patriot hideouts
in Lancaster County

To Columbia
and Charleston

N

= BRITISH

= AMERICANS

JDD and TPS

Williamson's Plantation
July 12, 1780

Plantation was but one of many) made it apparent the victory over South Carolina rebels the British had earlier proudly declared was premature.

For the Americans—and backwoods partisans in particular—the small but spectacular victory boosted morale and swelled pride and conviction. "Huck's Defeat," as it was known across the Carolinas, assisted Thomas Sumter's recruiting efforts, and his swelled ranks made it possible to assault Rocky Mount (part of the Camden Campaign), on August 1, 1780. During the next month more than a dozen similar engagements were fought across South Carolina as Patriots rose up against the invading British and their Tory allies. Some of these included: Brandon's Camp, Stallions, Cedar Spring's, Gowen's Old Fort, McDowell's Camp, Flat Rock, Thicketty Fort, Hunt's Bluff, Hanging Rock, Old Iron Work's, Port's Ferry, Wateree, and Rocky Mount. Similar events unfolded in the Northern theater. At rural locales such as Young's House on February 3 in Philipsburgh, New York, violent clashes involving militia units were a reoccurring affair.

Today: The site of this engagement is preserved within historic Brattonsville, which is on the National Register of Historic Places. A living history museum there interprets colonial life in the Carolinas. In 2000, Mel Gibson filmed *The Patriot* in and around Brattonsville.

Further Reading: Lumpkin, Henry, *From Savannah to Yorktown: The American Revolution in the South* (Paragon House, 1981); Ward, Christopher, *The War of the Revolution*, 2 vols. (MacMillian, 1952).

Hanging Rock, Battle of (Southern Campaign)

Date: August 6, 1780.
Region: Southern Colonies, South Carolina.
Commanders: British: Major John Carden; Tory: Colonel Thomas Brown and Lieutenant Colonel Samuel Bryan; American: Brigadier General Thomas Sumter, Colonels Edward Lacey, William Hill, and Robert Irwin, and Majors Richard Winn and William Davie.
Time of Day / Length of Action: 7:00 a.m. to 10:00 a.m.
Weather Conditions: Hot and humid.
Opposing Forces: British and Tory: 1,400; American: 800.

British Perspective: The British continued their push into South Carolina and established forward outposts throughout the region. One such position was located in Lancaster County at Hanging Rock, a rural community and hotbed of insurrectionist activities. The British knew Col. Thomas Sumter led a large force of partisan militia in the region and that these men were responsible for having attacked isolated detachments of British and Tory troops. The outpost at Hanging Rock included an encampment of 1,400 troops, including the 500-man Prince of Wales regiment commanded by Maj. John Carden, elements of Lt. Col. Banastre Tarleton's dragoons led by Capt. John Rousselet, and the Loyalist Militia led by Col. Thomas Brown; elements of Lt. Col. Samuel Bryan's Loyalist militia were also present. This post, which served as the main advanced column of the British army, was located atop a craggy ridgeline that was well defended by earthworks, alert sentinels, and artillery positions. Because it was located deep inside enemy territory, the Hanging Rock outpost remained on a constant war footing, with the British Legion infantry on the right, and the Loyalists holding the center and left flank.

On August 1, 1780, mounted rebels simultaneously attacked Loyalists posted on the outskirts of Hanging Rock and a unit posted at nearby Rocky Mount. These brazen assaults had caught the British and Tories flat-footed, though they still managed to inflict 120 rebel casualties. On August 6 the rebels moved to attack the main encampment at Hanging Rock.

American Perspective: South Carolina Governor John Rutledge, conducting government business from his office in exile at Hillsboro, North Carolina, promoted Thomas Sumter to the rank of brigadier general. Given command of the militia troops operating in the border counties of North and South Carolina, Sumter organized his 800-man army for an attack against British outposts. Together with Maj. William Davie, Sumter had led successful raids against the British posts at Rocky Mount and Hanging Rock on August 1, 1780. Sumter decided to combine the various partisan bands into a stronger force and attack the Hanging Rock garrison on August 6.

Sumter believed that if he could launch a surprise attack and drive directly into the camp simultaneously from three directions, he could destroy the enemy before they could effectively organize against him. On the night of August 5 Sumter's rebels rode toward the camp on horseback, dismounted once they reached its outskirts, and crept toward their assigned assault positions as planned.

Terrain: The battlefield is located 20 miles southeast of Lancaster, South Carolina, just below the town of Heath Springs. Hanging Rock Creek winds its way through the hilly terrain and the average elevation is 600 feet. The area along the creek is laden with brambles and the forested hills dominate the area. The precipice of Hanging Rock and the hills around them are strewn with large boulders. (There is some debate about the actual location of the battle.)

The Fighting: At dawn on August 6 Sumter sprung his three-prong attack against the British outpost at Hanging Rock. Within minutes he surmised his entire assault was being launched against solely the Tory left wing. As it turned out, the local guide had led the partisan warriors too far to the right. Assigned to that sector were North Carolina Loyalist militia under Col. Morgan Bryan. Hit on the front and one flank, the surprised defenders fled toward the center of the garrison, where they joined with other infantry and rangers.

At first, the chaotic fight in the center of the camp forced the British to fall back again, and the Americans continued pushing forward. Major John Carden led his small regiment of the Prince of Wales Loyal American Volunteers against Sumter's exposed left flank. Somehow (it is unclear exactly how) Sumter's men tactically survived the threat and with well-delivered fire killed or wounded much of Carden's outfit. According to some sources, the experience unnerved Major Carden, who turned over command to Captain Rousselet of the British Legion infantry. Many of Sumter's men began plundering Carden's overrun camp. What happened next, and when it happened, is open to some speculation.

On the British right side of the battlefield, a classic hollow square was formed, supported by a pair of light artillery pieces. Other Tories formed nearby in the woods. Although Major Davie is said to have attacked and scattered the defenders outside the square, the formation itself held against all efforts to take it. According to one credible source, it was at this point that reinforcements arrived for the defenders in the form of 40 legion mounted infantry. Major Davie's dragoons were routed off the field.

By this time several hours of fighting had elapsed. Unable to gather more than a couple hundred men to continue the fight, General Sumter decided it was time to conduct a tactical withdrawal. Many of the men had succumbed to the heat and many more were drunk on British rum and loaded down with stolen items. With some effort the various Patriot leaders corralled what was now essentially an armed mob and guided it back toward their original dismounted launch point. Major Davie provided security for the column's rear as Sumter led his men away from Hanging Rock toward the Waxhaws.

Casualties: British: 192 killed and wounded, and 70 captured; *American:* 12 killed and 41 wounded.

Outcome / Impact: The battle was an expensive quasi-success for the Americans. Sumter inflicted substantially more casualties than he suffered,

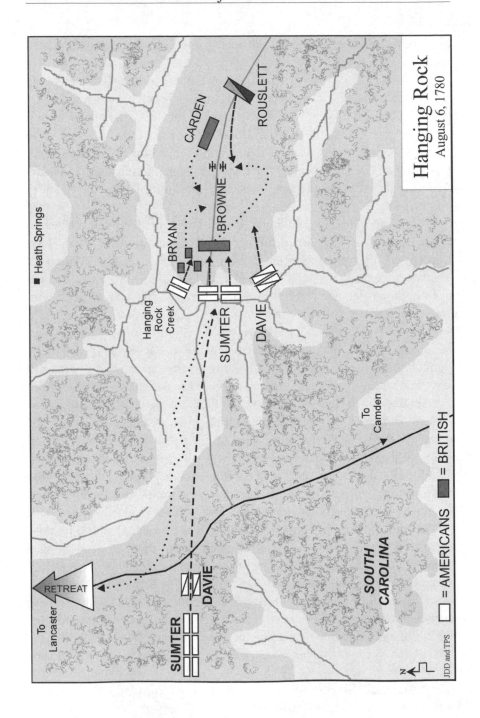

Hanging Rock
August 6, 1780

but failed in his objective to destroy the enemy and lost many of his best men, including several officers. He left the field with dozens of prisoners, 100 horses, and 250 muskets. The British repelled the American assault, but retreated from the forward base to join the main British army at Camden, South Carolina. The battle had no strategic effect on the course of the war.

Further Reading: Buchanan, John, *The Road to Guilford Courthouse: The American Revolution in the Carolinas* (John Wiley and Sons, 1999); Lumpkin, Henry, *From Savannah to Yorktown: The American Revolution in the South* (Paragon House, 1981).

Camden, Battle of (Southern Campaign)

Date: August 16, 1780.
Region: Southern Colonies, South Carolina.
Commanders: British: Lieutenant General Charles Earl Cornwallis; American: Major General Horatio Gates.
Time of Day / Length of Action: Morning, one hour.
Weather Conditions: Unremarkable, warm, and clear.
Opposing Forces: British: 2,239; American: approximately 3,700 (900 Continentals, 2,800 militia).

British Perspective: On May 12, 1780, Maj. Gen. Benjamin Lincoln surrendered Charleston, South Carolina, to a powerful combined British invasion force led by Sir Henry Clinton. Some 5,000 soldiers walked into captivity and tons of precious supplies were lost. Clinton sailed back to New York City leaving Gen. Charles Cornwallis in command. His orders to Cornwallis were to reduce and subjugate the rest of the Carolinas while maintaining a firm grasp on the port cities of Charleston and Savannah, Georgia.

Cornwallis's most important interior garrison and logistical supply depot was established at Camden. This small but strategically located crossroads town by the Wateree River and Catawba Indian Trail was about 115 miles northwest of Charleston. When Cornwallis learned Horatio Gates had been appointed to lead an American army that was threatening Camden, Cornwallis left Charleston to confront and defeat him in the field. Cornwallis made a night march from Camden on August 15-16 in an attempt to position his army for an attack the next morning, but halted when his cavalry struck the head of Gates's army.

American Perspective: A few days before the fall of Charleston the Continental Congress dispatched the victor of Saratoga, Maj. Gen. Horatio Gates, to take command of the small Continental field army in the South and stabilize the deteriorating situation there. Although Gates was credited with the tremendous New York victory against John Burgoyne's army, the true architects of that decisive strategic success were Benedict Arnold and a few other subordinate officers. The colonial cause needed a competent and tactically aggressive field commander in the Carolinas. Gates would prove soon enough that he was neither.

Gates arrived in late July 1780 at the Deep River camp and took command of a small, demoralized, and ill-equipped army composed largely of militia. Despite its deplorable condition, Gates marched on Camden on July 27 believing that only 700 men held it. He knew almost nothing about the region and marched his hungry men through unfriendly and difficult terrain. Though large numbers of militia reached him, he also weakened his army by detaching several hundred men on less important duties.

About 2:00 a.m. on August 16, advance cavalry elements of the opposing forces stumbled into one another on the old Waxhaws Road several miles north of Camden above Saunder's Creek. Both sides pulled back to await the dawn. When Gates discovered he faced Cornwallis and a veteran field army, he decided it was too late to retreat and prepared for combat.

Terrain: Gently undulating lightly wooded field of battle approximately three-quarters of a mile wide with both flanks covered with woods and swamp land. The Waxhaws Road bisected the length of this field.

The Fighting: Cornwallis formed his men before dawn on either side of the Waxhaws Road. His finest troops under Lt. Col. James Webster held the position of honor on the right wing. These men included the 23rd and 33rd Foot, with a pair of battalions from the 71st Highlanders behind them in reserve (perhaps astride the road). The left wing under Lord Rawdon was composed of his own Irish Volunteers, infantry from the British Legion, the Royal North Carolina Regiment, and Morgan Bryan's North Carolina militia. Banastre Tarleton's veteran legion of horse and foot formed in reserve. Four pieces of artillery bolstered the center of his line. Cornwallis was so certain of tactical victory he deployed his army with Saunder's Creek behind him.

Gates deployed his army in much the same manner. His right wing comprised some 900 veteran Maryland and Delaware infantry under the command of General Baron Jean de Kalb, one of the Continental Army's

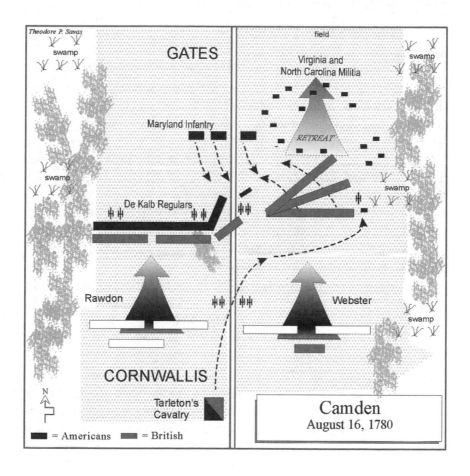

finest subordinate commanders. Three small Maryland regiments straddled the road in reserve 200 yards behind the front line. Gates joined them there with his staff—a critical mistake that kept him too far in the rear to affect the course of the fighting. His left front was entirely formed of untried militia from North Carolina and Virginia, about 2,500 strong, with a handful of cavalry and other light infantry behind them. Seven pieces of artillery dotted the line. Gates's foolhardy deployment positioned his least reliable troops in front of Cornwallis's finest Regulars. (Long established European tradition calls for the best troops to hold the right side of the line.)

Cornwallis opened the battle by advancing Webster's elite warriors against Gates's left. They advanced "with great vigour [and] in good order and with the cool intrepidity of experienced British soldiers," wrote Cornwallis after the battle. Except for one company the American militia fled almost without firing a shot. In a matter of minutes the left half of the American army had evaporated.

On the other flank, General de Kalb's Regulars held their own against a spirited advance by Lord Rawdon. General de Kalb, who was wounded early and often at Camden, launched a serious attack that forced Cornwallis himself to ride into the action and steady his men. Webster, meanwhile, pivoted his regiments to the left and pinned de Kalb and the advancing Maryland reserves into place. With Rawdon in front and Webster on one flank and swampy woodland on the other, Cornwallis recognized his opportunity and threw Tarleton's cavalry around the Continentals, sealing their doom. A few escaped into the swamp, but most were killed, wounded, or captured. Gates, who spent the entire battle deep in the rear, fled the field even before the mortally wounded de Kalb was surrounded. Tarleton's vigorous pursuit inflicted additional American casualties.

Casualties: British: 68 killed and 256 wounded, or about 14% of Cornwallis's effective force; American: losses seem never to have been officially reported. They are estimated at 250 killed and 800 wounded and captured. Many of the militia never returned to the ranks, and the American army lost the valuable services of General de Kalb, who died three days after the battle.

Outcome / Impact: The defeat at Camden was the worst loss suffered by an American army during the entire war. Morale dropped like a stone and the Southern army was reduced to a paltry few hundred men. South Carolina and Georgia were firmly, if temporarily, under the Crown's control. The most important consequence of the battle was the exposure of the hapless Gates as an incompetent field commander, and the appointment of Nathanael Greene to replace him.

Today: Historic Camden Revolutionary War Site can be visited in Camden, South Carolina. Several hundred acres of the battlefield have been preserved, and there is a museum on the site, walking trails, and regular historic living history programs and battle reenactments.

Further Reading: Buchanan, John, *The Road to Guilford Courthouse: The American Revolution in the Carolinas* (John Wiley and Sons, 1999); Landers, H. L. *The Battle of Camden, S.C., August 16, 1780* (Kershaw County Historical Society, 1997); Pancake, John S. *This Destructive War: The British Campaigns in the Carolinas, 1780-1782 (University of Alabama Press, 1985).*

Musgrove's Mill, Battle of (Southern Campaign)

Date: August 18, 1780.
Region: Southern Colonies, South Carolina.
Commanders: British: Colonel Alexander Innes and Captain Abraham DePeyster; Tory: Colonel Daniel Clary; American (militia): Colonels Isaac Shelby, James Williams, and Elijah Clark.
Time of Day / Length of Action: Afternoon, one hour.
Weather Conditions: Hot and humid.
Opposing Forces: British: 600; American: 300.

British Perspective: After General Cornwallis scored his decisive victory against Horatio Gates at the Battle of Camden (August 16, 1780), his efforts were focused on crushing the pockets of rebels who continued to harass British supply trains and outposts. Colonel Banastre Tarleton's dragoons caught up with rebel leader Thomas Sumter on the 18th of August, but the nimble backwoodsman escaped Tarleton's dragnet. That same day American rebels attacked the British outpost at Musgrove's Mill in South Carolina's rural Upcountry. Musgrove's Mill was being used as a staging ground by British and Tory troops based at nearby Fort Ninety Six. There, the Crown gathered and organized Loyalist units under British commander Maj. Patrick Ferguson.

Unbeknownst to the rebels, the British had just reinforced the outpost with 300 Loyalist rangers under Col. Alexander Innes. Local Tory militia led by Col. Daniel Clary numbered 150, and Capt. Abraham DePeyster of Major Ferguson's command led another 150 British troops. After three British sentinels were suddenly shot and the alarm rang, Colonel Innes organized his men into attack columns and marched northward up the road toward the rebels.

American Perspective: After the Battle of Hanging Rock (August 6, 1780), Brig. Gen. Thomas Sumter transferred a large group of his militia to serve with Horatio Gates, who wasted their lives in the disastrous combat at Camden ten days later. Sumter and his backwoods militiamen, meanwhile, continued launching partisan attacks throughout much of South Carolina. On August 18 the British nearly captured Sumter and his men as they rested along the banks of Fishing Creek in rural Chester County. Sumter made a narrow escape but lost all the British horses, supplies, and prisoners he had obtained during several weeks of fruitful raiding.

Meanwhile, Col. James Williams had moved his Laurens District South Carolina militia into the Upcountry of South Carolina to raid Tories in District Ninety Six. As Williams's command passed near Cherokee Ford on the Broad River, they met with partisans led by Col. Charles McDowell of North Carolina and Col. Elijah Clark of Georgia. Also present were men from the Overmountain region of North Carolina (present-day southwest Virginia and east Tennessee). These backwoods warriors were experienced Indian fighters led by Col. Isaac Shelby. At this meeting they learned Maj. Patrick Ferguson was leading the British effort to organize, train, and equip Loyalists throughout the region. The backwoodsmen decided to strike the British and Tory stronghold at Musgrove's Mill on the Enoree River. They rode through the night of August 17 to reach their objective.

On the 18th, scouts led by Georgia Capt. Shadrack Inman were dispatched to survey the enemy positions. Unfortunately for the rebels, they shot several British sentinels, killing one and wounding two others. While the element of surprise was lost, the scouts did gain valuable information concerning the enemy's strength and disposition. When the partisans realized the enemy was larger than expected, and fearing attack, they established hasty defensive positions using logs and brush. The barriers were erected along a ridge facing Ferguson's command, one-half mile north of the river. Hidden within the thick woods, Colonel Shelby's men secured the right (west) sector of the road while Colonel Clark's men secured the left (east) sector. Small detachments were sent into the woods on either flank to fire from concealed positions. The entire partisan line faced south. The command's horses were left 300 yards to the rear.

Terrain: This battlefield is located near the Enoree River on the border of rural Laurens and Union counties of South Carolina (only a few miles from the November 20, 1780, Blackstock's Plantation field). The wooded terrain is hilly, with an average elevation of 450 feet. Sumter National Forest lies just east of the battlefield. The soil is sandy loam and brambles and a wide variety of undergrowth dominate the lowlands and the hills. The main battle occurred on the dominant high ground at an elevation of 600 feet, one-half mile north of the river in Union County.

The Fighting: There is a dearth of reliable detailed information on this action. When the British and Loyalist troops were spotted advancing from the south, the partisans leveled their muskets and, showing tremendous discipline, waited for the enemy to close. A detachment of militia crept forward to skirmish with the advancing British and Loyalists, who formed lines in the woods on either side of the road and continued moving forward through the light by pesky fire as the partisan skirmish line fell back.

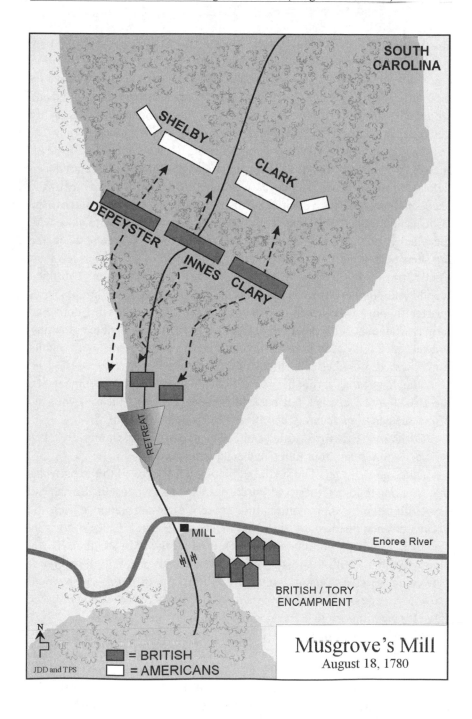

According to some accounts, Colonel Innes's men may have believed they were driving the main enemy line. When Innes's infantry advanced to within a few dozen yards of the primary defensive line, however, they discovered their error when the waiting partisans opened fire. The flying lead killed and wounded many of the attackers, who were now pinned down by a fire delivered from an enemy they could barely make out.

The battle continued for perhaps an hour, during which time Colonel Innes's infantry inflicted little or no damage against the entrenched defenders. His command, however, was being steadily whittled away by the excellent partisan sharpshooting skills. According to some sources, the British and Loyalists advanced with fixed bayonets in an effort to close with the enemy, and Colonel Shelby's men on the right wavered when the attackers neared their position. Colonel Clark's soldiers, however, left their light barricade to attack with hatchets, knives, and rifle butts. The thick woods and smoke obscured visibility and complicated the brutal close-quarter fighting. The accurate fire of the backwoods partisans, delivered largely from concealed positions at close range, inflicted terrible casualties. A lead ball fired by an unknown hand felled British commander Colonel Innes at what was likely the climax of the fighting.

Unable to break through, even with double the number of combatants, the British and Loyalists fell back to Musgrove's Mill. Pleased with the effort, the partisans secured their horses and rode northward.

Casualties: British: 63 killed and 160 wounded (70 of whom were taken prisoner); American: four killed and eight wounded.

Outcome / Impact: The small but bloody battle proved to the partisans that, working together, they could strike deadly blows against the British and Tories threatening their homes. Immediately after the action closed the backwoodsmen learned of the destruction of General Gates's army at Camden. The news prompted them to retreat northward to Gilbert Town, North Carolina. Still, the lesson learned was a vital one, and the compact between otherwise disparate groups of militia from different states would prove to be one of the most important arrangements of the war, setting the stage for the victories to come at Kings Mountain and Cowpens.

Meanwhile, the debacle that was Musgrove's Mill upset the British, who organized a pursuit of Shelby, Clark, and the other rebels. This time Cornwallis ordered Major Patrick Ferguson to take charge of all the Tories and British soldiers on the western frontier of the Carolinas. A professional soldier of Scottish descent, Ferguson set out to crush the enemy.

Today: The state's newest historic park, Musgrove's Mill State Historic Site, opened to visitors in 2003. It is 93 miles west of Camden and 15 miles north of Clinton, South Carolina. While the mill itself no longer stands, there is a stone marker just off SC Hwy. 56 on the south side of the river. The battlefield is about two miles north of Exit 52, off I-26, on Hwy. 56.

Further Reading: Buchanan, John, *The Road to Guilford Courthouse* (Wiley, 1997); Keller, S. Roger, *Isaac Shelby* (Burd Street Press, 2000); Lumpkin, Henry, *From Savannah to Yorktown: The American Revolution in the South* (Paragon House, 1981).

Augusta, Battle of (Southern Campaign)

Date: September 14-18, 1780.
Region: Southern Colonies, South Carolina.
Commanders: British: Colonel John Harris Cruger; Tory: Colonel Thomas Brown and Captain Andrew Johnston; American (Militia): Colonel Elijah Clark, Lieutenant Colonel James McCall, and Major Samuel Taylor.
Time of Day / Length of Action: Five days of intermittent fighting.
Weather Conditions: Clear and warm.
Opposing Forces: British: 600; Tory: 300; Indians: 250; American: 430.

British Perspective: After the rebels attacked the British outpost at Musgrove's Mill near Fort Ninety Six in South Carolina on August 18, 1780, the British initiated a ruthless campaign to crush the partisan bands operating in the rural backwoods of the Southern Theater. Major Patrick Ferguson arrived at Musgrove's Mill shortly after the fight and led a force of 1,000 soldiers north to Gilbert Town, North Carolina, in pursuit of the rebels. At Fort Ninety Six, Col. John Harris Cruger dispatched patrols of British and Tory units to hunt down rebels and hang them. General Cornwallis also issued orders for British officers to hang any Tories who displayed doubts concerning their loyalty to the Crown, or any paroled rebels who thereafter took up arms.

On September 4, 1780, Major Ferguson's forces clashed with some of the retreating partisans at Cane Creek, North Carolina. Ferguson spent the next three weeks fighting and hunting down the marauders in that region. While this was occurring Tory messengers reported on September 16 that rebels had attacked the British outpost at Augusta, Georgia. The post was commanded by Loyalist leader Col. Thomas Brown. Colonel Cruger organized a relief squadron and began the 60-mile march to assist in Augusta's defense.

At Augusta, meanwhile, Colonel Brown and another Loyalist officer, Col. James Grierson, commanded the "King's Rangers," a 300-man Loyalist militia unit. These Tories held the town and two posts named Fort Grierson and Fort Cornwallis. The former was about one-half mile northwest of town, while the latter was in Augusta along the Savannah River. Colonel Brown also served as the British Indian Agent in the region, a position he assumed following the death of the notorious John Stuart. As a result, Brown also had 250 Creek Indians under his command. The Creeks maintained a camp on the west end of town near Robert Mackay's Trading Post. While Augusta was important to the British, its influence was secondary to the overall plan of campaign that called for a sweep into North Carolina. Still, the Savannah River town was a Crown possession and the British were compelled to support their Tory allies.

American Perspective: After the small but stunning victory at the Battle of Musgrove's Mill, the Americans wisely rode for their lives with the British in vigorous pursuit. Moving northward to the safety of Col. Charles McDowell's camp in the mountains of North Carolina near Gilbert Town, the American militia made a pact of mutual support and went their separate ways. Colonel James Williams's South Carolinians moved on to Hillsboro, North Carolina, taking with them the prisoners they had captured in their recent battles; Col. Isaac Shelby returned with his "Overmountain Men" to the Watauga camp in what is today East Tennessee; Col. Elijah Clark's unit returned to northwest Georgia.

Soon after his return to Georgia, Clark discovered that Tories had been using forts in Augusta to launch raids into the frontier. These marauding Tories raped women, ransacked homes, and terrorized anyone who opposed them—and many who did not. Clark decided to organize an assault against the Augusta-based enemy. His command consisted of his own 350 Georgia militiamen and 130 South Carolinians led by Lt. Col. James McCall. The forces joined together about 40 miles northwest of Augusta before moving to the city's outskirts. By the morning of September 14 Clark was in position to open hostilities.

Terrain: Augusta, Georgia, was established as an early trading post on the Savannah River. The city was erected on a large sandy plateau along the river's west bank. Hills rose to the north, west, and east of the city, while the land to the south was generally flat (the Savannah River drains the region from northwest to southeast). Although the town became the seat of government for the colony in December of 1778, the British captured it in 1779. When they abandoned it later that year the Americans reoccupied the

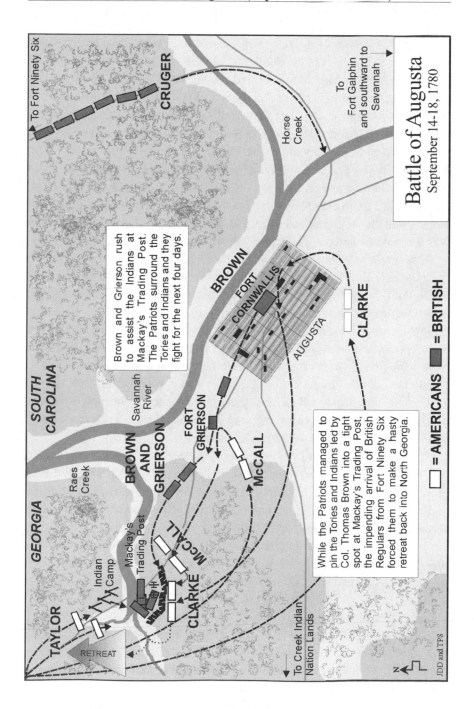

To Fort Ninety Six

CRUGER

To
Fort Galphin
and southward to
Savannah

Horse
Creek

Battle of Augusta
September 14-18, 1780

SOUTH
CAROLINA

Brown and Grierson rush to assist the Indians at Mackay's Trading Post. The Patriots surround the Tories and Indians and they fight for the next four days.

Savannah
River

BROWN

FORT
CORNWALLIS

CLARKE

AUGUSTA

GEORGIA

Raes
Creek

BROWN
AND
GRIERSON

FORT
GRIERSON

McCALL

Indian
Camp

Mackay's
Trading Post

McCALL

CLARKE

While the Patriots managed to pin the Tories and Indians led by Col. Thomas Brown into a tight spot at Mackay's Trading Post, the impending arrival of British Regulars from Fort Ninety Six forced them to make a hasty retreat back into North Georgia.

TAYLOR

RETREAT

To Creek Indian
Nation Lands

N

□ = AMERICANS   ■ = BRITISH

JDD and TPS

city until the spring of 1780, when Charleston, South Carolina, fell and British fortunes surged in the Southern colonies.

The battle unfolded in and around Augusta. There were three primary sites of heavy activity. One was on the west bank of the Savannah River in downtown Augusta at Fort Cornwallis, located at the present-day intersection of 11th and Reynolds streets. This stronghold was a traditional earthen and palisade fort originally known to the early pioneers as Fort Augusta. The second site was Fort Grierson, a fortified blockhouse about one-half mile west of Fort Cornwallis. The third site consisted of a fortified house known as Robert Mackay's Trading Post (also known as the White House) and the adjacent site known as Garden Hill. This defensive position was located one and one-half miles west of Fort Grierson.

The Fighting: The Americans advanced in three columns early on the morning of September 14. The left wing under Maj. Samuel Taylor initiated the fighting by moving against the Creek Indian camp west of town. Caught utterly off guard, the Indians offered only token resistance before seeking refuge at Robert Mackay's Trading Post. The sporadic fighting alerted the Tories posted in Forts Cornwallis and Grierson that there was trouble west of town. Brown and Grierson unwisely left the bastions and moved quickly to assist their Creek allies. With good timing and even better luck, James McCall led the main attack against these forts, which he occupied without much difficulty. Colonel Clark, meanwhile, led the third prong of the assault and entered the center of town from the south.

Leaving detachments sufficient to hold the captured forts, Clark pursued the Tories to Mackay's Trading Post, where a brisk and lengthy battle erupted. Tory leader Capt. Andrew Johnston was killed during the fighting and the Americans captured more prisoners. Brown and his command formed for battle on a rise of ground near the trading post called Garden Hill. On his right Brown deployed the King's Rangers, their bayonets fixed for bloody work. On Brown's left were his Creek allies, who were also armed with rifles. His small arms weaponry was supported by two light field pieces. Unable to piece the Tory defenses, Clark withdrew his men to the east and Colonel Brown took possession of the Mackay house, a stout structure constructed of heavy stones and fortified with firing ports. Entrenchments were dug around the house to bolster its defense. Knowing he faced serious opposition, that night Colonel Brown dispatched a rider to Fort Ninety Six (South Carolina) requesting assistance.

The next morning, September 15, Brown sent another urgent message to Fort Ninety Six seeking reinforcements. Colonel Clark's men drove in an Indian detachment and cut off the Tory's water supply. Determined to capture the stronghold, Clark ordered his men to dig their own line of defensive entrenchments while other soldiers rolled two field pieces from Fort Grierson into position. The guns opened fire, but the only qualified artillerist, Capt. William Martin, was killed early in the fight by small arms fire. The combat intensified and casualties mounted on both sides (Brown was wounded through both legs). As darkness approached Clark demanded Brown surrender, but the Tory adamantly refused and the fighting continued until darkness put an end to the combat. That evening about 50 additional Creek Indians arrived to assist Brown, but Clark's men interrupted the effort and kept them away.

On September 16, 600 professional British soldiers under Col. John Harris Cruger marched out of Fort Ninety Six en route to Augusta 60 miles to the south. By this time the fighting along the banks of the Savannah River had subsided into a pointless stand off. Brown was unable to break out and was unwilling to surrender, even though he and his Indian allies were suffering horribly from thirst (some reports have men drinking their own urine). Clark, on the other hand, was not strong enough to capture the reinforced stone structure. When rumors of British reinforcements began spreading through the ranks, some of Clark's men quietly slipped away and headed for home.

At 8:00 a.m. on September 18 Clark's scouts reported that British reinforcements were approaching Augusta. Determined to fight as long as he could, Clark ordered his men to fire everything they had against the trapped Tories and Indians. It was not enough, and another hour of fighting did not alter the outcome. By this time Colonel Cruger's British were crossing the river to assist the Tories and Clark reluctantly ordered his men to retreat into the woods, leaving to the mercy of the enemy those who were wounded and unable to travel. He nearly waited too long and his men were almost caught between the Tory defenders and the approaching British. The Creeks were dispatched to pursue the Americans.

Casualties: British (Tory and Indian): Precise casualties are difficult to tabulate. Colonel Brown was wounded and Captain Johnston was killed, as were 20 Indians. Certainly more men were killed and wounded, but figures do not exist to confirm this; American: Clark's attacking command lost 60 killed and wounded and many deserters.

Outcome / Impact: Clark's offensive, deemed by some to have been "ill-advised," failed to capture Augusta or inflict any loss of significance against the enemy. It did, however, succeed in inflaming Tory passions and triggered retribution against Patriot supporters. The result was an exodus of Patriots from northeast Georgia, most of whom spent the next few months in the "Overmountain" Watauga community (present-day East Tennessee). After the fighting, Colonel Cruger sent word to Maj. Patrick Ferguson that Colonel Clark was thought to near Gilbert Town, North Carolina. Although the British invested heavily in Clark's capture, he managed to evade the enemy and fight another day.

According to varying reports, 29 of Clark's men (a dozen of them wounded) were captured by the British. Captain Ashby and the wounded were cruelly hanged in a wide stairwell inside Robert Mackay's Trading Post as traitors, while the rest were handed over to the Tories and Indians, who took out their revenge upon them. South Carolina Governor John Rutledge claimed that Colonel Brown allowed the Indians to behead four of the Americans and kick the severed heads through the streets of Augusta. A bloody civil war was tearing through the Southern Colonies as divided Americans fought bitterly for their beliefs. The hatred between the Patriots and their Tory adversaries would soon reach a crescendo on a lonely mountain top in South Carolina.

Further Reading: Cashin, Edward J., *The King's Ranger: Thomas Brown and the American Revolution on the Southern Frontier* (University of Georgia Press, 1989); Lumpkin, Henry, *From Savannah to Yorktown: The American Revolution in the South* (Paragon House, 1981).

Kings Mountain, Battle of (Southern Campaign)

Date: October 7, 1780.

Region: Southern Colonies, South Carolina.

Commanders: British: Major General Charles Cornwallis, Major Patrick Ferguson, and Captain Abraham DePeyster; Tories: Colonels Ambrose Mills, Daniel Plummer, John Cotton, Sr., and Major Patrick Cunningham; American: Colonels William Campbell, Isaac Shelby, John Sevier, Edward Lacey, James Williams, Benjamin Cleveland, Joseph Hambright; Majors William Chronicle, William Candler, Joseph Winston, and Joseph McDowell.

Time of Day / Length of Action: 3:00 p.m. to 4:00 p.m.

Weather Conditions: Clear and cool, following a long rain.

Opposing Forces: British (Tory): 1,075; American: 910.

British Perspective: The near-destruction of the Patriot army at Camden (August 16, 1780) encouraged British soldiers and bolstered the morale of the loyalist movement throughout the Carolinas. As far as General Cornwallis was concerned, that decisive victory—together with the triumph at Charleston (April-May, 1780) and the purge of rebel bands operating in the Upcountry region of South Carolina—completed the Crown's conquest of the state. North Carolina was next on the aggressive commander's list of regions requiring subjugation.

Leaving behind the forces Lord Francis Rawdon had commanded at Camden to act as a foundational base, Cornwallis decided to swing his army northward in a broad hinge movement across the border into North Carolina. He would maintain the center of the main invading force as it moved into Charlotte Town (modern-day Charlotte), while farther west Maj. Patrick Ferguson's Loyalists advanced deep into North Carolina's Tryon County (modern-day Rutherford and Lincoln counties). There, Ferguson's militia would rally local inhabitants to British allegiance. Ferguson's command would also secure the mountainous region in the west while simultaneously covering Cornwallis's advancing strategic left flank. Cornwallis launched his invasion with a renewed vigor and a plan he was confident would work. He also sent word into North Carolina urging Loyalist allies to assist the British by capturing suspected rebels and seizing their arms and ammunition.

For many locals, the mere sight of Redcoats and Tories massed on North Carolina soil encouraged them to rally to the King's banner. Encouraged by his success, Ferguson decided to address the people on the western side of the Blue Ridge Mountains (a region which was known as the backwater or Overmountain region). He selected a rebel captive from the region to deliver a message threatening to hang everyone and lay waste to their homes if they did not swear allegiance to the Crown.

In pursuit of his odious goals, Ferguson sent out patrols to search for local rebels operating in Burke County under the command of Col. Charles McDowell. After a minor engagement at Cane Creek (Cowan's Ford) on September 12, 1780, resulted in a setback for the British, Ferguson concentrated his command around his headquarters at Gilbert Town, waited for the enemy, and gathered supplies. Ferguson next turned his Tory militia southeast to link up with Cornwallis's main army closing on Charlotte. While en route Ferguson learned a large group of rebels was following him. He turned the head of his command southward, making a deliberate hook maneuver onto a ridgeline 36 miles west of Charlotte, where he established his men in a defensive posture atop a ridge known locally as Kings

Mountain. Ferguson sent requests for reinforcements to Colonel Tarleton at Charlotte and Colonel Cruger at Fort Ninety Six, but Tarleton was sick with Yellow Fever and Cruger had no men to spare. Isolated on Kings Mountain, Ferguson for the first time probably felt some unease about his exposed position.

Loyalist tents and wagons occupied the northeastern corner of the mountain top while Ferguson arrayed his army in defensive positions along the ridge's long, narrow, and barren plateau. Sentries were posted below the rim of the hilltop to provide early warning of any enemy attack. Ferguson's command, comprised of 1,075 officers and men derived from elements of six "Loyalists Militia" regiments, was organized into four main units. Although his raw numbers were substantial, the composition of Ferguson's force left something to be desired. The bulk of his militia had been raised in and around District Ninety Six in South Carolina, and additional troops had swelled his ranks during his march through North Carolina. He had drilled them as well as possible under the circumstances, with a heavy emphasis on bayonet assaults. The units mirrored British organizational structure, formations, and tactics. Securely positioned on Kings Mountain, Ferguson and his Tories awaited the enemy's arrival.

American Perspective: When Ferguson's threat to hang civilians reached Patriot commander Isaac Shelby beyond the Blue Ridge, he contacted other militia leaders and urged them to combine their forces, march across the mountains, and destroy Ferguson's Loyalist army. The Patriots gathered at Sycamore Shoals on the banks of the Watauga River just below modern-day Elizabethton, Tennessee. On September 25, 1780, Shelby joined his militiamen with those of John Sevier, Joseph McDowell, and William Campbell in a meeting known today as the gathering of the "Overmountain Men." The massive rally of these frontier pioneers coalesced into a loosely organized army of hardy frontier Indian fighters outraged by the British invasion of the Carolinas and the threat to hang them and burn their homes.

The men rode steadily through high mountain passes and covered about fifteen miles a day. After crossing the mountains they were joined by additional troops from both Carolinas and Georgia. The Patriot commanders decided Colonel Campbell should retain command of the composite force. With little fanfare Campbell led 910 outstanding horsemen through a driving rain to find Ferguson before he reached the safety of the main British army. Locals informed the militia that the Loyalists were encamped on Kings Mountain. Campbell's militia approached the broad northern slope of the ridge, where the thick forest shielded their approach. Campbell divided his command into two divisions of nearly equal strength. The divisions were further divided into four linear columns to better maintain unit integrity during the approach to the high ground and to more rapidly reach their respective assault positions.

The so-called Left Division was ordered to surround the north side of Kings Mountain (which ran generally northeast to southwest) while the Right Division did the same on the south. The Left Division was organized from left (southwest) to right (northeast) as follows: Colonel Shelby's 120 men; the composite force of Colonel William's 30 men, Colonel Lacey's 100 men; Major Candler's 30 men; Colonel Cleveland's 110 men, and 50 men led by Colonel Hambright and Major Chronicle. The southern or Right Division was organized from left (southwest) to right (northeast) as follows: Colonel Campbell's 200 men; Colonel Sevier's 120 men; Major McDowell's 90 men, and Major Winston's 60 men. The Left Division on the northern face of the mountain would assault with about 440 men, while 470 men scaled the southern slope. Once these forces were in position the signal to commence the assault would be given: a loud Indian war-whoop. Once the battle began, everyone was under orders to press upward simultaneously and overwhelm the defenders hunkered down on the high ground.

At 2:00 p.m. on October 7, Colonel Campbell gave the order to advance. Major Joseph Winston led his men out first. His job was to ride hard and swing his men beyond the southwestern point of the ridge, cutting an arc about one mile beyond the mountain. He would then circle back and approach the objective from the northeast. Winston's assault sector was the extreme northeast corner of the high ground. His mission was important because the only road that led to the heights ran up the eastern side of Kings Mountain. If Ferguson attempted to retreat toward Charlotte, Winston's cavalry would block his move.

Once Winston was gone the rest of the Patriot columns moved toward their assigned attack positions. On the north side of the mountain, elements of the Left Division bogged down in marshy terrain several hundred yards from their objective. The only militia unit on the north side able to move largely unimpeded was Shelby's column. His route to the objective was dominated by high ground and so was more easily traversed. As Shelby approached his assault position, Campbell's column to the southwest was riding around the southwestern end of the mountain and closing in on its assigned position. Trailing behind Campbell were Sevier and McDowell, who were ordered to continue around the southern flank of the high ground to extend their lines northeast. Unbeknownst to Ferguson's Loyalists, the noose around them was tightening by the minute.

Terrain: Kings Mountain is located in York County, South Carolina, 36 miles west of Charlotte, North Carolina. This rural area just below the North Carolina border is dominated by hills with slow meandering brooks draining the areas below them. The battlefield consists of a single dominant piece of high ground forming the northern end of Brushy Ridge (known as Kings Mountain, elevation 1,000 ft.). The low-lying area around Long Branch Creek below the northern slope of the ridge is marshy and contains patches of thick cane and brambles. The opposite side of the ridge gently slopes to the south into a small valley. The crest of Kings Mountain is dominated by a plateau 600 yards long. It extends from the northeast, where it is about 120 yards wide, to the southwest, where it narrows to a width of only 70 yards. Ferguson parked his 17 wagons in a semi-circle on the northeast corner of this plateau, where he also established his headquarters and encampment.

The Fighting: About 3:00 p.m., Loyalist scouts detected movement in the woods on the northern side of Kings Mountain. At the same time pickets on the mountain precipice opened a sporadic long-range fire against Shelby's approaching column. As this fire was developing advance elements of other northern militia columns from the Left Division ran up against loyalist pickets near the base of the northeast sector of the mountain and a fitful firing also broke out there. Loyalist drums were beaten and Ferguson blew his whistle commands to order his Provincial Rangers (men raised in the colonies to fight for the British) to move rapidly to the southwest corner of the ridge to counter what Ferguson deemed to be the most serious threat. As events would prove he was correct about the threat about to engulf the narrow southwest plateau. In addition to the Provincial Rangers, his Loyalist militia included experienced men from District Ninety Six, South Carolinians Ferguson had enlisted and formed months earlier. They were well prepared for battle and Ferguson employed them skillfully.

Moving around the southwest base of the mountain, Campbell's rebel column was detected by a Loyalist who fired into approaching frontiersmen. Realizing the element of surprise was lost, Campbell made a command decision to turn and assault the heights. At nearly the exact same time, Major Winston's mounted force reached its assigned position on the northeast side, blocking the only road off Kings Mountain. Winston's men attacked from that position. Because the assault commenced prematurely, Sevier's following column became intermingled with Campbell's and ended up widely divided. All of Sevier's 120 men would assault up the narrow southwest end of the mountain, and the unit as a whole retained some company integrity. However, as the bulk of Sevier's men deployed into their assigned sector on Campbell's right (northeast), a large contingent broke off

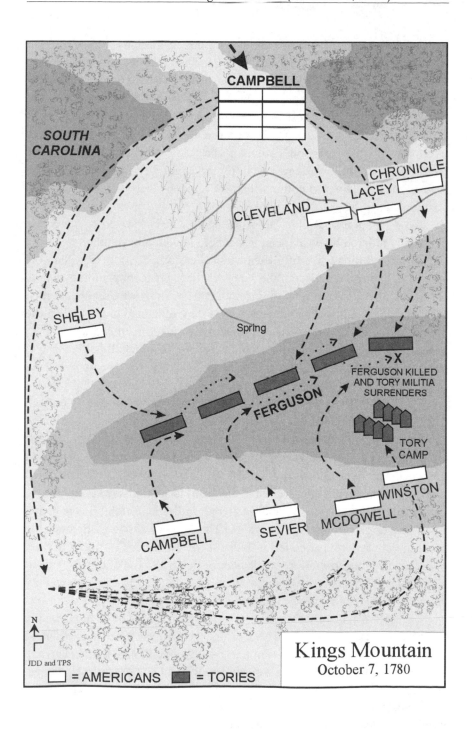

Kings Mountain
October 7, 1780

and ended up assaulting the mountain on Campbell's left, between Campbell and Shelby farther to the northeast on the northern side of the ridge.

Because Campbell's Right Division had not yet extended along the southern base of the mountain as planned, McDowell urged his 90 men to maneuver as quickly as possible around Campbell's right. Although most eventually reached their assigned position, some made the assault up the hill intermingled with Campbell's column. The result was that the first twenty minutes of the battle was carried out by the Right Division alone because none of the Left Division columns had yet achieved their assigned jump-off positions.

As Campbell's Right Division approached the crest Ferguson personally ordered his Provincial Rangers to launch a bayonet charge. The impact created by a wave of glistening steel rushing downhill into Patriots approaching from below sent the rebels reeling. Officers wielding swords cut down several of the retreating frontiersmen. Many of Campbell's men took shelter behind rocks and trees, where they remained hidden. Near the bottom Campbell and his officers rallied their shaken men and urged them back up the slope. When Ferguson blew his whistle to recall his Provincial Rangers to the summit, his South Carolina militia who had accompanied the charge became confused and did not immediately rally as intended.

The reinforced Loyalist assaults in the southwest stripped away enough defenders from the northwest slope for Shelby's men to gain ground there. Just as they neared the summit, however, Ferguson dispatched his bayonet wielding forces into their ranks. This time the result was not what Ferguson intended. The mountain men absorbed the bayonet assault and scampered part way down the hillside. Although their unit formations had been broken, the small pockets of men and scattered individual fighters created a swarming effect around the attackers. The tactical situation favored the partisan Patriots, who excelled in Indian-style fighting. Confident in their abilities, they began working their way back up the rock-strewn wooded slope, small knots of men supporting one another as they inexorably crawled, trotted, and crouched their way toward the crest.

The smoke and confusion made it difficult for Ferguson to immediately grasp what was happening. His Loyalists had been trained to fight in traditional linear European fashion. The unconventional battle that had suddenly erupted in their faces forced them to fight at a great disadvantage. As they quickly discovered, their drill in massed formations and dependence upon bulk musket fire was useless against dispersed militia hiding behind trees and rocks, picking them apart with accurate small arms fire.

Near the southwestern tip of the summit Campbell's, Sevier's, and Shelby's men pressed into the British lines, where a bloody hand-to-hand struggle ensued. Meanwhile, the heights to the northeast were threatened by the arrival of the other Patriot columns. Ferguson left Loyalist militia to defend the southwestern end of the ridge while he led his Provincial Rangers down the ridge (northeast) to address the new threat arriving in that sector.

It was approximately 3:30 p.m., and Ferguson was rushing to confront the arriving columns comprising the Left Division. The terrain there was especially difficult because the elevation was steeper and the vegetation denser than it was on the opposite flank. The arriving American militiamen were exhausted after their grueling march through the swampy lowlands and had already experienced a fitful fight against Loyalist sentries near the base of the northern slope. They had also formed under fire. Majors Winston and Chronicle formed and assaulted from the northeast, while Colonels Cleveland, Williams, and Lacey attacked along the northern slope. The men clambered over the craggy rock-strewn slopes while the Loyalists poured volleys of fire into them from above. Southwest of Chronicle's position (on his right) Colonels Cleveland, Williams, and Lacey guided their men up the slope. Ferguson's militia held the tactical advantage, lining the brow of the northern ridge while waiting for the enemy to close within killing range. Just as it had on the other end of the mountain, the inherent difficulty of climbing and fighting dispersed the once tightly-packed Patriot advance. The frontiersmen maneuvered in small pockets and fired well-aimed shots into the defenders hovering above them.

On the summit the Provincial Rangers launched another bayonet charge. Hambright's men were struggling up the steep northeast slope when the charge fell upon them. A few minutes later the Rangers withdrew while the Loyalist militia covered them from above. In Cleveland's sector, the Loyalists made only one other bayonet charge down the northern slope. The bloody work of the bayonet charges did nothing to dissuade the Patriots from their assault. The heavy pressure against the northeast summit forced Ferguson to shuttle men to the embattled sector or risk having it overrun.

Like a large vice, the pressure slowly but surely crushed Ferguson's position from every side. In the southwest corner of the ridge, dozens of frontiersmen from the Right Division finally reached the summit and began pushing Loyalist militia from their rocky strongholds along the crest. Elements of the Left Division began mounting the crest in the northern and northeastern sectors about the same time. The tide of battle was turning decisively in favor of the Patriot militia.

Ferguson's position was now desperate. His surviving soldiers were being pressed into an ever-constricting mass, surrounded by a deadly enemy within a shrinking enclave on the northeast end of Kings Mountain. Constrained within his own formations, tents, and wagons, Ferguson had little room to maneuver. His only option was to stand and die, or assault and try to turn the tide. Blowing on his silver whistle, Ferguson ordered the Provincial Rangers to assault the enemy charging up the ridge from the southwest. He also ordered some mounted men to charge into the approaching enemy, but they could not do so because the mountaineers picked them off too quickly.

Pressing forward, the swarming Patriots gained the upper hand quickly, picking off Tories milling about on the open plateau before them. The demise of the Provincial Rangers signaled the end of Ferguson's now demoralized command, which was now completely surrounded and running out of ammunition. Amidst the smoke and confusion Ferguson was killed by musket fire. Realizing there was no further hope in fighting, the surviving Tories began surrendering and begging for quarter. As is always true in close-quarter fighting, the killing continued for some time until violent passions subsided and control was established.

The Tory prisoners were marched first to Gilbert Town and then to Hillsboro, North Carolina. Many escaped along the way. Nine were hanged for committing heinous crimes, an act that perpetuated the cycle of retribution. Following the fighting the victorious frontiersmen disbanded and returned to their homes for the winter, while the British retreated to winter quarters around Winnsboro, South Carolina.

Casualties: British (Tories): 244 killed, 163 wounded, and 668 captured; American: 29 killed and 58 wounded.

Outcome / Impact: Kings Mountain was a significant Patriot victory and the turning point of the war in the Southern Theater. The decimation of Cornwallis's entire left wing stunned the British general and convinced him to abandon his invasion of North Carolina for several months. This, in turn, allowed Gen. Nathanael Greene (who would assume command of a shattered Southern army in December 1780) the time he needed to reorganize his army and assume the initiative. The battle also struck a fatal blow to the Loyalist movement in America while simultaneously inducing a Patriotic resurgence. It is interesting to note that except for the British officer Ferguson (a Scotsman), every man who fought at Kings Mountain was a native American. More than any other battle of the war, Kings Mountain reflects the passionate political and social differences that fanned the flames of the American Revolution.

Further Reading: Buchanan, John, *The Road to Guilford Courthouse: The American Revolution in the Carolinas* (John Wiley and Sons, 1999); Dameron, J. David, *Kings Mountain: The Defeat of the Loyalists* (Da Capo Press, 2003); Tarleton, Banastre, *A History of the Campaigns of 1780 and 1781, in the Southern Provinces of North America* (Cadell, 1787).

Blackstock's Plantation, Battle of (Southern Campaign)

Date: November 20, 1780.

Region: Southern Colonies, South Carolina.

Commanders: British: Lieutenant Colonel Banastre Tarleton and Major John Money; American (militia): Brigadier General Thomas Sumter and Colonels James Williams, Elijah Clark, Edward Lacey, William Bratton, and William Hill.

Time of Day / Length of Action: Evening, one hour.

Weather Conditions: Clear and cold.

Opposing Forces: British: 270; American: 1,000.

British Perspective: Following the stunning loss at the Battle of Kings Mountain on October 7, 1780, Lt. Col. Banastre Tarleton was ordered to track down and destroy the rebel militia operating in the Upcountry of South Carolina. On November 18 Tarleton learned rebel leader Thomas Sumter was operating within striking distance of Tarleton's mounted patrol. Informants told the British that Sumter and his men were planning to attack a Loyalist outpost at Williamson's Plantation, fifteen miles from Fort Ninety Six. Tarleton sped off with his dragoons toward the reported location, riding along the Enoree River to trap the rebels between him and Col. John Harris Cruger's troops at Fort Ninety Six. Tarleton caught up with Sumter's rear guard on the morning of November 20 as it was crossing the Tyger River, but the rebels escaped without any casualties except for a handful of British prisoners they had been holding who were accidentally killed by their attacking comrades.

Infuriated, Tarleton's men gave chase throughout the day and late that afternoon caught up with the rebels just west of the Tyger River and Blackstock's Plantation. Artillery and infantry trailing behind Tarleton's cavalry were still miles away when the opposing forces met. Tarleton rather imprudently decided to mount an immediate assault without waiting for his supports to arrive.

The rebels formed on clear high ground, allowing Tarleton to see that his 270 men were facing off against about four times their number. Bold to a fault, Tarleton hesitated not at all. He deployed his British Legion on the left (or west) side of Blackstock Road and the 63rd Regiment, commanded by Maj. John Money, on the right (or east) side. The dragoons moved on horseback; the 63rd Regiment dismounted to fight as infantry before fixing bayonets. Together, the British moved steadily northward to meet the waiting Rebels. Tarleton knew he faced steep odds, but believed he could engage and pin the rebels in place until his reinforcements arrived to seal the victory. Although some sources claim Tarleton planned to wait for his supporting troops, his own memoirs dispute this. He intended to attack without them, and his decision was wholly in line with his normal battlefield comportment.

American Perspective: Following the Kings Mountain fight, the Patriot Militia (the "Overmountain Men") returned to their homes on the far side of the Appalachian range. However, the South Carolina militiamen joined Gen. Thomas Sumter with the intent of launching raids against the British and Tories. Throughout November of 1780, Sumter and his men harassed the British west of the British camp at Winnsboro, while Francis Marion (known as the "Swamp Fox") conducted hit and run strikes east of the enemy camping grounds. Marion was also promoted to brigadier general and led numerous successful raids against the British in his assigned sector from the fall of 1780 through the spring of 1781. From actions such as Blue Savannah on September 4, 1780, to Fort Watson on April 23, 1781, Marion lived up to his "nom de guerre," repeatedly outfoxing larger enemy forces by conducting swift hit and run raids that helped erode British morale and control in South Carolina.

By late 1780 Sumter had earned the nickname "Gamecock" and had proven he was successful conducting unconventional assaults in the backwoods of the Upcountry. His men won a small victory at Fish Dam Ford on November 9, and the angry British were soon hot on his trail. By the 19th of that month his rebels learned the despised "Bloody Ban" Tarleton and his infamous dragoons were tracking them. Sumter decided to turn and offer battle. After consulting with local militia leaders who knew the area better than he did, Sumter placed his army in a defensive posture at Blackstock's Plantation. This site along the Tyger River provided an excellent position as well as an escape route if the fight turned against him. Sumter placed Col. Edward Lacey's troops in the front and center (facing south) as skirmishers while the bulk of his command assumed positions behind them. The Blackstock buildings and the Tyger River were beyond Sumter's left, east of his line of battle. Sumter also placed Capt. John Twiggs's Georgians at the Blackstock Plantation along a rail fence just southwest of the farm. The main road to the ford across the Tyger River was secured within Sumter's lines and provided him with an emergency exit from the field.

Late that afternoon the British appeared south of the American position, organized for battle, and moved against the American militia. Sumter coolly dispatched 400 skirmishers to meet Tarleton's advance. Although a militia commander, Sumter was conducting a conventional engagement against veteran enemy troops and an outstanding tactician.

Terrain: This battlefield is 45 miles south of Spartanburg, South Carolina, in rural Union County. The dominant high ground is just southwest of the Tyger River, which flows from northwest to southeast. The area around the battlefield is hilly with an average elevation of 500 feet. At least one major source claims the river was behind and on the right of Sumter's line. This is incorrect; the river winds its way from northeast to southwest north of the old plantation site.

The Fighting: The American skirmishers opened a premature fire against the advancing British about 5:00 p.m. The ineffective shooting was followed by a bayonet charge conducted by Major Money and his 63rd Regiment east of the road. Money's bayonet assaults were repulsed twice by the Americans. With each charge the British line faltered a bit and fell back a considerable distance. The charges also opened the British to flank fire from the plantation area, where American marksmen poured a torrent of accurate fire into the British formations. The Americans took deliberate aim at the British officers and killed not only Major Money but other senior officers of the 63rd Regiment. When the British infantry assault began to falter, Tarleton wheeled his dragoons north to northeast to reinforce his advance and charged into the Americans along Blackstock Road and on to the plantation.

Tarleton guided his dragoons into his own right flank to stabilize his line, and in doing so ended up attacking the grounds around the Blackstock house and outlying buildings. With cool discipline and precision, the British horse charged around the buildings, hacking at the dispersing American formations. The chaos worked to Tarleton's advantage and the Americans began running for their lives. Despite an overwhelming superiority in numbers, the undisciplined Americans could not hold their ground and remain in formation. General Sumter was wounded during the melee, which only added to the defenders' confusion. In the absence of organized leadership, the Americans broke completely and made a rapid retreat across the Tyger River.

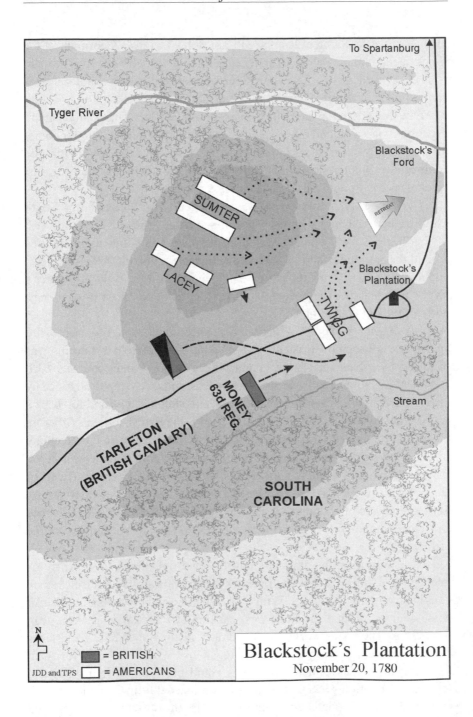

To Spartanburg

Tyger River

Blackstock's Ford

SUMTER

RETREAT

LACEY

Blackstock's Plantation

TWIGG

TARLETON (BRITISH CAVALRY)

MONEY 63d REG.

Stream

SOUTH CAROLINA

N

JDD and TPS   = BRITISH   = AMERICANS

Blackstock's Plantation
November 20, 1780

The 63rd Regiment, which had been checked by American fire, made a clumsy advance behind Tarleton's dragoons and reformed at the plantation. The soldiers began shooting at the fleeing enemy making for the river ford, but the Americans were beyond the range of British muskets. By this time darkness was approaching and Tarleton wisely halted his advance, moved his troops away from the battlefield toward his reinforcements, and regrouped his command. Sumter's Americans, meanwhile, streamed away from the field and disappeared into the night.

Casualties: British: 92 killed and 100 wounded; American: 100 killed and wounded and 50 captured.

Outcome / Impact: This battle was extremely frustrating for the British in general and Colonel Tarleton in particular. The battle offered Tarleton his first unpalatable taste of heavy losses. Although he had driven the enemy from the field, his initial attacks had been checked and he suffered significantly higher casualties than Sumter's ragtag militia force. Tarleton continued the chase for three days, his dragoons racing through the woods night and day trying to catch the elusive foe. Although badly wounded, the "Gamecock" successfully evaded the British by ordering his men to disperse. Sumter hid in friendly homes and barns to evade the British dragnet. After several months of recovery time Sumter returned to fight again.

The fight proved to the Americans that the dreaded "Bloody Ban" and his infamous dragoons were vulnerable and with a little luck and better discipline could be beaten. The results of the morale-boosting fight quickly spread across the countryside. The lesson was an obvious one: cavalry was very powerful and the British were expert horsemen and soldiers, but if the horsemen extended themselves too far from their main army, they were vulnerable to defeat in detail.

Today: The relatively small field where the fighting occurred is surrounded by the heavily wooded Sumter National Forest. The privately-held plantation site is a barren field marked with a single monument.

Further Reading: Buchanan, John, *The Road to Guilford Courthouse: The American Revolution in the Carolinas* (John Wiley and Sons, 1999); Dameron, J. David, *Kings Mountain: The Defeat of the Loyalists* (Da Capo Press, 2003); Tarleton, Banastre, *A History of the Campaigns of 1780 and 1781, in the Southern Provinces of North America* (Cadell, 1787).

Cowpens, Battle of (Southern Campaign)

Date: January 17, 1781.
Region: Southern Colonies, South Carolina.
Commanders: British: Lieutenant General Charles Cornwallis and Colonel Banastre Tarleton; American: Major General Nathanael Greene, Brigadier General Daniel Morgan, Colonel Andrew Pickens, Lieutenant Colonels John Howard and William Washington, Majors John McDowell and John Cunningham.
Time of Day / Length of Action: 7:00 a.m. to 8:00 a.m.
Weather Conditions: Cold, clear, and sunny.
Opposing Forces: British: 1,100; American: 1,065.

British Perspective: During the winter of 1780-1781, General Charles Cornwallis's army remained in cold weather quarters at Winnsboro, South Carolina. His ranks were swelled by an additional 2,000 troops from the Northern colonies. His soldiers actively patrolled the countryside around Winnsboro in order to keep rebel raiding parties led by Thomas Sumter and Francis Marion away from slow moving British supply trains. Lieutenant Colonel Banastre Tarleton's cavalry patrolled the western upcountry region of the state. On November 20, 1780, Tarleton encountered and narrowly defeated Sumter's rebel army at Blackstock's Plantation. The cavalry leader fought his command piecemeal against a rebel army that outnumbered his own by nearly four-to-one. The result was nearly disastrous for the British, who suffered heavy casualties in the expensive tactical victory.

When Cornwallis learned in early January of 1781 that Gen. Daniel Morgan was operating in the western part of the state, he dispatched Tarleton to find and defeat them. Gathering intelligence along the way, Tarleton pursued the rebels northward toward Cowpens, South Carolina, a few miles below the North Carolina border. Tarleton reported the rebel position and Cornwallis maneuvered part of his main army northwest to help Tarleton trap Morgan's Americans.

After the bloody lesson Sumter taught him at Blackstock's Plantation, Tarleton maintained a tighter reign on his troops. With his 1,100-man army and two small-bore cannon, the British cavalry leader approached Morgan's rebels from the southeast along Mill Gap (now Green River) Road. Tarleton had pushed his army through most of a long cold night's journey of 12 miles before catching up with Morgan at Cowpens about 6:30 a.m. on the 17th of January.

American Perspective: In 1780, two battles played a major role in changing America's Southern war strategy. The first was Camden (August 16), where tremendous losses embarrassed the Patriot cause and shattered the Continental Army's Southern Department. The second was at Kings Mountain (October 7), where a determined attack by a group of frontiersmen wiped out a 1,000-man Loyalist command and collapsed Cornwallis's bid to invade North Carolina. The victory revealed for the world that British were indeed vulnerable and offered a sliver of hope to the beleaguered rebel cause.

That setback notwithstanding, Gen. George Washington knew if Cornwallis continued moving north unchecked the Americans would be crushed between two giant British pincer arms (Cornwallis from the south and Gen. Henry Clinton from the north). Appreciating that the Southern Department was vital to the Patriot cause, and cognizant that good leadership could bring about more victories like Kings Mountain, Washington transferred key commanders and units to the Carolinas to rescue a war effort that was in real danger of foundering.

On October 30, Gen. Nathanael Greene replaced Camden's disgraced Horatio Gates as the commander of the Southern Department. One of Washington's most trusted veteran leaders, Greene quickly reorganized and revitalized the shattered command. Washington also promoted Virginian Daniel Morgan, one of his most dependable fighters and experienced backwoodsmen. Morgan and his rangers had successfully conducted Indian-style raids and stood the trials of traditional combat for years against Britain's finest soldiers. By making Morgan a brigadier general, Washington offered the Patriot cause a fighting leader the rank and file would willingly fight hard and die for. Morgan was aggressive, experienced, wise, and a natural combat officer—exactly what the Southern Department needed. Washington also transferred Lt. Col. Henry Lee and his cavalry corps of 350 men to the Carolinas.

Greene boldly divided his small army to better harass the British over a wider region. The general remained with the wing operating around an enemy outpost at Camden. With Greene's second wing, Morgan was ordered to operate against Ninety Six. Between these two positions were Cornwallis and 4,000 men at Winnsboro. Greene's bold plan risked a decisive move by Cornwallis against either Greene or Morgan, and thus a defeat in detail.

Morgan made camp on the Pacolet River along the border of North Carolina and South Carolina. When Cornwallis learned about Morgan's potentially exposed position, he ordered Tarleton and his light troops and dragoons to destroy him. On January 13, 1781, Lt. Col. William

Washington's cavalry was patrolling the vicinity of Fair Forest when they came upon a large band of Tories. The cavalry captured 40 prisoners and derived intelligence from them (and local inhabitants) that British troops were operating nearby at Musgrove's Mill. Morgan wisely maneuvered his forces away from his enemy until he reached the Broad River just below the North Carolina border at a local gathering place known as "Hannah's Cowpens."

Morgan decided to give battle at Cowpens because the position offered advantageous terrain for the type of combat he intended to wage against Tarleton. It was also a well known and easy gathering place, though an impassable river meandered five miles behind his rear. With him were about 1,000 soldiers (533 militiamen from Virginia, Georgia, and both Carolinas, 237 Continentals, 80 cavalrymen, and about 200 independent riflemen; estimates vary from 800 to 1,065). Morgan set about arranging his command into a clever deployment.

Some 150 militia riflemen were placed in front as a skirmish line under Maj. John McDowell and Maj. John Cunningham, the Green River (Mill Gap) Road dividing the line. The militiamen were outstanding marksmen but were not known as dependable front line soldiers. Knowing this, Morgan asked that they fire twice and retire firing back to the second line 150 yards to their rear. He knew he could not get much else out of his militia, and this arrangement would maximize their firepower and keep them in place if they knew they could retire quickly instead of having to stand and face British steel. The battle line the militiamen would fall back to reinforce 150 yards to the northwest was under the command of Col. Andrew Pickens. This second line, resting on the field's military crest, was comprised of 300 militia. Morgan had cautioned these men the night before to wait until the British were within easy range, aim at the officers, and then after two shots or "hits" retire around the left flank of the third or final line, where they could reform.

Lieutenant Colonel John Howard and his 450 riflemen (mostly Continentals) held the last line, a slightly higher position 150 yards behind Pickens. This base formation was flanked on both sides by 200 Virginia independent riflemen whose shooting skills were unsurpassed. William Washington (the general's cousin) and his cavalry were placed in the rear as a reserve beyond the range of both enemy fire and easy observation.

Terrain: The rolling Cowpens battlefield is four miles east of Chesnee, South Carolina, and 28 miles due west of Kings Mountain. The elevation at the highest point on the battlefield is 296 feet, and the region is drained by the Broad River, which flows from northwest to southeast five miles behind where Morgan took up his position. Divided by the Mill Gap Road, the

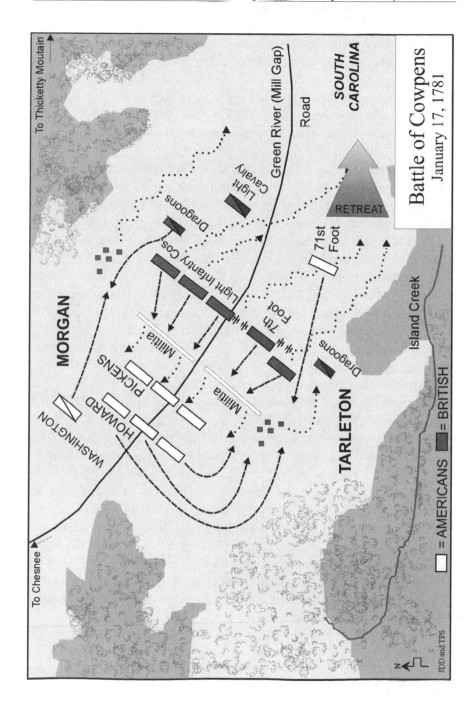

Battle of Cowpens
January 17, 1781

battlefield was essentially a broad pasture one-half mile wide (southwest to northeast) and one mile long (southeast to northwest). Light timber dotted the landscape, which was used to graze cattle (hence the name Cowpens). The terrain rises gently from southeast (British approach) to northwest (American defensive positions). Thickety Mountain is visible to the southeast, and the Blue Ridge Mountains rise in the north and dominate the horizon.

The Fighting: Pleased the Americans had decided to stand and fight, Tarleton arranged for immediate battle. He did not believe the terrain offered any special advantage to his opponent, and Morgan's flanks were not properly anchored. With an air of impatience Tarleton formed his tired command for battle with the 7th Regiment of Foot on the left and three light infantry companies extending the line to the right across the road. Two detachments of dragoons, about 50 in each, were posted to the flanks, one on each side. Tarleton formed his 280 light cavalry behind the main line, and on the left center unlimbered his pair of guns, one on either side of the Legion infantry. In his left rear was the 71st Highlander Regiment. So formed, the impetuous British commander ordered his men to charge the American lines. It was about 7:00 a.m.

When the British infantry stepped into killing range, the front rank of militia opened fire into the massed formations. Just as Morgan had asked of them, they fired two good volleys before easing rearward toward Colonel Pickens's second line. The move disturbed Pickens's formation, which he quickly reformed, augmented with breathless militia from the first line. At about 100 yards Pickens ordered his men to fire into the advancing British infantry. According to most accounts, the British losses at this stage of the battle were severe, especially in officers. Virginia riflemen posted on the flanks cut apart the dragoons and drove them back. With their duty done, the second line of militia scampered off to the left as ordered, though the movement was almost certainly more chaotic than usually portrayed. The 17th Dragoons on Tarleton's right believed the enemy was retreating and galloped forward to cut apart the militia. Washington's cavalry and Virginia riflemen tore them apart and drove the unit rearward in confusion.

Colonel Howard and his Continentals, meanwhile, waited for Tarleton's men in the third and last line of defense. In a repeat performance, the British marched into range and Howard's men greeted them with well delivered volleys. With the Virginia riflemen posted on the flanks, the British were now within a large and effective kill zone—exactly as Morgan had planned. This phase developed into an extended slugfest that Tarleton himself admitted "produced much slaughter." The climax of the battle was at hand.

Tarleton ordered up the Highlanders to crush Morgan's right flank. Howard's order to refuse the right side of his line to meet the attack resulted in some confusion, but when his men steadied themselves and fired into the advancing Highlanders at close range, Howard sensed the enemy was wavering. He ordered his men to follow it up with a charge with fixed bayonets. In conjunction with Washington's cavalry, Howard's assaulting troops surprised the British. Most turned and fled, but many threw down their arms and asked for quarter. Within a few minutes the retreat on Tarleton's left turned into a complete rout. The long night, poor rations, and rigorous fighting had drained away British will to continue the combat.

In one last desperate effort to save the day, Tarleton ordered his own cavalry command to charge the American riflemen. Exhausted and ill-disciplined, the 200 or so dragoons refused and rode off the field. With perhaps 55 riders Tarleton launched a forlorn hope. Washington's troopers countercharged and a short brutal fight was waged, the saber-wielding horsemen slashing at one another. Although it only lasted for a few minutes, the action was one of the most dramatic cavalry fights of the war.

With his army fleeing the field (the collapse was so sudden the pair of field pieces were abandoned) Tarleton had no choice but to admit defeat. His command had been nearly wiped out. Washington's cavalry pursued the beaten enemy for much of the day. With Cornwallis's command just 20 miles away and closing, Morgan paroled captive British officers, entrusted the wounded to the care of the locals, and retreated northward with his victorious—and elated—army.

Casualties: British: 110 killed, 200 wounded, and 529 captured; American: 12 killed and 60 wounded.

Outcome / Impact: Morgan's tremendous victory was achieved against one of the most notorious (though grudgingly respected) British officers. Rifle fire had picked apart the British officer corps, killing 39 and wounding 27. In addition to winning the field, Morgan's men captured 100 horses, 70 slaves, two sets of the King's colors, 800 muskets, two light field pieces, 35 wagons, and a large quantity of badly needed supplies. Immediately after the battle Morgan led his men safely into North Carolina, where he joined forces with General Greene to plot how best to defeat Cornwallis.

The victory raised the morale of American soldiers in every theater of war. Colonel Andrew Pickens was promoted to brigadier general, and Lieutenant Colonel Washington was awarded a Congressional Gold Medal for his outstanding tactical handling of the cavalry. Despite his stunning success, advanced age, fever, arthritis, and stress finally caught up with old Dan Morgan. The rugged frontiersman retired from active service.

The defeat angered Cornwallis. Not only did it revive enemy morale, but it effectively eviscerated his army's fast and light striking force (Tarleton). Leaving Lord Rawdon to defend South Carolina, Cornwallis pursued Morgan in an effort to destroy him. The frigid temperatures and rain-swollen rivers, however, prevented Cornwallis and his slow-moving army from catching up with Morgan, who marched quickly north across the Catawba River. Infuriated but committed to his policy of invading North Carolina, Cornwallis destroyed his wagon train and excess baggage in an effort to turn his army into a more mobile force to catch Morgan and Greene. The eventual result would be the combat at Guilford Courthouse on March 15, 1781.

Further Reading: Babits, Lawrence, *A Devil of a Whipping: The Battle of Cowpens* (Chapel Hill, 1998); Bearss, Edwin C., *The Battle of Cowpens* (Washington, D.C., 1967); Buchanan, John, *The Road to Guilford Courthouse: The American Revolution in the Carolinas* (John Wiley and Sons, 1999); Lumpkin, Henry, *From Savannah to Yorktown: The American Revolution in the South* (Paragon House, 1981); Tarleton, Banastre, *A History of the Campaigns of 1780 and 1781, in the Southern Provinces of North America* (Cadell, 1787).

Haw River, Battle of (Pyle's Defeat and Pyle's Hacking Match), Southern Campaign

Date: February 25, 1781.
Region: Southern Colonies, North Carolina.
Commanders: British (Tory): Colonel John Pyle; American: Brigadier General Andrew Pickens and Colonel Henry Lee.
Time of Day / Length of Action: Dusk, 10 minutes.
Weather Conditions: Cold and overcast.
Opposing Forces: British (Tory): 400; American: 600.

British Perspective: Loyalist recruits swelled the ranks of Gen. Charles Cornwallis's army as it marched through North Carolina in an effort to catch Gen. Nathanael Greene's Patriot army. By 1781, many North Carolina Tories had already been captured and paroled after swearing a loyalty oath to the state. However, when it appeared the Union Jack was again in the ascendant, locals rallied anew and assisted Cornwallis in the pursuit of the Patriots. One such man was Dr. John Pyle, who had served as a Tory commander on February 27, 1776, during the fight at Moores Creek Bridge.

Captured there with many of his men, Pyle took the loyalty oath and was eventually released.

As the British army approached Hillsborough, Pyle resumed his Tory affiliation. The Loyalist militia colonel raised a regiment of 400 men and sent a message to Cornwallis requesting an escort. Colonel Banastre Tarleton and his cavalry were ordered to conduct the operation. Tarleton advanced to a position west of Hillsborough and camped at O'Neal's Plantation (modern-day Burlington cemetery), five miles north of Alamance, North Carolina. Pyle and his Tory militia, meanwhile, were riding north along the Old Alamance Road when they came upon a mounted column of soldiers they mistakenly believed to be Tarleton's dragoons.

American Perspective: In February of 1781, General Greene moved his army north into Virginia. He sent his cavalry under Col. Henry "Light Horse Harry" Lee (father of Robert E. Lee) back into North Carolina to scout and harass the enemy. By February 23 Lee joined forces with Brig. Gen. Andrew Pickens's mounted infantry and together they operated around Hillsborough. Through a network of informants and scouts, the Patriots learned Tarleton was scheduled to link up with Colonel Pyle's Tories near Haw River. Knowing the countryside well, the Americans planned an ambush. While riding west from Hillsborough on February 24 they learned Tarleton intended to camp at O'Neal's Plantation. Lee and Pickens moved southwest along the Old Alamance Road until dusk, when they met with two of Colonel Pyle's scouts riding ahead of the Tory column in an effort to locate Colonel Tarleton. With darkness approaching the scouts mistook the Americans for British dragoons (both wore dark green jackets).

Thinking they had accomplished their mission, one Tory scout rode to inform Colonel Pyle while the other engaged in conversation with an officer he believed was Tarleton (it was actually Colonel Lee). Several minutes later the two columns approached one another and the Loyalists moved off the road in respect. Pickens's militia, meanwhile, moved quickly to take up a position in the woods. Lee's cavalry trotted past the Tories with swords drawn in salute. As Lee approached Pyle near the rear of the column and exchanged greetings, someone began shooting, triggering the engagement.

Terrain: The battle was fought in the central piedmont of Alamance County, North Carolina. The rural wooded area is three miles southwest of Graham and six miles southwest of Haw River. The fighting took place on the Old Alamance Road (modern-day State Route 1148 / Anthony Road), which connected Alamance to the southwest with Graham, Burlington, and Haw River to the northeast. The battlefield terrain consists of a level ridge northeast of Alamance and the Alamance River surrounded by a rough hilly

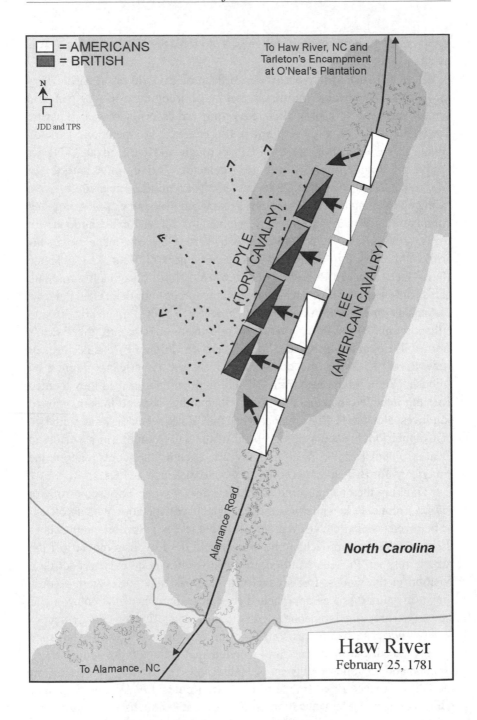

= AMERICANS
= BRITISH

N

JDD and TPS

To Haw River, NC and
Tarleton's Encampment
at O'Neal's Plantation

PYLE
(TORY CAVALRY)

LEE
(AMERICAN CAVALRY)

North Carolina

Alamance Road

To Alamance, NC

Haw River
February 25, 1781

countryside with an average elevation of about 500 feet. Creeks that empty southward into the Alamance River wind their way through the area, and the lowlands along the creeks are dominated by dense undergrowth. The hills are covered with tall long needle pines and oak trees.

The Fighting: There is no agreement in existing accounts as to which side initiated the fighting. Colonel Lee left the best firsthand account of the affair. According to that officer, the Tories discovered Pickens's militia taking up ambush positions and opened fire on them. Regardless of who fired first, the Americans were prepared for battle, knew it was coming, and had their swords drawn. Once the subterfuge was revealed, they slashed their way through the unsuspecting Tories. Realizing the hopelessness of his situation, Colonel Pyle yelled out for mercy but was knocked from his horse. As Lee explained it, the close proximity of enemies made calling for a halt impossible until the Tories had been too "disabled to offend." The combat lasted for several minutes, but the outcome was never in question. Some Tories managed to escape into the woods, but many more were killed or wounded before they could make good their escape. Charges circulated that the affair was little more than a massacre, which Lee steadfastly denied. The one-sided fighting, however, did not cost the Americans a single man.

Casualties: British (Tory): 90 killed and approximately 250 wounded; American: none reported.

Outcome / Impact: This was not a battle in the traditional sense, but the unconventional operation destroyed a Tory regiment and served as a brisk slap in the face for Colonel Tarleton. The British and Tories looked upon the Haw River fight as a blatant massacre. Whatever it was, it indicated in terms too clear to be ignored that the British were not in firm control of North Carolina. The American victory struck fear into the hearts of North Carolina Loyalists and even caused the cold-blooded Tarleton some apprehension.

During the night following the battle, several surviving Tories reached Tarleton's camp at O'Neal's Plantation to warn about the disaster. Fearing the American column was much larger than his command, Tarleton ordered his mounted men to make for the safety of the British army at Hillsborough. Pickens and Lee reached Tarleton's camp the next day, but were unable to catch the hated officer. The British army, meanwhile, moved west and camped at Haw River. Cornwallis was maneuvering to strike at General Greene's army, which had marched southward toward Guilford Courthouse. When Cornwallis finally caught up with Greene and engaged him in battle on March 15, several hundred Tories were conspicuous by their absence.

Today: A state historic marker entitled "Pyles's Defeat" denotes the site of the Haw River bloodshed. It reads as follows: "A body of Tories, going to join Cornwallis's Army at Hillsborough, was destroyed by a Whig force, Feb. 23, 1781." The marker is located three-quarters of a mile southwest of Graham, North Carolina, on NC Hwy. 49. However, the battle took place more than two miles southwest of the marker's current location.

Further Reading: Lumpkin, Henry, *From Savannah to Yorktown: The American Revolution in the South* (Paragon House, 1981); Whitaker, Walter, *Centennial History of Alamance County, 1849-1949* (Dowd Press, Inc., 1950).

Guilford Courthouse, Battle of (Southern Campaign)

Date: March 15, 1781.
Region: Southern Colonies, North Carolina.
Commanders: British: Lieutenant General Charles Cornwallis, Major General Alexander Leslie, Brigadier General Charles O'Hara, Colonel James Webster, and Lieutenant Colonel Banastre Tarleton; American: Major General Nathanael Greene, Brigadier Generals Isaac Huger, John Butler, and Pinkertham Eaton, and Colonels William Campbell and William Washington.
Time of Day / Length of Action: 1:00 p.m. to 2:30 p.m.
Weather Conditions: Cold and overcast (rain-soaked terrain).
Opposing Forces: British: 2,100; American: 4,500.

British Perspective: Lieutenant General Charles Cornwallis pushed his army hard as he marched through North Carolina intent on catching and destroying a diminished and divided Patriot army. As always, the rebels harassed the British whenever any opportunity presented itself. On February 1, 1781, the Americans attacked the British as they crossed the Catawba River at Cowan's Ford. Several Americans were killed in the skirmish, but the British admitted to 40 casualties. Frigid temperatures and rain-swollen rivers, coupled with dwindling supplies and exhaustion, added to the misery the British were experiencing in the rural Carolinas. As Cornwallis pushed his men northward, Loyalist volunteers joined his army.

When Greene withdrew north toward the Dan River on the border of North Carolina and Virginia, Cornwallis saw an opportunity to trap him against the flooded river. The lower (eastern) fords could not be crossed without the assistance of a large number of boats. If Greene could be caught south of the fords he could be destroyed. The British general drove his army northeast to cut Greene off from the upper fords, not realizing he was chasing a decoy force under Otho Williams. Colonel Banastre Tarleton's dragoons and Williams's rear guard fought a few spirited skirmishes that only served to frustrate and exhaust Cornwallis's men. What the British general did not know was that Greene had already gathered the boats he needed to cross the Dan River. Williams was leading Cornwallis in the wrong direction while Greene's main army was marching east to cross the lower fords. By mid-February Greene's army was safely in Virginia. When he learned Greene had outsmarted him, an outraged Cornwallis retreated south to Hillsborough, where he established his headquarters for several weeks to rest his army and recruit several companies of Tory militia.

In early March, friendly Loyalists and British patrols confirmed that the Americans had followed the British back into North Carolina. For ten days Cornwallis maneuvered his army in an effort to come to grips with Greene, to no avail. With his supplies dwindling (he had burned most of his wagons so he could move faster) and his men exhausted and ill, Cornwallis knew he would have to fight Greene soon or retire completely. To his satisfaction, he learned on the evening of March 14 that his opponent was camped just twelve miles distant at Guilford Courthouse. Anxious to crush the colonial officer, Cornwallis roused his army before daybreak and marched toward the Americans intent on having his battle.

American Perspective: After his stunning victory against Colonel Tarleton at Cowpens (January 17, 1781) Dan Morgan swung his small army northward away from General Cornwallis, who was pursuing him with 2,000 professional soldiers. Moving into the heart of North Carolina, Morgan was assisted by Gen. William Davidson, whose North Carolina militia harassed the British at every opportunity. During one of these actions on February 1 along the Catawba River, General Davidson and several of his men were killed obstructing Cowan's Ford. His efforts, however, slowed Cornwallis's pursuit, which enabled Greene to join forces with Morgan and move together across the Yadkin and Dan rivers into Virginia.

Greene used the respite north of the river to reorganize and rest his men, but reinforcements promised from Virginia did not arrive when expected, and his own enlistments were expiring. Many men had already left, and his army numbered barely 1,500 men. Intelligence that Cornwallis was retiring south prompted Greene to send a detachment to follow and harass him. When 600 Virginia militiamen arrived a few days later, Greene decided to re-cross the Dan and find a favorable opportunity to engage the British.

Once below the river and back into North Carolina, Greene's confidence grew as thousands of men funneled into his army from several sources.

About 400 Continentals from Virginia arrived with Col. Richard Campbell, as did more than 1,000 militiamen from North Carolina. Additional troops from Virginia, 1,700 militiamen divided between two brigades, also arrived to pitch their tents with Greene. By March 10 the once-small Patriot army had grown to 4,400 men. The time to fight had arrived. Two days later Greene moved his army 20 miles south to Guilford Courthouse, where he carefully chose his ground for a fight he hoped Cornwallis would give him.

Terrain: The battlefield lies in the heart of North Carolina on the northwest outskirts of Greensboro. In 1781 the county seat of Guilford County was the hub of the rural community and its peaceful farms occupied the lowland fields that dominate the gently rolling countryside. The wooded and in many places sharply undulating terrain steadily rises from west to east to a plateau near the courthouse itself, which forced the British to march and fight uphill in order to come to grips with the Patriot army.

The Fighting: It is important to understand how Greene deployed his men to appreciate how this battle unfolded. Greene had carefully surveyed the ground and, based upon the troops he had on hand and Morgan's success with militia at Cowpens, established his defensive position in depth in three successive lines of infantry supported by cavalry and artillery. Each line of battle was perpendicular to the New Garden Road, which ran through Greene's lines west to east before intersecting with the road from Reedy Fork behind the American army. The courthouse that gave the battle its name sat within a T-intersection formed by the junction of these roads.

Greene's militia, about 1,000 strong under Brig. Gen. John Butler and Col. Thomas Eaton, took up a position in the front line along the edge of some timber behind a split rail fence. In their front was an open field offering a good field of fire. Two small artillery pieces were deployed on the road in the middle of the line. Veteran infantry and cavalry took up positions on either flank. The second line took up position 350 yards behind the first. It was made up of 1,200 Virginia militiamen with a mixture of previously discharged Continental veterans. Five hundred yards farther to the rear on commanding ground near the courthouse was Greene's main line of battle consisting of 1,400 American Regulars from Virginia, Delaware, and Maryland on the west side of the road.

Cornwallis approached the American positions from the west along New Garden Road about midday. In his ranks were slightly less than 2,000 men, but they were tough experienced professionals. Four miles west of Guilford Courthouse some of Greene's cavalry and dismounted infantry initiated the fight with harassing fire against the approaching British. A running battle eastward broke out. About 1:00 p.m. the British crossed Little

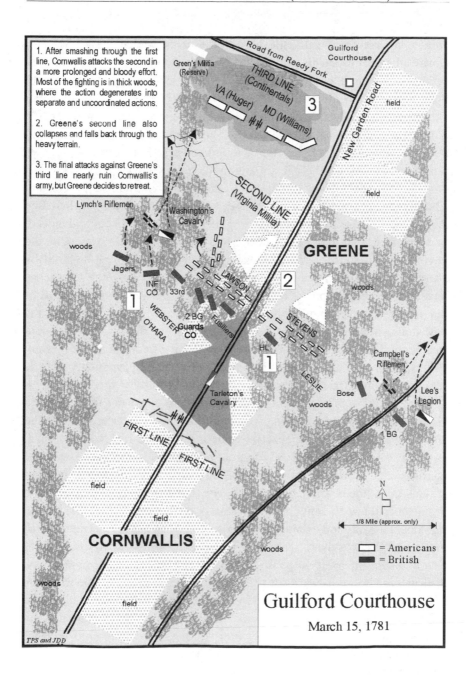

1. After smashing through the first line, Cornwallis attacks the second in a more prolonged and bloody effort. Most of the fighting is in thick woods, where the action degenerates into separate and uncoordinated actions.

2. Greene's second line also collapses and falls back through the heavy terrain.

3. The final attacks against Greene's third line nearly ruin Cornwallis's army, but Greene decides to retreat.

Guilford Courthouse
March 15, 1781

Horsepen Creek; one-half mile beyond the creek waited the Americans. Cornwallis had pushed his soldiers hard since before dawn. By the time they arrived on the field they were hungry and tired. He deployed them without being fed or rested. Cornwallis wheeled his artillery to the front to counter a fitful American fire while he divided his army into two wings on either side of the New Garden Road. Colonel James Webster took command of his more powerful left wing, while his right was led by Maj. Gen. Alexander Leslie. Tarleton's Legion was held in column in the rear as a reserve.

The well-disciplined British troops advanced with lockstep precision. The first line of American militia fired a volley into the redcoats when they approached within killing range, dropping many. The British advanced, fired off their own rather ineffective volley, and doubled forward with the bayonet. To the surprise of the attackers the militia stood strong—unlike the armed civilians they had faced at Camden. Instead of running, the Americans leveled their muskets on the fence and ripped apart the redcoats with one of the most effective single volleys of the entire war. Staggered by the devastating round, the officers steadied their men and the advance with cold steel continued. Their task done, the first line of militia melted away. American cavalry and infantry stationed on the flanks eventually did the same, siphoning British strength away from the unfolding main battle.

Cornwallis's veterans continued advancing in good order toward Greene's second line of Virginians. Because they were deployed on wooded and hilly rolling terrain, pockets of opposition were met without much advance warning. Fighting uphill through scattered but deadly resistance confused the exhausted British, who began losing their cohesion. The fight at the second line was much harder, longer, and even more deadly than the initial encounter. Eventually Cornwallis's left overlapped the American right, bent it back, and eventually collapsed the Virginia front. The fight for the second line was over.

Without much of a pause to reorganize, Cornwallis pushed his disorganized troops forward until he discovered Greene's third and final line 500 yards behind the second. Here were Greene's best men, the Continental Line and another two regiments of Virginia militiamen, supported by artillery, cavalry, and remnants from his militia. The aggressive Webster launched a quick uphill attack on Cornwallis's left, though without taking the time to protect his flanks. It was sharply repulsed and Webster was mortally wounded. On the other side of the field, British Gen. Charles O'Hara ordered a bayonet assault against Greene's left, which overran part of the line and captured two pieces of artillery. A hand-to-hand fight between Patriot cavalry and infantry and O'Hara's men eventually sealed the breach and recaptured the pieces. (Cornwallis was so desperate he had ordered his artillery to fire into the melee in an effort to salvage the deteriorating situation—knowing it would kill some of his own men.)

With his infantry utterly enervated, hungry, thirsty, and disorganized, Cornwallis called upon Tarleton's dragoons to win the day. Believing his own men were in danger of being driven from the field, and that he had accomplished all that was possible, Greene began a relatively orderly retreat northwest on the Reedy Road. Tarleton's cavalry, together with several Hessian units, swept what was left of the Patriot force from the field, ending the battle with nightfall.

Casualties: British: 93 killed, 413 wounded, and 26 missing; American: 70 killed, 185 wounded, and 1,046 missing. (The American casualty list was compiled on March 16; most of the missing were North Carolina militiamen who had simply left once the fighting ended.)

Outcome / Impact: Guilford Courthouse was one of the largest battles fought in the Southern Theater. Cornwallis held the field at the end of the day and is entitled to claim a victory. Another such "victory," however, would have extinguished his army. His severe casualties (25% of his force including Colonel Webster and many other fine officers) dulled his offensive capabilities and gained him nothing in terms of strategic advantage. Cornwallis's aggressive tactics bled his army in an expensive display of professionalism. He could no longer pursue Greene because his army lacked the food and supplies necessary to continue the campaign. The British buried their dead and moved southeast via Cross Creek (now Fayetteville) toward Wilmington, where they could obtain supplies and access to the sea. Cornwallis had torn across North Carolina in an imprudent rage; the losses he suffered at Guilford would haunt him for the remainder of the war and beyond.

For the Americans, the battle had the opposite effect. Although they abandoned the field, the Patriots knew they had severely mauled Cornwallis's army. Their withdrawal was not strategically relevant to final American success. Survival was important, and Greene's army had survived. The Americans could equally claim a "victory." The capable Greene pursued Cornwallis's retiring army for the next three weeks. The Americans now controlled all of North Carolina except for the small corner held by Cornwallis. Unable to come to grips with Cornwallis, Greene moved southward into South Carolina, intent on clearing the British from their strongholds in that state. Guilford Courthouse spun the war in a different direction. Fed up with the fighting in the Carolinas, Cornwallis set his eyes farther north on Virginia.

Today: Greensboro has grown into a large industrial center just below the battlefield, but the rustic field itself can still be seen and toured at the Guilford Courthouse National Military Park, where monuments, interpretive trails, and living history programs enhance the experience.

Further Reading: Buchanan, John. *The Road to Guilford Courthouse: The American Revolution in the Carolinas*. John Wiley & Sons, 1997; Golway, Terry, *Washington's General: Nathanael Greene and the Triumph of the American Revolution* (Henry Holt, 2005); Hairr, John. *Guilford Courthouse: Nathanael Greene's Victory in Defeat, March 15, 1781*. Da Capo, 2002; Tarleton, Banastre, *A History of the Campaigns of 1780 and 1781, in the Southern Provinces of North America* (Cadell, 1787).

Hobkirk's Hill, Battle of (Second Battle of Camden), Southern Campaign

Date: April 25, 1781.
Region: Southern Colonies, South Carolina.
Commanders: British: Lord Francis Rawdon; American: Major General Nathanael Greene, Brigadier General Isaac Huger, Colonels Otho Williams, John Howard, and Benjamin Ford, and Lieutenant Colonel William Washington.
Time of Day / Length of Action: 10:30 p.m. to 11:30 p.m.
Weather Conditions: Clear and warm.
Opposing Forces: British: 900; American: 1,550.

British Perspective: After the tactically successful but strategically devastating battle at Guildford Courthouse (March 15, 1781), General Cornwallis withdrew southeast to Wilmington, North Carolina, to reorganize and refit his shattered command. The bulk of the state was now under Patriot control, as was much of South Carolina. Once safe on the coast, Cornwallis decided the decisive theater was in Virginia, and he marched there that April. Although he hoped to draw Greene's army after him, the American moved south toward Camden, South Carolina.

When he initially retreated to Wilmington, Cornwallis ordered Lord Rawdon to defend South Carolina with a dispersed command of 9,000 British and Tory soldiers. Rawdon's primary post was in Camden, though the Crown maintained outposts across the state and in Georgia. Charleston, Camden, and Fort Watson were the principal British enclaves in the east, with Orangeburg, Fort Motte, Fort Granby, and Fort Ninety Six acting in a similar capacity in the central and western parts of the state. The British supply lines were lengthy and difficult to maintain against marauding rebels, who attacked them whenever the opportunity arose.

In an effort to chase down and eliminate one of the major rebel threats, Rawdon dispatched about 900 men (half of his Camden army) under Col. John Watson. Tory spies kept Rawdon informed of Greene's whereabouts. When intelligence revealed the American army was marching toward Camden, Rawdon recalled Watson and prepared to defend the important British supply center. By April 20 Greene's army had taken up a position on Hobkirk's Hill, a low sandy ridge less then two miles northwest of Rawdon's position. On the night of April 24, a deserter reached Camden with interesting news: Greene's artillery had been withdrawn, his army was divided, and he was low on supplies. The deserter also sketched out the deployment of the Patriot forces. Lord Rawdon decided the Americans would never be weaker than they were at that time, and that an attack was in order. Just before dawn on April 25, Lord Rawdon led 900 men northwest from Camden toward Hobkirk's Hill.

American Perspective: When General Cornwallis marched his British army northward to Virginia, General Greene refused to follow him. Instead, he decided to remain in the Southern Department and use the opportunity of Cornwallis's self-imposed absence to wrest South Carolina from British control. Although his own army numbered only 2,000 men and the Crown's 9,000, Greene knew his enemy was divided into numerous garrisons, stretched thin in an effort to hold territory. Greene detached Col. "Light Horse" Harry Lee's cavalry to assist Brig. Gen. Francis "Swamp Fox" Marion's raiders in the eastern part of South Carolina. If Marion and Lee could take Fort Watson, they would sever Lord Rawdon's supply line from Charleston. Greene also dispatched Col. Andrew Pickens with several hundred men west to assist Gen. Thomas Sumter in his fight with British outposts at Ninety Six and Augusta. Although his own army was divided, Greene marched what remained of his command (about 1,550 men) toward the British center at Camden, where he hoped to draw Lord Rawdon into battle. Although he anticipated Marion and his men would join him, the "Swamp Fox" refused to subordinate himself to Greene.

Greene arrived on the outskirts of Camden by April 20. Lord Rawdon was too well defended to successfully attack, so Greene established a base on Hobkirk's Hill to threaten the enemy post and sent word for his detached forces to join him. Marion and Lee took Fort Watson on April 23 with little trouble as Watson and his 500 men were moving west to rejoin Lord Rawdon at Camden. Thanks to the actions of the Patriot cavalry, Watson would not reach Camden in time for the pending battle.

The only way the British could reach Greene's position on Hobkirk's Hill was to march up the Great Road (Waxhaws Road) linking Camden with Waxhaws. Greene deployed his army accordingly, essentially camping in battle formation. However, he failed to prepare adequate defensive positions or make sure his advance outposts were positioned far enough away to sound an early alarm. The piney woods also made it possible for an enemy to creep within artillery range without being seen. On the morning of April 25 a fresh wagon train of food reached the Patriots, who spent the morning fixing breakfast and relaxing as the enemy approached their camp.

Terrain: Hobkirk's Hill was about one and one-half miles north of colonial Camden, South Carolina, the same distance east of the Wateree River, and three miles south of the Camden battlefield where Horatio Gates had been soundly defeated on August 16, 1780. Woods and low marshy terrain flanked the sandy ridge on the east and west. The battlefield is one-half mile deep (north to south) and about half again as wide from east to west. The Great Road (Waxhaws Road) runs through the center of the battlefield from north to south along a low ridge line. Pine Tree Creek and swamp lands dominate the area east below the battlefield.

The Fighting: Instead of following the road and conducting a traditional march, Lord Rawdon moved his small army alongside the swamp on the eastern side of the road. The British formed for battle facing uphill and northwest with a strong but narrow front. Three regiments were in the first line, from left to right: King's American Regiment of Foot, New York Volunteers (both Loyalist outfits organized in the North early in the war), and the 63rd (West Suffolk) Regiment of Foot. Behind the front line was essentially a mobile reserve second line composed of 50 convalescents on the left, gathered together by Lord Rawdon specifically for this action, and 140 men of the Volunteers of Ireland on the right, a provincial regiment raised in New York. In yet a third line were 60 mounted men from the New York Dragoons on the left and 130 South Carolina Tories on the right. A few dozen militiamen were divided and positioned on either flank. Two 6-pounder field pieces rolled north with Lord Rawdon. Hidden from view, the British advanced quietly until skirmishers opened fire with their American counterparts southeast of Hobkirk's Hill.

The initial firing startled Greene's army, which had not been expecting a battle that morning. The Americans quickly formed into a single line of battle along the brow of the hill facing south by southeast. This line was comprised of 950 men. General Isaac Huger's pair of Virginia regiments

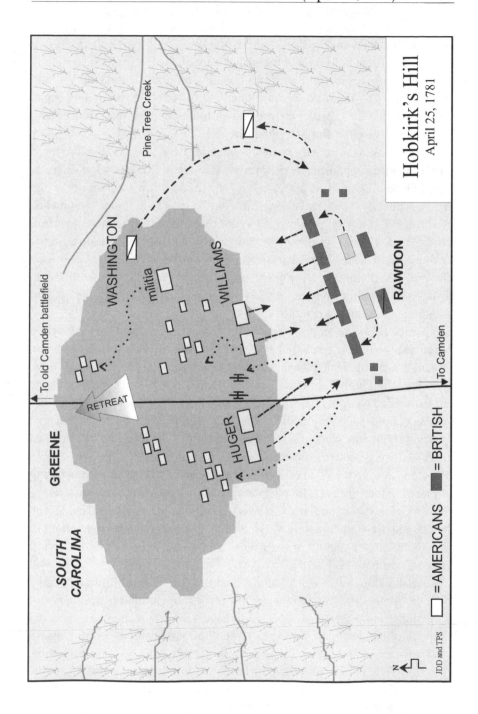

Hobkirk's Hill
April 25, 1781

were on the right (west) side of the road, and Col. Otho Williams's two Continental Regular Maryland regiments were on the left (east) side. Behind Williams was a reserve of 250 North Carolina militiamen and Col. William Washington's 85-man cavalry detachment. Shortly before the fighting began three 6-pounder field pieces arrived and unlimbered in the road facing south between the Virginia and Maryland troops.

Greene was an experienced commander who always looked for a weakness in his opponent. He believed he saw one in Lord Rawdon's narrow front. Greene decided to advance his lines and with his center strike the British directly, but envelope him with his two outer regiments. Washington's cavalry, meanwhile, would ride around to the east and attack Lord Rawdon's rear—a complex plan hastily developed. Although young, Lord Rawdon was a very capable field commander. When he saw what Greene was attempting he brought up his reserves and extended his own front, which within a few minutes was longer than Greene's. The tactical situation had suddenly reversed.

The battle, however, went well initially for the Americans when Huger's Virginians held their own and began forcing back the British left. It was on Greene's eastern flank that matters fell apart for reasons still in dispute. Colonel John Gunby's veteran 1st Maryland Regiment encountered some confusion and was pulled back to reorganize. An officer unnamed to history (perhaps Lord Rawdon) realized the opportunity and ordered a bayonet charge, which was launched with great aplomb. The Marylanders cracked apart and were routed from the field. Their sister unit on its left, the 5th Maryland, also retreated in confusion. Greene's front of veterans was falling to pieces before his eyes. Immediately on the west side of the road was the 5th Virginia, whose left flank was now exposed to enemy fire and cold steel. It, too, withdrew precipitately. Only the 1st Virginia on the far right seems to have held long enough to prevent what could have been the destruction of Greene's primary field army.

Washington, meanwhile, had reached the rear of Lord Rawdon's army with his dragoons, but dissipated his efforts by rounding up scores of noncombatants. When he discovered Greene's army was streaming from the field, Washington ordered his men to set their spurs and return to assist in covering the withdrawal. They arrived just in time to save the three American field pieces from capture. The army withdrew a few miles much as a mob might, with an organized rear guard holding back the pursuit. Greene went into camp near the Camden battlefield of 1780.

Casualties: British: 38 killed, 220 wounded; American: 18 killed, 236 wounded, and an undermined number of captured.

Outcome / Impact: Lord Rawdon's tactical victory at Hobkirk's Hill did nothing to alter the strategic situation in the South. It was, as Napoleon would later describe such a battle, nothing more than an "ordinary victory." Greene's handling of the battle was inept for a commander of his caliber. The defeat was eventually placed on Col. Gunby's shoulders for the tactical mistake he made with the 1st Maryland Regiment. A court of inquiry tagged him with causing the defeat, but did not call for his removal from command.

The three weeks after the battle witnessed raids against British supply lines and Tory garrisons that forced Lord Rawdon to abandon Camden and move his headquarters to Charleston and the protection of the Royal Navy. American pressure throughout the state forced Lord Rawdon to also give up the British outpost at Georgetown. On May 11 General Sumter captured the British outpost at Orangeburg; Forts Motte and Granby fell later that same month. British fortunes in the Southern colonies were at a low ebb.

Today: The battlefield is now part of northern Camden, and there is little left for the visitor to visualize except historic signs announcing the action.

Further Reading: Dann, John C., ed., *The Revolution Remembered: Eyewitness Accounts of the War for Independence* (University of Chicago Press, 1980); Kirkwood, Robert, *The Journal and Order Book of Captain Robert Kirkwood* (Historical Society of Delaware, 1910); Golway, Terry, *Washington's General: Nathanael Greene and the Triumph of the American Revolution* (Henry Holt, 2005).

Pensacola, Siege of (Spanish Campaign)

Date: March 9 – May 10, 1781.

Region: Spanish Territory (West Florida).

Commanders: British: Major General John Campbell; Spanish: Field Marshal Bernardo de Gálvez; French: Claude Anne, Marquis de St. Simon.

Time of Day / Length of Action: Two-month siege.

Weather Conditions: Warm, unremarkable.

Opposing Forces: British: 1,600 (two ships); Spanish: 7,025 (64 ships); French: 725 (8 ships).

British Perspective: In January of 1779, Maj. Gen. John Campbell waded ashore at Pensacola in the West Florida Territory (today's Florida) with an expeditionary column from Jamaica. His 1,200-man composite force of British Regulars, Hessian Waldeckers, and Loyalist (Provincial) militiamen bolstered the 1,500-man British defense force assigned to a territory extending from Pensacola in the east to the Mississippi River fortifications in the west. At that time, Pensacola was a small coastal town with roughly 400 citizens and a small garrison of troops who occupied a log and sand palisade protecting the port. Shortly after their arrival Spain entered the war as an American ally. Its entry prompted the British to improve their fortifications to better defend the region from Spanish aggression.

The Crown also maintained small garrisons and forts at Mobile (Alabama), Natchez (Mississippi), and Baton Rouge (Louisiana). The British alliance with the local Choctaw Indians was used to wage small engagements against Spanish troops in Louisiana and Florida. In 1780 the strategic situation changed when Spain organized a campaign to eliminate the British presence in West Florida. Campbell's troops notwithstanding, the Spanish dominated the fighting and in May and June of that year laid siege to British outposts across the region. The British garrison at Mobile surrendered in May; a six-week siege of Fort Panmure at Natchez resulted in the surrender of that place on June 22, 1780. General Campbell had sent reinforcements, but they did not reach the outposts in time to save them.

Certain that Pensacola was the next target on the Spanish wish list, Campbell bolstered the port's defenses at Fort George and at Red Cliffs (now known as Fort Barrancas at the entrance to the bay). He also raised reinforcements with assistance from the local Creek Indians, which increased the British defense force to nearly 2,000 men. The British had several warships in the bay defending the port city, but if the Spanish managed to slip a larger fleet past them and the Royal Navy redoubt gun emplacements at Red Cliffs, the city was doomed. Campbell knew he would be fighting alone, for there were no reinforcements available. The entry of France and now Spain in the American rebellion spread the Crown's resources dangerously thin.

At 8:00 a.m. on March 9, 1781, HMS *Mentor* fired her signal guns: the enemy fleet had sailed into sight. The Spanish fleet approaching Pensacola from the southern end of the bay was huge (38 warships in the initial wave), and prompted Campbell to send HMS *Childers* to Jamaica to seek reinforcements. The Spanish commander deployed troops onto neighboring Santa Rosa Island before sailing his fleet under the guns of the British Royal Navy Redoubt at Red Cliffs. Within a few hours Pensacola Bay was filled with Spanish warships. On the 24th of March, the fleet sailed north and launched an amphibious assault with small water craft to secure a position within Sutton's Lagoon. The beachhead was just two miles west of Fort George, a four-sided fortification well armed with artillery. Two main strongholds, Prince of Wales Redoubt and the Queen's Redoubt, guarded the approaches to the garrison.

On March 25 Campbell ordered a series of probing assaults against the Spanish. The probes gleaned but little information at the cost of a few casualties, and Campbell withdrew the men into the fort. During the next few weeks the Spanish continued landing troops and equipment, assembling a large assault column while the British looked on helplessly, their options limited to their resources on hand.

Spanish-Allied Perspective: Early in the American Revolution, the Spanish government provided covert aid to the Americans in the form of loans and war materiel. Once they formally allied themselves with the French and Americans in May of 1779, however, the Spanish aggressively fought the British for control of the Caribbean Isles, Louisiana, the Mississippi River Valley, and West Florida. Led by Governor Bernardo de Gálvez, the Spanish territorial authority based in New Orleans, the Spanish army prepared to make war against the British in a military campaign labeled by some historians as "Washington's second front."

Governor Gálvez was an effective 33-year-old leader who used his keen intellect and influence with local Indians to great advantage. Gálvez mobilized both local militias and regular Spanish forces for a campaign to eliminate the British threat in the region. By attacking isolated British outposts and shipping with overwhelming forces, the Spanish quickly dominated the Mississippi River Valley. By October of 1779 they secured Natchez (present-day Mississippi) and Baton Rouge (present-day Louisiana); in May of 1780 they defeated the British at Mobile (present-day Alabama). That June, the Spanish were forced into another battle at Natchez, which ended in their favor after a six-week siege. The British unsuccessfully attempted to retake Mobile in 1781, but the Spanish repulsed them. With the British defeated in the west, Gálvez focused on Pensacola. The King of Spain promoted Gálvez to field marshal and extended his command to include the entire territory. After establishing a strong presence at each of the former British garrisons in the Mississippi delta, Gálvez sailed to Cuba to prepare for the Pensacola operation.

In Havana, Gálvez took control of an armada that included thousands of Spanish infantry, his Louisiana militia, and dozens of Spanish warships to carry them across the gulf to attack Pensacola. Gálvez's army included elements of the King, Crown, Prince, Sorio, Mallorca, Guadalajara, Aragon, Cataluna, Navarra, Toledo, Louisiana, and Hibernia regiments, as well as the Royal Corps of Artillery and a contingent of naval marines. His thrust into the underbelly of England's American presence assisted America's struggle for independence by siphoning off British assets that could have otherwise been employed elsewhere.

After early attempts to deploy were hampered by hurricanes, the persistent Spaniards arrived off the coast of Santa Rosa Island on March 9, 1781. Slipping under the guns at Red Cliffs, which guarded the bay's entry to the Bay of Pensacola, the Spaniards landed on the mainland southwest of Pensacola and secured a base of operations there. The withdrawal of British ships provided freedom of movement for the Spanish fleet. By March 24 Gálvez outnumbered his enemy three to one on land and his vast fleet of ships dominated the bay.

Beginning on March 25, the British launched small hit and run assaults that did little other than irritate Gálvez's men, though Creek Indian forays behind the lines unnerved some of the Spanish troops. On April 19, 1,600 additional Spanish troops arrived, and three days later French troops commanded by Marquis de St. Simon reached Pensacola Bay. St. Simon had with him four frigates and four transport ships containing 725 additional troops. These French regiments had been stationed in nearby Haiti and Santo Domingo, and included the following regiments: Poitiou, Agénois, Orléans, Gâtinois, Cambrésis, Regiment le Cap, the Chasseur Company, and the Royal Corps of Artillery. Gálvez now had a combined force of 7,800 soldiers and several thousand seamen aboard 68 warships.

Gálvez's plan was to extend his position north and build a trench line running eastward onto higher ground around and behind Fort George. From this location he could employ artillery from dominant ground above the fort and bombard the British into submission.

Terrain: Today, Pensacola is a modern metropolitan center and a gulf coast beach resort city. In 1781 it was a small coastal port town. Pensacola is located in the northwest Panhandle region of Florida. Its beaches are sandy and the terrain is generally flat with marshy swamps along the inlets. The town is shielded from the Gulf of Mexico by narrow sandbars and Santa Rosa Island, a natural barrier island to the south. The Bay of Pensacola was about 30 feet deep in 1781, and the water over the bar measured 21 feet. Entrance to the bay was gained through a narrow passage southwest of Pensacola between Perdido Key to the west and Santa Rosa Island to the east. Ships moving into the bay had to run along a narrow strip of land at Red Cliffs (now known as Fort Barrancas and Pensacola Naval Air Station), with the bay opening wide to the north and east once past that point. Once inside, the bay measures six miles north to south (Pensacola to Santa Rosa Island) and six miles from east to west (from Gulf Breeze to Red Cliffs). Although

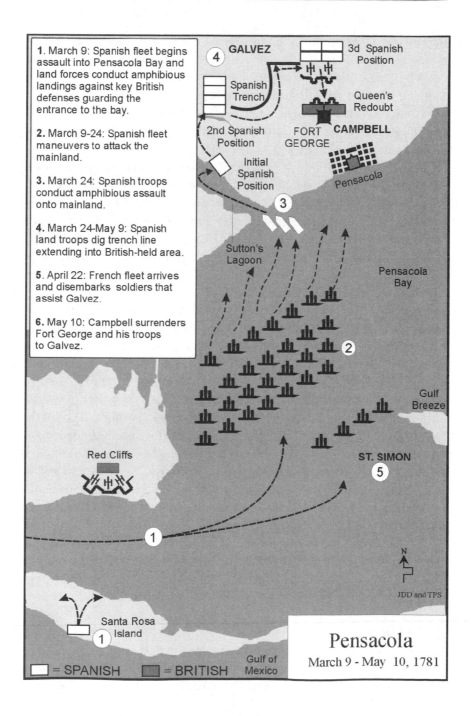

1. March 9: Spanish fleet begins assault into Pensacola Bay and land forces conduct amphibious landings against key British defenses guarding the entrance to the bay.

2. March 9-24: Spanish fleet maneuvers to attack the mainland.

3. March 24: Spanish troops conduct amphibious assault onto mainland.

4. March 24-May 9: Spanish land troops dig trench line extending into British-held area.

5. April 22: French fleet arrives and disembarks soldiers that assist Galvez.

6. May 10: Campbell surrenders Fort George and his troops to Galvez.

GALVEZ

3d Spanish Position

Spanish Trench

2nd Spanish Position

Initial Spanish Position

Queen's Redoubt

FORT GEORGE

CAMPBELL

Pensacola

Sutton's Lagoon

Pensacola Bay

Red Cliffs

Gulf Breeze

ST. SIMON

N

JDD and TPS

Santa Rosa Island

Gulf of Mexico

Pensacola

March 9 - May 10, 1781

☐ = SPANISH   ◼ = BRITISH

the bay was even larger to the north and east, the room to maneuver available during the siege of Pensacola was restricted to the area described above.

The Spanish mainland assault point at Bayou Chico (then known as Sutton's Lagoon) was two miles southwest of Fort George. The elevation above sea level at Fort George is 32 feet, the ground comprised of sandy soil. In 1781 Pensacola was restricted to the southern coast and Fort George was located north of it, about 1,000 yards inland.

The Fighting: Gálvez's men slowly dug a deep trench and dragged their field pieces through it onto new positions on the high ground. When the Spanish succeeded in placing a battery of six 24-pounders on this forward position, the British wasted no time attacking it. On May 1, from a redoubt between Fort George and the Spanish, British infantry assaulted Gálvez's advance positions. The fighting was sharp and killed and wounded dozens of men. Among the Spanish wounded was Field Marshal Gálvez, who suffered from injuries to his abdomen and hand.

Artillery duels occupied the next several days. On May 6, a combined force made up of the Hessian 3rd Waldeck Regiment and Provincial Tory Loyalists from Pennsylvania and Maryland assaulted the Spanish trenches with fixed bayonets. The attack caught the Spaniards off guard, their arms stacked while their owners ate lunch. Although they suffered dozens of casualties, the Spanish drove the British again. Two days later a Spanish artillery round scored a direct hit into a powder magazine dug into one of the forward British positions. The massive explosion killed and wounded scores of men and opened a gaping hole in General Campbell's defenses, through which Spanish infantry poured. The stunned British survivors retreated to Fort George or fled the scene of carnage as deserters. The Spaniards, meanwhile, rolled their artillery forward as fast as possible and began firing south into Fort George. The direct close range fire sealed Campbell's fate. Unable to shield his men from the bombardment, without the hope of reinforcements, and unable to retreat, Campbell raised a surrender flag at 3:00 p.m. on May 9. A formal surrender was concluded the following day.

Casualties: British: 105 men were reported killed and wounded (Indian losses unknown), 1,113 were captured and sent to New York as prisoners, and 300 men were paroled to Georgia; Spanish: 74 killed and 198 wounded.

Outcome / Impact: The multi-national Allied effort at Pensacola was eerily similar to what General Cornwallis was about to face in Virginia at Yorktown. In both instances control of the seas, coupled with a traditional siege on land, cut off defending British armies and forced their surrender. In both cases the British attempted traditional small-scale assault tactics, to no avail. After the victory Gálvez provided his French reinforcements with

100,000 pesos and urged them on to Virginia, where they joined the French fleet and participated in the naval blockade and siege of Yorktown.

Strategically, the siege of Pensacola played a minor (though notable and largely overlooked) role in America's struggle to cast Great Britain out of North America. The major campaign tied down precious British resources, forced the Crown to cast anxious eyes about much of the globe, and freed French troops to assist General Washington in Virginia. The British could not afford to dispatch any troops from the Caribbean or East Florida to west Florida for fear of the powerful Spanish presence.

Gálvez sealed his string of astounding victories by securing his stronghold at Pensacola, across West Florida and the Mississippi River Valley, and in the Caribbean. When he returned to Spain, King Carlos III promoted him to the rank of lieutenant general, made him the governor of West Florida and Louisiana, and bestowed several titles upon him, including Count of Gálvez and Viscount of Galveztown. Gálvez's victories during the American Revolution (and more direct Spanish aid as well) resulted in Spain being awarded both East and West Florida in the 1783 Treaty of Paris.

Because of the assistance rendered by the Spanish forces to the American cause of liberty, descendants of Hispanic troops who served in North America are eligible for membership in the Sons of the American Revolution and the Daughters of the American Revolution.

Further Reading: Caughey, John Walton, *Bernardo de Gálvez in Louisiana 1776-1783* (University of California Press, 1934); Lang, James, *Conquest and Commerce Spain and England in the Americas* (Academic Press, 1975); Langley, Lester D., *Struggle for the American Mediterranean: United States-European Rivalry in the Gulf-Caribbean, 1776-1904* (University of Georgia Press, 1969); McDermott, John Francis, ed., *The Spanish in the Mississippi Valley, 1762-1804* (University of Illinois Press, 1974); Thomson, Buchannon Parker, *Spain: Forgotten Ally of the American Revolution* (The Christopher Publishing House, 1976).

Ninety Six and Augusta, Siege of (Southern Campaign)

Date: May 22 – June 19, 1781.
Region: Southern Colonies, South Carolina and Georgia.
Commanders: (Ninety Six): British: Lord Francis Rawdon, Colonel John Harris Cruger; American: Major General Nathanael Greene, Brigadier General Isaac Huger, Brigadier General Thomas Sumter, and Lieutenant

Colonel William Washington; (Augusta): British: Colonel Thomas Brown; American: Colonels Andrew Pickens, Elijah Clark, Pinkertham Eaton, and Lieutenant Colonel Henry Lee.

Time of Day / Length of Action: May 22 – June 19, 1781.

Weather Conditions: Warm and unremarkable.

Opposing Forces: (Ninety Six): British (Tories): 550; American: 1,000; (Augusta): British (Tories): 500; American: 600.

British Perspective: In the spring of 1781, Lord Francis Rawdon and the British were forced to loosen their grip on South Carolina. As outposts fell and British strength waned, the people of the Southern colonies increased the tempo of rebellion, rallying in greater numbers to the American cause. Lord Rawdon sent messengers to Ninety Six ordering Col. John Harris Cruger to abandon his position and move his men to Augusta, Georgia, to assist Tory leader Col. Thomas Brown. Unbeknownst to Lord Rawdon, the message was intercepted by rebels and Cruger did not vacate his position.

The Augusta outpost consisted of several interconnected strong points, including Forts Grierson and Cornwallis. Some 400 Tory militiamen and an unknown number of Indians defended these forts. They remained organized, as they had been when attacked by the Americans nearly a year earlier (September 14-18, 1780). While the Americans remained a threat beyond the walls of the forts, the Tories were a potent force and controlled Augusta throughout the war.

At Fort Ninety Six, Colonel Cruger commanded a composite force of 900 troops. The need for patrols and Loyalist outposts in the region required a garrison of 550 men to permanently man Ninety Six. Even the Regular troops were Loyalists from the Northern colonies, thus the outpost served as a regional Tory hub in which Loyalist companies were trained and organized. It also served as a forward base for the British and a launching point for offensive operations during the war. The families of these soldiers lived in the adjacent town; black labor supplied the work necessary to turn the fort into a citadel.

During the war, British engineers had steadily improved the classically designed Fort Ninety Six. Built of earth and logs, it was shaped like an eight-pointed star with log palisade walls, complete with a large ditch and abatis around it. The fort was connected with the adjacent town and laborers dug interconnecting earthworks around it. Several large bomb proofs were established at strategic locations inside the defenses to protect the defenders from artillery fire. A set of large blockhouses guarded the northern and southern entrances to the fort and town. While Fort Ninety Six was a formidable bastion, it had one obvious weakness: a lack of artillery. The British had equipped the fort with just three light field pieces.

On May 22, 1781, Colonel Cruger was suddenly greeted with the arrival of Gen. Nathanael Greene and the American army. Greene allowed women and children to evacuate to Charleston before the commencement of hostilities. Cruger's wife refused the offer, though she did stay with Greene's wife at a farmhouse outside the fort while the siege was underway.

American Perspective: By the middle of May, General Greene controlled all of South Carolina above the Congaree River. His partisan warriors had struck deeply into British territory throughout the state. As British outposts fell to Generals Sumter and Marion, dispatches were obtained and messengers intercepted that provided valuable intelligence for the Americans. It was in this manner that General Greene learned Colonel Cruger was ordered to abandon Fort Ninety Six, cross the Savannah River, and strengthen Augusta. On the basis of this news Greene moved his army toward Ninety Six while dispatching Lt. Col. Henry Lee and his cavalry toward Augusta. Once there, Lee joined with Cols. Andrew Pickens and Elijah Clark and initiated a siege against the Augusta-based Tories and Indians. Greene, meanwhile, moved his 1,000-man army west and by the 22nd of May both British outposts in the west (August and Fort Ninety-Six) were under siege.

Terrain: The forts at Ninety-Six and Augusta were established in the western frontier region along strategic positions. The latter guarded the Savannah River and the settlements of northeast Georgia, while the former offered some protection to the important Upcountry region of South Carolina and the settlements in that region. Ninety Six was 60 miles north of Augusta, which was 200 miles northwest of Charleston. When the British also controlled Camden, South Carolina, the outposts formed an important triangular network connecting and defending the key locations until it all unraveled in 1781. The terrain in both areas consisted of dense woods and flat terrain surrounded by gently rolling hills. With excellent growing seasons, both locations were prime settlement areas and thus hotly contested terrain.

The Fighting: The siege commenced at both locations on the same date: May 22, 1781. Augusta was the first to fall on June 5. The Americans surrounded the defenders of Augusta and repeatedly attacked from various directions until Colonel Brown and his Tories could no longer maintain a credible defense. Two weeks of steady firing left the combatants of both sides exhausted, and the isolated Brown agreed to terms of surrender.

Despite the bitter hatred the Americans had for Brown they did not hang him; he was instead taken prisoner.

For the operation against Fort Ninety Six, Greene brought with him the Polish Patriot Col. Thaddeus Kosciusko. This brilliant engineer advised the Americans to dig a series of parallel entrenchments from the northwest to threaten a weak point in the fort's construction. The entrenchments were constructed very close to the fort, and Colonel Cruger countered the traditional European siege tactic by focusing artillery fire against the Americans. Kosciusko refocused his efforts farther from the fort's walls, building trench lines, gabions (wicker baskets filled with dirt), and fascines (wooden poles bound together) to provide his workers with more protection. Inching closer and digging night and day, the Americans finished a third parallel on June 3 within just 60 yards of the fort's wall. Both sides erected parapets for their artillery and continued bombarding the other until June 8, when the Patriot victors from Augusta marched within view of Fort Ninety Six with their Tory prisoners. This act, probably designed to crush the morale of the defenders, backfired. Instead of dampening spirits it infuriated Colonel Cruger and reinvigorated his Tories in their quest to hold the fort.

The arrival of the Americans from Augusta gave Greene adequate numbers to launch an assault against the fort with a reasonable hope of success. In an effort to preempt any such attack, the Tories launched an assault late on June 9 against the Patriot entrenchments. The strike wounded Colonel Kosciusko, who was inspecting a mine his men were digging beneath the fort. Their intent was to pack it with gunpowder and blow a large hole in Cruger's wall. The Tory raids continued nightly in an effort to keep Greene's men off balance and delay the completion of their tunnels. On June 11, Greene and Cruger learned Lord Rawdon was rushing 2,000 British reinforcements from Charleston to Fort Ninety Six.

The welcome news emboldened the besieged Tories and forced Greene to make some tough choices. He attempted to stall the approaching British column by dispatching Col. William Washington's cavalry and General Sumter's militia to stop them. He also ordered his men to work harder to complete the siege parallels. By the morning of June 18, Kosciusko's siege lines were ready. The American artillery opened a tremendous preparatory attack on the fort and at noon, two assault groups advanced armed with tools to breach the walls and climb over the parapets. This first wave was supposed to be followed by the main assault group comprised of Continental soldiers. Cruger's Tories, however, were well and aggressively led. Instead of waiting passively inside a trap, they counterattacked from the rear of the fort and swung around both sides and flanked the Americans trying to breach

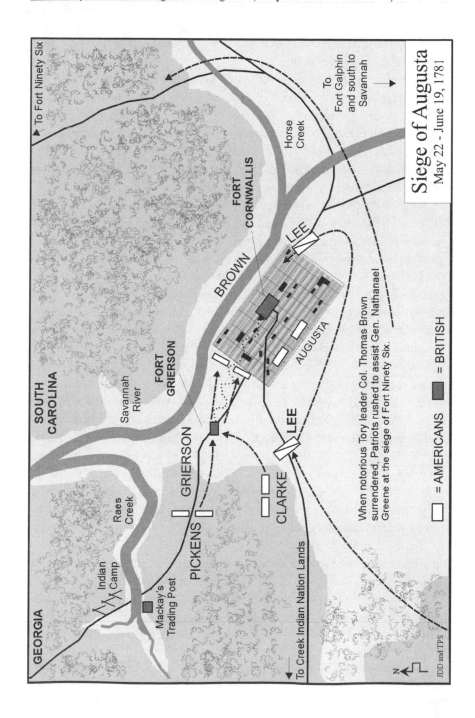

Siege of Augusta
May 22 - June 19, 1781

To Fort Ninety Six

To Fort Galphin and south to Savannah

Horse Creek

FORT CORNWALLIS

BROWN

LEE

AUGUSTA

FORT GRIERSON

Savannah River

SOUTH CAROLINA

GRIERSON

PICKENS

CLARKE

LEE

Raes Creek

Indian Camp

Mackay's Trading Post

GEORGIA

To Creek Indian Nation Lands

When notorious Tory leader Col. Thomas Brown surrendered, Patriots rushed to assist Gen. Nathanael Greene at the siege of Fort Ninety Six.

☐ = AMERICANS   ■ = BRITISH

N

JDD and TPS

the walls. The attackers inflicted heavy casualties and successfully returned to the fort, ending the assault.

Greene's interdiction mission did not go any better. General Sumter and Colonel Washington failed to halt the British relief column, which continued its rapid advance toward Fort Ninety Six. Finding himself between two strong forces Greene had little choice but to order a retreat; he did so on the evening of June 19. Lord Rawdon and his 2,000 reinforcements arrived shortly after the Americans withdrew. A pursuit of several days' duration failed to catch Greene's withdrawing column.

Casualties: (Ninety Six): British (Tories): 52 killed and 70 wounded; American: 57 killed and 70 wounded; (Augusta): British (Tories): 16 killed and 58 wounded; American: 16 killed and 35 wounded.

Outcome / Impact: The Augusta siege was successful, but the 27-day effort against Ninety Six was a humiliating failure. It was also proved pointless because the British soon abandoned the fort, destroyed its walls, and marched toward Charleston. Lord Rawdon decided to consolidate his strength closer to his supply depot. The tragedy of these sieges is that all the combatants were Americans, be they Tory or Patriot. After years of fighting the bitter hatred in the Southern colonies remained as palpable as ever.

As the southern summer heat bore down hard on the combatants, Lord Rawdon marched his army to Charleston; the Americans followed at a respectable distance. Several small skirmishes erupted on the outskirts of Charleston that summer. On July 17, Generals Sumter and Marion clashed with British Lt. Col. John Coates at Quinby's Bridge, but the American attack was mismanaged and ended in another frustrating retreat. On August 13 at Parker's Ferry, Francis Marion's men ambushed a British column trying to attack the Americans there. These small actions had no impact on larger strategic questions, and the British remained in complete control of the strategic port cities of Savannah and Charleston. The Americans remained determined to find a way to remove the British from the Southern colonies.

Today: Ninety Six National Historic Site in South Carolina covers nearly 1,000 acres and offers a modern visitor center, reconstructed palisade walls, walking trails, living history programs, and artifact displays.

Further Reading: Buchanan, John, *The Road to Guilford Courthouse* (Wiley, 1997); Lumpkin, Henry, *From Savannah to Yorktown: The American Revolution in the South* (Paragon House, 1981); Christopher Ward, *The War of the Revolution*, 2 vols. (MacMillan, 1952).

Green Spring, Battle of (Yorktown Campaign)

Date: July 6, 1781.
Region: Southern Colonies, Virginia.
Commanders: British: Lieutenant General Charles Cornwallis and Lieutenant Colonel Banastre Tarleton; American: Marquis de Lafayette and Major General Anthony Wayne.
Time of Day / Length of Action: 3:00 p.m. to 6:00 p.m.
Weather Conditions: Hot and humid.
Opposing Forces: British: 3,000; American: 1,100.

British Perspective: After his bloody tactical victory at Guilford Courthouse against Nathanael Greene in March, General Cornwallis moved his exhausted army to Wilmington, North Carolina. Satisfied he could not achieve decisive victory in the Southern colonies, Cornwallis concluded Virginia offered better opportunities to defeat the Patriot field armies and bring the war to a successful close. His strategy called for combining his army in Virginia with reinforcements sent from New York by General Sir Henry Clinton. Cornwallis would assume overall command in Virginia and open a new campaign. In May 1781, after refitting and resting his command along the North Carolina coast, Cornwallis marched his army northward.

By the spring of 1781 the British navy had brushed aside Virginia's tiny state navy and occupied Chesapeake Bay. Some 2,000 British soldiers commanded by Maj. Gen. Edward Matthews and Brig. Gen. Benedict Arnold moved easily into Norfolk and Suffolk and established a post at Portsmouth. From this base, troops led by Arnold moved west along the James River, raiding towns and plantations along the historic waterway. Arnold, the notorious traitor who had once served his nation so proudly, had resorted to pillaging and burning properties of his fellow countrymen. Major General William Phillips, meanwhile, led another 2,600 troops west from Portsmouth along a land route south and generally parallel to the James River.

Driving the outnumbered Virginia militia before them, the British twin-pronged advance moved through Williamsburg, Richmond, occupied Petersburg, and joined forces with Cornwallis on May 20. The conjunction swelled Cornwallis's command to more then 7,000 men. The victor of Camden spent the next five weeks scouting the countryside, gathering supplies, and maneuvering to gain advantage against a smaller American army under Maj. Gen. Marquis de Lafayette, who had been dispatched south to Virginia to counter Cornwallis.

On June 4 Col. Banastre Tarleton raided north and west to Charlottesville in an attempt to capture Governor Thomas Jefferson and the Virginia legislature. The Patriot leaders escaped just minutes before Tarleton's dragoons arrived. For the next several weeks Cornwallis unsuccessfully attempted to lure Lafayette into a pitched battle. On June 16 Cornwallis moved his headquarters to Richmond and was planning to strike at Lafayette when Clinton changed his orders. Concerned that a combined French and American force under George Washington was about to assault him in New York, the Crown's commander in chief asked Cornwallis to return 3,000 troops to him. In order to comply with this order, Cornwallis had to march his army southeast toward Portsmouth, where his men could board ships and sail to New York.

The march to Portsmouth carried the British onto the narrow peninsula between the York and James rivers. American troops cautiously approached Cornwallis's men camped in the vicinity of Williamsburg. Both armies were now operating within a narrow arena dangerously close to one another. American cavalry struck British troops on the left (northern) wing of the army north of Williamsburg on June 26. The combat at Spencer's Ordinary (Williamsburg) was a small but brisk affair that caught the British off guard and killed and wounded several dozen men. More ominously, it served as a warning to all concerned that the armies were in proximity and serious fighting was in the offing.

Disappointed that he could not come to decisive grips with Lafayette, Cornwallis decided to continue marching toward Portsmouth. He had grown somewhat disillusioned with his decision to occupy Virginia and wanted to return to Charleston and reinvigorate his Southern campaign strategy. On July 7 his army was at Jamestown Island Ford in preparation for crossing the wide waterway. Concerned lest the enemy assault his army during the river crossing, Cornwallis sent only a small force across the James while concealing his main army along the near shoreline. His hope was that the young and less experienced Lafayette would strike out toward the ford in the mistaken belief he was assaulting a vulnerable rear guard. If all went well, he would instead find himself facing the bulk of Cornwallis's command. To add credence to the ruse Cornwallis released two "deserters" to confirm the main body of the British army had crossed the river.

American Perspective: The general stalemate that developed in the Northern colonies after the close of the 1778 campaigns continued through the spring of 1781. George Washington had every reason to be pleased with the turnaround in the Southern colonies, where Patriot armies had achieved important victories at Kings Mountain (October 7, 1780) and Cowpens (January 17, 1781). Although Nathanael Greene had been driven from the field at the end of the day at Guilford Courthouse (March 15, 1781), the fighting had so crippled Cornwallis's army (which was already exhausted by hard marching and a shortage of supplies) that it was unfit for further field service. Cornwallis made for the coastal port of Wilmington; Greene headed south into South Carolina.

When reports from Virginia reached Washington that Cornwallis was moving north with a large field army, Washington dispatched Maj. Gen. Marquis de Lafayette (assisted by Maj. Gen. Baron von Steuben) from New York to Virginia with 1,200 men to join forces with militia operating there and defend the state against British incursions. As the Americans marched south into Virginia the French navy was to move into Chesapeake Bay to provide Lafayette with naval support. British warships beat them there, however, leaving the much smaller American army to its own devices. In addition to the large British navy in Virginia water that May of 1781, three separate British land columns were converging at Petersburg. The threat facing Lafayette was serious and growing more so by the day.

In early June Washington sent Maj. Gen. Anthony Wayne with an 800-man brigade to strengthen Lafayette's Virginia command. A brigade of 600 Virginia militia led by Brig. Gen. William Campbell, the heroic leader of Kings Mountain, also joined Lafayette's army. When it became clear Lafayette was facing a more serious threat than originally believed, Washington sent additional reinforcements until the Virginia army swelled to 5,000 men. Cornwallis was still significantly stronger, however, so Lafayette kept his troops at a safe distance north of the British position.

When Cornwallis began moving southeast toward Williamsburg, Lafayette followed at a respectful distance. Pickets from both sides skirmished now and again as the two armies marched along the peninsula. When Lafayette learned the enemy was trying to get to Portsmouth to send troops back to New York, the Frenchman pursued with the hope of striking a blow. He stopped his army between Williamsburg and Green Spring plantation, where he decided to lash out at the enemy's isolated rear column as the main body crossed the James. Unbeknownst to Lafayette, his information was based upon a British deception. General Wayne and about 900 troops moved forward to strike what they believed was the exposed enemy rear.

Terrain: This area of Virginia is located in what is known as the Tidewater region on the peninsula between the James River on the south and the York River on the north. The land along the rivers is comprised of tidal marshes and the entire peninsula is low, densely forested terrain. The battle took place on a narrow neck of land about three-quarters of a mile wide (east to west) by two miles long (north to south), between Jamestown Island (in the southeast) and Green Spring plantation (in the northwest). Powhatan Creek in the east and tidal flat marshes in the west forced the combatants to fight on a level but narrow arena. The action began at Green Spring plantation and a running battle developed that moved southeast along the road connecting Jamestown Island with Green Spring plantation (present-day State Route 614).

The Fighting: Early on the afternoon of July 6, General Wayne moved southeast between Powhatan Creek on his left and the James River on his right with a composite force of 500 men. His task was to keep contact with the British. Ahead, he believed, was a weak rear guard composed of bored British soldiers waiting their turn to cross the James River just south of Green Spring. Lafayette joined Wayne after the first skirmishing erupted. Intelligence as to whether the main enemy body had actually crossed or not was contradictory. Lafayette ordered up reinforcements of Continentals and light infantry, about 1,100 men, from six miles in the rear at Norrell's Mills. The militia remained miles behind the American army. The afternoon hours passed as Wayne's men pressed slowly forward, British pickets falling slowly back toward the river.

Unbeknownst to Lafayette or Wayne, who were undoubtedly pleased with the steady advance, Cornwallis had no intention of offering a firm defensive line. He had stretched out the bulk of his large army along the northern shore of the river and was only slowly ferrying troops to the southern side. He had also deployed infantry along a natural causeway formed by marshes to prevent the Americans from attacking in strength across a wide front.

Wayne was apparently sanguine but Lafayette grew suspicious. Cornwallis, he feared, might be baiting a trap and, if so, Wayne was driving his men directly into it. The French officer wisely withheld a pair of light battalion reinforcements in the rear at Green Spring plantation while shuttling forward three battalions to strengthen Wayne, who now had about 950 men at the front. While Wayne slowly advanced Lafayette performed a daring reconnaissance along the river. To his horror he uncovered the bulk of the waiting British infantry: Wayne was stumbling into a trap.

As the British infantry fell back before Wayne's strengthened advance, bait in the form of a cannon emplacement was set out for easy capture. The artillery piece had been placed at a strategic point against which Cornwallis

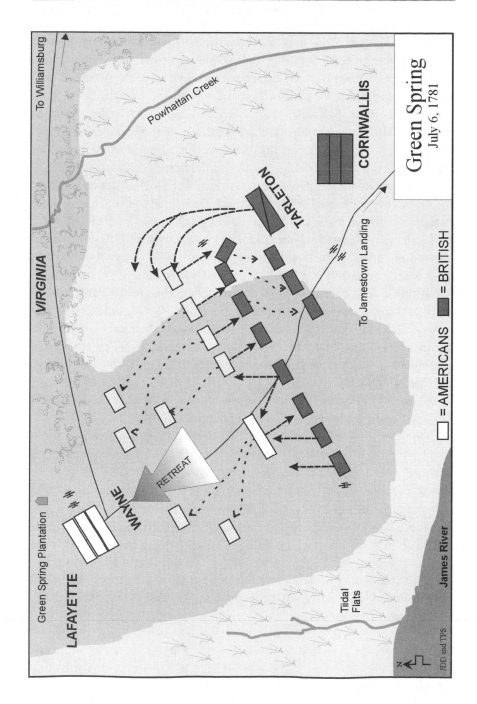

To Williamsburg

Powhattan Creek

VIRGINIA

Green Spring Plantation

LAFAYETTE

WAYNE

RETREAT

TARLETON

CORNWALLIS

To Jamestown Landing

Tidal Flats

James River

□ = AMERICANS   ■ = BRITISH

Green Spring
July 6, 1781

N

JDD and TPS

intended to counterattack once the Americans had advanced deep enough into his ambush. An American effort to take the piece was beaten back. Cornwallis was an outstanding tactician and in this case, a very patient one. He could have attacked much earlier, but instead waited until as many of Lafayette's men as possible had taken the field. The British leader wanted to make sure his hammer fell hard when he struck. With about 3,000 men he turned to the offensive against his unwitting American prey. As he would soon learn and live to regret, his attack was delivered two hours too late.

The stunned Wayne showed tremendous force of character by ordering an attack, even though he was outnumbered three-to-one. As he later explained, a retreat under the circumstances would have likely turned into a panicked rout. The sudden American attack took the British by surprise and held up the advance for many critical minutes. Still, Wayne's left flank melted under a heavy assault that pressed its advantage to the fullest. Lafayette arrived on the field about this time and helped peel off units that he sent marching to the reserve line near the plantation. By this time the sun was setting. Cornwallis had only allowed himself about sixty minutes of daylight to finish a task that, under the best of circumstances, would have required several hours. Lafayette and Wayne regrouped at Green Spring and retired. There was no pursuit.

Casualties: British: 75 killed and wounded; American: 28 killed, 99 wounded, and 12 missing, and two field pieces.

Outcome / Impact: The tactical British victory was a small one that could have been devastating to American arms. Colonel Tarleton urged Cornwallis to remain north of the James and destroy Lafayette, but the British commander decided instead to continue crossing and march on to Portsmouth as originally intended. It was a fateful decision. If Cornwallis had heeded Tarleton's advice, or if he had attacked earlier in the day, it is far less likely that his army would have ended up trapped inside Yorktown's defenses. Years later Tarleton expressed his belief that if Cornwallis had destroyed the American army at Green Spring the course of events would have been very different. Such a conclusion is difficult to argue with.

The next morning, July 7, the Americans contented themselves with observing the British army from their lines at Green Spring plantation. Lafayette decided against challenging the Earl to battle. Cornwallis completed his crossing without mishap. Additional and conflicting messages from General Clinton, however, evinced uncertainty as to General Washington's strategy in New York. Moreover, Clinton had also received intelligence that a large French fleet was sailing toward Chesapeake Bay.

On July 20 Clinton ordered Cornwallis to establish defensive positions on the James River peninsula and hold reinforcements bound for New York. Cornwallis complied by building fortifications at Old Point Comfort, Virginia, where he settled down to await further orders from Clinton.

Further Reading: Johnston, Henry P, *The Yorktown Campaign and the Surrender of Cornwallis 1781* (Harper & Brothers, 1881); Greene, Jerome A., *The Guns of Independence: The Siege of Yorktown, 1781* (Savas Beatie, LLC, 2005); Wickwire, Franklin B., *Cornwallis: The American Adventure* (Houghton Mifflin, 1970).

The Capes, Battle of (Yorktown Campaign)

Date: September 5-8, 1781.
Region: Southern Colonies, Virginia (offshore naval battle).
Commanders: British: Rear Admirals Thomas Graves, Samuel Hood, and Francis Samuel Drake; French: Lieutenant General le Count de Grasse, and Admirals De Latouche-Treville, Le Sieur de Monteil, and Le Sieur de Bougainville.
Time of Day / Length of Action: 3:45 p.m. to 6:30 p.m.
Weather Conditions: Fair with a northeasterly wind.
Opposing Forces: British: 27 ships, 13,000 sailors, and 1,400 guns; French: 23 ships, 18,000 seamen, and 1,600 guns.

British Perspective: The American Revolution was quickly moving toward a climax by the late summer of 1781. General Charles Cornwallis had abandoned his efforts in the Southern colonies to seek a decisive engagement in Virginia. General Sir Henry Clinton, meanwhile, holed up around New York City, was keeping an eye on Gen. George Washington's Continental army in upstate New York. Clinton ordered Cornwallis to secure a deep water port for the British fleet and to establish defensive positions in southeastern Virginia to secure it. Cornwallis held an excellent port at Portsmouth and had fortified positions at Old Point Comfort. A survey conducted by his best engineers, however, convinced him to focus his efforts along the York River. On August 1 Cornwallis moved toward Yorktown with 4,500 men and established a new base of operations there. During the next few days he transferred his entire army and naval operations to that vicinity.

Cornwallis spent the next several weeks constructing field fortifications around Yorktown and across the river on Gloucester point. Shore batteries were established to defend the port and redoubts were constructed to defend the approaches by land. About this time the British learned a major French fleet was sailing toward Chesapeake Bay to assist and reinforce the growing American presence in Virginia. In response to this threat, Rear Admiral Thomas Graves sailed the British fleet southward from New Jersey on August 31 to block the French naval armada.

On September 5 the British fleet sailed into Chesapeake Bay, only to discover the French fleet was already on station there. French troops were being landed and the James and York rivers (access to Cornwallis) were blockaded by enemy warships. Admiral Graves ordered his fleet to prepare for action. By noon the British warships were organized into three sections commanded by Admirals Graves, Samuel Hood, and Francis Samuel Drake. From his 98-gun flagship *London* Graves commanded 27 ships (19 ships of the line, including *London*, all of which would attempt to directly partake in the fighting, and eight frigates). In addition to *London*, Graves's fleet consisted of the following warships: *Barfleur, Shrewsbury, Monarch, Centaur, America, Resolution, Royal Oak, Solebay, Montagu, Terrible, Ajax, Princessa, Europe, Sybil, Fortunée, Bedford, Nymphe, Santa Monica, Alfred, Belliqueux, Invincible, Richmond, Salamander, Adamant, Alcide,* and *Intrepid.*

French Perspective: After the Battle of Green Spring (July 6, 1781), Maj. Gen. Marquis de Lafayette and his 5,000-man American army shadowed British army operations in Virginia. Lafayette moved the bulk of his army to Malvern Hill, Virginia, while Maj. Gen. Anthony Wayne observed the British operating around Portsmouth. Other American troops were tasked with watching and containing Col. Banastre Tarleton's dragoons, who were conducting reconnaissance operations and raids against American positions.

In August, the British sailed away from Portsmouth and Lafayette learned from intelligence reports that Cornwallis was moving to Yorktown. Lafayette marched his army to a new position on the Pamunkey River 30 miles northwest of the British just outside West Point, Virginia. As August drew to a close the Americans learned a French fleet commanded by Count de Grasse was sailing for Virginia with 3,200 soldiers to assist the Americans. Meanwhile, General Washington had reached the conclusion that Cornwallis had placed his army in a potentially precarious position, and urged the French to assist him in trapping the general and his men around Yorktown. To that end, Washington and his French counterpart, Count de

Rochambeau, embarked on a 450-mile march from Newport, Rhode Island, with a combined Franco-American army of 8,000 men. Their plan was to seal off the land route with the army, and use the French navy to cut off Cornwallis's sea communications. Major General William Heath and 4,000 men were left in New York to defend the Highlands and deceive General Clinton in New York City about what was transpiring.

De Grasse's French fleet arrived off the Virginia Capes on August 30. Enemy warships were guarding the entrance to Chesapeake Bay. The British frigate *Guadaloupe* was chased up the York River and the corvette *Loyalist* was taken in battle. With the bay secured, 3,200 French soldiers led by Marquis de St. Simon landed and moved inland to join Lafayette. From his 110-gun flagship *Le Ville de Paris* de Grasse deployed his fleet into three sections commanded by Admirals De Latouche-Treville, Le Sieur de Monteil, and Le Sieur de Bougainville.

By September 2 de Grasses's ships were guarding the rivers and patrolling the capes. However, on the morning of September 5 Admiral Graves's British fleet appeared to challenge French control of the vital sea access to Virginia. Although many French sailors were involved with other operations ashore, de Grasse ordered his fleet to prepare for action. The French fleet was comprised of the following 24 ships: *Le Cesar*; *Le Hector*; *Le Bourgogne*; *Le Diademe*; *Le Auguste*; *Le Caton*; *Le Reflechi*; *Le Magnanime*; *Le Destin*; *La Ville de Paris*; *La Victoire*; *Le Sceptre*; *Le Begue*; *Le Northumberland*; *Le St. Esprit*; *Le Marseillais*; *Le Palmier*; *Le Pluton*; *Le Solitaire*; *Le Citoyen*; *Le Hercule*; *Le Zele*; *Le Scipion*, and *Le Souverain*.

Terrain: The entrance to the Chesapeake Bay is ten miles wide from Cape Henry in the south to Cape Charles in the north. Numerous rivers (including the York and James) drain into the bay, which empties into the Atlantic Ocean. Yorktown is on the southern shore of the York River 35 miles inland (northwest) of Cape Henry. The battle began just north of Cape Henry and the combatants sailed to the southeast into the Atlantic Ocean as the combat unfolded. During the next four days the combatants drifted southward and parallel to the coast until both fleets reached Cape Hatteras, North Carolina, 100 miles from where the battle initially began.

The Fighting: French patrol boats spotted the sails of the enemy at 8:00 a.m. on the 5th of September. The French vessels were forced to work against an ebb tide and had to tack several times before they could reach a favorable position. With fair weather and a northeasterly wind, the full sails and alert crews of the British fleet drove into the bay with the advantage. While they varied in size and speed, all of the British vessels arrayed for battle were ships of the line, and none were armed with fewer than 64 guns.

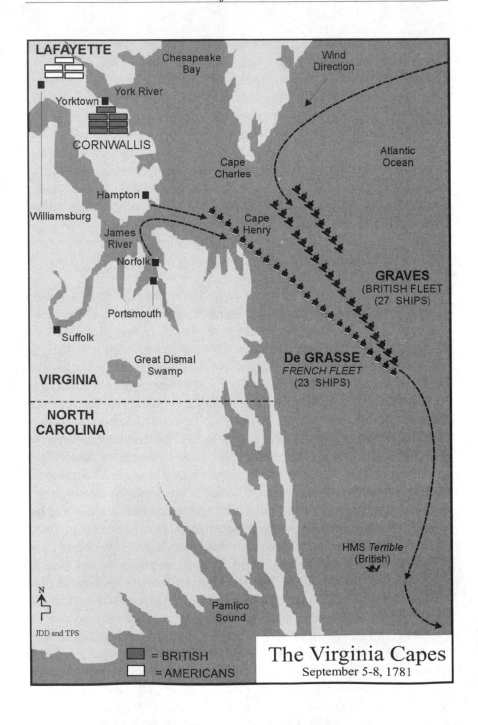

LAFAYETTE

Chesapeake
Bay

Wind
Direction

York River

Yorktown

CORNWALLIS

Atlantic
Ocean

Williamsburg

Hampton

Cape
Charles

James
River

Cape
Henry

Norfolk

GRAVES
(BRITISH FLEET
(27 SHIPS)

Portsmouth

Suffolk

Great Dismal
Swamp

De GRASSE
FRENCH FLEET
(23 SHIPS)

VIRGINIA

NORTH
CAROLINA

HMS *Terrible*
(British)

N

Pamlico
Sound

JDD and TPS

= BRITISH
= AMERICANS

The Virginia Capes
September 5-8, 1781

The British armada boasted 13,000 sailors and at least 1,400 guns, while the French fleet had 19,000 seamen and 1,600 cannon.

Once the opposing fleets lined up and maneuvered for battle, the British lead or "van" signaled the fleet to "line ahead" at 3:45 p.m. The French did likewise and moved on a parallel course southeast, with the distance between the combatants narrowing by the minute. With the wind driving them together, the two lines formed a sideways "V." When the van ships were nearly together at the tip of the formations (one French naval officer described the distance as "almost within pistol shot"), Admiral Graves signaled for his men to "bear down and engage the enemy." Admiral Hood's ship, however, continued to fly the signal "line ahead," which took precedence over all other signals. The result was that some British ships failed to engage because naval tactics dictated they should fire broadsides into their respective enemy ship as they passed in line of battle.

For the next 90 minutes the ships pummeled each other with artillery fire, though the British communication snafu left only leading ships to fire into their French counterparts. At 5:20 p.m. Admiral Graves signaled "close action" and the other British ships moved to join the fight. It was too late, and the random shots that resulted were ineffectual. Because of shifting winds and the poor alignment of the British fleet, only the first eight British ships and just the front fifteen French ships exchanged shots within decisive range. By 6:30 p.m. nightfall arrived and all hostile action ceased.

The day had gone against the British. Admiral Graves's *London* was heavily damaged by de Grasse's *La Ville de Paris*, and three other British ships were badly mauled, including the 64-gun *Terrible*, which the British scuttled on the night of September 9. As the sun set that evening, the two navies pulled apart but remained within striking distance of one another while waiting for dawn.

Casualties: British: 90 killed and 246 wounded (six ships badly damaged, one scuttled); French: 200 killed and wounded.

Outcome / Impact: During the first night following the battle the two fleets maintained a safe distance as they slowly drifted south and east into the Atlantic Ocean. Neither side wanted to immediately re-engage the other, and a stalemate ensued for several days, drifting more than 100 miles to the outer reaches of Cape Hatteras by September 10. De Grasse lost sight of the British ships and returned the French fleet to the Chesapeake Bay. More good news reached the Americans when they learned another French squadron led by Comte de Barras had arrived from its base at Newport, Rhode Island, to deliver siege equipment to the Patriot army. With the French in complete control of the Chesapeake Bay, Admiral Graves returned to New York with the British fleet.

The Battle of the Capes was a tremendous victory for Franco-American arms. For the British, it was an inept debacle whose consequences would soon become apparent when Cornwallis surrendered his army to Washington the following month at Yorktown.

Further Reading: Coggins, Jack, *Ships and Seamen of the American Revolution* (Dover Publications, 2002); Greene, Jerome A., *The Guns of Independence: The Siege of Yorktown, 1781* (Savas Beatie, 2005); Johnston, Henry P., *The Yorktown Campaign and the Surrender of Cornwallis 1781* (Harper & Brothers, 1881).

New London, Battle of (also known as Fort Griswold and Groton Heights) (Arnold's Expedition)

Date: September 6, 1781.
Region: Northern Colonies, Connecticut.
Commanders: British: Brigadier General Benedict Arnold, Lieutenant Colonel Edmund Eyre, and Major William Montgomery; American: Lieutenant Colonel William Ledyard and Captain Adam Shapley.
Time of Day / Length of Action: 11:00 a.m. to 11:45 a.m.
Weather Conditions: Warm, unremarkable morning.
Opposing Forces: British: 1,400; American: 175.

British Perspective: When the British learned the Americans were pressing south into Virginia to confront General Cornwallis's army, Brig. Gen. Benedict Arnold (who had changed his allegiance and was fighting for the Crown) suggested to Gen. Sir Henry Clinton that an amphibious assault be launched against New London, Connecticut. Arnold selected New London because it was easily reachable by sea from New York (140 miles), was loaded with American supplies, and he knew the area well. Arnold was under the impression his attack would divert Franco-American strength from Washington's army. New London was also an important shipping center harboring American privateers who frequently struck British ships on the open sea. Clinton agreed with Arnold's plan.

Arnold's armada approached the harbor in the pre-dawn darkness of September 6. He intended to launch a night attack, but shifting winds kept him out of the river until long after dawn. At 10:00 a.m., Arnold's men disembarked on both banks of the Thames River. Arnold's column, which landed on the western bank, consisted of the 34th Foot, two Loyalist regiments, a detachment of Hessian Jägers, and field artillery. Lieutenant Colonel Edmund Eyre's command landed on the eastern bank. It was comprised of the 40th and 54th Foot, a battalion of Loyalists, Hessian Jägers, and field artillery. Both wings, about 1,400 men, moved quickly northward paralleling the river toward two small American forts—the only defenses between New London and the Crown's military forces.

American Perspective: New London, Connecticut, was on the west bank of the Thames River three miles from its mouth. The river feeds into the Atlantic Ocean. Patriot privateers used the harbor to launch raids into the Atlantic against unsuspecting enemy supply ships. As events would quickly prove, the Connecticut city was woefully unprepared to repel a serious attack. About one mile below the town on the same side of the river was Fort Trumbull, an unfinished and undermanned earthwork positioned to protect the harbor. Unfortunately, its landside was open to attack and only two dozen defenders under Capt. Adam Shapley were available to hold it. On the east side of the river on Groton Heights overlooking the harbor was Fort Griswold, manned by 150 men under Lt. Col. William Ledyard. Fort Griswold was the more powerful of the two main forts. It was roughly square with projections that gave it a pentagonal appearance. It had 12-foot walls of earth, the bottom portions covered with stone. Wall embrasures held artillery. A deep ditch lined with obstacles surrounded three sides. Several trenches connected the main fort to distant batteries below the bastion via a sally port to fortify the area to the southwest.

Terrain: The New London harbor is one mile wide and three miles from the ocean. The western bank of the Thames River was swampier and more heavily wooded than the eastern side. In addition to the forts described, another small fort, Fort Nonsense, had been established on the road and high ground west of Fort Trumbull to guard against a land incursion. When Arnold attacked, however, it was unmanned.

The Fighting: Fort Trumbull fell first, and quickly. Arnold dispatched four companies from the 38th Foot to overrun it. Captain Shapley's Patriot defenders knew their position was hopeless. They stayed put long enough to fire one round in the enemy's direction before fleeing across the river to reinforce Fort Griswold. Arnold, meanwhile, continued moving north to New London in the face of minimal opposition. A handful of defenders armed with a small old field piece fired it once at the British invaders before

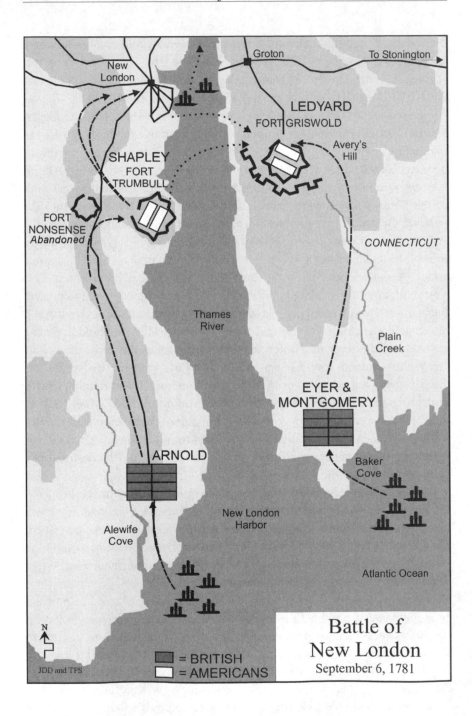

New London

Groton

To Stonington

LEDYARD
FORT GRISWOLD

Avery's
Hill

SHAPLEY
FORT
TRUMBULL

FORT
NONSENSE
Abandoned

CONNECTICUT

Thames
River

Plain
Creek

EYER &
MONTGOMERY

ARNOLD

Baker
Cove

Alewife
Cove

New London
Harbor

Atlantic Ocean

N

JDD and TPS

= BRITISH
= AMERICANS

**Battle of
New London**
September 6, 1781

the town was overrun by hundreds of enemy soldiers. American privateers sailed upriver to escape the British.

Lieutenant Colonel Edmund Eyre's command on the western bank of the Thames had a rougher time of it. The terrain there was swampy and more heavily wooded, which slowed down the advance toward Fort Griswold. Lieutenant Colonel Eyre reached Groton Heights and found the Americans ready to defend the fort. When he received a dispatch from Arnold to attack, Eyre extended an offer of surrender to Lieutenant Colonel Ledyard. When the offer was refused, Eyre extended the option a second time, supposedly adding (according to American sources) that no quarter would be given if he was forced to attack. Arnold later claimed to have believed the fort was unfinished, and when he realized his mistake tried to recall Eyre, but the battle was already underway.

Eyre's infantry assault engulfed the fort on three sides. Artillery and small arms fire ripped through their ranks, and for a few minutes the ditches kept the enemy away from the walls. Eyre was mortally injured early in the attack. His troops were forced to hoist one another above the fraise, which prevented them from flooding into the moat. When the fighting finally reached the walls one of Eyre's field officers, Maj. William Montgomery of the 40th Foot, was stabbed to death (either by a bayonet wielded by Captain Shapley or a pike thrust by an unnamed black man) trying to enter the fort. The American defense crumbled once the British managed to climb over the ramparts. Several redcoats forced open the gate and scores of soldiers poured inside (according to one source "in formation," though this is doubtful).

When Ledyard realized the fight was lost he ordered his men to lay down their arms. He turned over his sword to Lt. Col. Abraham Van Buskirk, a Loyalist with the New Jersey Volunteers. It is at this point the sources begin to widely diverge. According to American accounts, Ledyard was killed with his own sword after surrendering it (either by Van Buskirk or another man, depending upon the source). When an outraged American officer killed the offender, the angry British began indiscriminately putting the surrendered garrison to the bayonet. British sources do not mention anything about a massacre, although Arnold's own report notes that "85 men were found dead in Fort Griswold, and 60 wounded, most of them mortally." Given that only 175 or so men were defending the fort, 145 killed or mortally wounded can only mean that no quarter was extended for some period of time.

In New London, meanwhile, ten American privateer vessels were captured, tons of supplies were captured, and a few British prisoners released. Arnold plundered New London and, according to American sources, deliberately set it ablaze, destroying scores of homes and buildings and leaving 100 families homeless. According to Arnold, an exploding powder magazine aboard a ship triggered the fire, which because of the wind jumped from structure to structure "notwithstanding every effort to prevent it." An American postwar committee assessed the damage in New London at nearly $500,000.

Casualties: British and Tory: 53 killed, 146 wounded; American: 85 killed, 72 wounded (60 of them mortally), and 71 prisoners.

Outcome / Impact: The last sizable action in the Northern department, New London (also commonly called Groton Heights) had absolutely no effect on the war. Within six weeks General Cornwallis surrendered at Yorktown, Virginia, effectively moving the war from the battlefield to the diplomacy table. The wanton destruction of New London was thorough and several innocent civilians died as a result of the fire. Although the debate still rages about whether atrocities took place inside Fort Griswold, reliable accounts exist that comport with the horrendous casualty figures. Benedict Arnold's infamy, already cast in iron by his defection to the British, was only deepened by this needless and cruel affair.

Today: Fort Griswold State Park, complete with a walking trail and a museum, is open to the public. The fort is well preserved. A granite monument was erected to its defenders in 1830.

Further Reading: Mackenzie, Frederick, *Diary of Frederick Mackenzie* (Harvard University Press, 1930); Wilson, Barry K., *Benedict Arnold: A Traitor in Our Midst* (McGill-Queen's University, 2001).

Eutaw Springs, Battle of (Southern Campaign)

Date: September 8, 1781.

Region: Southern Colonies, South Carolina.

Commanders: British: Lieutenant Colonel Alexander Stewart; American: Major General Nathanael Greene, Brigadier General Francis Marion, Brigadier General Jethro Sumner, and Colonels Andrew Pickens, Richard Campbell, Otho Williams, and Lieutenant Colonel Wade Hampton.

Time of Day / Length of Action: Early morning, two hours.

Weather Conditions: Hot and humid.

Opposing Forces: British: 2,300; American: 2,100.

British Perspective: After his tactical victory over Nathanael Greene at Hobkirk's Hill (April 21, 1781), the young but capable Lord Francis Rawdon was forced to withdraw his small army to Charleston, South Carolina. He returned to England exhausted, ill, and disgusted with the war. The Crown's Southern strategy was in disarray, and Cornwallis and his veteran army were in Virginia about to be trapped on a narrow peninsula by a combined Franco-American army. The British, however, still maintained a firm grip on Charleston and the surrounding region. Insignificant enemy raids that spring and summer did little to break the tedium of the southern stalemate, with the highlight of the summer being the lynching of a handful of rebels. That event only made matters worse by inflaming Carolina locals, who were weary of years of British occupation. That same September Lt. Col. Alexander Stewart encamped his 2,100 troops northwest of Charleston at Eutaw Springs, where they enjoyed a bountiful supply of water and harvested sweet potatoes. Stewart learned on the night of September 7 that Greene's reinforced army was moving against him. Instead of withdrawing, Stewart formed his men for battle early on the morning of the 8th and awaited Greene's arrival.

Stewart's front faced generally west, with his right flank near the Santee River and Eutaw Creek, which flowed out of the larger waterway. His main line was bisected by the River Road, which paralleled the river and would serve as the enemy's obvious line of advance. Stewart placed an artillery battery in the center and formed his regiments in long ranks on either side of the road in a strong defensive line. The British center was held by Col. John Harris Cruger's Tories. The right (north) wing was comprised of the 3rd Regiment, and the left (south) flank of the 63rd and 64th regiments. On the extreme right flank in the elbow formed by the confluence of Eutaw Creek and the Santee River, Stewart posted Maj. John Majoribanks with several light infantry companies. Additional artillery was posted in strategic locations between the road and the creek, as were additional reserves and artillery well to the rear near the juncture of the Charleston and River roads.

American Perspective: After retreating into the safety of the Upcountry of South Carolina, General Greene pushed around to the east before moving southward, passing Camden as he marched his command southeast toward British-held Charleston. Before and during this journey Greene called in various partisan bands and formed his militia and Continentals into a small but respectable 2,200-man army. The British maintained several large bodies of troops north and northwest of Charleston to protect the British stronghold and forage across the countryside. When Greene's scouts reported British retreating southward toward the Santee River and Eutaw

Springs the American commander followed, intent on bringing the enemy to battle. Greene roused his army an hour before dawn on September 8 and marched east along the River Road, each step closing the distance to a waiting enemy army at Eutaw Springs.

When he began running into delaying parties sent out to obstruct his approach, Greene formed his men for battle facing east into the early morning sun. In front on either flank he placed his South Carolina militiamen under Col. Andrew Pickens and Brig. Gen. Francis Marion, with North Carolina militia arrayed in the center. Three regiments of Continental infantry formed behind the militia: Brig. Gen. Jethro Sumner's 350 North Carolinians on the right (south), Col. Richard Campbell's 350 Virginians in the center, and Col. Otho Williams's 250 Marylanders on the left (north) closest to the Santee River. Behind the Continentals Greene placed his reserve, Col. William Washington's cavalry and a small Delaware Continental unit. Each line was supported with field artillery. Lee's Legion took up a position beyond the army's right, while smaller outfits of infantry and cavalry formed on the left.

Terrain: This area of South Carolina's low country is predominantly flat. In the extreme northeast corner of the battlefield, Eutaw Springs gushed forth a heavy flow of cool water into a deep ravine and creek that flowed south out of the Santee before turning sharply ninety degrees to the east and running parallel to the River Road (which ran east to west). The road connected the plantation to St. John's Parish, with the Charleston Road arcing diagonally southeast at the plantation on the east side of the battlefield. The surrounding area beyond the plantation was densely wooded with heavy thickets sprinkled with small patches of open ground.

The Fighting: About 9:00 a.m. Greene ordered his army through the woods against Stewart. When the distance closed to killing range the opposing lines, from the American right to left, opened fire. This began what would be several distinct phases of fighting at Eutaw Springs. The better concealed British poured a steady fire into the rebel militia, who held fast for as many as 17 volleys before wavering in the face of mostly professional soldiers. A half-hearted effort by Lee's Legion to find the British left flank was beaten back. The second phase began when the British left (63rd and 64th regiments) advanced without orders. Unable to stand the pressure, the rebel militia broke and ran, prompting Greene to order up his right flank North Carolina Continentals to steady the front. The Patriot bayonet charge that followed forced some of the Crown's finest infantry to the rear.

The third or middle phase of the fighting got underway when Stewart called up his reserves to steady his left and center and re-anchor his line of

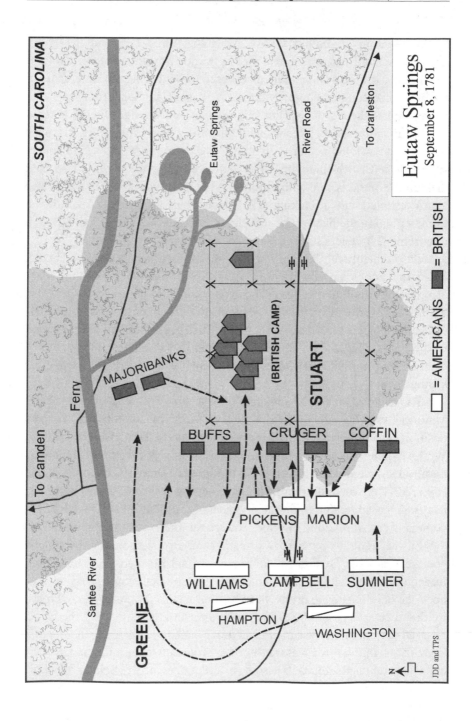

Eutaw Springs
September 8, 1781

battle. Fighting on both flanks was heavy. While Lee and the North Carolinians held fast on Greene's right, Major Majoribanks led his light infantry in a charge near the river that succeeded in driving the American left backward. A countercharge by Lt. Col. Wade Hampton drove back the enemy. When the North Carolina infantry on Greene's right finally faltered and began falling back, Greene had little choice but to order his best troops forward to save his center and right. The Virginians and Marylanders smashed the British line with a well-delivered close range volley, leveled their empty muskets, and with bayonets at the ready charged the enemy. The attack, coupled with a flanking effort against Stewart's exposed left, was a turning point in the battle. The British line, from left to center, collapsed in utter retreat. Greene's star seemed in the ascendant.

Unfortunately for Greene, who had thus far fought an exceptional battle, when his troops on the right pursued the retreating enemy into their campground, they stopped to engage in rampant pillaging and drinking. This drained away critical strength at the moment it was most needed. The rebels were also subjected to a deadly fire from British posted around the plantation to the north. The loss of momentum turned these soldiers into a mob of disorganized individuals who eventually ran for their lives to escape the killing zone.

The tide also turned against Greene on his left, where Major Majoribanks, who had been earlier thrown back by Hampton, maintained a position in heavy terrain with the protection of the creek to his right and rear. While looking for a way to turn Majoribanks's position, Washington's cavalrymen were slaughtered and Washington himself bayoneted and captured. The wooded area made maneuvering, especially on horseback, nearly impossible. Safe for the moment, Majoribanks slid his infantry command eastward along the creek toward the final climatic fighting.

In the center, a massed formation of British soldiers eventually coalesced among the farm buildings, where a large two-story home was turned into a field citadel. Two American artillery pieces brought up to blast open the buildings were driven back by musket fire. Majoribanks, who had by this time arrived on the British right after his journey along the creek, charged and captured the cannon and drove back the remainder of Greene's organized fighting force, but was mortally wounded in the attempt. Greene's exhausted remnants fell back in some disorder, leaving the field in Stewart's hands.

Casualties: British: 85 killed, 350 wounded, and 257 missing; American: 251 killed, 367 wounded, and 74 missing.

Outcome / Impact: Eutaw Springs has fallen into undeserved obscurity. Much like Bentonville at the end of the American Civil War, Eutaw Springs was waged within the shadows of more momentous events. In Bentonville's case it was the final fighting around Richmond and Petersburg, the retreat of the Army of Northern Virginia, the surrender at Appomattox Courthouse, and the assassination of Abraham Lincoln. Eutaw Springs was fought during the opening days of the climatic Yorktown Campaign.

The battle inflicted horrendously high casualties on both sides. Indeed, Eutaw Spring was one of the bloodiest and most hotly contested close-quarter fights of the war. The retreating Americans regrouped and later returned to Eutaw Springs, but the British were already marching for the safety of Charleston. Greene followed his enemy to the outskirts of the city, but he wisely decided he could not successfully attack them in their heavily defended positions. Both sides claimed victory in what would be the last major battle in the Carolinas. The focus of the war had shifted north to Virginia, where General Cornwallis would surrender to General Washington at Yorktown the following month.

Today: This battle is preserved and interpreted at the Eutaw Springs Battleground Park (two miles east of Eutawville on SC 6 and 45) with trails, historic markers, marked grave sites, and living history programs.

Further Reading: Buchanan, John, *The Road to Guilford Courthouse: The American Revolution in the Carolinas* (Wiley, 1999); De Peyster, J. Watts, *The Battle of Eutaw Springs, South Carolina,: Saturday, 8, September, 1781* (n.p., n.d.); Edgar, Walter B., *Partisans and Redcoats: The Southern Conflict That Turned the Tide of the American Revolution* (Harper, 2003); Golway, Terry, *Washington's General: Nathanael Greene and the Triumph of the American Revolution* (Henry Holt, 2005).

Yorktown, Siege of (Yorktown Campaign)

Date: September 28 – October 18, 1781.

Region: Southern Colonies, Virginia.

Commanders: British: Lieutenant General Charles Cornwallis, Brigadier General Charles O'Hara, and Lieutenant Colonels Banastre Tarleton and Robert Abercrombie; Hessians: Colonel F.A.V. Voit von Salzburg and Lieutenant Colonel de Deybothen; American: General George Washington, Major General Benjamin Lincoln and Major Generals Marquis Maria Joseph de Lafayette and Baron Frederich Wilhelm von Steuben;

French: Lieutenant Generals le Counts Francois Joseph Paul de Grasse and Jean de Vimeur de Rochambeau, and Comte Claude Gabriel de Choisey.

Time of Day / Length of Action: 21-day siege.

Weather Conditions: Mild and generally unremarkable fall weather.

Opposing Forces: British: 8,000 (soldiers and sailors); Franco-American: 15,845 (American: 8,845; French: 7,800).

British Perspective: After his exhausting campaign in the Carolinas and bloody tactical "victory" at Guilford Courthouse in March 1781, Lt. Gen. Charles Cornwallis refitted his army in Wilmington, North Carolina, before marching north into Virginia, believing that decisive victory was more likely in that quarter. He reached Williamsburg in late June and after a flurry of contradictory and confusing orders from his superior, General Sir Henry Clinton, began establishing a base of operation on the York River in August. His main position was in and around Yorktown, Virginia, a small prosperous city of several hundred houses and an important inland port with strategic value to the British. The key to holding Yorktown rested with the British navy. On September 5 at the Battle of the Capes, however, French warships severely damaged a British fleet and blocked England's access to the Chesapeake. With a Franco-American army now blocking a move inland, Cornwallis's position at Yorktown began to assume the look of a self-imposed trap.

Cornwallis set his army to improving its defensive line of works around Yorktown, which were wholly unready to stand a serious siege. Gloucester Point on the north side of the York River was also fortified. On September 28 the combined Franco-American army left Williamsburg and arrived outside Yorktown.

With 7,200 men, including a large contingent of Hessian troops, Cornwallis established a strong inner line of entrenchments around Yorktown supported by detached redoubts and other fortifications in an outer ring of defenses. The outer line encircled the main line from Yorktown Creek in the west and southwest all the way around to the south and back to Wormeley's Creek and Pond in the east and southeast. The creeks were deep natural obstacles with marshy banks that wound their way around Yorktown and emptied to the north in the York River. Four redoubts were placed along the outer line in the south, but they were primarily to guard the roads leading into town and were not connected to the inner line of trenches. To the northwest, where the Williamsburg Road crossed Yorktown Creek, was a large strong star-shaped redoubt. The fortification blocked access to Yorktown along the main road, with the river immediately behind it. It was manned primarily by the 23rd Regiment ("Royal Welch Fusiliers") and often referred to as the "Fusiliers' Redoubt." Cornwallis's troops had cleared deep fields of fire around and beyond the detached works to assist the artillery and the aim of small arms fire against an approaching enemy. The inner line was much stronger and contained interconnecting trenches, redoubts, and batteries. Cornwallis had 65 field pieces, including several 18-pounders removed from the British ships anchored off Yorktown.

North of Yorktown on the other side of the York River was the small town of Gloucester on a spit of land called Gloucester Point. A fortified line to defend the area from a northerly assault was established. It consisted of a single trench line with four redoubts and three batteries, and ran from east to west across the narrow base of the peninsula. Colonel Banastre Tarleton and 700 men from his British Legion manned this line. In addition to the army, Cornwallis also had 800 sailors and a dozen naval vessels that had been trapped in the York River by the French sea victory. The frigates *Charon* and *Guadaloupe*, assisted by supply ships and a few transports, were available to assist in Cornwallis's defense, but their ability to move was restricted.

With little or no access to the sea Cornwallis could not be reinforced, re-supplied, or withdrawn. Each day that passed reduced his food and water supply. His thousands of animals needed forage and grain that was available in limited supplies. His men suffered from bad water, rotting food, and a wide assortment of maladies associated with such hardships. Cornwallis remained curiously passive about his predicament, allowing the enemy to encircle him on the land side without attempting to either march or fight his way out. On September 29, the day after the Franco-American army arrived outside Yorktown, Cornwallis received a message from General Clinton promising reinforcements and the return of the British fleet to assist him. This news convinced Cornwallis he could hold out at Yorktown until reinforcements arrived. Unfortunately for the British, it also convinced him to abandon much of his outer line and concentrate his troops within the inner fortifications. It was a decision that would haunt Cornwallis for the rest of his life.

Franco-American Perspective: George Washington, who was operating in New York, believed Cornwallis's move into Virginia was a strategic mistake. When he learned on August 14 that French Admiral de Grasse's fleet and marines were available until the middle of October, Washington decided on a bold plan. He feinted against New York to confuse General Clinton and stole a march south into Virginia. Bolstered by Comte de Rochambeau's French troops, who had arrived in the colonies in the summer of 1780, Washington moved his army into Williamsburg on September 14, blocking Cornwallis's ready access inland. The French naval victory off the Capes blocked British access to the bay and Cornwallis, while guaranteeing Washington that French artillery and siege equipment could be landed.

With his enemy trapped at Yorktown, Washington and his French allies moved swiftly to establish a traditional siege. On September 17 Washington and Rochambeau met with de Grasse aboard his flagship *La Ville de Paris* to coordinate the joint operation. Washington was assured the French would remain in position until at least October 31. On September 28 the siege of Yorktown was officially begun with French warships blocking the Chesapeake Bay and the Franco-American army positioned outside the British fortifications.

The Allied army was organized into three divisions. Rochambeau commanded the French contingent of about 7,800 men. They occupied the left wing, or northwestern sector, of the siege line. Rochambeau's army consisted of three infantry brigades, a heavy cavalry corps, and a large artillery corps. Duke Armand Louis de Lauzun led the cavalry and Col. François-Marie d'Aboville commanded the artillery. The right or southern sector of the siege line formed the base of the two wings boasting 8,845 American troops. These were divided into three divisions led by Major General Lincoln (commanding the American wing and his own division), and Maj. Gens. Lafayette and von Steuben. Colonel Henry Knox was in charge of the American artillery, engineers, sappers, and miners, and Col. Stephen Moylan led the cavalry. The third division of the Allied army was comprised of 3,200 Virginia militiamen. It occupied the southeastern sector or far right wing of the siege line. Brigadier General Thomas Nelson, Jr., commanded these men; his unit commanders were Brig. Gens. George Weedon, Edward Stevens, and Robert Lawson.

The Franco-American siege line was initially established two miles below Yorktown in a giant arc, with the French on the west (left) and the Americans in the south (center) and east (right). Additionally, Washington dispatched four regiments led by Comte Claude Gabriel de Choisey to the northern side of the York River to lay siege to the British troops operating on Gloucester Point. There, 1,500 Virginia militiamen commanded by Brig. Gen. George Weedon, aided by 1,400 French troops under Duke de Lauzun, joined forces to bottle up the enemy.

Terrain: Located in the Tidewater region of Virginia, Yorktown rests on the northern border of a large peninsula formed by the James River on the south and the York River on the north. Yorktown is on the southern shore of the York River, and Gloucester Point is on the opposite bank. Both positions are 35 miles inland, northwest of Cape Henry, and 15 miles east of

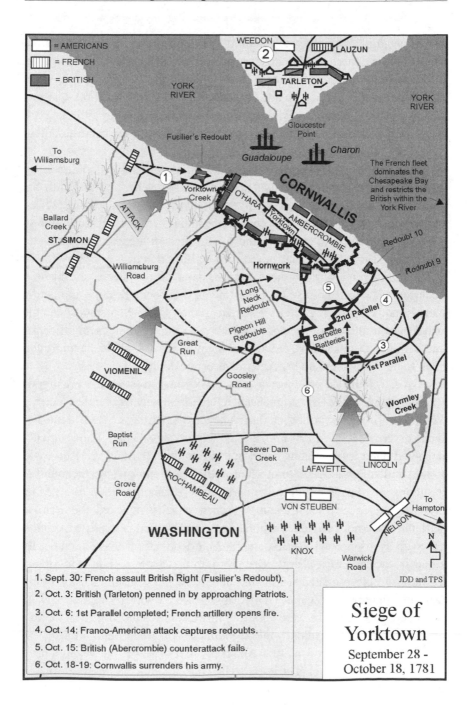

Map Legend
- □ = AMERICANS
- ▥ = FRENCH
- ▧ = BRITISH

YORK RIVER

WEEDON

② LAUZUN

TARLETON

YORK RIVER

Gloucester Point

Guadaloupe   Charon

The French fleet dominates the Chesapeake Bay and restricts the British within the York River

Fusilier's Redoubt

To Williamsburg

① Yorktown Creek

ATTACK

CORNWALLIS

O'HARA   Yorktown   AMBERCROMBIE

Redoubt 10

Redoubt 9

Ballard Creek

ST. SIMON

Williamsburg Road

Hornwork

Long Neck Redoubt

⑤

④

2nd Parallel

Great Run

Pigeon Hill Redoubts

Barbette Batteries

③

1st Parallel

VIOMENIL

Goosley Road

⑥

Wormley Creek

Baptist Run

Beaver Dam Creek

LAFAYETTE   LINCOLN

Grove Road

ROCHAMBEAU

VON STEUBEN

To Hampton

WASHINGTON

NELSON

KNOX

Warwick Road

N

JDD and TPS

1. Sept. 30: French assault British Right (Fusilier's Redoubt).
2. Oct. 3: British (Tarleton) penned in by approaching Patriots.
3. Oct. 6: 1st Parallel completed; French artillery opens fire.
4. Oct. 14: Franco-American attack captures redoubts.
5. Oct. 15: British (Abercrombie) counterattack fails.
6. Oct. 18-19: Cornwallis surrenders his army.

Siege of Yorktown
September 28 - October 18, 1781

Williamsburg. Yorktown was a natural inland port, with access to both the sea lanes to the east and Williamsburg and other points inland. It was thus an important transshipment hub for the state of Virginia. The river between the British defenses at Yorktown and Gloucester Point was about three-quarters of a mile wide. Gloucester Point extends from north to south into the York River, which made it an ideal location to guard the port from a land assault in the north.

The land around Yorktown is generally flat with some undulation. In 1781 the countryside was cultivated with corn, tobacco, and grains to the south, while the land west and east of the city was cut by meandering creeks, ravines, and dense patches of woods. Four main roads served Yorktown in 1781, two to the north and west and two to the south and east. The water above and below the town anchored Cornwallis's defenses.

The Fighting: During the first few days of the siege, skirmishing occurred at various points along the line as the troops began establishing patrols and organizing their assigned sectors. On September 29 the Americans in the eastern sector (right wing) began reconnoitering the area and a minor skirmish broke out at Wormeley Creek. The British simply fell back to their trenches and the Americans broke contact.

On the 30th of September a heavier skirmish west of the Fusiliers's Redoubt between the British and French forces resulted in several casualties. To the surprise of the Allies, on that same day the British evacuated most of their outer works, which French and Americans happily and quickly occupied. On October 3, the small but fascinating Battle of the Hook was fought north of Gloucester Point when Colonel Tarleton and a detachment of dragoons guarding foraging wagons ran into advancing Allied forces. The brisk fight began when Lauzon's French cavalry attacked the British. Tarleton was knocked from his horse and nearly killed or captured, only to be saved by his men at the last moment. American militia arrived and boldly stood in the face of a charge. British infantry was also lightly involved. Tarleton wisely retreated within the defensive lines on Gloucester Point. Casualty figures vary widely. Allied losses were about five killed and 27 wounded. British losses were about 50 killed and wounded. It was the last battle the despised Tarleton would fight in the American Revolution.

The construction of the first Allied parallel or siege line began during the first week of October. The line was laid out in a concave arc from west of the Hampton Road in the French sector east and then northeast into the American sector, anchored at each end by, respectively, the Grand French Battery Complex and the American Grand Battery. The line was about 800-1,000 yards from the main line of British works and roughly the same one evacuated by the British. Allied troops worked night and day on the construction of gabions (large woven baskets filled with earth) to bolster the trenches, fascines (bundled timbers), fraises (sharpened stakes directed at the enemy), and saucissons (large sharpened logs pointed at the enemy) to improve their lines. The British ineffectually bombarded the Allies with artillery fire during its construction. On the night of October 6, a French diversion on the left toward the Fusiliers Redoubt helped focus attention on that distant flank and away from the digging of the first parallel. Once the line was finished and artillery was emplaced, the Allies opened a relentless bombardment against British positions. The fire inflicted scores of casualties and sank, burned, or drove off several ships anchored off Yorktown.

It was now time to dig a second siege line to further strangle Cornwallis's defenders. The line was begun on October 11 and spotted by Cornwallis at dawn the following morning. This line, about 750 yards long, was within musket and easy artillery range of the British main line. The British response drove the workers to ground and brought work, temporarily, to a halt. On the east or right wing sector of the field work was made doubly difficult by the presence of two strong British forts: Redoubts 9 and 10. Both were well defended and blocked the extension of the siege line in that direction. Washington decided to assault and capture the strongholds. The French were ordered to conduct a feint in the western sector against the Fusiliers Redoubt to distract the enemy, while a simultaneous action was conducted at Gloucester Point. Under cover of darkness on October 14, meanwhile, two columns (one French and one American) would attack Redoubts 9 and 10, respectively.

At 8:00 p.m., 400 Americans led by Col. Alexander Hamilton stormed Redoubt 10, the fort closest to the York River. The Continentals climbed up, over, and through the British fraises, abatis, and saucissons ringing the redoubt. The fight only lasted about 10 minutes before the Americans were in possession of it. American losses were nine dead and 25 wounded; British casualties were about eight killed and wounded and 20 captured, the rest escaping back to the main line. On Hamilton's left was the 400-man French column under Col. William Deux Ponts. These men attacked and captured British Redoubt Number 9. Their losses were heavier with 15 killed and 77 wounded. British losses were 18 killed and as many as 50 captured.

That night the Allies began incorporating the forts into the right wing of the second parallel. The batteries could fire and hit any point within Yorktown. A massed Allied infantry column, at a distance of only 400 or so yards, threatened to penetrate the British lines. Unless Cornwallis did something quickly to turn the tide of the siege, the end was in sight. Before dawn on October 16, 350 British troops commanded by Lt. Col. Robert Abercrombie attacked the center of the American line. The British captured several dozen Americans and spiked a few cannon, but were not strong enough to do more than that before being driven back to their lines. That feeble attempt was all Cornwallis could muster.

That same night Cornwallis ordered the evacuation of his troops to Gloucester Point, but bad weather, a lack of adequate transports, and the Allied bombardment forced him to abort the effort. Cornwallis had decided to attempt a breakthrough and a march northward to New York, but it was simply too little, too late. On October 17 Cornwallis opened surrender negotiations that eventually led to the capitulation of his entire army.

Casualties: British: 156 killed, 326 wounded, and 7,157 prisoners; Franco-American: 274 casualties (French: 52 killed and 134 wounded; American: 23 killed and 65 wounded).

Outcome / Impact: On October 19, 1781, at 2:00 p.m., the British and Hessian defenders of Yorktown officially surrendered. About 2,000 of the surrendered troops were sick or wounded and unable to march. However, 7,157 soldiers, 840 sailors, and 80 camp followers walked out of Yorktown, passing between the French and American soldiers lining the Yorktown-Hampton Road. General Cornwallis claimed he was ill, so Brig. Gen. Charles O'Hara led the surrendered in his absence. The British officers were allowed to keep their side arms, papers, and property, and select officers (including Cornwallis) were given their freedom on parole. However, the British soldiers and sailors were sentenced as prisoners of war to camps in Virginia and Pennsylvania.

Cornwallis boarded the sloop *Bonetta* and sailed to New York, where he officially informed General Clinton of the surrender at Yorktown. When the British fleet carrying the reinforcements Cornwallis so badly needed learned of his capitulation, it returned to New York. Admiral de Grasse returned the French fleet to the West Indies, and the Americans began their return march to the Hudson Highlands of New York on November 1, 1781.

It is impossible to overstate the ramifications of the Allied victory at Yorktown. Without qualification it was the most decisive campaign of the American Revolution. It also demonstrated General Washington's brilliance as a field commander. However, without the assistance of his French allies, the campaign would not have been possible.

British armed forces remained in New York until November 25, 1783, and several minor skirmishes occurred before a final peace was achieved, but the victory at Yorktown assured the end of the war and the beginning of a hard-won peace for a new nation.

Further Reading: Freeman, Douglas Southall, *George Washington: A Biography*. 7 vols. (Augustus Kelly Publishers, 1948); Greene, Jerome A., *The Guns of Independence: The Siege of Yorktown*, 1781 (Savas Beatie, 2005); Morrissey, Brandon, *Yorktown 1781: The World Turned Upside Down* (Osprey, 1997); Johnston, Henry P., *The Yorktown Campaign and the Surrender of Cornwallis 1781* (Harper & Brothers, 1881).

Blue Licks, Battle of (Western Territories Campaign)

Date: August 19, 1782.
Region: Southern Colonies, Virginia (present-day Kentucky).
Commanders: British: Lieutenant Colonel John Butler and Captain William Caldwell; Tory: Captains Alexander McKee and Simon Girty; Indian: Chief "Captain" Joseph Brant; American: Colonels John Todd and Stephen Trigg, Lieutenant Colonel Daniel Boone, and Majors Hugh McGary and Silas Harlan.
Time of Day / Length of Action: 7:30 a.m. to 7:45 a.m.
Weather Conditions: Warm, unremarkable summer morning.
Opposing Forces: British: 300; Indian: 1,000; American: 181.

British Perspective: Both John Butler and William Caldwell served the Crown throughout the American Revolution as provincial militia officers. Their service as "rangers" in the frontier regions of New York and Pennsylvania provided them with notoriety because of their actions at the Wyoming Massacre and during similar raids along the frontier. Following the Battle of Newtown (August 29, 1779) and the destruction of the Iroquois Nation during Sullivan's Campaign that year, the British forces abandoned their operations in the northeast and moved west from Fort Niagara, New York, to Fort Detroit in present-day Michigan. From there, "Butler's Rangers" and their long-time Mohawk ally Chief "Captain" Joseph Brant sought alliances with the Ohio Indian Nations.

In early August of 1782, the Ohio Indian Nations (Algonquin, Delaware, Wyandot, Shawnee, Mingo, Miami, Chippewa, and Sauk) held a meeting at Chalahgawtha, a Shawnee town on the Little Miami River in what is today the state of Ohio. During the Revolutionary War, the Ohio Indian Nations were allied with the British and frequently raided American frontier settlements south of the Ohio River and east into Pennsylvania. The Indians sought many things, including retribution for the massacre of nearly 100 Delaware Indians at Gnadenhutten (present-day Ohio), where American pioneers had systematically slaughtered the Delaware (also known as the Moravian Massacre). Numbered among the dead were 39 Indian children. In addition to these outrages, throughout the Revolution pioneers continued encroaching into the Ohio territory and especially south of the Ohio River in the mountainous outback of western Virginia (present-day states of Kentucky, West Virginia, and Virginia).

Several battles were waged in the Ohio Indian lands, including Sandusky (also known as the Sandusky Expedition) on June 4-5, 1782, and Olentangy, which took place the following day. This fighting resulted in the deaths of at least 250 Americans, many of whom were tortured and burned at the stake. The blatant encroachment of whites into Indian Territory and the Moravian Massacre helped trigger the formation of a significant war party. At a meeting that August a former Patriot-turned-Tory leader named Simon Girty urged the Indians to join forces with the British in an organized campaign to raid the frontier settlements to the south. Girty's encouragement convinced the Ohio tribes to join forces with "Butler's Rangers." Together, they launched a large-scale raid.

Simon Girty was a former Irish immigrant captured by the Senecas while still quite young. He convinced the British to set a trap to lure out the American militiamen to a designated spot where they could be ambushed. By splitting their force into two elements, urged Girty, the British could lay siege to the American fort at Brant's Station, an outpost five miles northeast of modern-day Lexington, Kentucky. By doing so, various militiamen stationed in central Kentucky would rush to the fort's aid. On August 16 Girty led 500 Indians in an attack against Brant's Station. He purposefully allowed messengers to leave the outpost and spread word throughout the countryside that the hated turncoat Girty and hundreds of Indians were on the warpath in Kentucky. After conducting a siege for several days Girty and his Indians retreated northward to join their waiting comrades who hoped to ambush the pursuing Americans.

The main ambush force was under the command of Capt. William Caldwell of "Butler's Rangers." Caldwell established position on the high ground north of Blue Licks, a destination popular with pioneers for harvesting salt. He concealed his command on both sides of the sole footpath coursing through the area. His plan was to lure the Americans down the path and annihilate them. As Girty and his Indians retreated to Blue Licks, they intentionally left a readily identifiable trail for the Americans to follow. Reassembled on the high ground north of Blue Licks, the British and Indians awaited the arrival of the unsuspecting Americans.

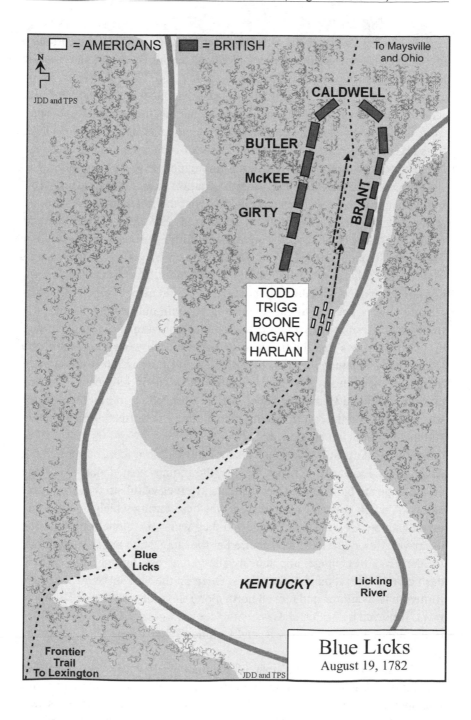

Blue Licks
August 19, 1782

American Perspective: Colonel George Rogers Clark successfully invaded the Northwest Territory and defeated a joint British/Indian force at Fort Sackville (modern-day Vincennes, Indiana) in 1779. However, all of Ohio territory north of Virginia (present-day Kentucky and West Virginia) remained in Indian hands. Frequent raids threatened the frontier settlements from that quarter. Nonetheless, the stalwart pioneers held onto their little forts and settlements. One of the best-known frontiersmen in this area was Daniel Boone, who served as the militia commander at Fort Boonesborough.

When word arrived that Brant's Station was under attack, 181 militiamen of central Kentucky rallied to assist their neighbors. When they arrived at the besieged fort they discovered the Indians had retreated northward toward Blue Licks. The ranking militia officers were Cols. John Todd and Stephen Trigg, Lt. Col. Daniel Boone, Maj. Hugh McGary, and Maj. Silas Harlan. The overall militia commander, Col. Benjamin Logan, had not yet arrived with the main contingent of 400 men, but the militiamen already present decided to pursue their enemy without waiting. The militia followed the trail for fifty miles even though Boone urged caution, warning his fellow officers that the trail was too obvious. However, several of the leaders had lost family members to the Indian raid and passions were running high. Revenge lingered in the air and clouded their judgment. As they pushed northward Boone continued warning his fellow militia there was a strong likelihood they were heading into a trap. His words fell on deaf ears and the hasty pursuit continued.

Early on August 19 the militia reached the southern shore of the Licking River and the lower Blue Licks. On cue, the Indians posted along the ridge on the opposite bank of the river made themselves visible to the Americans below. A quick council of the officers was held during which Boone again urged caution. Colonel Todd suggested they wait for Colonel Logan's men to arrive. Major McGary, who scoffed at the suggestion and insulted them for their lack of courage, impetuously charged across the river. His spirited dash carried with it most of the others. Once on the far bank the Americans formed into a column and moved north along the trail with Major Harlan in front, followed by Major McGary in the center, Colonel Todd's men on the right, Boone's force on the left, and Colonel Trigg's men bringing up the rear.

Terrain: In 1782, this area of Kentucky (then considered part of Virginia) was wilderness forest with several small settlements and farms interspersed along fertile river valleys. The Licking River carves its way through the north central highlands of Kentucky as it empties northward into the Ohio River. Terrain in the northern outer bluegrass region averages 750 feet in elevation and rises sharply above the rivers below. The Blue Licks lie in a natural crook in the Licking River, which had been used for centuries by wildlife as a natural salt lick; early pioneers harvested salt there. Blue Licks is located fifty miles northeast of Lexington, Kentucky, and sixty miles southeast of Cincinnati, Ohio. Daniel Boone erected a chain of small forts and outpost stations along the river valleys in this region in 1775, and the area was filled with buffalo, elk, bears, deer, and Indians.

The Fighting: As the Americans moved northward on horseback along the trail from lower Blue Licks to the high ground above, the Indians were no where to be seen. When the militia reached the top of the high ridgeline with the river surrounding them to the east, west, and south, gunfire poured opened on them from all sides. The Indians and British sprung their well-planned ambush while hidden within the ravines jutting down from the heights above. The Americans could do little more than try and escape the killing zone. The right and rear militia formations bore the brunt of the short fight and it was impossible for them to organize either an effective defense or counterattack. The battle quickly turned into a rout, with each man for himself. Individual escape and evasion saved 92 of the 181. The balance were killed, wounded, or captured. Among the casualties were Colonels Todd and Trigg, and Majors McGary and Harlan. Daniel Boone's son, Israel Boone, was among the killed. Many historians regard this brief but bloody fight as the last action of the American Revolution.

Casualties: British and Tory: one killed; Indian: six killed and 10 wounded; American: 77 killed and 12 wounded.

Outcome / Impact: Daniel Boone escaped by rushing toward the vacated enemy positions in a ravine as the Indians clambered onto high ground to scalp their victims. Once the survivors joined with Colonel Logan's main force at the Lower Blue Licks they cautiously returned to the scene of carnage only to discover the enemy had moved northeast. Continuing their swath through the American settlements on the frontier, they ultimately struck at Fort Henry and Rice's Fort (present-day Wheeling, West Virginia). From September 11-13, 1782, the Americans repulsed hundreds of Indians in a successful defense of the forts. Rebuffed, the British and Indians retreated north and returned to the safety of the Ohio Indian lands.

Both the Battle of Blue Licks and Siege of Fort Henry are often referred to as the "final" battles of the Revolution. They were the last major actions waged by American soldiers against British provincial troops, but several minor engagements were fought in the rural areas across the Southern states during the latter months of 1782 (some also occasionally described as the "last" battle of the war). These included clashes in South Carolina at Combahee Ferry (August 27) and John's Ferry (November 4).

The fight at Blue Licks and similar frontier "massacres" echoed in continuing frontier violence for many years. These struggles for territorial control of a fertile region are reflected in the immediate postwar struggle that followed the American Revolution, when the fight with the Indians for the Ohio territory opened a new chapter in American history.

Further Reading: Mason, Augustus Lynch, *The Romance and Tragedy of Pioneer Life* (Jones Brothers and Company, 1883); Ranck, George W., *History of Lexington, Kentucky: Its Early Annals and Recent Progress* (Robert Clarke & Co, 1872); Doddridge, John, *The Settlement and Indian Wars of the Western Parts of Virginia and Pennsylvania, 1763-1783* (Heritage Books, 2004).

Arkansas Post, Battle of (Colbert's Raid), Spanish Campaign

Date: April 17, 1783.
Region: Spanish Territory (Louisiana and West Florida).
Commanders: British: Captain James Logan Colbert; Spanish: Captain Jacobo Dubreuil and Indian Chief Angaska.
Time of Day / Length of Action: 2:30 a.m. to noon.
Weather Conditions: Cool and unremarkable.
Opposing Forces: British: 81; Indians: 100; Spanish: 40.

British Perspective: Throughout the Revolution, the hinterlands of West Florida and Louisiana were contested regions where the British, Spanish, and Indians engaged in little known but bloody struggles. The British and Spanish governments encouraged people to settle in the Mississippi Valley. The British occupied the eastern side of the Mississippi, the Spanish the western. In 1779 the British sent Maj. Gen. John Campbell from Jamaica to West Florida with 1,200 troops. Campbell was ordered to protect settlers from Indians, Spanish, and American raiders. His force was primarily one of Hessian troops and Tories from Maryland and Pennsylvania. Most of his men occupied forts at Pensacola (Florida) and Mobile (Alabama), though 400 troops under Lt. Col. Alexander Dickson were sent into the frontier region around Natchez (Mississippi) and Baton Rouge (Louisiana).

When Spain formally sided with America in 1779, the British became increasingly alarmed about Spain's presence along the Gulf Coast. Control of the area was important to both nations. The British enlisted the aid of the

Choctaw Indians to assist them. A series of minor engagements between the Spanish and British erupted across Louisiana and Florida. In 1780, small-scale actions were fought at Baton Rouge, Mobile, and Natchez. The Spanish dominated the fighting and the British outpost of Fort Panmure at Natchez became the focus of Spain's efforts. The Spanish laid siege to the British outpost in May and June of 1780. After six weeks of warfare Capt. John Blommart formally surrendered Natchez on June 22, 1780.

Fighting continued for British posts at Mobile Bay and Pensacola Bay. Campbell surrendered the region to the Spanish in March 1781. The conflict was a decisive British strategic loss, though partisan bands (with Indian assistance) continued to stubbornly, if ineffectively, resist Spanish efforts to control the area. One of these partisans was Scotsman Capt. James Logan Colbert, who organized and allied British forces with the Chickasaw. From 1781 through 1783, Colbert's men raided Spanish outposts and shipping along the Mississippi River. Colbert took hostages and offered them in exchange for Captain Blommart and other British prisoners lost at Natchez. The Spanish refused Colbert's offer of prisoner exchanges and did their best to hunt down and exterminate his partisan bands.

In 1782 Colbert set his sights on Arkansas Post, a seemingly vulnerable Spanish fort that served as the westernmost outpost in the region. The small palisade fort with blockhouses was named as Fort Carlos III and manned by a garrison of only 40 Spanish soldiers. Colbert organized his command for a raid and in April of 1783 set out to assault the Spanish at Arkansas Post.

Spanish-American Perspective: During the Revolution, Spain provided aid for a pair of secret American expeditions into the Louisiana and Mississippi region. The Spanish assisted Col. George Rogers Clark and Capt. James Willing during their 1778 campaigns by supplying arms and protection. This aid was before an alliance was signed between the two countries. Without this assistance it would have been much more difficult for Colonel Rogers to have won the Battle of Fort Sackville (present-day Vincennes, Indiana), and for Captain Willing to have successfully raided British shipping and plantations throughout the Mississippi Valley.

In 1779, after the Spanish formally joined with America as an ally, Governor José de Gálvez, the Spanish territorial authority based in New Orleans, organized a campaign against the British. The Spanish had limited resources to engage in head-to-head warfare. Gálvez, however, was an influential and effective leader and he capitalized on his alliances with local Indians to organize troops for war. His plans were to attack British outposts and shipping in Louisiana and Florida. By October of 1779 the Spaniards had secured Natchez and Baton Rouge; by May of 1780 they had defeated the British at Mobile. The next month the Spanish were forced into another battle at Natchez that ended successfully for them after a six-week siege. All of this fighting assisted the Americans by siphoning off British resources.

The British failed to retake Mobile in 1781, and during February and March of that year the Spanish laid siege against Pensacola Bay (Florida), which surrendered on March 9. These battles secured the lower Mississippi Valley of Louisiana and Florida for Spain, though pockets of resistance remained. The British army in the region was reduced to marauding bands aligned with Indians to harass Spanish shipping on the Mississippi River, and occasional attacks were launched against isolated outposts and patrols.

Terrain: Arkansas Post (Fort San Carlos III) was built along the Arkansas River 34 miles west of the Mississippi River. The rural outpost was constructed of log palisades and fortified blockhouses. An important frontier trading town, Arkansas Post jutted into Indian Territory—the westernmost civilized point in North America in the 1780s. There were several outposts and trading centers established by the French, Spanish, and English, but the region was still considered "untamed." By 1779, Spain had wrested control of the area in the western colonies called "Louisiana" (land west of the Mississippi River) and East and West Florida, which included the provinces of Mobile, Pensacola, St. Augustine (Florida), and the Natchez district (present-day Mississippi). Spain established a capital at New Orleans and the Mississippi River Valley was patrolled by Spanish troops. The area was so vast that no one entity was powerful enough to fully "rule" it.

The Fighting: About 2:30 a.m. on April 17, Captain Colbert and 100 British soldiers and Indian raiders maneuvered seventeen small boats with muffled oars toward the Spanish garrison at Arkansas Post (Fort San Carlos III). Landing his small armada on the north bank of the Arkansas River (Red Bank) at 2:30 a.m., Colbert stealthily aligned his men and launched a ground assault by moving quickly among the garrison's quarters outside the fort. Within a few moments the raiders had killed two Spanish soldiers, wounded three more, and captured several dozen men and their family members.

Spanish commander Capt. Jacobo Dubreuil called out his small garrison and a detachment of Quapaw Indians, who fired at the shadows moving outside the fort. The raiders took up positions in a ravine and for a few hours gunfire was exchanged. The Spanish used their artillery to dissuade the raiders from approaching the walls. An engineering defect with the fort, however, made it impossible to hit the raiders in the shallow ravine. By the time the fighting ended 300 artillery rounds had been expended.

Trapped by small arms and cannon fire, Colbert's raiders were unable to attack or safely retreat. At 9:00 a.m. the Spanish opened the main gate to counterattack. Outside was a small party advancing with a flag of truce and hostages—including the wife of Spanish Lieutenant de Villars, Doña Marie Luisa de Villars. The note she delivered probably surprised Dubreuil. Instead of surrendering, Colbert demanded the immediate capitulation of the fort and its garrison. An indignant Dubreuil refused and the Spanish and Indians launched their assault in a driving rainstorm.

By this time it is likely Colbert had lost control of his men, most of whom were already withdrawing (with their Spanish hostages) to their boats. The exhausted raiders climbed aboard as fast as they could and set off down the Arkansas River. Just before leaving, Colbert delivered a threat to return at noon with 500 Chickasaw Indians (some accounts claim he said British troops). If Dubreuil did not surrender, threatened Colbert, the men, women, and children he was holding hostage would be killed.

Meanwhile, at the nearby Quapaw village of Kappa, Chief Angaska (a Spanish ally) ordered 100 warriors and 20 Spanish soldiers to pursue Colbert, who was bluffed into thinking he was outnumbered. Colbert freed most of his prisoners but escaped with some of his men. During the next four months the Spanish authorities attempted to persuade Colbert that a peace treaty had been signed between the warring nations (which was true) and that the remaining captives should be returned. Colbert refused to either surrender or believe the war was over. After reaching Florida and reporting to British authorities, he was thrown from his horse and killed.

Casualties: British: Unknown; Spanish: Unknown.

Outcome / Impact: Colbert's raid was unsuccessful, but Spanish, French, and American forces had delivered heavy blows against the Crown across the globe. Coupled with Yorktown, these losses convinced British politicians to make peace. Hostilities subsided in the Mississippi Valley in 1783 and Spain regained control of Florida and Louisiana. The United States did not achieve the right to freely ship goods on the Mississippi until France regained control of the Louisiana Territory from Spain and America bought it in 1803. President Thomas Jefferson's Louisiana Purchase eventually established the bulk of the western United States.

Today: Arkansas Post National Memorial Park preserves and interprets the rich history of the fort, including its role during the Civil War.

Further Reading: Caughey, John., "Willing's Expedition down The Mississippi, 1778," in *The Louisiana Historical Quarterly* (January 1932); Bearss, Edwin C., Special History Report (NPS 851), *The Colbert Raid, Arkansas Post National Memorial, Arkansas* (National Park Service, November 1974); English, William Hayden, *Conquest of the Country Northwest of the River Ohio 1778-1783 and Life of Gen. George Rogers Clark* (Bowen-Merrill Company, 1897).

Appendix

Battles and Campaigns by
State and Territory

Alabama, Arkansas, Mississippi, and Florida

Year	Major Engagements	Actions	Campaign
1778		1st, 2nd, and 3rd Florida Expeditions, Alligator Creek, Trout River	1st (British) Southern Expedition
1781	Pensacola		Spanish Campaign (Gálvez's Expedition)
1783	Arkansas Post, (also known as Colbert's Raid)	Mobile (Alabama), Natchez (Ft. Panmure)	Spanish Campaign (Gálvez's Expedition)

Canada

Year	Major Engagements	Actions	Campaign
1775	Ft. St. John	Chambly	Canadian Campaign
1775	Montreal		Canadian Campaign
1775	Québec		Canadian Campaign

Caribbean Sea

Year	Major Engagements	Actions	Campaign
1776	Nassau (1st Battle of)	Ft. Montagu, Ft. Nassau, HMS Glasgow, HMS Hawk, and HMS Boloton v. American Fleet	Caribbean Campaign

1778-1782	Caribbean, Battles of the	2nd Battle of Nassau, Yarmouth (naval battle), Martinique, St. Lucia, Tobago, St. Kitts, Nevis, Ft. San Juan de Nicaragua, and the Battle of the Saints (naval battle), Fort San Fernando de Omoa and Black River Fort, Honduras	Caribbean Campaign

Connecticut

Year	Major Engagements	Actions	Campaign
1781	New London	Fts. Trumbull and Griswold (Groton Heights)	Arnold's Expedition

Georgia

Year	Major Engagements	Actions	Campaign
1778	Savannah	1st, 2nd, and 3rd Florida Expeditions, and Fts. McIntosh, Howe, Sunbury, and Morris	1st (British) Southern Expedition
1779	Kettle Creek		Southern Campaign
1779	Brier Creek		Southern Campaign
1779	Savannah (siege and 2nd battle of)		Southern Campaign
1780	Augusta		Southern Campaign

Great Britain Home Islands

Year	Major Engagements	Actions	Campaign
1777	Battle of the British Isles	Ushant, HMS *Drake* v. *Ranger* (naval battle), HMS *Serapis* v. *Bonhomme Richard* (naval battle), Whitehaven, St. Mary's Island	American Naval Campaign (John Paul Jones's Expedition), Europe

Illinois

Year	Major Engagements	Actions	Campaign
1779	Ft. Sackville, Battle of	Kaskaskia and Cohokia	Illinois Campaign

Kentucky, Ohio, West Virginia

Year	Major Engagements	Actions	Campaign
1782	Blue Licks, Battle of	Moravian Massacre, Ft. Henry, Rice's Ft., Olentangy, Sandusky Expedition, Combahee Ferry, John's Ferry	Western Territories Campaign

Maine

Year	Major Engagements	Actions	Campaign
1779	Penobscot Bay	New Haven, Norwalk, and Green's Farms	Penobscot Expedition

Massachusetts

Year	Major Engagements	Actions	Campaign
1775	Lexington and Concord		Boston Campaign
1775	Boston (siege)		Boston Campaign
1775	Hog and Noodle Islands		Boston Campaign
1775	Bunker Hill		Boston Campaign

New Jersey

Year	Major Engagements	Actions	Campaign
1776	Trenton		New Jersey Campaign
1777	Princeton	Stony Creek	New Jersey Campaign

| 1777 | Fts. Mercer and Mifflin (also known as the Siege of Philadelphia) | | Philadelphia Campaign |
| 1778 | Monmouth Court House | | New Jersey Campaign |

New York

Year	Major Engagements	Actions	Campaign
1775	Ft. Ticonderoga	Crown Point	Canadian Campaign
1776	Long Island		New York Campaign
1776	New York (Siege of New York)	Kip's Bay, Harlem Heights, and Ft. Washington	New York Campaign
1776	Lake Champlain (Valcour Island)	Skenesborough	Canadian Campaign
1776	White Plains		New York Campaign
1777	Ft. Ticonderoga (2nd battle), and Hubbardton		New York Campaign
1777	Fts. Stanwix and Oriskany		Saratoga Campaign
1777	Freeman's Farm		Saratoga Campaign
1777	Hudson Highlands (also known as the Battle of Fts. Montgomery and Clinton)		Saratoga Campaign
1777	Bemis Heights, (also known as the 2nd Battle of Freeman's Farm)		Saratoga Campaign
1779	Stony Point		New York Campaign
1779	Newtown	Broadhead's Expedition, Chemung Massacre	Sullivan's Campaign

North Carolina

Year	Major Engagements	Actions	Campaign
1776	Moores (Moore's) Creek Bridge		1st (British) Southern Expedition
1781	Haw River (also known as Pyle's Defeat and Pyle's Hacking Match)		Southern Campaign
1781	Guilford Court House		Southern Campaign
1781	Hobkirk's Hill		Southern Campaign

Pennsylvania

Year	Major Engagements	Actions	Campaign
1777	Brandywine Creek	Amboy, Broad Brook, Crooked Billet, Barren Hill, and Cooch's Bridge	Philadelphia Campaign
1777	"The Clouds"		Philadelphia Campaign
1777	Paoli (also known as the Massacre of Paoli)		Philadelphia Campaign
1777	Germantown		Philadelphia Campaign
1777	Whitemarsh (Edge Hill)		Philadelphia Campaign
1778	Wyoming (also known as the Massacre of Wyoming)	Fts. Wintermoot, Jenkins, and Forty Fort	Sullivan's Campaign

Rhode Island

Year	Major Engagements	Actions	Campaign
1778	Rhode Island		Rhode Island Campaign

South Carolina

Year	Major Engagements	Actions	Campaign
1775	Snow Campaign (battles of the)	Ninety Six and Great Cane Brake	Snow Campaign
1776	Ft. Sullivan (1st Battle of Charleston)		1st (British) Southern Expedition
1779	Stono Ferry		Southern Campaign
1780	Charleston (siege)	Monck's Corner	Southern Campaign
1780	Waxhaws	Stallions, Cedar Springs, Gowan's Ferry, Port's Ferry, Thicketty Fort, Old Iron Works, Wateree, and Rocky Mount	Southern Campaign
1780	Williamson's Plantation (also known as Huck's Defeat)	Ramsour's Mill, Brandon's Camp, Old Fort, McDowell's Camp, Flat Rock, Hunt's Bluff, Wateree	Southern Campaign
1780	Hanging Rock		Southern Campaign
1780	Camden		Southern Campaign
1780	Musgrove's Mill	Fishing Creek	Southern Campaign
1780	Kings Mountain	Cane Creek (Cowan's Ford)	Southern Campaign
1780	Blackstock's Plantation	Blue Savannah and Ft. Wilson	Southern Campaign
1781	Cowpens		Southern Campaign
1781	Ninety Six (siege)	Siege of Augusta, Parker's Ferry, Quinby's Bridge	Southern Campaign
1781	Eutaw Springs		Southern Campaign

Vermont

Year	Major Engagements	Actions	Campaign
1777	Bennington		Saratoga Campaign

Virginia and Tennessee

Year	Major Engagements	Actions	Campaign
1775	Great Bridge		1st (British) Southern Expedition
1776	Cherokee Campaign (also known as the Second Cherokee War)	Lyndley's Fort, Long Island Flats, Hiwassee, Chickamauga, Ft. Nashborough, and Boyd's Creek	Cherokee Campaign
1781	Green Spring	Norfolk, Suffolk, Richmond, Williamsburg, Charlottesville, Spencer's Ordinary (Williamsburg)	Yorktown Campaign
1781	The Capes (Yorktown Campaign, French and British naval battle)		Yorktown Campaign
1781	Yorktown (siege)		Yorktown Campaign

Index*

---

* This index includes individuals, ships, and unit organizations. Battles and campaigns will be found in
the table of contents.

About the Authors

Theodore P. Savas graduated from The University of Iowa College of Law in 1986 (With Distinction) and practiced in Silicon Valley for twelve years. He is the author or editor of many books (published in six languages) including *Silent Hunters: German U-boat Commanders of World War II* (Campbell, 1997; Naval Institute Press, 2003), *Hunt and Kill: U-505 and the U-Boat War in the Atlantic* (Spellmount, 2004; Naval Institute Press, 2004), and *Nazi Millionaires: The Allied Search for Hidden SS Gold* (Casemate, 2002), as well as a score of articles in a variety of journals and magazines.

J. David Dameron received his education at the University of North Carolina. He is retired from the U.S. Army, where he served with the 82nd Airborne Division and the 7th Special Forces Group. Dave teaches evening classes in American History at Troy University and works as a civilian weapons research specialist at the U.S. Army Infantry School. He is the author of several books, including *General Henry Lewis Benning: This was a Man* (2001), and *The Battle of Kings Mountain* (2003).